Barron's Review Course Series

Let's Review:

Sequential Mathematics, Course II

Second Edition

Lawrence S. Leff

Assistant Principal, Mathematics Supervision
Franklin D. Roosevelt High School
Brooklyn, New York

BARRON'S

To Rhona
For the understanding,
for the love,
and with love.

All inquiries should be addressed to:
Barron's Educational Series, Inc.
250 Wireless Boulevard
Hauppauge, New York 11788

Library of Congress Catalog Card No. 95-25198

International Standard Book No. 0-8120-9051-9

Library of Congress Cataloging-in-Publication Data

Leff, Lawrence S.
    Let's review : sequential mathematics, course II / Lawrence S.
Leff.—2nd ed.
        p.   cm.—(Barron's review course series)
    Includes index.
    ISBN 9-8120-9051-9
    1. Mathematics.   2. Mathematics—Study and teaching (Secondary)
—New York (State)   I. Title.   II. Series.
QA39.2.L422   1996
510'.76—dc20   95-25198
                                                                 CIP

PRINTED IN THE UNITED STATES OF AMERICA

6789   8800   987654321

TABLE OF CONTENTS

*Chapter includes material that is optional in the Revised New York State Course II syllabus.

PREFACE

For which course can this book be used?

This book offers complete topic coverage and Regents Exam preparation for Course II of the New York State Three-Year Sequence in High School Mathematics. The straightforward approach, the numerous guided and independent practice exercises, and the built-in Regents Examination preparation make this book suitable for use in *any* Course II class either as the primary textbook or as a supplementary study aid.

What special features does this book have?

- *A Compact Format Designed for Self-Study and Rapid Learning*
  For easy reference, the major topics of the book are grouped by the branch of mathematics involved. The clear writing style quickly identifies essential ideas while avoiding unnecessary details. Helpful diagrams, convenient summaries, and numerous step-by-step demonstration examples facilitate learning. These features will be greatly appreciated by students who want to use this book to help prevent or resolve difficulties that may arise as they move from topic to topic in their Course II classrooms or in their Regents Exam preparation.

- *Key Ideas*
  Each section of each chapter begins with a KEY IDEAS box that highlights and motivates the material that follows. The KEY IDEAS, together with the annotated demonstration examples that follow the explanatory text, try to anticipate and answer students' "why" questions.

- *Regents Examination Preparation*
  The guided and independent practice exercises at the end of each section include Regents Exam types of questions. Each chapter closes with a set of REGENTS TUNE-UP exercises selected from actual past Course II Regents Examinations. These Regents problems provide a comprehensive review of the material covered in the chapter while previewing the types and the levels of difficulty of problems on actual Regents Examinations. As a culminating activity, several full-length Course II Regents Examinations with answers appear at the end of the book.

- *Answers To Selected Practice Exercises*
  Each set of practice exercises includes questions at different levels of difficulty that are designed to build understanding, skill, and confidence. The answers to many of these practice exercises are given at the end of each chapter, providing students with valuable feedback that will lead to greater mastery of the material.

- *Glossary of Course II Terms*
  Important Course II terms are collected for easy reference in a glossary at the end of the book.

Who should use this book?

Students who wish to improve their classroom performance and test grades will benefit greatly from the straightforward explanations, helpful examples, numerous practice exercises, and past Regents problems organized by topic. Students studying for classroom exams or preparing for the Course II Regents Examination will find this book a handy resource whenever they need further explanation or more practice on a troublesome topic.

Teachers who desire an additional instructional resource that is convenient to use will want this book in their personal and school libraries. Teachers will find it to be an ideal companion to any of the existing Course II textbooks, providing a valuable lesson-planning aid as well as a source of classroom exercises, homework problems, and test questions.

LAWRENCE S. LEFF
October, 1995

Unit One	**LOGIC AND MATHEMATICAL SYSTEMS**

CHAPTER 1

LOGIC

1.1 LOGICAL CONNECTIVES AND TRUTH VALUES

KEY IDEAS

An **open sentence** such as
        "He is an honor student"
cannot be judged to be true or false until the pronoun *he* is replaced
with the name of a particular person.
        Unlike an open sentence, a **statement** such as
        "The Earth is the third planet from the sun"
is based on a fact that can be verified, so it has a **truth value** of either
TRUE or FALSE, but not both.
        Much of your work in logic will involve determining the truth val-
ues of combinations of statements.

Conjunction and Disjunction

A statement formed by connecting two or more statements with the word
and is called a **conjunction**. Each of the other two statements that make up
a conjunction is called a **conjunct**. The conjunction $p \wedge q$ is read as "p and
q" and is true when conjunct p and conjunct q are both true.
    A **disjunction** is a statement formed by connecting two or more other
statements with the word *or*. Each statement that forms a disjunction is
called a **disjunct**. The disjunction $p \vee q$ is read as "p or q" and is true when
either disjunct p is true or disjunct q is true, or when both disjuncts are true.

Conditional Statement

A compound statement of the form "If p, then q" is called a **conditional
statement** (or *implication*), where statement p is the **antecedent** (*hypothesis*) and statement q is the **consequent** (*conclusion*). For example,

If today is Friday, then tomorrow is Saturday.

antecedent   consequent
(hypothesis)   (conclusion)

A conditional is true for all truth values of p and q except in the single instance in which the antecedent p is true and the consequent q is false.

Biconditional Statement

The biconditional of statements p and q is written as $p \leftrightarrow q$ and is read as "p if and only if q." The biconditional of two statements is true when both statements have the same truth value.

Table 1.1 summarizes the truth values for the logical connectives.

TABLE 1.1 TRUTH VALUES FOR THE LOGICAL CONNECTIVES

		Conjunction	Disjunction	Conditional	Biconditional
p	q	$p \wedge q$	$p \vee q$	$p \rightarrow q$	$p \leftrightarrow q$
T	T	T	T	T	T
T	F	F	T	F	F
F	T	F	T	T	F
F	F	F	F	T	T

Examples

1. Let p represent the statement "x is an even number," and let q represent the statement "x is a prime number." What is the truth value of each of the following statements when $x = 7$?

    (a) $p \leftrightarrow q$ **(b)** $p \wedge q$ **(c)** $p \vee q$ **(d)** $q \rightarrow p$

Solutions: When $x = 7$, statement p is false and statement q is true.

    (a) False. A biconditional is false when its left and right members have opposite truth values.

    (b) False. A conjunction is false when one of the conjuncts is false.

    (c) True. A disjunction is true when at least one of the disjuncts is true.

    (d) False. A conditional is false when the antecedent is true and the consequent is false.

2. In Example 1, for what value of x is $p \leftrightarrow q$ true?

    (1) 8   (2) 9   (3) 10   (4) 11

Solution: A biconditional is true when its left and right members have the same truth value. When $x = 9$, statement p is false and statement q is false, so $p \leftrightarrow q$ is true. The correct answer is **choice (2)**.

3. If $h \rightarrow k$ is false, which statement must be true?

    (1) $h \leftrightarrow k$ (2) $h \wedge k$ (3) $h \vee k$ (4) k

Solution: Since $h \rightarrow k$ is false, h is true and k is false. Therefore, $h \vee k$ is true. The correct answer is **choice (3)**.

4. If $t \vee s$ is false and $r \rightarrow s$ is true, which statement is always true?

    (1) $s \wedge r$ (2) $t \vee s$ (3) $t \vee r$ (4) $t \leftrightarrow r$

Solution: If the disjunction $t \vee s$ is false, then each disjunct must be false, so statement t is false and statement s is false. If the consequent (s) of a conditional is false, then, in order for the conditional to be true, its antecedent (r) must be false. Since statements t and r have the same truth value (both are false), their biconditional is true. The correct answer is **choice (4)**.

Tautology

A **tautology** is a compound statement that is always true regardless of the truth value of each of its component statements. A truth table can be constructed to determine whether a compound statement is a tautology.

Example

5. Determine whether the following statement is a tautology: $(p \wedge q) \rightarrow (p \vee q)$.

Solution: Construct a truth table.

p	q	$p \wedge q$	$p \vee q$	$(p \wedge q) \rightarrow (p \vee q)$
T	T	T	T	T
T	F	F	T	T
F	T	F	T	T
F	F	F	F	T

The last column of the truth table shows that the statement $(p \wedge q) \rightarrow (p \vee q)$ is always true, so **it is a tautology**.

Exercise Set 1.1

1. If p represents "Math is fun," q represents "Math is difficult," and r represents "Math is easy," write each of the following in symbol form, using p, q, and r:

  (a) Math is fun or math is difficult.

  (b) Math is fun and math is easy.

  (c) If math is easy, then it is fun.

  (d) Math is fun if and only if it is easy.

2. Let p represent "A square has three sides," and q represent "2 is a prime number." Determine the truth value of each statement.
   (a) $p \wedge q$ **(b)** $p \vee q$ **(c)** $p \rightarrow q$ **(d)** $p \leftrightarrow q$ **(e)** $q \rightarrow p$

3. Let p represent "x is a prime number," and q represent "$x + 2$ is a prime number." Determine the truth value of each statement when $x = 25$.
   (a) $p \wedge q$ **(b)** $p \vee q$ **(c)** $p \rightarrow q$ **(d)** $p \leftrightarrow q$ **(e)** $q \rightarrow p$

4. If p represents "x is divisible by 3," and q represents "x is the least common multiple of 4 and 6," determine the truth value of each statement when $x = 24$.
   (a) $p \wedge q$ **(b)** $p \vee q$ **(c)** $p \rightarrow q$ **(d)** $p \leftrightarrow q$ **(e)** $q \rightarrow p$

5. If p represents "$x > 5$," and q represents "x is divisible by 3," which statement is true if $x = 10$?
   (1) $p \rightarrow q$ (2) $(p \vee q) \rightarrow q$ (3) $(p \wedge q) \rightarrow p$ (4) $p \leftrightarrow q$

6. If $p \wedge q$ is true, which of the following statements is (are) *always* true?
   (1) $p \leftrightarrow q$ (2) $p \rightarrow q$ (3) $p \vee q$ (4) All of these

7. If $p \rightarrow q$ is false, which statement is *never* true?
   (1) $q \rightarrow p$ (2) p (3) $p \vee q$ (4) $p \leftrightarrow q$

8. If $p \rightarrow q$ is true and $p \leftrightarrow q$ is false, then:
   (1) p is true, q is false   (3) both p and q are true
   (2) p is false, q is true   (4) both p and q are false

9. If $p \leftrightarrow q$ is true, which statement is *always* true?
   (1) p (2) $p \vee q$ (3) $p \wedge q$ (4) $p \rightarrow q$

10. If $r \vee s$ is true and $r \wedge s$ is false, which statement is *always* false?
   (1) $r \rightarrow s$ (2) $r \leftrightarrow s$ (3) r (4) s

11–14. For each of the following statements, (a) construct a truth table, and (b) determine whether the statement is a tautology:

11. $[(p \rightarrow q) \wedge p] \rightarrow q$ **13.** $(p \rightarrow q) \leftrightarrow (p \vee q)$
12. $(p \rightarrow q) \vee (q \rightarrow p)$ **14.** $[(p \vee q) \wedge (p \wedge q)] \leftrightarrow (p \leftrightarrow q)$

1.2 STATEMENT NEGATIONS AND DE MORGAN'S LAWS

$$\wedge$$
KEY IDEAS

The **negation** of a statement can be formed by inserting the word *not,* so that the original statement and its negation have opposite truth values.

The negation of statement p is written as $\sim p$ and read as "not p." If statement p is true, then $\sim p$ is false; if p is false, then $\sim p$ is true.

Forming the Negation of a Statement

The negation of a statement may be written in more than one way. For example,

Statement:	Two plus two is equal to four.	(True)
Negation 1:	Two plus two is *not* equal to four.	(False)
or		
Negation 2:	It is *not* the case that two plus two is equal to four.	(False)

Example

1. If $p \vee \sim q$ is true and p is false, which of the following statements is true?

(1) $\sim p \wedge q$ (2) $\sim q \rightarrow p$ (3) $p \leftrightarrow q$ (4) q

Solution: Since the disjunction $p \vee \sim q$ is true and disjunct p is false, disjunct $\sim q$ must be true, and therefore statement q is false. Since statements p and q have the same truth value (both are false), their biconditional is true. The correct answer is **choice (3)**.

Law of Double Negation

The negation of $\sim p$ is written as $\sim (\sim p)$ and is referred to as the **double negation** of statement p. The first and second columns of the accompanying truth table illustrate that a statement and its negation have opposite truth values, so they are *logically contradictory.* The first and third columns of the truth table show that p and $\sim (\sim p)$ always have the same truth value and are, therefore, logically equivalent. This fact is sometimes referred to as the **Law of Double Negation**. The last column of the truth table illustrates that the *biconditional of two logically equivalent statements is always a tautology.*

p	$\sim p$	$\sim(\sim p)$	$p \leftrightarrow \sim(\sim p)$
T	F	T	T
F	T	F	T

Negation of a Compound Statement

The negation of a conjunction is a disjunction, and the negation of a disjunction is a conjunction.

MATH FACTS

DE MORGAN'S LAWS

- $\sim(p \wedge q)$ is logically equivalent to $\sim p \vee \sim q$.
- $\sim(p \vee q)$ is logically equivalent to $\sim p \wedge \sim q$.

To apply De Morgan's laws to the negation of a conjunction (or disjunction):

- Write the negation of each of the original conjuncts (or disjuncts).
- Then change the original logical connective so that a conjunction becomes a disjunction or a disjunction becomes a conjunction.

Examples

2. Using De Morgan's laws, write the negation of each compound statement.
   (a) She is wealthy or she is wise.
   (b) He is handsome and he is not famous.
   (c) $\sim(\sim p \wedge q)$.

Solutions: **(a) She is not wealthy *and* she is not wise.**
(b) He is not handsome *or* he is famous.
   (c) Apply the appropriate De Morgan's law, so that $\sim(\sim p \wedge q)$ becomes $\sim(\sim p) \vee \sim q$. Then use the Law of Double Negation to rewrite $\sim(\sim p)$ as p; the negation of $\sim(\sim p \wedge q)$ is $\boldsymbol{p \vee \sim q}$.

3. Which of the following statements is logically equivalent to $\sim(k \vee \sim t)$?
   (1) $\sim k \vee \sim t$ (2) $\sim k \wedge t$ (3) $\sim k \vee t$ (4) $\sim k \wedge \sim t$

Solution: Apply the appropriate De Morgan's law, so that $\sim(k \vee \sim t)$ becomes $\sim k \wedge \sim(\sim t)$. Next, use the Law of Double Negation and replace $\sim(\sim t)$ by t: $\sim k \wedge t$. The correct answer is **choice (2)**.

Exercise Set 1.2

1. What is the truth value of ~*p* if *p* represents the statement "13 is a prime number"?

2. What is the truth value of ~*q* if *q* represents the statement "A square has three sides"?

3. What is the truth value of *t* if ~*t* represents the statement "Odd numbers are *not* evenly divisible by 2"?

4. Let *p* represent the statement "He is a snob," and *q* represent the statement "He likes caviar." Replacing the symbols by words, express each of the following as a sentence:
   (a) ~*p* ∧ *q*   **(c)** ~*p* → ~*q*
   (b) ~*q* → ~*p*   **(d)** ~*p* ↔ *q*

5. Which statement is the negation of "It rains or it shines"?
   (1) It rains and it shines.
   (2) It rains or it does not shine.
   (3) It does not rain or it does not shine.
   (4) It does not rain and it does not shine.

6. Let *p* represent the statement "The quotient of *x* and 4 has a remainder of 1," and *q* represent the statement "*x* is divisible only by itself and 1." Which statement is true when *x* = 17?
   (1) ~ (*p* ∨ *q*)   (2) *p* → ~*q*   (3) ~*q* → *p*   (4) ~ (*p* ∧ *q*)

7. Which statement is logically equivalent to ~ (*c* ∨ ~*d*)?
   (1) ~*c* ∨ *d*   (2) ~*c* ∨ ~*d*   (3) ~*c* ∧ *d*   (4) ~*c* ∧ ~*d*

8. If *p* represents the statement "It is January," and *q* represents the statement "I have a cold," which statement is logically equivalent to ~ (*p* ∧ *q*)?
   (1) It is January and I have a cold.
   (2) It is not January and I do not have a cold.
   (3) It is not January or I do not have a cold.
   (4) It is January or I have a cold.

9. The statement ~*r* ∧ *s* is logically equivalent to:
   (1) ~ (*r* ∧ *s*)   (2) ~ (*r* ∨ *s*)   (3) ~ (~*r* ∨ *s*)   (4) ~ (*r* ∨ ~*s*)

10. Let *p* represent the statement "A rhombus is a parallelogram," and *q* represent the statement "A circle has three sides." Which of the following statements is true?
   (1) *p* → (*p* ∨ *q*)   (3) (*p* ∨ *q*) → (*p* ∧ *q*)
   (2) ~*q* → *q*   (4) ~*q* → ~ (*p* ∨ *q*)

7

11. Which of the following statements is a tautology?

(1) $\sim (p \rightarrow \sim p)$ (3) $q \rightarrow \sim q$

(2) $\sim (p \rightarrow q)$ (4) $(p \rightarrow q) \vee (q \rightarrow p)$

12. Which statement is true for all possible truth values of p and q?

(1) $p \rightarrow \sim q$ (3) $p \rightarrow (q \vee \sim q)$

(2) $(p \vee \sim p) \rightarrow q$ (4) $\sim (p \wedge \sim p) \rightarrow q$

13. Construct a truth table to verify that:

(a) $\sim (p \wedge q)$ is logically equivalent to $\sim p \vee \sim q$.

(b) $\sim (p \vee q)$ is logically equivalent to $\sim p \wedge \sim q$.

14–15. For each of the following, construct a truth table to show the following pairs of statements are logically equivalent:

14. $(p \wedge q) \leftrightarrow p$ and $p \rightarrow q$ **15.** $[(p \rightarrow q) \wedge \sim q]$ and $\sim p$

1.3 FORMING THE CONVERSE, INVERSE, AND CONTRAPOSITIVE

KEY IDEAS

By interchanging or negating both parts of a conditional, or by doing both, three conditionals of special interest—the **converse**, the **inverse**, and the **contrapositive**—can be formed.

Related Conditionals

Let p represent the statement "$x = 2$," and q represent the statement "x is even." Then four related conditionals can be formed:

Statement	Symbolic Form	Example
Original	$p \rightarrow q$	If $x = 2$, then x is even. (True)
Converse	$q \rightarrow p$	If x is even, then $x = 2$. (False)
Inverse	$\sim p \rightarrow \sim q$	If $x \neq 2$, then x is not even. (False)
Contrapositive	$\sim q \rightarrow \sim p$	If x is not even, then $x \neq 2$. (True)

Logically Equivalent Conditionals

A conditional $(p \rightarrow q)$ and its contrapositive $(\sim q \rightarrow \sim p)$ will always have the same truth value and are, therefore, logically equivalent. The converse $(q \rightarrow p)$ and inverse $(\sim p \rightarrow \sim q)$ of a conditional are also logically equivalent statements.

Examples

1. What is the inverse of $\sim p \rightarrow q$?

Solution: Forming the inverse requires negating both parts of the conditional: $\sim (\sim p) \rightarrow \sim (q)$. The hypothesis of this conditional may be simplified by keeping in mind that consecutive negations cancel out since one undoes the effect of the other. The correct answer is $\boldsymbol{p \rightarrow \sim q}$.

2. Let p represent "It is raining," and q represent "I have my umbrella." Express in words the contrapositive of $q \rightarrow p$.
Solution: The contrapositive of $q \rightarrow p$ is $\sim p \rightarrow \sim q$, so that:

$q \rightarrow p$: If I have my umbrella, then it is raining.

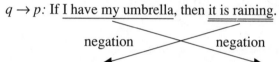

negation   negation

$\sim p \rightarrow \sim q$: **If it is not raining, then I do not have my umbrella.**

3. Which statement is logically equivalent to $r \rightarrow \sim s$?
(1) $\sim s \rightarrow r$ (2) $r \rightarrow s$ (3) $\sim s \rightarrow \sim r$ (4) $s \rightarrow \sim r$

Solution: A conditional and its contrapositive are logically equivalent. Choice (1) represents the converse. Negating both parts of the converse leads to the statement in choice (4), which is the contrapositive of the original statement. The correct answer is **choice (4)**.

4. Given the true statement "If a figure is a square, then the figure is a rectangle," which statement is also true?
(1) If a figure is not a rectangle, then it is a square.
(2) If a figure is a rectangle, then it is a square.
(3) If a figure is not a rectangle, then it is not a square.
(4) If a figure is not a square, then the figure is not a rectangle.

Solution: A conditional and its contrapositive always have the same truth value. The contrapositive of a true statement is also true. Since choice (3) is the contrapositive of the given statement, the correct answer is **choice (3)**.

Exercise Set 1.3

1. Which statement is logically equivalent to the statement "If it is sunny, then it is hot"?
   (1) If it is hot, then it is sunny.
   (2) If it is not hot, then it is not sunny.
   (3) If it is not sunny, then it is not hot.
   (4) If it is not hot, then it is sunny.

2. Which statement is logically equivalent to $\sim p \to q?$
   (1) $p \to \sim q$ (2) $\sim q \to p$ (3) $q \to \sim p$ (4) $\sim q \to \sim p$

3. In which of the following pairs are the statements logically equivalent?
   (1) $k \to h$ and $\sim h \to \sim k$ (3) $k \to h$ and $\sim k \to \sim h$
   (2) $h \to k$ and $\sim h \to \sim k$ (4) $h \to k$ and $k \to h$

4. Which statement is logically equivalent to the statement "If $n \le 5$, then $n \le 8$"?
   (1) If $n > 8$, then $n > 5$.   (3) If $n > 5$, then $n > 8$.
   (2) If $n \le 5$, then $n \le 8$.   (4) If $n \le 8$, then $n \le 5$.

5. Which statement is logically equivalent to the statement "If she says it, she does not mean it"?
   (1) If she means it, she does not say it.
   (2) If she means it, she says it.
   (3) If she does not say it, she means it.
   (4) If she does not mean it, she says it.

6. Which statement is logically equivalent to the *inverse* of the statement "If I study hard, then I will pass"?
   (1) If I do not study hard, then I will pass.
   (2) If I do not pass, then I will not study hard.
   (3) If I will pass, then I study hard.
   (4) If I will pass, then I do not study hard.

7. Construct a truth table to show that the biconditional is logically equivalent to the conjunction of a conditional statement and its converse.

1.4 LAWS OF REASONING

Logical inference involves arriving at a *conclusion* as a result of applying valid methods of reasoning to a set of assumptions called **premises.** This section presents some of the more commonly used laws of reasoning and illustrates how they can be applied to draw conclusions.

Format of an Argument

Assume $p \leftrightarrow q$ is true (*premise 1*), and also assume statement q is true (*premise 2*). Then statement p is true (*conclusion*) because p and q must have the same truth value. A set of premises with a valid conclusion forms an *argument,* which can be concisely summarized using the following format:

Premise 1: $p \leftrightarrow q$ (Biconditional is true).
Premise 2: q (Statement q is true.)
_____

Conclusion: p ($\therefore p$ is true.)

In the argument above, the symbol $\therefore$ is read as "therefore" and is sometimes used in place of the word *conclusion.*

Law of Disjunctive Inference

If a disjunction is true, then at least one of the disjuncts must also be true. This means that, if a disjunction is true and one disjunct is false, you can conclude that the remaining disjunct must be true. This argument, referred to as the **Law of Disjunctive Inference**, takes the following form:

Premise 1: $p \lor q$ (Disjunction is true.)
Premise 2: $\sim p$ (Negation of p is true.)
_____

Conclusion: q ($\therefore$ other disjunct is true.)

Note that the second premise states that $\sim p$ is true, so p must be false. Since p is false, q must be true in order for $p \lor q$ to be true.

The Law of Disjunctive Inference may be represented symbolically as follows:

$$[(p \lor q) \land \sim p] \to q \quad \text{or} \quad [(p \lor q) \land \sim q] \to p.$$

Law of Conjunctive Simplification

If the conjunction of two statements is true, then each conjunct is true, that is,

Premise: $p \wedge q$

Conclusion: p (or q)

This fact is called the **Law of Conjunctive Simplification** and may be represented symbolically as follows:

$$(p \wedge q) \rightarrow p \qquad \text{or} \qquad (p \wedge q) \rightarrow q.$$

Example

1. Draw a valid conclusion from the following set of true premises:

I will go skiing or I will stay at home.
I do not stay at home.

Solution: The second premise tells us that the right-hand disjunct of the first premise ("I will stay at home") is false. By the Law of Disjunctive Inference, the left-hand disjunct must be true. Therefore, a valid conclusion is **"I will go skiing."**

Law of Contrapositive Inference

Starting with the true premise $p \rightarrow q$, you can conclude that $\sim q \rightarrow \sim p$ is also true since a conditional and its contrapositive always have the same truth value. This rule of logic is known as the **Law of Contrapositive Inference**. For example,

Premise: If it rains, then it pours,   (True)

Conclusion: If it doesn't pour, then it doesn't rain   (True)

Example

2. Give the law of reasoning that can be used to justify each conclusion.

    (a) $m \vee \sim h$ **(c)** $\sim t \vee \sim w$

           h t

Conclusion: m Conclusion: $\sim w$

    (b) $R \wedge T$ **(d)** $\sim r \rightarrow k$

Conclusion: R Conclusion: $\sim k \rightarrow r$

Solutions: **(a) Law of Disjunctive Inference.** According to the second premise, statement h is true, so the right-hand disjunct of the first premise ($\sim h$) is false. Therefore, the left-hand disjunct (m) must be true.

(b) Law of Conjunctive Simplification. Since the conjunction is true, each conjunct is true.

(c) Law of Disjunctive Inference. The second premise states that statement *t* is true. Therefore, the left-hand disjunct of the first premise (*~t*) is false, so the right disjunct (*~w*) is true.

(d) Law of Contrapositive Inference. A conditional (*~r → k*) and its contrapositive (*~k → r*) are logically equivalent. [***Note:*** *r* and ~ (*~r*) are logically equivalent.]

The Chain Rule (Law of the Syllogism)

The **Chain Rule** states that, if the consequent of one conditional and the antecedent of another conditional are related in such a way that the two conditionals take the form

$$p \rightarrow q$$

$$q \rightarrow r,$$

then a third conditional, *p → r,* must also be true. For example,

Premise 1:	If it rains, then I will study.
Premise 2:	If I study, then I will do well in math.

Conclusion:	If it rains, then I will do well in math.

Example 3 shows that it is sometimes necessary to apply the Law of Contrapositive Inference before the Chain Rule can be used.

Example

3. For each set of premises draw a valid conclusion.

(a) *~h → j*
    h → f

(b) If it rains, then I will go to the movies.
    If I study, then I will not go to the movies.

Solutions: **(a)** Form the contrapositive of the first premise and then apply the Chain Rule:

	~j → h	(Contrapositive of *~h → j*)
	h → f	(Second premise)
Conclusion:	*~j → f*	(Application of the Chain Rule)

(b) Form the contrapositive of the second premise and then apply the Chain Rule:

If it rains, then I will go to the movies.
If I go to the movies, then I will not study.

Conclusion: **If it rains, then I will not study.**

Law of Detachment (*Modus Ponens*)

The **Law of Detachment** states that, if a conditional ($p \rightarrow q$) and its antecedent (p) are true, then its consequent (q) must also be true. For example,

Premise 1: If today is hot, then I will go swimming.
Premise 2: Today is hot.

Conclusion: I will go swimming.

Law of *Modus Tollens*

This law of reasoning states that, if a conditional ($p \rightarrow q$) is true and its consequent (q) is false, then its antecedent (p) must be false. For example,

Premise 1: If today is hot, then I will go swimming.
Premise 2: I will *not* go swimming.

Conclusion: Today is *not* hot.

Example

4. Given the following true statements: $\sim a \vee b$, $\sim b$, and $c \rightarrow a$, which statement is also true?
 (1) $c \wedge b$ (2) $\sim b$ (3) $\sim c$ (4) a

Solution: Since $\sim b$ is true, b is false. By the Law of Disjunctive Inference, $\sim a$ is true so a is false. Since $c \rightarrow a$ is true and a is false, $\sim c$ is true by the Law of *Modus Tollens*. The correct answer is **choice (3)**.

Summary of Reasoning Laws Involving Conditionals

Table 1.2 summarizes the laws of reasoning involving conditionals in symbolic and argument forms.

TABLE 1.2 LAWS OF REASONING INVOLVING CONDITIONALS

Law	Symbolic Form	Argument Form
Contrapositive Inference	$(p \rightarrow q) \leftrightarrow (\sim q \rightarrow \sim p)$	$p \rightarrow q$ $\therefore \sim q \rightarrow \sim p$
Detachment (*Modus Ponens*)	$[(p \rightarrow q) \wedge p] \rightarrow q$	$p \rightarrow q$ p $\therefore q$
Modus Tollens	$[(p \rightarrow q) \wedge \sim q] \rightarrow \sim p$	$p \rightarrow q$ $\sim q$ $\therefore \sim p$
Chain Rule	$[(p \rightarrow q) \wedge (q \rightarrow r)] \rightarrow (p \rightarrow r)$	$p \rightarrow q$ $q \rightarrow r$ $\therefore p \rightarrow r$

Examples

5. Let p represent the statement "Today is Saturday."
Let q represent the statement "I stay up late."
Let r represent the statement "I go to school."
Represent each of the following sets of premises symbolically, using the letters p, q, and r and the proper logical connectives. In each case, use both premises to draw a valid conclusion, if possible, and state the law(s) of reasoning being applied.

(a) I go to school or I stay up late.
I do not stay up late.

(b) If I go to school, then today is not Saturday.
Today is Saturday.

(c) If I stay up late, then I do not go to school.
I stay up late.

(d) If today is Saturday, then I do not go to school.
I do not go to school.

Solutions: **(a)** $r \vee q$
$\sim q$

Conclusion: r **(Law of Disjunctive Inference)**

(b) $r \rightarrow \sim p$
p

Conclusion: $\sim r$ **(Law of *Modus Tollens*.** Since the consequent of the given conditional is false, the antecedent of the conditional must also be false.)

(c) $q \rightarrow \sim r$
q

Conclusion: $\sim r$ **(Law of Detachment.** The antecedent of the given conditional is true, so its consequent must also be true.)

15

(d) $p \rightarrow \sim r$
$\sim r$
_____

No valid conclusion is possible. Since the consequent is true $(\sim r)$, the antecedent may be either true or false.

6. The statement $[(a \rightarrow \sim b)] \wedge (c \rightarrow b)]$ is logically equivalent to:
(1) $a \rightarrow c$ (2) $a \rightarrow \sim c$ (3) $\sim a \rightarrow c$ (4) $c \rightarrow a$

Solution: Since a conditional and its contrapositive are logically equivalent, the original statement may be rewritten as $[(a \rightarrow \sim b)] \wedge (\sim b \rightarrow \sim c)]$. When the Chain Rule is applied, the conclusion $a \rightarrow \sim c$ follows. The correct answer is **choice (2)**.

Exercise Set 1.4

1. Which of the following is logically equivalent to the statement "If I watch TV, then I will not do my homework"?
(1) If I do not watch TV, then I will do my homework.
(2) If I do my homework, then I will not watch TV.
(3) If I do not do my homework, then I will watch TV.
(4) If I do my homework, then I will watch TV.

2. Given these true statements: "If a boy plays high school football, he must be passing at least three subjects" and "Bob is not passing three subjects," it follows that:
(1) Bob plays on the football team.
(2) Bob does not play on the football team.
(3) Few boys try out for the team.
(4) No conclusion can be reached.

3. Given these true statements: "Mark goes shopping or he goes to the movies" and "Mark doesn't go to the movies," which statement *must* also be true?
(1) Mark goes shopping.
(2) Mark doesn't go shopping.
(3) Mark doesn't go shopping and he doesn't go to the movies.
(4) Mark stays home.

4. Given these true statements: "If you take a swim, then you don't catch a fish" and "If you row a boat, then you catch a fish," which statement *must* also be true?
(1) If you don't row a boat, then you don't take a swim.
(2) If you take a swim, then you don't row a boat.
(3) If you don't take a swim, then you catch a fish.
(4) If you don't catch a fish, then you don't take a swim.

5. Given the true statement $[(s \lor t) \land \sim s]$, which statement is true?
(1) t (2) $\sim t$ (3) s (4) $s \land \sim t$

6. If $\sim r \to s$ and $\sim s$ are given, which statement *must* be true?
(1) r (2) $\sim r$ (3) $r \to s$ (4) $s \land \sim s$

7. If $a \to b$ and $\sim c \to \sim b$ are true statements, which statement *must* also be true?
(1) $\sim c \to \sim a$ (2) $\sim a \to \sim c$ (3) $a \to \sim c$ (4) $\sim c \to a$

8. If $p \to q$, $p \lor \sim r$, and r are all true statements, which statement *must* also be true?
(1) q (2) $\sim p$ (3) $\sim q$ (4) $\sim r$

9–14. For each set of premises, draw a valid conclusion and state the law(s) of reasoning being applied.

9. $\sim e \lor q$
  e

10. $\sim w \to a$
  $\sim a$

11. $h \to \sim b$
  $c \to b$

12. $x \to \sim y$
  y

13. $A \land \sim B$
  $C \to B$

14. $\sim (r \lor s)$
  $t \to s$

15. Given these true statements: $\sim S \lor T$, $W \to S$, and $\sim T$, explain why:
(a) S is false.   **(b)** W is false.

1.5 LOGIC PROOFS

KEY IDEAS

An argument that gives a step-by-step explanation of how valid methods of reasoning can be used to reach a conclusion from a given set of premises is called a **logic proof**. Although a proof may be presented in different ways, only the statement-reason, two-column proof will be illustrated in this section.

Two-Column Format of Logic Proofs

More complicated arguments that involve several laws of reasoning are sometimes presented as a sequence of numbered statements with corresponding reasons that show, in step-by-step fashion, how principles of logic are used to reach a conclusion. For example,

Given: $\sim (p \wedge \sim q) \big\}$ Premises
$\qquad\qquad\quad p$

Prove: $\quad q \qquad\qquad$ Conclusion

PROOF

Statement	Reason
1. $\sim (p \wedge \sim q)$	1. Given.
2. $\sim p \vee q$	2. De Morgan's laws.
3. p	3. Given.
4. $\sim p$ is false.	4. A statement and its negation have opposite truth values.
5. q	5. Law of Disjunctive Inference (2,4).

Notice that in this form of logic proof:

- Statements and reasons are presented side by side in a two-column arrangement.
- Each numbered statement has a corresponding reason preceded by the same number.
- When a premise appears in the "Statement" column, the corresponding reason is "given."
- The last numbered statement of the proof is the desired conclusion.
- When a law of reasoning appears in the "Reason" column, it is followed by a pair of numbers, inside parentheses, that identify the statements to which the law is being applied. For example, in the preceding proof the Law of Disjunctive Inference is followed by (2, 4), indicating that it is being applied to the second and the fourth statements.

Examples

1. Given: $r \rightarrow t$
$\qquad\qquad r \vee \sim s$
$\qquad\qquad s$
$\quad$ Prove: $\ t$

Solution: Since statement s is true, look in the "Given" for another statement involving statement s. Then use a law of reasoning to draw a conclusion about the truth value of the other letter in the second statement. For example, consider the truth value of $r \vee \sim s$. Since statement s is true, $\sim s$ is false; therefore, by the Law of Disjunctive Inference, r is true. Next, look for a statement in the "Given" involving r. Continue this process until a conclusion is reached about the truth value of statement t.

PROOF

Statement	Reason
1. *s*	1. Given.
2. ~*s* is false.	2. A statement and its negation have opposite truth values.
3. *r* ∨ ~*s*	3. Given.
4. *r*	4. Law of Disjunctive Inference.
5. *r* → *t*	5. Given.
6. *t*	6. Law of Detachment (4, 5).

2. Given: $l \rightarrow \sim j$
$\sim l \rightarrow k$
j
Prove: k

Solution: Begin with statement *j* since it is a simple statement (single letter). Look for another statement in the "Given" that contains letter *j*, and draw a conclusion about the truth value of the other letter in the second statement. Continue this process until a conclusion can be reached about the truth value of statement *k*.

PROOF

Statement	Reason
1. *j*	1. Given.
2. *l* → ~*j*	2. Given.
3. ~*l*	3. Law of *Modus Tollens* (1, 2).
4. ~*l* → *k*	4. Given.
5. *k*	5. Law of Detachment (3, 4).

3. Given: Michael is an athlete.
Michael is not a professional.
If Michael is an athlete and he is salaried, then Michael is a professional.

Let *A* represent: "Michael is an athlete."
Let *P* represent: "Michael is a professional."
Let *S* represent: "Michael is salaried."

Prove: Michael is not salaried.

Solution: Step 1. Write each of the given statements in symbolic form.

- "Michael is an athlete":   *A*
- "Michael is not a professional" is the negation of statement *P:*   ~*P*

- "If Michael is an athlete and he is salaried,
  then Michael is a professional" is the conditional
  that the conjunction of A and S implies P: $\qquad (A \wedge S) \to P$

Step 2. Write the "Prove" in symbolic form.
"Prove: Michael is *not* salaried" is the negation of statement S: $\quad \sim S$

Step 3. Write the two-column proof. Since a conditional, $(A \wedge S) \to P$, and the negation of the conclusion, $\sim P$, are true statements, begin the proof by applying the Law of *Modus Tollens*.

PROOF

Statement	Reason
1. $(A \wedge S) \to P$	1. Given.
2. $\sim P$	2. Given.
3. $\sim(A \wedge S)$	3. Law of *Modus Tollens* (1, 2).
4. $\sim A \vee \sim S$	4. De Morgan's Law.
5. A	5. Given.
6. $\sim S$	6. Law of Disjunctive Inference (4, 5).

4. Given: (1) If Jill studies, then she will know the work.
        (2) If Jill goes out to play, then she will not know the work.
        (3) Jill studies or her parents will not be happy.
        (4) Jill's parents are happy or she will not be allowed to go to the party.
        (5) Jill is allowed to go to the party.

Let S represent: "Jill studies."
Let W represent: "Jill will know the work."
Let P represent: "Jill goes out to play."
Let H represent: "Jill's parents are happy."
Let A represent: "Jill is allowed to go to the party."

  (a) Using S, W, P, H, A, and proper connectives, express each statement in symbolic form.

  (b) Prove: Jill does not go out to play.

Solutions:
(a) Given: (1) $S \to W$
              (2) $P \to \sim W$
              (3) $S \vee \sim H$
              (4) $H \vee \sim A$
              (5) A

(b) The "Prove" can be written in symbolic form as $\sim P$.
    Since letter A in the "Given" stands alone, work "backward" by finding

a compound statement that involves statement A and draw a conclusion about the truth value of the other letter in the second statement. Continue this process until a conclusion can be reached about the truth value of ~P.

PROOF

Statement	Reason
1. A	1. Given.
2. $H \vee \sim A$	2. Given.
3. H	3. Law of Disjunctive Inference (1, 2).
4. $S \vee \sim H$	4. Given.
5. S	5. Law of Disjunctive Inference (3, 4).
6. $S \rightarrow W$	6. Given.
7. W	7. Law of Detachment (5, 6).
8. $P \rightarrow \sim W$	8. Given.
9. $\sim P$	9. Law of *Modus Tollens* (7, 8).

Exercise Set 1.5

1–6. In each case, write a two-column proof.

1. Given: $B \wedge C$
    $C \rightarrow D$
 Prove: D

2. Given: $R \vee \sim T$
    $W \rightarrow T$
    W
 Prove: R

3. Given: $x \vee \sim y$
    $z \rightarrow y$
    $\sim x$
 Prove: $\sim z$

4. Given: $H \vee E$
    $H \rightarrow K$
    $\sim K$
  Prove: E

5. Given: $r \rightarrow s$
    $s \rightarrow t$
    $\sim t$
 Prove: $\sim r$

6. Given: $f \wedge g$
    $f \rightarrow \sim h$
    $i \rightarrow h$
  Prove: $\sim i$

7. Given: Either I do the geometry question or I do the algebra question.
    If I do the algebra question, I get it correct.
    If I get the algebra question correct, I do not lose points.
    However, it is known that I lost points.
    Therefore, I did the geometry question.

Let G represent: "I do the geometry question."
Let A represent: "I do the algebra question."

Let *C* represent: "I get the algebra question correct."
Let *P* represent: "I lose points."

(a) Using *G, A, C, P,* and proper connectives, express each statement in symbolic form.
(b) Using laws of inference, show that a valid conclusion has been reached.

8. Given: I study hard or I do not take Regents mathematics.
     If I take Course II, then I take Regents mathematics.
     If I do not take Course II, then I did not pass Course I.
     I passed Course I.

Let *P* represent: "I study hard."
Let *Q* represent: "I take Regents mathematics."
Let *R* represent: "I take Course II."
Let *S* represent: "I passed Course I."

Using laws of inference, prove that I study hard.

9. Given: If the programmer is skilled, the computer will be accurate.
     Either the programmer is skilled, or the employees are lazy.
     If the employees are lazy, John will be fired.
     If the computer is accurate, Harry will get a raise.
     John did not get fired.

Let *P* represent: "The programmer is skilled."
Let *C* represent: "The computer is accurate."
Let *E* represent: "The employees are lazy."
Let *J* represent: "John will be fired."
Let *H* represent: "Harry will get a raise."

(a) Using *P, C, E, J, H,* and proper connectives, express each statement in symbolic form.
(b) Using laws of inference, prove that Harry will get a raise.

10. Given: Either a crime was committed or Arthur is not telling the truth.
     If the dog howled, a crime was not committed.
     If the dog did not howl, the butler did it.
     Arthur is telling the truth.

Let *A* represent: "Arthur is telling the truth."
Let *B* represent: "The butler did it."
Let *C* represent: "A crime was committed."
Let *D* represent: "The dog howled."

(a) Using *A, B, C, D,* and proper connectives, express each statement in symbolic form.
(b) Using the laws of inference, prove that the butler did it.

REGENTS TUNE-UP: CHAPTER 1

Each of the questions in this section has appeared on a previous Course II Regents Examination. Here is an opportunity for you to review the material in Chapter 1 and, at the same time, prepare for the Course II Regents Examination.

1. Which statement is logically equivalent to $\sim(p \vee \sim q)$?
   (1) $\sim p \vee \sim q$ (2) $\sim p \wedge \sim q$ (3) $\sim p \wedge q$ (4) $p \wedge q$

2. If the statement $[(p \vee q) \wedge (\sim p)]$ is true, then which statement *must* also be true?
   (1) $p \wedge q$ (2) p (3) $\sim q$ (4) q

3. Which statement is logically equivalent to the statement "If she does not mean it, she does not say it"?
   (1) If she says it, she means it.
   (2) If she means it, she says it.
   (3) If she does not say it, she means it.
   (4) If she does not mean it, she says it.

4. If $r \vee t$ and $\sim t$ are true statements, then which statement is true?
   (1) $\sim r$ (2) r (3) t (4) $r \rightarrow t$

5. Which statement is the inverse of "If it rains, then I do not go fishing?"
   (1) If it rains, then I go fishing.
   (2) If I do not go fishing, then it rains.
   (3) If it does not rain, then I go fishing.
   (4) If I go fishing, then it does not rain.

6. Given these true statements: $J \vee \sim N$ and $N,$ which statement *must* also be true?
   (1) J (2) $\sim J$ (3) $J \wedge \sim N$ (4) $\sim J \wedge N$

7. If $a \rightarrow b$ and $\sim c \rightarrow \sim b$ are both true statements, which statement *must* also be true?
   (1) $a \rightarrow c$ (2) $b \rightarrow c$ (3) $c \rightarrow a$ (4) $c \rightarrow b$

8. Which statement is logically equivalent to $\sim (p \vee \sim q)$?
   (1) $p \wedge \sim q$ (2) $\sim p \wedge q$ (3) $\sim p \vee q$ (4) $\sim p \wedge \sim q$

9. Given these true statements: "Jay loves the math team" and "If the math team does not win, then Jay does not love the math team," which statement *must* also be true?
   (1) The math team loses.   (3) The math team loves Jay.
   (2) The math team wins.   (4) Jay does not love the math team.

10. Which conclusion logically follows from these true statements: "If the negotiations fail, the baseball strike will not end" and "If the World Series is played, the baseball strike has ended"?
 (1) If negotiations fail, the World Series will not be played.
 (2) If negotiations fail, the World Series will be played.
 (3) If the baseball strike ends, the World Series will be played.
 (4) If negotiations do not fail, the baseball strike will not end.

11. Which statement is logically equivalent to $(a \vee b) \to c$?
 (1) $\sim c \to (\sim a \wedge \sim b)$
 (2) $\sim c \to (\sim a \vee \sim b)$
 (3) $\sim c \to (\sim a \vee b)$
 (4) $\sim c \to (a \wedge \sim b)$

12. *On your answer paper,* write the letters (a) through (e). Next to each letter, write a valid conclusion that can be deduced from each set of true statements. If no valid conclusion can be deduced, write "No conclusion."

 (a) $A \vee \sim B$ **(d)** $\sim A \to B$
    $\sim A$ $C \to \sim B$

 (b) $\sim P \to Q$ **(e)** $\sim A \to \sim B$
     P B

 (c) $\sim X \vee \sim Y$
     $\sim X$

13. Given: $A \to \sim (B \wedge C)$
       $C \vee E$
       $\sim A \to \sim D$
       B
       D
 Prove: E

14. Given: If the figure is a rhombus, then it is a parallelogram.
       If the figure is a quadrilateral and a parallelogram, then it is a square.
       The figure is not a square.
       The figure is a quadrilateral.

 Let R represent: "The figure is a rhombus."
 Let P represent: "The figure is a parallelogram."
 Let Q represent: "The figure is a quadrilateral."
 Let S represent: "The figure is a square."

 Prove: The figure is *not* a rhombus.

15. Given: If Kim and Lynette play soccer, then Glenda plays golf.
       If Glenda plays golf, then Helen does not play field hockey.
       Lynette plays soccer.
       Helen plays field hockey.

Let K represent: "Kim plays soccer."
Let L represent: "Lynette plays soccer."
Let G represent: "Glenda plays golf."
Let H represent: "Helen plays field hockey."

Prove: Kim does *not* play soccer.

16. Given: If laws are good and strictly enforced, then crime will diminish.
If laws are not strictly enforced, then the problem is critical.
Crime has not diminished.
Laws are good.

Let G represent: "Laws are good."
Let S represent: "Laws are strictly enforced."
Let D represent: "Crime has diminished."
Let P represent: "The problem is critical."

Using G, S, D, and P, prove: The problem is critical.

ANSWERS TO SELECTED EXERCISES: CHAPTER 1

Section 1.1
1. (a) $p \vee q$ **(b)** $p \wedge q$ **(c)** $r \to p$ **(d)** $p \leftrightarrow r$
2. (a) F   **(b)** T   **(c)** T   **(d)** F   **(e)** T
3. (a) F   **(b)** F   **(c)** T   **(d)** T   **(e)** T
4. (a) F   **(b)** T   **(c)** F   **(d)** F   **(e)** T
5. (3)   **6.** (4)   **7.** (4)   **8.** (2)   **9.** (4)   **10.** (2)

Section 1.2
1. F   **2.** T   **3.** F
4. (a) He is not a snob and he likes caviar.
    (b) If he is not a snob, then he does not like caviar.
5. (4)   **7.** (3)   **9.** (4)   **11.** (4)
6. (3)   **8.** (3)   **10.** (1)   **12.** (3)

Section 1.3
1. (2)   **2.** (2)   **3.** (1)   **4.** (1)   **5.** (1)   **6.** (3)

Section 1.4
1. (2)   **5.** (1)   **9.** q **13.** $\sim C$
2. (2)   **6.** (1)   **10.** w **14.** $\sim t$
3. (1)   **7.** (1)   **11.** $h \to \sim c$
4. (2)   **8.** (1)   **12.** $\sim x$

Section 1.5

1.

Statement	Reason
1. $B \wedge C$	1. Given.
2. C	2. Law of Conjunctive Simplification.
3. $C \rightarrow D$	3. Given.
4. D	4. Law of *Modus Ponens* (2, 3).

3.

Statement	Reason
1. $\sim x$	1. Given.
2. $x \vee \sim y$	2. Given.
3. $\sim y$	3. Law of Disjunctive Inference (1, 2).
4. $z \rightarrow y$	4. Given.
5. $\sim z$	5. Law of *Modus Tollens* (3, 4).

10. (a) Given: $C \vee \sim A$
$\qquad D \rightarrow \sim C$
$\qquad \sim D \rightarrow B$
$\qquad A$

(b) Prove: B

Statement	Reason
1. A	1. Given.
2. $C \vee \sim A$	2. Given.
3. C	3. Law of Disjunctive Inference (1, 2).
4. $D \rightarrow \sim C$	4. Given.
5. $\sim D$	5. Law of *Modus Tollens* (3, 4).
6. $\sim D \rightarrow B$	6. Given.
7. B	7. Law of *Modus Ponens* (5, 6).

Regents Tune-Up: Chapter 1

1. (3)   **6.** (1)   **11.** (1)

2. (4)   **7.** (1)   **12.** **(a)** ~B

3. (1)   **8.** (2)   **(b)** No conclusion

4. (2)   **9.** (2)   **(c)** No conclusion

5. (3)   **10.** (1)   **(d)** $\sim A \rightarrow \sim C$

                                               (e) A

13.

Statement	Reason
1. D	1. Given.
2. $\sim A \rightarrow \sim D$	2. Given.
3. A	3. Law of *Modus Tollens* (1, 2).
4. $A \rightarrow \sim (B \wedge C)$	4. Given.
5. $\sim (B \wedge C)$	5. Law of *Modus Ponens* (3, 4).
6. $\sim B \vee \sim C$	6. De Morgan's Law.
7. B	7. Given.
8. $\sim C$	8. Law of Disjunctive Inference (6, 7).
9. $C \vee E$	9. Given.
10. E	10. Law of Disjunctive Inference (8, 9).

## CHAPTER 2

MATHEMATICAL SYSTEMS*

2.1 THE REAL NUMBERS AND MATHEMATICAL SYSTEMS

KEY IDEAS

A **mathematical system** includes the following:
- A set.
- At least one operation.
- Rules for applying the operation(s) to members of the set.

The set of real numbers, together with any of the four arithmetic operations, is an example of a mathematical system. This chapter discusses different mathematical systems and their properties.

Sets and Subsets

A **set** is a collection of objects, called **elements,** which are listed within braces, { }. If set S contains the first three letters of the alphabet, then $S = \{a, b, c\}$. Since the order of the elements within the braces does not matter, $\{b, a, c\} = \{a, b, c\}$.

If each element of set B is also an element of set A, then set B is a **subset** of set A. If $B = \{2, 4\}$ and $A = \{1, 2, 3, 4, 5\}$, then set B is a subset of set A.

The Set of Integers

The numbers $0, 1, 2, 3, 4, \ldots$ are called **whole numbers**. The set of integers includes the whole numbers and their negatives. Thus,

$$\{\text{Integers}\} = \{\ldots, -3, -2, -1, 0, 1, 2, 3, \ldots\}.$$

The three dots indicate that the pattern continues without ending. The **positive integers** are the numbers $1, 2, 3, \ldots$, and the **negative integers** are the numbers $-1, -2, -3, \ldots$. The set of **nonnegative integers** includes 0 and the positive integers.

---

*This chapter includes material that represents optional topics in the New York State Syllabus.

The Set of Rational Numbers

Numbers such as 3, –8, $\frac{4}{9}$, 0.5, and 0.3333 are rational numbers. A **rational number** is any number that can be written in fractional form as a quotient of two integers, provided that the denominator is not 0. Integers are rational numbers since each integer can be put into this form by writing it as a fraction with a denominator of 1. For example, 3 and –8 are rational numbers since $3 = \frac{3}{1}$ and $-8 = -\frac{8}{1}$.

Decimal numbers that can be expressed as the quotient of two integers also represent rational numbers. For example, terminating decimals such as 0.5 $(= \frac{1}{2})$ and repeating decimals such as $0.33333 \ldots (= \frac{1}{3})$ are examples of rational numbers.

The set of whole numbers is a subset of the set of integers, and the set of integers is a subset of the set of rational numbers.

The Set of Real Numbers

Numbers such as $\sqrt{2}$ and π (approximately 3.14) cannot be expressed as the ratio of two integers. These numbers are called **irrational**. Decimal numbers such as $0.1010010001 \ldots$ that are nonterminating and nonrepeating are irrational. Every real number is either rational or irrational, as shown in Figure 2.1.

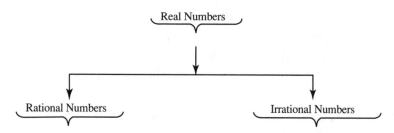

Figure 2.1   The Real Numbers

Binary Operations

A **binary operation,** such as ordinary addition or multiplication, works on exactly two numbers of a set at a time. If the outcome of the binary operation is also a member of the same set, then the set is said to be **closed** under that operation. The set of whole numbers is closed under addition since the sum of any two whole numbers is another whole number. The set of whole numbers is *not* closed under division since the quotient of two whole numbers may not be a whole number, as in $3 \div 2 = 1.5$.

Defining Operations

A new binary operation may be defined in one of two ways:

- By writing a formula that expresses the new operation in terms of familiar operations. As an example, consider the operation $\square$, which is defined by the formula

$$a \square b = \sqrt{a^2 + b^2}.$$

To find the value of $3 \square 4$, replace a by 3 and b by 4 in the formula $\sqrt{a^2 + b^2}$:

$$a \square b = \sqrt{a^2 + b^2}$$
$$3 \square 4 = \sqrt{3^2 + 4^2}$$
$$= \sqrt{9 + 16} = \sqrt{25}$$
$$= \mathbf{5}$$

- By presenting a table that shows the result of performing the operation on every possible pair of elements in the set for which the operation is defined. To illustrate, the accompanying table defines the operation $\diamond$ for the set $\{A, C, T\}$. The table is read in the same way that an ordinary "times table" (multiplication table) is read.

$\diamond$	A	C	T
A	C	T	W
C	A	T	T
T	A	A	C

To find the value of $T \diamond C$, locate T in the column headed by the operation symbol $\diamond$ and follow the same row to the right until it meets the column headed by C. The table entry that represents the value of $T \diamond C$ is located by drawing imaginary lines from T and C, as shown in the accompanying table. Since these lines intersect at A, $T \diamond C = A$.

$\diamond$	A	C	T
A			
C			
T		$\rightarrow A$	

Here are some additional examples that use the same table.

Example 1: Is the set $\{A, C, T\}$ closed under $\diamond$?

The set $\{A, C, T\}$ is **not closed** under operation $\diamond$ because $A \diamond T = W$ and W is *not* a member of the set.

Example 2: What is the value of $(C \diamond T) \diamond A?$

Evaluate $(C \diamond T) \diamond A$ by working from left to right.

$$(\underline{C \diamond T}) \diamond A = T \diamond A = A$$

Example 3: Solve for x: $A \diamond x = T$.

Locate A in the column headed by the operation symbol, $\diamond$. Move along the A row until the value T is encountered. Then determine the corresponding column heading, which is C. Since $A \diamond C = T$, $x = C$. The solution set is $\{C\}$.

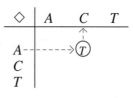

Example 4: Solve for x: $C \diamond x = T$.

From the table, $C \diamond C = T$ and $C \diamond T = T$, so that $x = C$ or $x = T$. The solution set is $\{C, T\}$.

Example 5: Solve for x: $T \diamond x = T$.

Since the third row of table values does not contain a T, there is *no* value of x that makes the equation $T \diamond x = T$ true. Therefore, the solution set is the empty set, $\{\ \}$.

Examples

1. If $a \otimes b$ is defined as $\left(\frac{a}{b}\right)^2$, what is the value of $6 \otimes 2$?

Solution: Let $a = 6$ and $b = 2$. Then

$$a \otimes b = \left(\frac{a}{b}\right)^2$$

$$6 \otimes 2 = \left(\frac{6}{2}\right)^2 = 3^2 = 9$$

2. Compute $(z * y) * x$ in the system defined by the accompanying table.

*	x	y	z
x	x	z	z
y	z	y	z
z	x	y	x

Solution: $(\underline{z * y}) * x$

Compute $z * y$: $\underline{y * x}$

Compute $y * x$: z

3. Using the accompanying table, find y if $a * y = c * d$.

*	a	b	c	d
a	b	c	d	a
b	c	d	a	b
c	d	a	b	c
d	a	b	c	d

Solution: First use the table to compute the right side of the equation.

$$a * y = \underline{c * d}$$
$$= c$$

To find the value of y, move along the a row until the value c is encountered. Then determine the corresponding column heading, which is b. Therefore $y = \boldsymbol{b}$ since $a * b = c$.

*	a	b	c	d
a		→ ⓒ		
b				
c				
d				

Identity and Inverses for Addition

If 0 is added to any real number, the sum is that number. For example, $4 + 0 = 4$ and $0 + 4 = 4$. The number 0 is called the **additive identity**.

If the sum of two numbers is 0, then either number is called the **additive inverse** of the other number. Thus, the additive inverse of any real number is the *opposite* of that number. For example, –5 is the additive inverse (opposite) of 5 since $5 + (-5) = 0$, and 5 is the additive inverse (opposite) of –5 since $(-5) + 5 = 0$.

Identity and Inverses for Multiplication

The number 1 has the same properties for multiplication that 0 has for addition. If any real number is multiplied by 1, the product is that number. For example, $4 \times 1 = 4$ and $1 \times 4 = 4$. The number 1 is called the **multiplicative identity**.

If the product of two numbers is 1, then either number is called the **multiplicative inverse** of the other number. For example, the multiplicative inverse of 5 is $\frac{1}{5}$ since $5 \times \frac{1}{5} = 1$, and the multiplicative inverse of $\frac{2}{3}$ is $\frac{3}{2}$ since $\frac{2}{3} \times \frac{3}{2} = 1$. Thus, the multiplicative inverse of a nonzero number is the *reciprocal* of that number.

Finding the Identity Element for a Binary Operation

The **identity element** for a set under a binary operation is the element of that set that always produces the same element as the one on which it operates.

Table (a) in Figure 2.2 defines the binary operation Ω for the set $\{T, A, B, L, E\}$. The identity element under this operation is an element i such that

$$x\,\Omega\,i = x \quad \text{and} \quad i\,\Omega\,x = x$$

for $x = T, A, B, L,$ or E.

Ω	T	A	B	L	E
T	L	E	T	A	B
A	E	T	A	B	L
B	T	A	B	L	E
L	A	B	L	E	T
E	B	L	E	T	A

(a)

Ω	T	A	B	L	E
T	L	E	T	A	B
A	E	T	A	B	L
B	T	A	B	L	E
L	A	B	L	E	T
E	B	L	E	T	A

(b)

Figure 2.2 The Binary Operation Ω for the Set $\{T, A, B, L, E\}$

The identity element for the set $\{T, A, B, L, E\}$ is B since

- $T\,\Omega\,B = T$ and $B\,\Omega\,T = T;$
- $A\,\Omega\,B = A$ and $B\,\Omega\,A = A;$
- $B\,\Omega\,B = B;$
- $L\,\Omega\,B = L$ and $B\,\Omega\,L = L;$
- $E\,\Omega\,B = E$ and $B\,\Omega\,E = E.$

Table (b) in Figure 2.2 shows how to pick out the identity element at a glance. The elements under column heading B are identical to those in the column to the left of the vertical line. Thus, $x\,\Omega\,B = B$ for $x = T, A, B, L,$ or E. Similarly, the row for B is identical to the row in the top heading. Hence, $B\,\Omega\,x = B$ for $x = T, A, B, L,$ or E.

Finding the Inverse of an Element for a Binary Operation

The identity element of a set is the *same* for each member of the set, while the **inverse** of an element depends on the particular element. Under a binary

33

operation, an element and its inverse produce the identity element for that operation. For the binary operation defined in table (a) in Figure 2.2, the inverse of element T is element E since

$$T \,\Omega\, E = E \,\Omega\, T = B = \text{identity element.}$$

To find the inverse of element A, look in row A for B, the identity element. Element B is at the intersection with the column headed L. Thus, $A \,\Omega\, L = B$. Similarly, in the column for A, B is at the intersection with row L, so $L \,\Omega\, A = B$. Hence, L is the inverse of A. You should verify that the inverse of element B is B.

Example

4. Using the accompanying table, find the following:
(a) The identity element for operation $\square$.
(b) The inverse of 2.

$\square$	1	2	3	4
1	3	4	1	2
2	4	1	2	3
3	1	2	3	4
4	2	3	4	1

Solutions: **(a)** The identity element for a set always produces the same number as the one on which it operates.

Step 1. Find the row in the table that duplicates the column headings to the right of the operation symbol. Notice that:

$$
\begin{array}{l}
3\ \square\ 1 = 1 \\
3\ \square\ 2 = 2 \\
3\ \square\ 3 = 3 \\
3\ \square\ 3 = 3
\end{array}
\longmapsto
$$

$\square$	1	2	3	4
1				
2				
3	(1	2	3	4)
4				

Step 2. Find the column in the table that duplicates the column headed by the operation symbol, $\square$. Notice that:

$$
\begin{array}{l}
1\ \square\ 3 = 1 \\
2\ \square\ 3 = 2 \\
3\ \square\ 3 = 3 \\
4\ \square\ 3 = 4
\end{array}
$$

$\square$	1	2	3	4
1			(1	
2			2	
3			3	
4			4)	

Step 3. Apply the information gained in Steps 1 and 2. Step 1 tells you that $3\ \square\ x = x$ for all x in the set. Step 2 tells you that $x\ \square\ 3 = x$ for all x in the set. Therefore,

$$3\ \square\ x = x\ \square\ 3 = x \quad \text{for all } x \text{ in the set.}$$

The identity element for operation $\square$ is **3**.

(b) Let x = inverse of 2.
Then, $2 \square x = 3$ (the identity element) and $x \square 2 = 3$.
From the table, $x = 4$ since $2 \square 4 = 3$ and $4 \square 2 = 3$.
Therefore, the inverse of 2 is **4**.

Keep in mind that, before you can determine the inverse of an element of a set under a particular operation, you must know the identity element for that set under that operation.

Exercise Set 2.1

1. Which is *not* a rational number?
   (1) $\sqrt{36}$ (3) $\sqrt{200}$
   (2) 1.25   (4) 0.121212 . . .

2. For which operation is the set $\{-1, 0, 1\}$ closed?
   (1) addition   (3) multiplication
   (2) subtraction   (4) division

3. Which set is *not* closed under the operation of multiplication?
   (1) {odd integers}   (3) {prime numbers}
   (2) {even integers}   (4) {rational numbers}

4. Excluding 0, which set does *not* have a multiplicative inverse for each of its elements?
   (1) {integers}   (3) {real numbers}
   (2) {rational numbers}   (4) $\{-1, \frac{1}{2}, 2, 1\}$

5. If Ω is a binary operation defined as $a \, \Omega \, b = a^2 + b^2 - 2ab$, evaluate $7 \, \Omega \, 4$.

6. If $\Diamond$ is a binary operation defined as $r \Diamond s = \dfrac{r^2}{s}$, evaluate $6 \Diamond 3$.

7. If $x * y$ is defined as $x^2 - 3y$, find the value of $4 * 2$.

8. If $a \circledast b$ is a binary operation defined as $\dfrac{a+b}{a}$, evaluate $2 \circledast 4$.

9. Find the value of $(B \, \# \, S) \, \# \, S$ within the system defined below.

#	B	E	S	T
B	T	S	E	B
E	S	T	B	E
S	E	B	T	S
T	B	E	S	T

10. What is the identity element in the system defined by the accompanying table?

#	L	U	C	K
L	K	C	U	L
U	C	K	L	U
C	U	L	K	C
K	L	U	C	K

Exercise 10

*	1	2	3	4
1	4	1	2	3
2	1	2	3	4
3	2	3	4	1
4	3	4	1	2

Exercise 11

11. Solve the equation $3 * y = 1$ for y in the accompanying table.

12. Using the accompanying table, find x if $x \oplus 4 = 3$.

$\oplus$	1	2	3	4
1	2	3	4	1
2	3	4	1	2
3	4	1	2	3
4	1	2	3	4

Exercise 12

$\square$	a	b	c	d
a	c	d	a	b
b	d	a	b	c
c	a	b	c	d
d	b	c	d	a

Exercise 13

13. Using the accompanying table, find the inverse element of b.

14. The accompanying table defines the operation @ on the set $\{N, I, T, A\}$. What is the inverse of T?

@	N	I	T	A
N	I	T	A	N
I	T	A	N	I
T	A	N	I	T
A	N	I	T	A

2.2 SOME ADDITIONAL PROPERTIES OF MATHEMATICAL SYSTEMS

Real numbers behave in predictable ways. The order in which real numbers are added or multiplied does not matter. The **commutative law** states that this property holds for any pair of real numbers. The **associative law** states that this property works also for sums or products of three real numbers.

The **distributive property** links the operations of multiplication and addition by stating that the parentheses in an expression such as $3(2 + 4)$ can be removed by writing $3(2 + 4) = 3 \cdot 2 + 3 \cdot 4$.

The Commutative and Associative Properties

A particular binary operation may or may not be a commutative or an associative operation.

- If the order in which any *two* members of set are operated on does not matter, then the operation is **commutative**.
- If the order in which any *three* members of a set are operated on does not matter, then the operation is **associative**.

Diagonal Test for Commutativity

A binary operation that is defined by a table is commutative if and only if the table values are symmetric with respect to a diagonal line drawn from the operation symbol to the opposite corner of the table. In the accompanying table, the operation Ω is commutative on $\{Q, U, A, D\}$ since it passes the diagonal test for commutativity. Notice that the same elements appear in corresponding positions (that is, positions that have their row and column numbers interchanged) on either side of the diagonal.

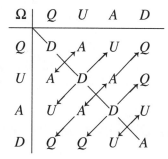

Example

#	M	A	T	H
M	A	T	H	M
A	T	H	M	A
T	H	M	A	T
H	M	A	T	H

1. Give the elements {M, A, T, H} and the operation # as shown in the accompanying table:

(a) What is the identity element for the operation #?
(b) What is the inverse of M?
(c) Determine whether the set {M, A, T, H} is commutative under #.
(d) Find the value of M # [A # (T # H)].
(e) Find x if H # x = A.

Solutions: **(a)** *H* is the identity element for # since the row for *H* duplicates the column headings and the column for *H* duplicates the column headed by the operation symbol, #.

(b) The element at the intersection of the *M* row with the *T* column is *H*, so M # T = H, where *H* is the identity element. Also, the element at the intersection of the *T* row with the *M* column is *H*, so T # M = H. Since

$$M \# T = H \text{ and } T \# M = H,$$

the inverse of *M* is **T.**

(c) As shown in the accompanying diagram, the table that defines # passes the diagonal test for commutativity, so the set **{M, A, T, H} is commutative under #.**

(d) M # [A # (T # H)]

M # [A # T]

M # M

A

(e) The element at the intersection of the *H* row with the *A* column is *A*, so H # A = A. Therefore, x = **A.**

The Distributive Property

The distributive property of real numbers links the operations of multiplication and addition so that, if *a*, *b*, and *c* are real numbers, then $a \cdot (b + c) = a \cdot b + a \cdot c$.

Example

2. Using the set {0, 2, 4, 6, 8} and the operations # and @ as shown in the accompanying tables, verify that

$$4 @ (6 \# 8) = (4 @ 6) \# (4 @ 8).$$

#	0	2	4	6	8
0	0	2	4	6	8
2	2	4	6	8	0
4	4	6	8	0	2
6	6	8	0	2	4
8	8	0	2	4	6

@	0	2	4	6	8
0	0	0	0	0	0
2	0	4	8	2	6
4	0	8	6	4	2
6	0	2	4	6	8
8	0	6	2	8	4

Solution: Evaluate and then compare each side of the given equation. Evaluate left side of equation: $4 @ \underbrace{(6 \# 8)}$

$$4 @ \underbrace{(\quad 4 \quad)}_{6}$$

Evaluate right side of equation: $\underbrace{(4 @ 6)} \# \underbrace{(4 @ 8)}$

$$\underbrace{(\quad 4 \quad) \# (\quad 2 \quad)}_{6}$$

Since each side of the given equation evaluates to 6, the statement $4 @ (6 \# 8) = (4 @ 6) \# (4 @ 8)$ is **true**.

Exercise Set 2.2

1. Using the accompanying tables, find the value of $(C \triangle A) * (A \triangle C)$.

△	A	C	T
A	C	A	T
C	T	A	C
T	A	C	T

*	A	C	T
A	A	A	A
C	A	C	T
T	T	T	T

2. If the accompanying table defines a commutative operation, find the value of $b \oplus c$.

⊕	w	a	b	c
w	w		w	
a		c		
b			a	
c	w	a	b	c

#	w	x	y	z
w	x	z	w	x
x	z	y	x	w
y	w	x	y	z
z	x	w	z	y

Exercise 2   **Exercise 3**

39

3. Given the set $\{w, x, y, z\}$ and the operation # as shown in the accompanying table, which statement is *not* true?
(1) The identity for the system is y.
(2) The set is closed under #.
(3) The set is commutative under #.
(4) Every element of the set has an inverse under #.

4. Given the set $\{a, b, c, d\}$ and the operation $\triangle$ as shown in the accompanying table, except for the second row, which has been omitted. If the operation is commutative, which could be the second row?
(1) $a\,b\,c\,d$ (2) $b\,c\,d\,a$ (3) $c\,d\,a\,b$ (4) $d\,a\,b\,c$

$\triangle$	a	b	c	d
a	b	c	d	a
b				
c	d	a	b	c
d	a	b	c	d

Exercise 4

$\circledast$	0	1	2	3
0	0	1	2	3
1	1	2	3	4
2	4	5	6	7
3	9	10	11	12

Exercise 5

5. Given the set $\{0, 1, 2, 3\}$ and the accompanying table for the operation $\circledast$, which is true of the operation?
(1) The operation is commutative.
(2) The identity element is 0.
(3) The operation $\circledast$ is not a binary operation.
(4) The set is not closed for the operation $\circledast$.

6. Using the accompanying table, determine which is the solution set for $y^2 = 9$.
(1) $\{3\}$ (2) $\{7\}$ (3) $\{3, 7\}$ (4) $\{3, 7, 9\}$

$\bullet$	3	5	7	9
3	9	5	1	7
5	5	5	5	5
7	1	5	9	3
9	7	5	3	1

Exercise 6

$\square$	c	d	e	f
c	c	d	e	f
d	d	e	f	c
e	e	f	c	d
f	f	c	d	e

Exercise 7

7. The accompanying table represents the operation $\square$ for the set $\{c, d, e, f\}$.
(a) What is the identity element of this system?
(b) What is the inverse of f?
(c) Find the value of $(e \square e) \square d$.
(d) Solve for x: $(f \square e) \square x = f$.

8. Given: set $S = \{A, N, G, L, E\}$ and the commutative operation @ as shown in the accompanying table.

@	A	N	G	L	E
A	A	A		N	A
N		N			N
G	N	L	G	G	G
L		E		L	L
E	A	N	G	L	E

(a) Complete the table.
(b) What is the identity element for operation @?
(c) What is the inverse of L under operation @?
(d) Evaluate: $[G @ (L @ N)] @ A$.
(e) Find x if $(G @ N) @ x = N$.

9. Given the elements $d, e, f,$ and g and the operations $\oplus$ and $\otimes$ as defined by the accompanying tables.

$\oplus$	d	e	f	g
d	g	d	e	f
e	d	e	f	g
f	e	f	g	d
g	f	g	d	e

$\otimes$	d	e	f	g
d	f	g	d	e
e	g	d	e	f
f	d	e	f	g
g	e	f	g	d

(a) What is the identity element for $\otimes$?
(b) What is the inverse of element g under the operation $\otimes$?
(c) Find the value of $(d \oplus e) \otimes (f \oplus g)$.
(d) Solve for y: $(f \oplus g) \otimes y = e$.

2.3 FIELD PROPERTIES OF REAL NUMBERS

KEY IDEAS

All of the properties that hold for the addition and multiplication of real numbers are collectively referred to as the **field properties** of real numbers. Since algebraic expressions represent real numbers, the field properties of real numbers determine the operations that can be performed on algebraic expressions.

Field Properties of Real Numbers

The various properties of the set of real numbers under the operations of addition and multiplication are summarized in the accompanying table. If the six properties listed in the table hold for *any* set of numbers with two operations defined on that set, then that system is called a **field**.

Although the set of real numbers forms a field under the operations of addition and multiplication, a subset of the real numbers is not necessarily a field. Thus, the set of integers is not a field since it lacks field property F_5. Although each integer has an additive inverse, each integer lacks a multiplicative inverse. For example, the multiplicative inverse (reciprocal) of 2 is $\frac{1}{2}$, which is *not* a member of the set of integers.

FIELD PROPERTIES FOR THE SET OF REAL NUMBERS

Field Property	Addition	Multiplication
F_1: Closure	$a + b$ is a real number.	$a \cdot b$ is a real number.
F_2: Commutative	$a + b = b + a$	$a \cdot b = b \cdot a$
F_3: Associative	$a + (b + c) = (a + b) + c$	$a(b \cdot c) = (a \cdot b)c$
F_4: Identity	0 is the real number such that $a + 0 = 0 + a = a.$	1 is the real number such that $a \cdot 1 = 1 \cdot a = a.$
F_5: Inverse	For each real number a, $-a$ exists such that $a + (-a) = (-a) + a = 0.$	For each real number a except 0, $\frac{1}{a}$ exists such that $a\left(\frac{1}{a}\right) = \left(\frac{1}{a}\right)a = 1.$
F_6: Distributive	$a(b + c) = a \cdot b + a \cdot c$ and $(b + c)a = b \cdot a + c \cdot a$	

Importance of the Field Properties

Field properties provide the underlying rationale for many familiar arithmetic and algebraic operations. Here are three illustrations.

- Factoring is based on the distributive property.

  Example: $xy + 5x = x(y + 5)$.

- Changing a fraction into an equivalent fraction having a desired denominator is based on the use of a multiplicative identity element.

42

Example: $\dfrac{2}{ax} + \dfrac{3}{a} = \dfrac{2}{ax} + \dfrac{3}{a} \cdot 1$

$$= \dfrac{2}{ax} + \dfrac{3}{a} \cdot \dfrac{x}{x} = \dfrac{2 + 3x}{ax}$$

$\dfrac{x}{x} = 1 = $ identity ⟍

- Solving various types of equations by isolating variables makes use of the field properties of the real numbers.

Example: Solve the equation $3x = 7$.

Step in Solution	Reason
1. $3x = 7$	1. Given.
2. $\dfrac{1}{3} \cdot 3x = \dfrac{1}{3} \cdot 7$	2. If both sides of an equation are multiplied by the same nonzero number, an equivalent equation results.
3. $\left(\dfrac{1}{3} \cdot 3\right)x = \dfrac{1}{3} \cdot 7$	3. Associative property.
4. $1 \cdot x = \dfrac{1}{3} \cdot 7$	4. The product of a number and its multiplicative inverse is 1.
5. $x = \dfrac{1}{3} \cdot 7$	5. The product of a number and the multiplicative identity is the number.

Exercise Set 2.3

1–4. Determine whether the given set of numbers forms a field under the operations of addition and multiplication. If a field is not formed, state a field property that is lacking.

1. $\{-1, 0, 1\}$

2. The set of rational numbers

3. The set of irrational numbers

4. The set of irrational numbers of the form $p + q \sqrt{2}$, where p and q are rational numbers

5. The statement $(x + y) + z = z + (x + y)$ illustrates which of the following properties of real numbers?
(1) commutative property   (3) distributive property
(2) associative property   (4) closure property

43

6. The statement $2x + 2y = 2(x + y)$ uses which of the following properties of real numbers?

(1) commutative property   (3) distributive property

(2) associative property   (4) closure property

7. To add $\frac{1}{2} + \frac{1}{x}$, where $x \neq 0$, the first step is to write

$$\frac{1}{2} + \frac{1}{x} = \frac{1}{2} \cdot \left(\frac{x}{x}\right) + \frac{1}{x} \cdot \left(\frac{2}{2}\right).$$

This step can be justified by which of the following properties of real numbers?

(1) commutative property   (3) distributive property

(2) addition property of 0   (4) multiplication property of 1

REGENTS TUNE-UP: CHAPTER 2

Each of the questions in this section has appeared on a previous Course II Regents Examination. Here is an opportunity for you to review the material in Chapter 2 and, at the same time, prepare for the Course II Regents Examination.

---

1. If $e \odot f$ is defined as $\dfrac{e^2 + f}{2}$, find the value of $4 \odot 6$.

2. Using the accompanying table, compute $6 \dagger (4 \dagger 8)$.

†	2	4	6	8
2	4	8	2	6
4	8	6	4	2
6	2	4	6	8
8	6	2	8	4

3. Find the value of $O \, \alpha \, (I \, \alpha \, L)$ in the system defined.

α	F	O	I	L
F	I	L	F	O
O	L	F	O	I
I	F	O	I	L
L	O	I	L	F

Exercise 3

*	r	s	t
r	s	t	r
s	t	r	s
t	r	s	t

Exercise 4

4. Based on the accompanying table, what is the inverse of r?

44

5. If 😊 is a binary operation defined by $s \;😊\; t = \dfrac{2(s+t)}{3...}$, find the value of $5 \;😊\; 4$.

6. Solve the equation $y \, ¢ \, 5 = 5$ for y in the system defined in the accompanying table.

¢	1	3	5	7
1	3	1	7	3
3	1	3	5	7
5	7	5	3	1
7	5	7	1	3

Exercise 6

♡	e	f	g	h
e	e	f	g	h
f	f	h	e	g
g	g	e	h	f
h	h	g	f	e

Exercise 7

7. The accompanying table defines the operation $♡$ for the set $\{e, f, g, h\}$. Using the table, solve for x: $g \; ♡ \; x = h$.

8. If $x * y = x^y + \dfrac{x}{y}$, find the value of $4 * 2$.

9. If a, b, and c are real numbers, which statement is *always* true?
(1) $a \div b = b \div a$
(2) $a(b + c) = (a + b) \times (a + c)$
(3) $a(b \times c) = (a \times b)c$
(4) $a \times 0 = a$

10. In the step-by-step simplification of the expression below, which property is *not* used?

$$3(1 + x)$$
$$3(x + 1)$$
$$3 \cdot x + 3 \cdot 1$$
$$3x + 3$$

(1) associative (3) distributive
(2) commutative (4) identity

11. The operation $*$ is commutative in the accompanying table.
(a) Copy and complete the table.
(b) What is the identity element for the operation $*$?
(c) What is the inverse of O under the operation $*$?
(d) Evaluate: $[O * (G * L)] * C$.
(e) Solve for x: $(C * I) * (G * x) = C$.

*	L	O	G	I	C
L	L	L	O	O	L
O		O		C	O
G		I	G	G	G
I				I	I
C	L	O	G		C

ANSWERS TO SELECTED EXERCISES: CHAPTER 2

Section 2.1
1. (3)	**5.** -1	**9.** B	**13.** d
2. (3)	**6.** 12	**10.** K	**14.** N
3. (3)	**7.** 10	**11.** 4	
4. (1)	**8.** 3	**12.** 3	

Section 2.2
1. T **7. (a)** c **(b)** d **(c)** d **(d)** e
3. (4)   **9. (a)** f **(b)** e **(c)** f **(d)** g
5. (4)

Section 2.3
1. No field; lacks F_1 under addition.   **5.** (2)
3. No field; lacks F_1 under multiplication.   **7.** (4)

Regents Tune-Up: Chapter 2
1. 11   **6.** 3

2. 2   **7.** h

3. I **8.** 18

4. s **9.** (3)

5. 6   **10.** (1)

11. (a)

$*$	L	O	G	I	C
L	L	L	O	O	L
O	L	O	I	C	O
G	O	I	G	G	G
I	O	C	G	I	I
C	L	O	G	I	C

(b) C **(c)** I **(d)** O **(e)** L

<table>
<tr><td>Unit
Two</td><td># REVIEW AND EXTENSION OF
ALGEBRAIC METHODS</td></tr>
</table>

| Unit Two | **REVIEW AND EXTENSION OF ALGEBRAIC METHODS** |

CHAPTER **3**

POLYNOMIALS AND ALGEBRAIC FRACTIONS

3.1 EXPONENTS AND MONOMIALS

KEY IDEAS

The numbers that are multiplied together to form a product are called **factors.** In the product $2 \cdot 2 \cdot 2 \cdot 2$, the number 2 appears as a *factor* four times. Repeated multiplication of the same quantity may be written in a more compact form by using an *exponent* that tells the number of times the quantity appears as a factor in a product. Thus,

$$2 \cdot 2 \cdot 2 \cdot 2 = 2^4 = 16.$$

The notation 2^4 is read as "2 raised to the fourth power," where 2 is the **base** and 4 is the **exponent** of that base.

Powers that have the same nonzero base can be multiplied and divided using the laws summarized in the following table:

Law	Rule	Example
Multiplication	$a^x \cdot a^y = a^{x+y}$	$n^5 \cdot n^2 = n^7$
Division	$a^x \div a^y = a^{x-y}$	$n^5 \div n^2 = n^3$
Power of a power	$(a^x)^y = a^{xy}$	$(n^5)^2 = n^{10}$
Power of a product	$(ab)^x = a^x b^x$	$(mn^5)^2 = m^2 n^{10}$

Exponents

The notation x^n is read as "x raised to the nth power," where x is the *base* and n is the *exponent* of that base. Special rules apply when an exponent is equal to 1, 0, or a negative integer.

- When a variable appears without an exponent, the exponent is understood to be 1. Thus, x and x^1 mean the same thing.
- Any nonzero quantity raised to the zero power is 1. For example, $3^0 = 1$. The expression 0^0 is undefined.

- Any nonzero quantity that has a negative exponent is equal to the reciprocal of the same quantity with the exponent changed to its opposite. For example,

$$5^{-2} = \frac{1}{5^2} = \frac{1}{25} \qquad \text{and} \qquad \frac{a^2}{a^5} = a^{2-5} = a^{-3} = \frac{1}{a^3}.$$

MATH FACTS

- $x^1 = x$
- $x^0 = 1$, where $x \neq 0$
- $x^{-a} = \dfrac{1}{x^a}$, where a is a positive integer and $x \neq 0$

Example

1. Evaluate: **(a)** $(-2)^3$ **(b)** $2x^0$ **(c)** $(2x)^0$

Solutions: **(a)** $(-2)^3 = (-2)(-2)(-2) = (+4)(-2) = \mathbf{-8}$

Keep in mind that a negative number raised to an *odd* integer power will always have a negative value. A negative number raised to an *even* integer power will always have a positive value.

(b) $2x^0 = 2 \cdot 1 = \mathbf{2}$ **(c)** $(2x)^0 = \mathbf{1}$

Monomials and Like Terms

A number, a variable, or the indicated product of a number and one or more variables with positive integer exponents is called a **monomial**. Thus, 3, x^2, and $-5ab^2$ are monomials.

The numerical part of a monomial is its **coefficient**. The numerical coefficient of $-3ab$ is -3. The numerical coefficient of x^2 is 1 since $x^2 = 1 \cdot x^2$.

Monomials that have the same variables raised to the same powers, but may have different numerical coefficients, are called **like terms**. Thus, $2xy$ and $3xy$ are like terms, as are $3a^2b$ and $-5a^2b$. Monomials such as xy^2 and x^2y and *not* like terms, however, since they contain different powers of x and y.

Combining Like Terms

Like terms can be added or subtracted by combining their numerical coefficients while keeping the same variable factors.

Example 1: $2x + 3x = (2 + 3)x = 5x$
Example 2: $4a^2b - a^2b = (4 - 1)\, a^2b = 3a^2b$
Example 3: $5c - (3b - 4c) = 5c + (-1)(3b - 4c)$
Use the distributive property: $= 5c - 3b + 4c$
Add like terms: $\qquad\qquad\quad = 9c - 3b$

Multiplying Monomials

To multiply monomials, first multiply their numerical coefficients. Then multiply powers having the same base by *adding* their exponents. For example, to multiply $3x^5$ by $2x^3$, proceed as follows:

Group like factors: $\qquad\qquad (3x^5)(2x^3) = (3 \cdot 2)(x^5 x^3)$
Multiply numeral factors: $\qquad\qquad\qquad\; = 6(x^5 x^3)$
Multiply literal factors with the same base: $\; = 6x^{5+3} = 6x^8$

Example

2. Multiply: $(3a^2b)\,(-4a^3)$.

Solution: $(3a^2b)(-4a^3) = (3)(-4)(a^2a^3)b$
$\qquad\qquad\qquad\quad = -12(a^2a^3)b$
$\qquad\qquad\qquad\quad = \mathbf{-12a^5b}$

Dividing Monomials

To divide monomials, first divide their numerical coefficients. Then divide powers having the same base by *subtracting* their exponents. For example, to divide $\dfrac{20y^3}{4y^2}$, proceed as follows:

Group like factors: $\qquad \dfrac{20y^3}{4y^2} = \left(\dfrac{20}{4}\right)\left(\dfrac{y^3}{y^2}\right)$

Divide numerical factors: $\qquad = 5\left(\dfrac{y^3}{y^2}\right)$

Divide variable factors
with the same base: $\qquad\quad = 5y^{3-2} = 5y$

Example

3. Divide: $\dfrac{-24a^4b^2c^3}{3ab^2c^5}$.

49

$$Solution: \frac{-24a^4b^2c^3}{3ab^2c^5} = \left(\frac{-24}{3}\right)\left(\frac{a^4}{a}\right)\left(\frac{b^2}{b^2}\right)\left(\frac{c^3}{c^5}\right)$$

$$= (-8)(a^{4-1})(1)(c^{3-5})$$

$$= -8a^3c^{-2} \text{ or } -\frac{8a^3}{c^2}$$

Exercise Set 3.1

1–12. Perform the indicated multiplication or division.

1. $x^2 \cdot x^5 \cdot x$ **4.** $(-b^3)(-3a^2)$ **7.** $\dfrac{x}{x^3}$ **10.** $\dfrac{-32r^2s^3}{6rs^2}$

2. $(xy^3)^2$ **5.** $(4ab^2)(-2ab^2)$ **8.** $\dfrac{a^3}{2a^3}$ **11.** $\dfrac{4p^5q^3}{8pq^4}$

3. $(2a^3)(-3a^2)$ **6.** $\dfrac{-12x^7}{3x^4}$ **9.** $\dfrac{a^3b^2}{ab}$ **12.** $-\dfrac{12ab^6c^3}{3b^2c^3}$

13–15. Simplify by combining like terms, if any.

13. $ab + 2ab + 3ab$ **14.** $5xy - xy + 2xy$ **15.** $2x^3y + 3xy^2$

16–21. Simplify by removing parentheses and then combining like terms.

16. $7b - (8b + 3c)$ **18.** $a - 3(a + 4)$ **20.** $3rs - r(s - 2r)$

17. $3(x^2 + y) - 2x^2$ **19.** $4b + \frac{1}{3}(12b - 3)$ **21.** $3(x - y) + 2(x + y)$

3.2   OPERATIONS WITH POLYNOMIALS

KEY IDEAS

Variables and numbers may be multiplied and their products combined to produce expressions called **polynomials**. Since polynomials represent real numbers, they can be added, subtracted, multiplied, and divided by using the properties of real numbers.

Definition of a Polynomial

A **polynomial** is a monomial or the sum or difference of two or more monomials. Each monomial of a polynomial is called a **term**.

A polynomial having two unlike terms, such as $2x + 3y$, is called a **binomial**. Since the polynomial $x^2 - 3x + 7$ has three unlike terms, it is called a **trinomial**.

The **degree** of a polynomial in one variable is the largest exponent of any of its terms. Thus, the degree of $2x^4 - 7x^2 + 5x$ is 4.

Adding and Subtracting Polynomials

To add polynomials, collect and then add their like terms. For example,

$$(4x^2 + 3y - 8) + (5x^2 - 2y + 7) = (4x^2 + 5x^2) + (3y - 2y) + (-8 + 7)$$
$$= 9x^2 + y - 1$$

To subtract polynomials, change to an addition operation by taking the opposite of each term of the polynomial that is being subtracted. Then add the two polynomials. For example;

$$(3a^2 - 7a + 5) - (2a^2 - 4a - 1) = (3a^2 - 7a + 5) + (-2a^2 + 4a + 1)$$
$$= (3a^2 - 2a^2) + (-7a + 4a) + (5 + 1)$$
$$= a^2 - 3a + 6$$

Multiplying a Polynomial by a Monomial

To multiply a polynomial by a monomial, multiply each term of the polynomial by the monomial. Then add the resulting products.

Example 1: $\quad 3a(2a - 1) = 3a(2a) + 3a(-1)$
$$= 6a^2 - 3a$$

Example 2: $\quad 4x^2(3x^2 - 5x + 1) = 4x^2(3x^2) + 4x^2(-5x) + 4x^2(1)$
$$= 12x^4 - 20x^3 + 4x^2$$

Dividing a Polynomial by a Monomial

To divide a polynomial by a monomial, divide each term of the polynomial by the monomial and then add the quotients. For example,

$$\frac{72x^3 - 32x^2}{8x} = \frac{72x^3}{8x} - \frac{32x^2}{8x}$$

$$= \left(\frac{72}{8}\right)\left(\frac{x^3}{x}\right) - \left(\frac{32}{8}\right)\left(\frac{x^2}{x}\right)$$

$$= 9x^{3-1} - 4x^{2-1}$$

$$= \mathbf{9x^2 - 4x}$$

Multiplying Binomials

To multiply a binomial by another binomial, write one binomial underneath the other. Then multiply the binomial on top by each term of the binomial below. For example;

$$3x + 7$$
$$2x + 5$$

Multiply each term of $3x + 7$ by $2x$: $\quad 6x^2 + 14x$

Multiply each term of $3x + 7$ by 5: $\quad \underline{ + 15x + 35}$

Add like terms in each column: $\quad 6x^2 + 29x + 35$

You can also multiply two binomials by writing one binomial next to the other and then using the **FOIL** method. To use FOIL, add the products obtained by multiplying the *F*irst pair of terms, the *O*uter pair of terms, the *I*nner pair of terms, and the *L*ast pair of terms of the two binomials, as shown below:

$$
\begin{array}{cccc}
\textit{First} & \textit{Outer} & \textit{Inner} & \textit{Last}
\end{array}
$$

$$
\begin{aligned}
(3x + 7)(2x + 5) &= (3x)(2x) &+ (3x)(5) &+ (7)(2x) &+ (7)(5) \\
&= \quad 6x^2 &+ (15x &+ 14x) &+ \quad 35 \\
&= \quad 6x^2 &+ &29x &+ \quad 35
\end{aligned}
$$

Example

4. Use the FOIL method to find each of the following products:

(a) $(x - 2)(x - 6)$ **(c)** $(5x - 9)(2x + 3)$

(b) $(y + 3)^2$ **(d)** $(w - 6)(w + 6)$

Solutions:

$$\qquad\qquad \textbf{F} \quad\ \textbf{O} \quad\ \textbf{I} \quad\ \textbf{L}$$

(a) $(x - 2)(x - 6) = x^2 + [(-6x) + (-2x)] + 12 = \boldsymbol{x^2 - 8x + 12}$

(b) Rewrite the square of the binomial as the product of two identical binomials.

$$\qquad\qquad\qquad \textbf{F} \quad\ \textbf{O} \quad\ \textbf{I} \quad\ \textbf{L}$$

$$(y + 3)^2 = (y + 3)(y + 3) = y^2 + [3y + 3y] + 9 = \boldsymbol{y^2 + 6y + 9}$$

$$\qquad\qquad\qquad \textbf{F} \quad\ \textbf{O} \quad\ \textbf{I} \quad\ \textbf{L}$$

(c) $(5x - 9)(2x + 3) = 10x^2 + [15x + (-18x)] - 27 = \boldsymbol{10x^2 - 3x - 27}$

$$\qquad\qquad\qquad \textbf{F} \quad\ \textbf{O} \quad\ \textbf{I} \quad\ \textbf{L}$$

(d) $(w - 6)(w + 6) = w^2 + [6w + (-6w)] - 36$

$$\qquad\qquad\qquad = w^2 + 0w - 36 = \boldsymbol{w^2 - 36}$$

Notice that the product of two binomials is *not* always a trinomial.

Exercise Set 3.2

1–2. Simplify.

1. $-2(x^2 - 7x - 9) + 10$ **2.** $3(2a^3 - 5a + 1) + 15a$

3–6. After studying the following example, find, in each case, the value of y for the indicated value of x.

Example: Given $y = 3x^2 - 5x + 9$, find the value of y when $x = -2$.

$$7 = 3(-2)^2 - 5(-2) + 9$$
$$= 3 \cdot 4 \ + 10 \ \ + 9$$
$$= 31$$

3. $y = x^2 - 3x + 7; x = 3$ **5.** $y = (x - 2)^2 + 9; x = 0$

4. $y = 3x^2 - 4x - 1; x = -2$ **6.** $y = -3x^2 - 3x + 12; x = -3$

7–10. Add.

7. $(5y - 8) + (3y - 2)$

8. $(4x^2 + 1) + (3x^2 - 7)$

9. $(2n^2 - 7n + 8) + (8n^2 - 3n - 11)$

10. $(-8m^2 - 7m) + (8m^2 + 3m + 2)$

11–13. Subtract.

11. $(-2y - 9) - (-8y + 6)$

12. $(4n^2 + 11) - (10n^2 + 7)$

13. $(2x^3 - 4x^2 + 9x) - (5x^3 + x^2 - 2x)$

14. From $5x^2 - 2x + 3$, subtract $3x^2 + 4x + 3$.

15–20. Multiply.

15. $3x(x^2 - 5x + 7)$ **18.** $(9x^3 - 2x^2 + 7)(4x - 1)$

16. $-4a(a^3 + 6a - 9)$ **19.** $(5w + 8)(5w - 8)$

17. $0.06c^3(0.5c^2 - 0.8)$ **20.** $(2c - 2)^2$

21–26. Divide.

21. $\dfrac{32a^5 - 8a^2}{4a}$ **23.** $\dfrac{t^4 + t^3 + 5t^2}{t^2}$

22. $\dfrac{15p^3 - 45p^2 + 9p}{3p}$ **24.** $\dfrac{30y^6 + 5y^3 - 10y^2}{-5y^2}$

53

25. $\dfrac{h^3k^2 + h^2k^3 - 7hk}{hk}$ **26.** $\dfrac{0.14a^3 - 1.05a^2b}{0.7a}$

27–44. Use FOIL to find each of the following products:

27. $(x - 4)(x - 7)$

28. $(y + 3)(y + 10)$

29. $(t - 8)(t + 8)$

30. $(2x + 1)(x + 4)$

31. $(2y - 1)(4y - 3)$

32. $(a + 7)(a - 7)$

33. $(n + 9)(n + 9)$

34. $\left(x - \dfrac{1}{4}\right)\left(x + \dfrac{1}{4}\right)$

35. $(8m - 7)(5m + 9)$

36. $(2x - 5)(2x + 5)$

37. $(5 - 6p)(8 - 3p)$

38. $(10 - x)(10 + x)$

39. $(0.6y - 5)(0.4y + 8)$

40. $(x + y)(x - y)$

41. $(x - 7)^2$

42. $(2n - 3)^2$

43. $(x + 2y)^2$

44. $(0.3n - 5)^2$

3.3   FACTORING POLYNOMIALS

KEY IDEAS

Factoring reverses multiplication.

Operation	Example
Multiplication	$3x(x + 2) = 3x^2 + 6x$
Factoring	$3x^2 + 6x = 3x(x + 2)$

If all the terms of a polynomial contain the same monomial factor, then that common monomial can be factored out using the reverse of the distributive property. When we factor a polynomial that has integer coefficients, we look for polynomial factors that also have integer coefficients.

The Factoring Process

Factoring a polynomial means writing the polynomial as the product of two or more lower degree polynomials each of which is called a **factor** of the original polynomial. Since $3x^2 + 6x$ can be written as $3x(x + 2)$, the two factors of $3x^2 + 6x$ are $3x$ and $x + 2$.

A polynomial that cannot be factored except by writing it as the product of itself and 1 (or negative itself and –1) is called a **prime polynomial**. Thus, $12x + 7y$ is a prime polynomial.

Finding the Greatest Common Factor

To find the *Greatest Common Factor* (GCF) of the terms of a polynomial, form the product of the greatest numerical and variable factors that are contained in all of the terms. For example, to find the GCF of the terms of $21a^5 + 14a^3$, follow these steps:

Step 1. Find the largest integer that divides evenly into 21 and 14:   7

Step 2. Find the greatest power of a that is contained in both a^5 and a^3: a^3

Step 3. Form the product of the factors determined in Steps 1 and 2: $7a^3$ is the GCF.

Factoring a Polynomial by Removing the GCF

If we know that 5 is a factor of 30, we can find the other factor by dividing 30 by 5 to obtain 6. Similarly, if we know the GCF of the terms of a polynomial, we can find the other factor by dividing the polynomial by the GCF. For example, to factor $21a^5 + 14a^3$, follow these steps:

Step 1. Determine the GCF of $21a^5$ and $14a^3$:   The GCF is $7a^3$.

Step 2. Find the factor that corresponds to the GCF by dividing the original polynomial by the GCF:

$$\frac{21a^5 + 14a^3}{7a^3} = \frac{21a^5}{7a^3} + \frac{14a^3}{7a^3}$$

$$= 3a^2 + 2$$

Step 3. Write $21a^5 + 14a^3$ as the product of the GCF of the terms and its corresponding factor: $21a^5 + 14a^3 = 7a^3(3a^2 + 2)$

You should always check that the factorization of a polynomial is correct by multiplying the two factors together and then comparing the product with the original polynomial. Since

$$7a^3(3a^2 + 2) = 7a^3(3a^2) + 7a^3(2) = 21a^5 + 14a^3$$

the factorization in the example above is correct.

Examples

1. Factor: $6kp^2 - 21p^2$.

Solution: Compare the numerical and the variable factors of $6kp^2$ and $21p^2$. Since 3 is the largest number that divides 6 and 21 evenly and p^2 is the greatest power of p in both $6kp^2$ and $21p^2$, the GCF of $6kp^2$ and $21p^2$ is $3p^2$. To find the other factor, divide the given polynomial by $3p^2$:

$$\frac{6kp^2 - 21p^2}{3p^2} = \frac{6kp^2}{3p^2} - \frac{21p^2}{3p^2}$$

$$= 2k - 7$$

Thus, $6kp^2 - 21p^2 = \mathbf{3p^2\ (2k - 7)}$.

2. Factor: $-2rs - 10$.

Solution: The GCF of $-2rs$ and -10 is -2. Find the other factor by dividing the polynomial by -2:

$$\frac{-2rs - 10}{-2} = \frac{-2rs}{-2} + \left(\frac{-10}{-2}\right) = rs + 5$$

Thus, $-2rs - 10 = \mathbf{-2(rs + 5)}$.

3. Factor: $9x^4 - 3x^3 + 12x$

Solution: The GCF is $3x$. Find the other factor by dividing $9x^4 - 3x^3 + 12x$ by $3x$:

$$\frac{9x^4 - 3x^3 + 12x}{3x} = \frac{9x^4}{3x} - \frac{3x^3}{3x} + \frac{12x}{3x}$$

$$= 3x^3 - x^2 + 4$$

Thus, $9x^4 - 3x^3 + 12x = \mathbf{3x(3x^3 - x^2 + 4)}$.

4. Factor: $x(x - 3) + 7(x - 3)$.

Solution: To factor $x(x - 3) + 7(x - 3)$, treat $(x - 3)$ as a common *monomial* factor by letting $A = x - 3$.

$$x(x - 3) + 7(x - 3) = xA + 7A$$

Factor out A: $= A\ (x + 7)$

Replace A with $(x - 3)$: $= (x - 3)(x + 7)$

Thus, $x\ (x - 3) + 7(x - 3) = \mathbf{(x - 3)(x + 7)}$.

Factoring by Grouping Terms

Some polynomials can be factored by grouping together pairs of terms that have a common monomial factor. For example, to factor $2x^2 - 3x + 4x - 6$:

Group the first two terms and
the last two terms together: $\quad 2x^2 - 3x + 4x - 6 = (2x^2 - 3x) + (4x - 6)$

Factor out x from the first pair
of terms and 2 from the second
pair of terms: $\qquad\qquad\qquad\qquad = x(2x - 3) + 2(2x - 3)$

Factor again by removing the
common binomial factor, $(2x - 3)$: $\qquad\quad = (2x - 3)(x + 2)$

Exercise Set 3.3

1–18. Factor each of the following polynomials so that one of the factors is the GCF:

1. $5x^2 + 11x$

2. $6a^3 - 9a^2$

3. $4p^2q + 12p^2q^2$

4. $7n^2 + 7t^2$

5. $x^3 + x^2 + x$

6. $14x - 7x^2$

7. $n^4 - 2n^3 + 5n^2$

8. $4s^3 - 12s^2 + 8s - 20$

9. $3y^7 - 6y^5 + 12y^3$

10. $-3a - 3b$

11. $8u^5w^2 - 40u^2w^5$

12. $-14t^3 - 21t^5$

13. $p^2k^4 - p^3k^2 + (pk)^2$

14. $\frac{1}{4}a^2b - \frac{3}{4}ab^2$

15. $x(x + 2) - 3(x + 2)$

16. $(x + a)^2 - a(x + a)$

17. $x(3x + 4) + 2(3x + 4)$

18. $4x(x - 1) + 7(x - 1)$

19. If the area of a rectangle is $14x^3 - 21x^2$ and the width is $7x^2$, what is the length?

20. If the area of a rectangle is $45h^4 - 18h^2$ and the length is $5h^2 - 2$, what is the width?

21–22. Factor by grouping.

21. $xz + yz + xw + yw$

22. $ax^2 - 4a + bx^2 - 4b$

3.4   FACTORING QUADRATIC TRINOMIALS

Some quadratic trinomials can be factored by using the reverse of FOIL.

Operation	Example
Multiplication	$(x+2)(x+5) = x^2 + 7x + 10$
	$10 = 2 \cdot 5$
Factoring	$x^2 + 7x + 10 = (x+2)(x+5)$
	$7 = 2+5$

Factoring $ax^2 + bx + c$ ($a = 1$)

FOIL can be used to verify that the product of $(x + 2)$ and $(x + 5)$ is $x^2 + 7x + 10$. The binomial factors of the quadratic trinomial $x^2 + 7x + 10$ may, therefore, be written as follows:

$$x^2 + 7x + 10 = (x + 2)(x + 5).$$

— *product of 2 and 5*

— *sum of 2 and 5*

Observe that there is a relationship between the terms of the binomial factors and the values of the coefficients of the terms of the quadratic trinomial. For example, the product of 2 and 5 is 10 (c term), and the sum of 2 and 5 is 7 (bx term). This suggests a convenient method by which similar types of quadratic trinomials may be expressed in factored form.

When attempting to factor a quadratic trinomial of the form $x^2 + bx + c$, think: "What *two* numbers when multiplied give c *and* when added give b?" If two such numbers, say p and q, exist, then write

$$x^2 + bx + c = (x + p)(x + q), \text{ where } p + q = b \text{ and } pq = c.$$

Examples

1. Factor $x^2 + 11x + 18$ as the product of two binomials.

Solution: Step 1. Write $x^2 + 11x + 18 = (x \ \Box)(x \ \Box)$.

Step 2. Think: "What two numbers when multiplied give 18, *and* when added give 11?" Since the product and the sum of these factors are both positive, each factor must be positive. List the set of all possible pairs of positive integers whose product is 18. Then choose the pair of factors that satisfy the additional condition that their sum is 11.

The desired numbers are 2 and 9, so there is no need to test other pairs of factors of 18.

Step 3. Write the binomial factors.

$$x^2 + 11x + 18 = (x + 2)(x + 9)$$

Step 4. Check by multiplying the factors using FOIL.

$$(x + 2)(x + 9) = x^2 + 9x + 2x + 18$$
$$= x^2 + 11x + 18$$

2. Factor $y^2 - 7y + 12$.

Solution: Since the product of the two numbers you are seeking is +12, they must have the same sign. Since their sum is –7, both factors must be negative. Thus,

$$y^2 - 7y + 12 = (y\ \square)(y\ \square).$$

The possible factors of +12 are limited to –1 and –12, –2 and –6, –3 and –4. Use –3 and –4 as the factors of +12 since $(-3) + (-4) = -7$. Hence,

$$y^2 - 7y + 12 = (y - 3)(y - 4).$$

The check is left for you.

3. Factor $n^2 - 5n - 14$ as the product of two binomials.

Solution: The numbers you are seeking have different signs since their product is negative. Write

$$n^2 - 5n - 14 = (n + \square)(n - \square).$$

Think: "What two numbers when multiplied give –14, *and* when added give –5?" The desired numbers are +2 and –7. Hence,

$$x^2 - 5x - 14 = = (x + 2)(x - 7).$$

The check is left for you.

Factoring $ax^2 + bx + c$ ($a > 1$)

A quadratic trinomial of the form $ax^2 + bx + c$ can be factored if there are two integers whose sum is b and whose product is ac. If integers p and q satisfy these conditions, then $ax^2 + bx + c$ can be factored by replacing bx with $px + qx$.

For example, to factor $3x^2 + 10x + 8$, you need to find two integers whose sum is +10 (the coefficient of x) and whose product is $3 \cdot 8 = 24$. Since these integers are 4 and 6, write

$$3x^2 + 10x + 8 = 3x^2 + \underbrace{4x + 6x}_{+10x} + 8$$

Group the first and last
   pairs of terms: $\qquad = (3x^2 + 4x) + (6x + 8)$

Factor out the GCF of each
   pair of terms: $\qquad = x(3x + 4) + 2(3x + 4)$

Factor out the common
   binomial factors: $\qquad = (3x + 4)\,(x + 2)$

Thus, $3x^2 + 10x + 8 = (3x + 4)\,(x + 2)$.

Example

4. Factor $4x^2 + 3x - 7$.

Solution: The coefficient of the middle term is +3. The product of the coefficient of x^2 and the constant term is $4(-7) = -28$.

Step 1. Find two integers whose sum is +3 and whose product is –28. The integers that have these properties are –4 and +7.

Step 2. Replace the linear term of the original quadratic trinomial with the sum of –4x and 7x.

$$4x^2 + 3x - 7 = 4x^2 \underbrace{-4x + 7x}_{+3x} - 7$$

Step 3. Group the first pair of terms and the last pair of terms. Then factor out the GCF of each pair.

$$4x^2 + 3x - 7 = (4x^2 - 4x) + (7x - 7)$$
$$= 4x(x - 1) + 7(x - 1)$$

Step 4. Factor out the common binomial factor.

$$4x^2 + 3x - 7 = 4x(x - 1) + 7(x - 1)$$
$$= \mathbf{(x - 1)(4x + 7)}$$

Since the order in which the factors in a product are written does not matter, you could also write $4x^2 + 3x - 7 = \mathbf{(4x + 7)(x - 1)}.$

Exercise Set 3.4

1–21. Factor.

1. $x^2 + 8x + 15$

2. $x^2 - 10x + 21$

3. $x^2 + 4x - 21$

4. $y^2 + 6y + 9$

5. $n^2 + 3n - 88$

6. $a^2 - 4a - 45$

7. $w^2 - 13w + 42$

8. $t^2 - 7t - 60$

9. $y^2 - 9y + 8$

10. $s^2 - s - 56$

11. $x^2 - 19x + 90$

12. $y^2 - 2y + 1$

13. $a^2 + a - 20$

14. $2a^2 + 5a - 3$

15. $3x^2 + 2x - 21$

16. $5s^2 + 14s - 3$

17. $5t^2 + 18t - 8$

18. $3n^2 + 29n - 44$

19. $7x^2 + 52x - 32$

20. $-x^2 + x + 12$

21. $-h^2 - h + 30$

22. If $2x - 3$ is a factor of $4x^2 + 4x - 15$, what is the other binomial factor?

23. If $x + 8$ is a factor of $4x^2 + 27x - 40$, what is the other binomial factor?

24. If $5x - 8$ is a factor of $30x^2 - 38x - 16$, what is the other binomial factor?

25. If the binomial factors of $4x^2 - 36x + 81$ are identical, what is each factor?

26–31. Factor as the product of two binomials.

26. $4x^2 - 10x - 50$

27. $6m^2 + m - 12$

28. $10p^2 - 33p - 7$

29. $8n^2 + 9n - 14$

30. $8d^2 - 22d + 15$

31. $6a^2 - 13a + 5$

3.5 MULTIPLYING CONJUGATE BINOMIALS AND FACTORING THE DIFFERENCE OF TWO SQUARES

KEY IDEAS

Binomial pairs such as $(x + 3)$ and $(x - 3)$, $(m + 7)$ and $(m - 7)$, and $(2y + 5)$ and $(2y - 5)$ are examples of conjugate binomials. **Conjugate binomials** are binomials that take the sum and difference of the same two terms.

Multiplying Conjugate Binomials

Observe the pattern in the following examples, in which pairs of conjugate binomials are multiplied:

$$\begin{array}{cccccc} & \text{F} & \text{O} & \text{I} & \text{L} & \\ (x+3)(x-3) = & x^2 - 3x & + 3x & - & 9 = x^2 - 9; \\ (m+7)(m-7) = & m^2 - 7m & + 7m & - 49 = & m^2 - 49; \\ (2y+5)(2y-5) = & 4y^2 - 10y & + 10y & - 25 = 4y^2 - 25. \end{array}$$

Notice that the sum of the outer and inner products will always be equal to 0, so that the product always lacks a "middle" term. *The product of a pair of conjugate binomials is a binomial formed by taking the difference of the squares of the first and last terms of each of the original binomials.*

MATH FACTS

MULTIPLYING CONJUGATE BINOMIALS

$$(a + b)(a - b) = a^2 - b^2$$

Example

1. Find the product of $(x - 3y)$ and $(x + 3y)$.

Solution: $(x - 3y)(x + 3y) = x^2 - (3y)^2 = \boldsymbol{x^2 - 9y^2}$

Factoring the Difference of Two Squares

Reversing the pattern observed in multiplying two conjugate binomials provides a method for factoring a binomial that represents the difference of two squares. To illustrate, since $(x + 5)(x - 5) = x^2 - 25$, then $x^2 - 25$ can be factored by observing that

$$x^2 - 25 = (x)^2 - (5)^2 = (x + 5)(x - 5).$$

To factor a binomial that is the *difference* of two squares, write the product of the corresponding pair of conjugate binomials.

MATH FACTS

FACTORING THE DIFFERENCE OF TWO SQUARES

$$p^2 - q^2 = (p + q)(p - q)$$

Examples

2. Factor: $n^2 - 100$.

Solution: $n^2 - 100 = (n)^2 - (10)^2 = \boldsymbol{(n + 10)(n - 10)}$

3. Factor: $4a^2 - 25b^2$.

Solution: $4a^2 - 25b^2 = (2a)^2 - (5b)^2 = \boldsymbol{(2a + 5b)(2a - 5b)}$

4. Factor: $0.16y^2 - 0.09$.

Solution: $0.16y^2 - 0.09 = (0.4y)^2 - (0.3)^2 = \boldsymbol{(0.4y + 0.3)(0.4y - 0.3)}$

5. Factor: $p^2 - \frac{36}{49}$.

Solution: $p^2 - \frac{36}{49} = (p)^2 - \left(\frac{6}{7}\right)^2 = \boldsymbol{\left(p + \frac{6}{7}\right)\left(p - \frac{6}{7}\right)}$

Exercise Set 3.5

1–16. Multiply.

1. $(x + 2)(x - 2)$

2. $(y - 10)(y + 10)$

3. $(3a - 1)(3a + 1)$

4. $(-n + 6)(-n - 6)$

5. $(4 - x)(4 + x)$

6. $(1 - 2y)(1 + 2y)$

7. $(0.8n - 7)(0.8n + 7)$

8. $\left(x - \frac{2}{3}\right)\left(x + \frac{2}{3}\right)$

9. $\left(2y - \frac{1}{5}\right)\left(2y + \frac{2}{10}\right)$

10. $\left(0.2p - \frac{3}{8}\right)\left(0.2p + \frac{3}{8}\right)$

11. $(0.5n + 0.3)(0.5n - 0.3)$

12. $(a - 7b)(a + 7b)$

13. $(x^2 - 8)(x^2 + 8)$

14. $(y^3 - z)(y^3 + z)$

15. $(m^2 - n^2)(m^2 + n^2)$

16. $(2w - 3)^2$

17–32. Factor

17. $x^2 - 144$

18. $y^2 - 0.49$

19. $25 - a^2$

20. $p^2 - \frac{1}{9}$

21. $16a^2 - 36$

22. $64x^2 - 1$

23. $h^2 - k^2$

24. $121w^2 - 25z^2$

25. $\frac{4}{9}x^2 - 49$

26. $0.36y^2 - 0.64x^2$

27. $0.09h^2 - 0.04$

28. $\frac{1}{4}y^2 - \frac{1}{9}$

29. $100a^2 - 81b^2$

30. $n^4 - 49$

31. $x^6 - y^4$

32. $h^2x^2 - h^2$

3.6 FACTORING COMPLETELY

$$\bigwedge$$
KEY IDEAS
$$\diagdown\diagup$$

A polynomial is **factored completely** when *each* of its factors cannot be factored further. Sometimes it is necessary to apply more than one factoring technique in order to factor a polynomial completely.

A Strategy for Factoring Completely

To factor a polynomial completely, proceed as follows:
1. Factor out the GCF, if any.
2. If there is a binomial, determine whether it can be factored as the difference of two squares.
3. If there is a quadratic trinomial, determine whether it can be factored as the product of two binomials by using the reverse of FOIL.

Examples

1. Factor completely: $3x^3 - 75x$.

Solution: First factor out the GCF of $3x$.

$$3x^3 - 75x = 3x(x^2 - 25)$$
$$= 3x(x - 5)(x + 5)$$

2. Factor completely: $t^3 + 6t^2 - 16t$.

Solution: First factor out the GCF of t.

$$t^3 + 6t^2 - 16t = t(t^2 + 6t - 16)$$
$$= t(t + 8)(t - 2)$$

3. Factor completely: $x^4 - y^4$

Solution: Factor as the difference of two squares.

$$x^4 - y^4 = (x^2)^2 - (y^2)^2$$
$$= (x^2 - y^2)(x^2 + y^2)$$
$$\text{Factor } (x^2 - y^2)\text{:} = (x - y)(x + y)(x^2 + y^2)$$

Exercise Set 3.6

1–16. Factor completely.

1. $2y^2 - 50$

2. $b^3 - 49b$

3. $x^3 + x^2 - 56x$

4. $8w^3 - 32w$

5. $-x^2 - 7x - 10$

6. $3y^2 - 9y + 6$

7. $4x^2 - 4y^2$

8. $ax^2 - a + bx^2 - b$

9. $12s^3 - 2s^2 - 4s$

10. $10y^3 + 50y^2 - 500y$

11. $3t^4 + 12t^3 - 15t^2$

12. $p^4 - 1$

13. $2x^3 - 12x + 18x$

14. $-5t^2 + 5$

15. $x^3 + x^2 - 4x - 4$

16. $a^2y^2 - 4a^2 - y^2b^2 + 4b^2$

3.7 SIMPLIFYING ALGEBRAIC FRACTIONS

 KEY IDEAS

A fraction is in *simplest form* or *lowest terms* when the numerator and denominator have no factors in common other than 1 and –1.

To change a fraction into lowest terms, factor the numerator and denominator and then use the multiplication property of 1. For example,

$$\frac{12}{15} = \frac{4 \cdot 3}{5 \cdot 3} = \frac{4}{5} \cdot \frac{3}{3} = \frac{4}{5} \cdot 1 = \frac{4}{5}.$$

To consolidate steps, it is customary to "cancel" the quotient of common factors, as in

$$\frac{12}{15} = \frac{4 \cdot \overset{1}{\cancel{3}}}{5 \cdot \cancel{3}} = \frac{4}{5}$$

The rules for working with algebraic fractions are the same as the rules for working with fractions in arithmetic.

Fractions with Variable Denominators

Since division by 0 is not defined, always assume that a variable in the denominator of a fraction can never have a value that will make the denominator of that fraction equal 0. For example, the denominator of the fraction $\dfrac{3}{x+1}$ has a value of 0 when $x = -1$. When working with this fraction, assume that x cannot equal -1.

Reducing Algebraic Fractions

Writing an algebraic fraction in lowest terms depends on factoring. To write $\dfrac{14a^3}{21a^5}$ in lowest terms, factor the numerator and denominator by removing their GCF. Thus,

$$\frac{14a^3}{21a^5} = \frac{\overset{1}{\cancel{7a^5}} \cdot 2}{\cancel{7a^5} \cdot 3a^2} = \frac{2}{3a^2}.$$

Examples

1. Write in lowest terms: $\dfrac{3x+6}{x^2+2x}$.

Solution:

Factor the numerator and denominator:
$$\frac{3x+6}{x^2+2x} = \frac{3(x+2)}{x(x+2)}$$

Cancel common factors:
$$= \frac{3\overset{1}{\cancel{(x+2)}}}{x\cancel{(x+2)}}$$

Write the remaining factors:
$$= \frac{3}{x}$$

2. Write in lowest terms: $\dfrac{18a^4 - 30a^3}{3a^2}$.

Solution:

Factor the numerator:
$$\frac{18a^4 - 30a^3}{3a^2} = \frac{6a^3(3a-5)}{3a^2}$$

Divide the numerator and denominator by their GCF, $3a^2$:
$$= \frac{\overset{2a}{\cancel{6a^3}}(3a-5)}{\cancel{3a^2}}$$

Write the remaining factors:
$$= \mathbf{2a\,(3a-5)}$$

Alternative Method: Divide each term of the polynomial in the numerator by the *monomial* in the denominator. Thus,

$$\frac{18a^4 - 30a^3}{3a^2} = \frac{18a^4}{3a^2} - \frac{30a^3}{3a^2} = 6a^2 - 10a = \mathbf{2a\,(3a-5)}.$$

3. Write in lowest terms: $\dfrac{y^2 - 25}{y^2 + 4y - 5}$.

Solution:

Factor the numerator and denominator: $\qquad \dfrac{y^2 - 25}{y^2 + 6y + 5} = \dfrac{(y-5)(y+5)}{(y+1)(y+5)}$

Cancel common factors: $\qquad\qquad\qquad = \dfrac{(y-5)\overset{1}{\cancel{(y+5)}}}{(y+1)\cancel{(y+5)}}$

Write the remaining factors: $\qquad\qquad = \dfrac{\boldsymbol{y-5}}{\boldsymbol{y+1}}$

4. Write in lowest terms: $\dfrac{2x + 2y}{x^2 - y^2}$.

Solution:

$$\dfrac{2x + 2y}{x^2 - y^2} = \dfrac{2\overset{1}{\cancel{(x+y)}}}{(x-y)\cancel{(x+y)}} = \dfrac{\boldsymbol{2}}{\boldsymbol{x-y}}$$

5. Write in lowest terms: $\dfrac{9 - x^2}{x^2 - 3x}$.

Solution:

$$\dfrac{9 - x^2}{x^2 - 3x} = \dfrac{\overset{-1}{\cancel{(3-x)}}(3+x)}{x\,\cancel{(x-3)}} = \dfrac{\boldsymbol{-(3+x)}}{\boldsymbol{x}}$$

Exercise Set 3.7

1–24. Write each fraction in lowest terms.

1. $\dfrac{28a^5}{4a^2}$

2. $\dfrac{-52x^3y}{-13xy}$

3. $\dfrac{2x - 16}{x^2 - 64}$

4. $\dfrac{a^2 - 16}{3a + 12}$

5. $\dfrac{2ab^2 - 2a^2b}{4ab}$

6. $\dfrac{-x - y}{x + y}$

7. $\dfrac{10y^3 - 5y^2}{15y}$

8. $\dfrac{12x^3 - 21x^4}{9x^2}$

9. $\dfrac{0.48xy - 0.16y}{0.8y}$

10. $\dfrac{21r^2s - 7r^3s^2}{14rs}$

11. $\dfrac{-3x - 6}{x + 2}$

12. $\dfrac{y^2 + 4y}{2y + 8}$

13. $\dfrac{3x + 15}{x^2 + 5x}$

14. $\dfrac{x^2 - 4}{x + 2}$

15. $\dfrac{10y + 30}{y^2 - 9}$

16. $\dfrac{-6a + 18}{a^2 - 3a}$

17. $\dfrac{x + 1}{x^2 - x - 2}$

18. $\dfrac{x^2 - x - 6}{x^2 - 4x + 3}$

19. $\dfrac{x^2 - 9}{x^2 + 4x + 3}$

20. $\dfrac{1 - x^2}{3x + 3}$

21. $\dfrac{2x^2 - 50}{2x^2 + 14x + 20}$

22. $\dfrac{x^2 - x - 42}{x^2 + 7x + 6}$

23. $\dfrac{4r - 4s}{r^2 - 2rs + s^2}$

24. $\dfrac{x^2 - y^2}{(x - y)^2}$

3.8 MULTIPLYING AND DIVIDING ALGEBRAIC FRACTIONS

=== KEY IDEAS ===

Algebraic fractions are multiplied and divided in much the same way that fractions in arithmetic are multiplied and divided.

To multiply fractions, use the rule

$$\frac{a}{b} \cdot \frac{c}{d} = \frac{ac}{bd},$$

where a, b, c, and d stand for real numbers except that $b \neq 0$ and $d \neq 0$. It is usually easier to write the product of two or more fractions in lowest terms by canceling pairs of common factors whose quotient is 1 *before* multiplying. For example,

$$\frac{4}{9} \times \frac{3}{10} = \frac{2 \cdot \overset{1}{\cancel{2}}}{3 \cdot \cancel{3}} \times \frac{\overset{1}{\cancel{3}}}{2 \cdot 5} = \frac{2}{15}.$$

To divide fractions, invert the second fraction and then multiply.

Multiplying Fractions

To multiply fractions, write the product of the numerators over the product of the denominators. Then simplify, if possible. For example,

$$\frac{8y}{3x} \cdot \frac{15y^3}{4x^2} = \frac{\overset{10}{\cancel{120}y^4}}{\cancel{12}x^3} = \frac{10y^4}{x^3}.$$

If you eliminate common factors from the numerators and denominators *before* multiplying, the product that results will be in lowest terms. For example, to find the product

$$\frac{12y^2}{x^2 + 7x} \cdot \frac{x^2 - 49}{2y^5}$$

begin by factoring the denominator of the first fraction and the numerator of the second fraction. Thus,

$$\frac{12y^2}{x^2 + 7x} \cdot \frac{x^2 - 49}{2y^5} = \frac{12\,y^2}{x(x + 7)} \cdot \frac{(x + 7)(x - 7)}{2y^5}$$

Divide out (cancel) any factor
that appears in both a numerator
and a denominator:

$$= \frac{\overset{6}{\cancel{12}}\,\overset{1}{\cancel{y^2}}}{x\,\cancel{(x+7)}} \cdot \frac{\cancel{(x+7)}(x-7)}{\underset{y^3}{\cancel{2y^5}}}$$

Multiply together the remaining
factors in the numerators, and multiply
together the remaining factors in the
denominators:

$$= \frac{6(x-7)}{xy^3}$$

Dividing Fractions

Algebraic fractions, like arithmetic fractions are divided by inverting the second fraction and then multiplying.

Examples

1. Write the quotient in lowest terms: $\dfrac{8m^2}{3} \div \dfrac{6m^3}{3m-12}$.

Solution: To begin, change from division to multiplication by taking the reciprocal of the second fraction. Then, where possible, factor.

$$\frac{8m^3}{3} \div \frac{6m^3}{3m-12} = \frac{8m^2}{3} \cdot \frac{3m-12}{6m^3}$$

Cancel pairs of common factors in
the numerator and denominator:

$$= \frac{\overset{4}{\cancel{8m^2}}}{\underset{1}{\cancel{3}}} \cdot \frac{\overset{1}{\cancel{3}}(m-4)}{\underset{3m}{\cancel{6m^3}}}$$

Multiply the remaining factors:

$$= \frac{4(m-4)}{3m}$$

2. Divide and express in simplest form: $\dfrac{x^2-2x-8}{x^2-25} \div \dfrac{x^2-4}{2x+10}$.

Solution: Change to a multiplication example, and factor the numerator and denominator of each fraction.

$$\frac{x^2-2x-8}{x^2-25} \div \frac{x^2-4}{2x+10} = \frac{x^2-2x-8}{x^2-25} \cdot \frac{2x+10}{x^2-4}$$

$$= \frac{(x+2)(x-4)}{(x-5)\cancel{(x+5)}} \cdot \frac{2\cancel{(x+5)}}{(x-2)\cancel{(x+2)}}$$

$$= \frac{2(x-4)}{(x-5)(x-2)}$$

69

Exercise Set 3.8

1–16. Write each product or quotient in simplest form.

1. $\dfrac{12a^2}{5c} \cdot \dfrac{15c^3}{8a}$

2. $\dfrac{3y}{4x} \cdot \dfrac{8x^2 - 4x}{9y}$

3. $\dfrac{5y + 10}{x^2} \cdot \dfrac{3x^2 - x^3}{15}$

4. $\dfrac{8}{rs} \cdot \dfrac{r^2s - rs^2}{12}$

5. $\dfrac{3x}{5y} \div \dfrac{12x^2 - 15x}{20y^2}$

6. $\dfrac{2b^2 - 2b}{3a} \cdot \left(\dfrac{2a}{3b}\right)^2$

7. $\dfrac{18}{x^2 - y^2} \div \dfrac{9}{x + y}$

8. $\dfrac{(a + b)^2}{4} \div \dfrac{a + b}{2}$

9. $\dfrac{2x + 6}{8} \div \dfrac{x + 3}{2}$

10. $\dfrac{4x + 12}{x^2 - x - 20} \cdot \dfrac{x^3 + 4x^2}{2x^2 - 18}$

11. $\dfrac{x^2 + 6x}{x^2 y - 4y} \div \dfrac{x^2 + 12x + 36}{5xy - 10y}$

12. $\dfrac{3 - 3r}{r^2 - 10r + 25} \div \dfrac{r^3 - r}{6r - 30}$

13. $\dfrac{(x - 7)^2}{x^2 - 6x - 7} \cdot \dfrac{5x + 5}{x^2 - 49}$

14. $\dfrac{a^2 - b^2}{2ab} \div \dfrac{a - b}{a^2}$

15. $\dfrac{x^2 - 9}{x^2 - 8x} \cdot \dfrac{x - 8}{x^2 - 6x + 9}$

16. $\dfrac{x^2 - 3x}{x^2 + 3x - 10} \div \dfrac{x^2 - x - 6}{x^2 - 4}$

17. The area of a rectangle is represented by $p^2 - 2p - 35$, and the length is represented by $p + 5$. In terms of p, what is the width of the rectangle?

3.9 ADDING AND SUBTRACTING ALGEBRAIC FRACTIONS

KEY IDEAS

To add (or subtract) arithmetic fractions that have the same denominator, write the sum (or difference) of the numerators over the common denominator:

$$\frac{2}{7} + \frac{3}{7} = \frac{2 + 3}{7} = \frac{5}{7}.$$

If the fractions have *different* denominators, each fraction must first be changed to an equivalent fraction having the LCD (lowest common denominator) as its denominator.

The addition and subtraction of algebraic fractions are handled in much the same way.

Combining Fractions with the Same Denominator

To combine algebraic fractions having the same denominator, write the sum or difference of the numerators over the common denominator and then simplify.

Examples

1. Write the difference in lowest terms: $\dfrac{5a+b}{10ab} - \dfrac{3a-b}{10ab}$.

Solution:

$$\dfrac{5a+b}{10ab} - \dfrac{3a-b}{10ab} = \dfrac{5a+b-(3a-b)}{10ab}$$

$$= \dfrac{5a+b-3a+b}{10ab}$$

$$= \dfrac{(5a-3a)+(b+b)}{10ab}$$

$$= \dfrac{2a+2b}{10ab}$$

$$= \dfrac{\overset{1}{\cancel{2}}(a+b)}{\underset{5}{\cancel{10}}ab} = \dfrac{a+b}{5ab}$$

2. Express as a single fraction in lowest terms: $\dfrac{4x}{x^2-4} + \dfrac{x+6}{4-x^2}$.

Solution: Rewrite $4-x^2$ as $-x^2+4$. Then factor out -1 so that $-x^2+4 = -(x^2-4)$.

$$\dfrac{4x}{x^2-4} + \dfrac{x+6}{4-x^2} = \dfrac{4x}{x^2-4} + \dfrac{x+6}{-(x^2-4)}$$

Write the negative sign in front of the second fraction:

$$= \dfrac{4x}{x^2-4} - \dfrac{x+6}{x^2-4}$$

Write the numerators over the common denominator:

$$= \dfrac{4x-(x+6)}{x^2-4}$$

Simplify the numerator:

$$= \dfrac{4x-x-6}{x^2-4}$$

Write the fraction in lowest terms:

$$= \dfrac{3x-6}{x^2-4}$$

Factor, and cancel common factors:

$$= \dfrac{3\overset{1}{\cancel{(x-2)}}}{\underset{1}{\cancel{(x-2)}}(x+2)}$$

$$= \dfrac{3}{x+2}$$

71

Combining Fractions with Unlike Denominators

To combine fractions with unlike denominators, first determine their LCD. Then change each fraction into an equivalent fraction with the LCD as its denominator.

Examples

3. Express as a single fraction in lowest terms: $\dfrac{x}{2} - \dfrac{5x}{12} + \dfrac{x}{4}$.

Solution: The LCD of 2, 12, and 4 is 12 since 12 is the smallest positive integer into which 2, 12, and 4 divide evenly. Consider the first fraction. Since $12 \div 2 = 6$, change the first fraction into an equivalent fraction that has the LCD as its denominator by multiplying it by 1 in the form of $\frac{6}{6}$. Similarly, since $12 \div 4 = 3$, multiply the last fraction by $\frac{3}{3}$.

$$\frac{x}{2} - \frac{5x}{12} + \frac{x}{4} = \frac{6}{6}\left(\frac{x}{2}\right) - \frac{5x}{12} + \frac{3}{3}\left(\frac{x}{4}\right)$$

$$= \frac{6x}{12} - \frac{5x}{12} + \frac{3x}{12}$$

$$= \frac{6x - 5x + 3x}{12}$$

$$= \frac{4x}{12}$$

$$= \frac{\overset{1}{\cancel{4x}}}{\underset{3}{\cancel{12}}}$$

$$= \frac{x}{3}$$

4. Add: $\dfrac{2x+1}{6} + \dfrac{3x-5}{8}$.

Solution: The LCD of 6 and 8 is 24. Multiplying the first fraction by 1 in the form of $\frac{4}{4}$ will produce an equivalent fraction having the LCD of 24 as its denominator. Multiplying the second fraction by 1 in the form of $\frac{3}{3}$ will also give an equivalent fraction having 24 as its denominator.

$$\frac{2x+1}{6} + \frac{3x-5}{8} = \left(\frac{2x+1}{6}\right)\frac{4}{4} + \left(\frac{3x-5}{8}\right)\frac{3}{3}$$

Write the numerators over the LCD:

$$= \frac{4(2x+1) + 3(3x-5)}{24}$$

Combine like terms in
the numerator:

$$= \frac{8x + 4 + 9x - 15}{24}$$

$$= \frac{17x - 11}{24}$$

5. Write the difference in simplest form: $\dfrac{3}{10xy} - \dfrac{10x - y}{5xy^2}$.

Solution: Factor each denominator into its prime factors. Prime factors are expressions that cannot be factored further. Thus,

$$10xy = 2 \cdot 5 \cdot x \cdot y$$
$$5xy^2 = 5 \cdot x \cdot y^2$$

The LCD is the product of the different factors of the denominators with each raised to the greatest power to which that factor appears in any of the denominators. The factors 2, 5, and x appear only to the first power, but the highest power for the factor y is y^2. Hence,

$$\text{LCD} = 2 \cdot 5 \cdot x \cdot y^2 = 10xy^2.$$

Now, compare each of the factored denominators to the LCD. Multiply the numerator and denominator of each fraction by the factors contained in the LCD that are missing from the denominators of that fraction.

$$\left(\frac{3}{10xy}\right)\frac{y}{y} - \left(\frac{10x - y}{5xy^2}\right)\frac{2}{2} = \frac{3y}{10xy^2} - \frac{2(10x - y)}{10xy^2}$$

$$= \frac{3y - 20x + 2y}{10xy^2}$$

$$= \frac{5y - 20x}{10xy^2}$$

$$= \frac{\overset{1}{\cancel{5}}(y - 4x)}{\underset{2}{\cancel{10}xy^2}}$$

$$= \frac{y - 4x}{2xy^2}$$

6. Subtract: $\dfrac{7x - 2}{4} - x$.

Solution: Rewrite x as $\dfrac{x}{1}$. Since the LCD of 4 and 1 is 4, multiply the second fraction by $\dfrac{4}{4}$.

$$\frac{7x-2}{4} - x = \frac{7x-2}{4} - \left(\frac{x}{1}\right)\left(\frac{4}{4}\right)$$

$$= \frac{7x-2}{4} - \frac{4x}{4}$$

$$= \frac{7x-2-4x}{4}$$

$$= \frac{3x-2}{4}$$

7. Express the difference in simplest form: $\dfrac{a^2+1}{a^2-1} - \dfrac{a}{a+1}$.

Solution: Factor each denominator into its prime factors.

$$a^2 - 1 = (a+1)(a-1)$$
$$a + 1 = a + 1$$

The LCD is $(a + 1)(a - 1)$. The first fraction already has the LCD as its denominator. The denominator of the second fraction lacks the factor $(a - 1)$. Multiplying the second fraction by 1 in the form of $\left(\dfrac{a-1}{a-1}\right)$ changes it into an equivalent fraction that has the LCD as its denominator.

$$\frac{a^2+1}{a^2-1} - \frac{a}{a+1} = \frac{a^2+1}{(a+1)(a-1)} - \frac{a}{a+1}\left(\frac{a-1}{a-1}\right)$$

$$= \frac{a^2+1-a(a-1)}{(a+1)(a-1)}$$

$$= \frac{a^2+1-a^2+a}{(a+1)(a-1)}$$

$$= \frac{\overset{1}{\cancel{(a+1)}}}{\underset{1}{\cancel{(a+1)}}(a-1)}$$

$$= \frac{1}{a-1}$$

8. Express the difference in simplest form: $\dfrac{5y+7}{y^2-4} - \dfrac{3}{4y+8}$.

Solution: Factor each denominator.

$$y^2 - 4 = (y+2)(y-2)$$
$$4y + 8 = 4(y+2)$$
$$\text{LCD} = 4(y+2)(y-2)$$

74

Compare each of the factored denominators to the LCD. The denominator of the first fraction is missing a factor of 4, while the denominator of the second fraction lacks the factor $(y - 2)$. Therefore, multiply the numerator and denominator of the first fraction by 4, and multiply the numerator and the denominator of the second fraction by $(y - 2)$.

$$\frac{5y + 7}{y^2 - 4} - \frac{3}{4y + 8} = \left(\frac{4}{4}\right) \cdot \frac{5y + 7}{(y + 2)(y - 2)} - \frac{3}{4(y + 2)} \cdot \left(\frac{y - 2}{y - 2}\right)$$

Write the numerators over the LCD:
$$= \frac{4(5y + 7) - 3(y - 2)}{4(y + 2)(y - 2)}$$

Simplify:
$$= \frac{20y + 28 - 3y + 6}{4(y + 2)(y - 2)}$$

$$= \frac{17y + 34}{4(y + 2)(y - 2)}$$

Factor the numerator:
Cancel the common factor:
$$= \frac{17\overset{1}{\cancel{(y + 2)}}}{4\underset{1}{\cancel{(y + 2)}}(y - 2)}$$

Simplify:
$$= \frac{17}{4(y - 2)}$$

Exercise Set 3.9

1–28. Write each of the following sums or differences as a single fraction in simplest form.

1. $\dfrac{2x}{3} + \dfrac{5x}{6}$

2. $\dfrac{7}{12x} - \dfrac{1}{3x}$

3. $\dfrac{4b}{5x} - \dfrac{3b}{10x}$

4. $\dfrac{4a + 1}{2} - \dfrac{a}{3}$

5. $\dfrac{3y - 5}{5xy} - \dfrac{1}{10x}$

6. $\dfrac{1}{a} + \dfrac{1}{b}$

7. $\dfrac{a}{b} - \dfrac{b}{a}$

8. $\dfrac{3x - 1}{7x} + \dfrac{x + 9}{14x}$

9. $\dfrac{3x + 1}{5x} - \dfrac{x + 2}{10x}$

10. $\dfrac{y - x}{x^2y} + \dfrac{y + x}{xy^2}$

11. $\dfrac{a}{a - b} + \dfrac{b}{a + b}$

12. $\dfrac{b - 5}{10b} + \dfrac{b + 10}{15b}$

13. $\dfrac{a - 2}{2a} + \dfrac{3a + 5}{5a}$

14. $\dfrac{3c + 1}{c^2 + 3c} - \dfrac{c - 3}{c - 3c^2}$

15. $\dfrac{3a+5}{a^2+2a} - \dfrac{1}{2a+4}$

16. $\dfrac{10x+1}{14x} - \dfrac{x+5}{21x}$

17. $\dfrac{x^2}{(x+1)^2} - \dfrac{x-1}{x+1}$

18. $\dfrac{2y+1}{3y^2-3y} + \dfrac{5}{2y-2}$

19. $\dfrac{3}{a^2+4a+4} - \dfrac{1}{a^2-4}$

20. $\dfrac{y}{y^2-9} - \dfrac{1}{2y+6}$

21. $\dfrac{3}{ab} - \dfrac{4a+1}{a^2b} + \dfrac{b+2}{ab^2}$

22. $\dfrac{x}{x+3} + 2$

23. $\dfrac{3}{x-1} - \dfrac{2}{x}$

24. $\dfrac{5}{x^2-1} + \dfrac{3}{(x-1)^2}$

25. $\dfrac{3}{x^2-4} + \dfrac{2}{x^2+5x+6}$

26. $\dfrac{x^2}{2x^2-9x+4} - \dfrac{3x^2}{x^2+4x}$

27. $\dfrac{4}{2n^2-18} + \dfrac{1}{n^2+6n+9}$

28. $\dfrac{5}{p^2-3p-10} + \dfrac{3p-2}{p^2-25} - \dfrac{3p}{3p+6}$

REGENTS TUNE-UP: CHAPTER 3

Each of the questions in this section has appeared on a previous Course II Regents Examination. Here is an opportunity for you to review the material in Chapter 3 and, at the same time, prepare for the Course II Regents Examination.

---

1. Factor completely: $2a^2 + 2a - 84$.

2. Factor completely: $2x^2 - 50$.

3. Factor completely: $x^3 + 5x^2 + 6x$.

4. If $(x+k)^2 = x^2 + 10x + k^2$, find the value of k.

5. What are the factors of $3x^2 + 7x - 20$?
  (1) $(3x+5)(x-4)$ (3) $(3x-5)(x+4)$
  (2) $(3x-4)(x+5)$ (4) $(3x+4)(x-5)$

6. Expressed in simplest form, $\dfrac{x-7}{2} + \dfrac{x+2}{6}$ is equivalent to

  (1) $\dfrac{2x-5}{8}$ (2) $\dfrac{4x-19}{6}$ (3) $\dfrac{8x-5}{12}$ (4) $\dfrac{x^2-14}{12}$

7. For all values of x for which the expressions are defined, perform the indicated operations and express the result in simplest form.

$$\frac{x^2 + 4x + 4}{2x - 3} \div \frac{x^2 - 4}{2x^2 - 7x + 6}$$

8. For all values of x for which the expressions are defined, perform the indicated operations and express the result in simplest form.

(a) $\dfrac{3x + 1}{x^2 - 1} - \dfrac{1}{x + 1}$ (b) $\dfrac{x^2 - 3x}{x^2 + 2x} \div \dfrac{x^2 - 5x + 6}{x^2 - 4}$

ANSWERS TO SELECTED EXERCISES: CHAPTER 3

Section 3.1
1. x^8

3. $-6a^5$

5. $-8a^2b^2$

7. $\dfrac{1}{x^2}$

9. a^2b

11. $\dfrac{p^4}{2q}$

13. $6ab$

17. $x^2 + 3y$

19. $8b - 1$

21. $5x - y$

Section 3.2
1. $-2x^2 + 14x + 28$

3. 7

5. 13

7. $8y - 10$

9. $10n^2 - 10n - 3$

11. $6y - 15$

13. $-3x^3 - 5x^2 + 11x$

15. $3x^3 - 15x^2 + 21x$

17. $0.03c^5 - 0.048c^3$

19. $25w^2 - 64$

21. $8a^4 - 2a$

23. $t^2 + t + 5$

25. $h^2k + hk^2 - 7$

27. $x^2 - 11x + 28$

29. $t^2 - 64$

31. $8y^2 - 10y + 3$

33. $n^2 + 18n + 81$

35. $40m^2 + 37m - 63$

37. $40 - 63p + 18p^2$

39. $0.24y^2 + 2.8y - 40$

41. $x^2 - 14x + 49$

43. $x^2 + 4xy + 4y^2$

Section 3.3
1. $x(5x + 11)$

3. $4p^2q(1 + 3q)$

5. $x(x^2 + x + 1)$

7. $n^2(n^2 - 2n + 5)$

9. $3y^3(y^4 - 2y^2 + 4)$

11. $8u^2w^2(u^3 - 5w^3)$

13. $p^2k^2(k^2 - p + 1)$

15. $(x + 2)(x - 3)$

17. $(3x + 4)(x + 2)$

19. $2x - 3$

21. $(x + y)(z + w)$

Section 3.4
1. $(x + 5)(x + 3)$

3. $(x + 7)(x - 3)$

5. $(n + 11)(n - 8)$

7. $(w - 7)(w - 6)$

9. $(y - 1)(y - 8)$

11. $(x - 10)(x - 9)$

13. $(a + 5)(a - 4)$

15. $(3x - 7)(x + 3)$

17. $(5t - 2)(t + 4)$

19. $(7x - 4)(x + 8)$

21. $-(h + 6)(h - 5)$

23. $(4x - 5)(x + 8)$

25. $2x - 9$

27. $(3m - 4)(2m + 3)$

29. $(8n - 7)(n + 2)$

31. $(3a - 5)(2a - 1)$

Section 3.5

1. $x^2 - 4$

3. $9a^2 - 1$

5. $16 - x^2$

7. $0.64n^2 - 49$

9. $4y^2 - \dfrac{1}{25}$

11. $0.25n - 0.09$

13. $x^4 - 64$

15. $m^4 - n^4$

17. $(x + 12)(x - 12)$

19. $(5 + a)(5 - a)$

21. $(4a + 6)(4a - 6)$

23. $(h + k)(h - k)$

25. $\left(\dfrac{2}{3}x + 7\right)\left(\dfrac{2}{3}x - 7\right)$

27. $(0.3h + 0.2)(0.3h - 0.2)$

29. $(10a + 9b)(10a - 9b)$

31. $(x^3 + y^2)(x^3 - y^2)$

Section 3.6

1. $2(y + 5)(y - 5)$

3. $x(x + 8)(x - 7)$

5. $-(x + 5)(x + 2)$

7. $4(x + y)(x - y)$

9. $2s(3s - 2)(2s + 1)$

11. $3t^2(t + 5)(t - 1)$

13. $2x(x - 3)^2$

15. $(x + 1)(x + 2)(x - 2)$

Section 3.7

1. $7a^3$

3. $\dfrac{2}{x + 8}$

5. $\dfrac{b - a}{2}$

7. $\dfrac{y(2y - 1)}{3}$

9. $6x - 0.2$

11. -3

13. $\dfrac{3}{x}$

15. $\dfrac{10}{y - 3}$

17. $\dfrac{1}{x - 2}$

19. $\dfrac{x - 3}{x + 1}$

21. $\dfrac{x - 5}{x + 2}$

23. $\dfrac{4}{r + s}$

Section 3.8

1. $\dfrac{9ac^2}{2}$

3. $\dfrac{(y + 2)(3 - x)}{3}$

5. $\dfrac{4y}{4x - 5}$

7. $\dfrac{2}{x - y}$

9. 1

11. $\dfrac{5x}{(x + 2)(x + 6)}$

13. $\dfrac{5}{x + 7}$

15. $\dfrac{x + 3}{x(x - 3)}$

17. $p - 7$

Section 3.9

1. $\dfrac{3x}{2}$

3. $\dfrac{b}{2x}$

5. $\dfrac{y - 2}{2xy}$

7. $\dfrac{a^2 - b^2}{ab}$

9. $\dfrac{1}{2}$

11. $\dfrac{a^2 + 2ab - b^2}{(a + b)(a - b)}$

13. $\dfrac{11}{10}$

15. $\dfrac{5}{2a}$

17. $\dfrac{1}{(x + 1)^2}$

19. $\dfrac{2(a - 4)}{(a + 2)^2(a - 2)}$

21. $\dfrac{2a - b}{a^2b^2}$

23. $\dfrac{x + 2}{x(x - 1)}$

25. $\dfrac{5(x + 1)}{(x + 2)(x - 2)(x + 3)}$

27. $\dfrac{3(n + 1)}{(n - 3)(n + 3)^2}$

Regents Tune-Up: Chapter 3

1. $2(a + 7)(a - 6)$ **4.** 25   **7.** $x + 2$

2. $2(x + 5)(x - 5)$ **5.** (3)

3. $x(x + 3)(x + 2)$ **6.** (2)   **8. (a)** $\dfrac{2}{x - 1}$ **(b)** 1

CHAPTER 4

SOLVING LINEAR AND QUADRATIC EQUATIONS

4.1 SOLVING LINEAR EQUATIONS

KEY IDEAS

Equations that have the same solution are **equivalent.** The equations

$$x + 1 = 4, \qquad 2x = 6, \qquad \text{and} \qquad x = 3$$

are equivalent since 3 is the solution of each equation.

When solving an equation, our goal is to try to obtain an equivalent equation in which the variable is "isolated" on one side, so that the solution can be read from the opposite side, as in $x = 3$.

An equation in which the greatest exponent of the variable is 1 is called a **first-degree** or **linear equation.** This section will illustrate how to solve various types of linear equations.

Solving Equations with Two Arithmetic Operations

In the equation $2n + 5 = -11$, the variable is involved in two operations: multiplication ($2n$) and addition ($2n + 5$). In solving this equation, you should undo the addition before the multiplication.

Examples

1. Solve and check: $2n + 5 = -11$.

Solution:
$$2n + 5 - 5 = -11 - 5$$
$$2n + 0 = -16$$
$$\frac{2n}{2} = \frac{-16}{2}$$
$$\boldsymbol{n = -8}$$

Check:
$$2n + 5 = -11$$
$$2(-8) + 5$$
$$-16 + 5$$
$$-11 = -11 \checkmark$$

2. Solve and check: $\frac{x}{3} - 2 = 13$.

Solution: $\dfrac{x}{3} - 2 + 2 = 13 + 2$

$\dfrac{x}{3} + 0 \quad = 15$

$\quad$ *Check:* $\quad \dfrac{x}{3} - 2 = 13$

$\dfrac{1}{\cancel{3}}\left(\dfrac{x}{\cancel{3}}\right) = 3(15)$

$\dfrac{45}{3} - 2$

$x = 45$

$15 - 2$

$13 = 13\checkmark$

Solving Equations with Parentheses

If an equation contains parentheses, remove them by applying the distributive property of multiplication over addition (or subtraction).

Examples

3. Solve and check: $3(1 - 2x) = -15$.

Solution: $3(1 - 2x) = -15$
$3 - 6x = -15$
$3 - 6x - 3 = -15 - 3$
$\dfrac{-6x}{-6} = \dfrac{-18}{-6}$
$x = 3$

Check: $3(1 - 2x) = -15$
$3(1 - 2 \cdot 3)$
$3(1 - 6)$
$3(-5)$
$-15 \overset{?}{=} -15\checkmark$

4. Solve for x and check: $\dfrac{2}{3} = \dfrac{x + 9}{21}$. *Check:* $\dfrac{2}{3} = \dfrac{x + 9}{21}$

Solution: Cross-multiply and then simplify.

$3(x + 9) = 2 \cdot 21$
$3x + 27 = 42$
$3x + 27 - 27 = 42 - 27$
$3x = 15$
$\dfrac{3x}{3} = \dfrac{15}{3}$
$x = 5$

$\dfrac{5 + 9}{21}$

$\dfrac{14}{21}$

$\dfrac{14 \div 7}{21 \div 7}$

$\dfrac{2}{3} = \dfrac{2}{3}\checkmark$

Solving Equations with Variable Terms on the Same Side

To solve an equation in which the variable appears in more than one term on the same side of the equation, first combine like terms. Then solve the resulting equation as usual.

Example

5. Solve and check: $5x + 3x = -24$.

Solution: Begin by combining like terms.

$$8x = -24$$
$$\frac{8x}{8} = \frac{-24}{8}$$
$$x = -3$$

Check: $5x + 3x = -24$
$$5(-3) + 3(-3)$$
$$-15 + (-9)$$
$$-24 = -24\checkmark$$

Solving Equations with Variable Terms on Different Sides

If variable terms appear on opposite sides of an equation, work toward collecting variables on the same side of the equal sign and constant terms (numbers) on the other side.

Examples

6. Solve and check: $5w + 14 = 3(w - 8)$.

Solution:

	$5w + 14 = 3(w - 8)$
Apply the distributive property:	$5w + 14 = 3w - 24$
Subtract $3w$ from each side:	$-3w + 5w + 14 = -3w + 3w - 24$
Simplify:	$2w + 14 = -24$
Subtract 14 from each side:	$2w + 14 - 14 = -24 - 14$
Divide each side by 2:	$\dfrac{2w}{2} = \dfrac{-38}{2}$

$$w = -19$$

Check: $5w + 14 = 3(w - 8)$
$$5(-19) + 14 \mid 3(-19 - 8)$$
$$-95 + 14 \mid 3(-27)$$
$$-81 = -81\checkmark$$

7. Solve $3x + 0.9 = 1.3 - 7x$

Solution:

Method 1	**Method 2**
$10(3x) + 10(0.9) = 10(1.3) - 10(7x)$	$3x + 0.9 = 1.3 - 7x$
$30x + 9 = 13 - 70x$	$7x + 3x + 0.9 = 1.3 - 7x + 7x$
$70x + 30x + 9 = 13 - 70x + 70x$	$10x + 0.9 = 1.3$
$100x + 9 = 13$	$10x + 0.9 - 0.9 = 1.3 - 0.9$
$100x + 9 - 9 = 13 - 9$	$10x = 0.4$
$\dfrac{100x}{100} = \dfrac{4}{100}$	$\dfrac{10x}{10} = \dfrac{0.4}{10} = 0.04$
$x = \dfrac{1}{25}$ or 0.04	$x = 0.04$

The check is left for you.

Exercise Set 4.1

1–40. Solve for the variable in each equation, and check.

1. $2x - 0.4 = 1.8$

2. $3x - 1 = -16$

3. $32 = 3w + 5$

4. $2x + 3 = 8$

5. $2(x + 3) = 8$

6. $3(2x - 5) = -28$

7. $3x + 4x = -21$

8. $5x - 2x + 1 = -26$

9. $-2(1 - x) = 16$

10. $0.2x + 0.3 = 8.1$

11. $-(8x - 3) = 19$

12. $8 - 5r = -7$

13. $-12 + 3k = -6$

14. $7t = t - 42$

15. $0.54 - 0.07y = 0.2y$

16. $3(x + 4) = x$

17. $7 - (3n - 5) = n$

18. $4c - (c + 7) = 5$

19. $5(6 - q) = -3(q + 2)$

20. $\frac{3}{4}x - 1 = 14$

21. $\frac{2t}{3} + 5 = 13$

22. $\frac{x}{2} + 5 = -17$

23. $13 - \frac{3x}{4} = -8$

24. $7 - 3(x - 1) = -17$

25. $-5(2p + 6) + 3 = -12$

26. $18 - 2(h + 1) = 0$

27. $\frac{a - 2}{3} = a - 6$

28. $\frac{n - 5}{2} = 3n - 5$

29. $7(2p - 1) = 4(1 - 2p)$

30. $y - 6 = 3(2y + 9) + y$

31. $6\left(x + \frac{1}{2}\right) = 33$

32. $6\left(\frac{x}{2} + 1\right) = 33$

33. $5(n + 2) - 2(n + 2) = -9$

34. $-(11 + 5m) = 4(7 - 2m)$

35. $0.7(x - 0.2) + 0.3(x - 0.2) = 0.4$

36. $x(x - 3) = 24 + x + x^2$

37. $\dfrac{x + 5}{4} = \dfrac{x + 2}{3}$

38. $\dfrac{4}{x + 3} = \dfrac{1}{x - 3}$

39. $\dfrac{10 - x}{5} = \dfrac{7 - x}{2}$

40. $\dfrac{4}{11} = \dfrac{x + 6}{2x}$

41–47. Solve each problem algebraically.

41. The length of a rectangle exceeds twice its width by 5. If the perimeter of the rectangle is 52, find the dimensions of the rectangle.

42. The number 45 is 9 greater than twice the difference obtained by subtracting 7 from another number. What is the other number?

43. A 72-inch board is cut into two pieces so that the larger piece is seven times as long as the shorter piece. Find the length of each piece.

44. The product of 3 and 1 less than a number is the same as twice the number increased by 14. What is the number?

45. How old is David if his age 6 years from now will be twice his age 7 years ago?

46. Three years ago Rosita was one-half as old as she will be 2 years from now. What is Rosita's present age?

47. The denominator of a fraction is 2 less than the numerator. The fraction when expressed in simplest form is $\dfrac{6}{5}$. What is the numerator of the original fraction?

4.2 SOLVING LINEAR EQUATIONS WITH FRACTIONS

KEY IDEAS

To solve an equation that contains fractions, change the equation into an equivalent equation that does not contain fractions by multiplying each side of the equation by the LCD of all of its fractional terms.

Solving Fractional Equations

In the equation

$$\frac{3y}{4} + \frac{7}{12} = \frac{y}{6}$$

The variable appears only in the numerator of the fractional terms. The equation

$$\frac{2}{y} - \frac{9}{10} = \frac{1}{5y}$$

is called a **fractional equation** because the variable is contained in the denominator of a fractional term.

To solve either type of equation, first clear the equation of its fractions.

Examples

1. Solve and check: $\frac{3y}{4} + \frac{7}{12} = \frac{y}{6}$.

Solution: The LCD of all of the fractional terms of the equation is 12 since 12 is the smallest positive number into which each of the denominators divides evenly.

$$\frac{3y}{4} + \frac{7}{12} = \frac{y}{6}$$

Clear the equation of its fractions by multiplying each term on both sides of the equation by 12:

$$\overset{3}{\cancel{12}}\left(\frac{3y}{\cancel{4}}\right) + \overset{1}{\cancel{12}}\left(\frac{7}{\cancel{12}}\right) = \overset{2}{\cancel{12}}\left(\frac{y}{\cancel{6}}\right)$$

$$9y \quad + \quad 7 = 2y$$

$$7y = -7$$

$$y = \frac{-7}{7} = -1$$

The solution is **−1.** The check is left for you.

2. Solve for y: $\frac{2}{y} - \frac{9}{10} = \frac{1}{5y}$.

Solution: The LCM of y, 10, and $5y$ is $10y$.

Multiply each term by $10y$: $\overset{1}{\cancel{10y}}\left(\dfrac{2}{\cancel{y}}\right) - \overset{1}{\cancel{10y}}\left(\dfrac{9}{\cancel{10}}\right) = \overset{2}{\cancel{10y}}\left(\dfrac{1}{\cancel{5y}}\right)$

$$20 - 9y = 2$$
$$-9y = 2 - 20$$
$$\frac{-9y}{-9} = \frac{-18}{-9}$$
$$y = 2$$

The solution is **2**. The check is left for you.

3. When a number is divided by that number increased by 2, the result is 1 decreased by the reciprocal of the original number. Find the original number.

Solution: Let x = original number. Then

Number divided by that number increased by 2 $\quad$ Reciprocal of original number

$$\frac{x}{x+2} \quad = \quad 1 - \quad \frac{1}{x}$$

Since the LCD of $x + 2$ and x is $x(x + 2)$, multiply each side of the equation by $x(x + 2)$: $\quad \left(\dfrac{x}{x+2}\right) \cdot x(x+2) = (1) \cdot x(x+2) - \left(\dfrac{1}{x}\right) \cdot x(x+2)$

$$(x) \cdot x = x(x+2) - (x+2)$$
$$x^2 = x^2 + 2x - x - 2$$
$$0 = x - 2$$
$$2 = x$$

The number is **2**. You should verify that 2 satisfies the conditions of the problem.

Exercise Set 4.2

1–10. Solve for the variable and check.

1. $\dfrac{n}{2} - 3 = \dfrac{n}{5}$

2. $\dfrac{x+1}{4} - \dfrac{2}{3} = \dfrac{1}{12}$

3. $\dfrac{3b}{4} = \dfrac{2b}{5} + \dfrac{21}{20}$

4. $\dfrac{y-2}{2} + \dfrac{2y-1}{20} = \dfrac{y}{4}$

5. $\dfrac{x}{4} + \dfrac{x+2}{12} = \dfrac{x-2}{3}$

6. $\dfrac{1}{5} - \dfrac{1}{3x} = \dfrac{1}{15x}$

7. $\dfrac{3}{5r} - \dfrac{2}{6r} = \dfrac{1}{15}$

8. $\dfrac{1}{2a} + \dfrac{5}{9} = -\dfrac{1}{18a}$

9. $\dfrac{12}{x+1} + \dfrac{x-1}{2} = \dfrac{x+3}{2}$

10. $\dfrac{5}{x} + \dfrac{2x}{x+3} = 2$

11. Two numbers are in the ratio of 2 : 3. If the sum of their reciprocals is $\frac{5}{12}$, find the smaller of the two numbers.

12. If $\frac{1}{2}$ is added to the reciprocal of a number, the result is 1 less than twice the reciprocal of the original number. Find the number.

13. If the reciprocal of a number is multiplied by 3, the result exceeds the reciprocal of the original number by $\frac{1}{3}$. Find the number.

14. If the reciprocal of a number is multiplied by 1 less than the original number, the result exceeds one-half the reciprocal of the original number by $\frac{5}{8}$. Find the number.

4.3 SOLVING QUADRATIC EQUATIONS BY FACTORING

KEY IDEAS

If the product of two numbers equals 0, then the first number equals 0, or the second number equals 0, or both numbers equal 0. This is sometimes referred to as the **zero product rule.**

The zero product rule provides a method of solving an equation that can be written in such a way that one side is 0, while the other side is written in factored form. For example, if

$$x(x-5) = 0,$$

then $x = 0$ or $x - 5 = 0$. Hence, the two roots of $x(x-5) = 0$ are 0 and 5.

The equation $x(x-5) = 0$ can also be written as $x^2 - 5x = 0$. Since this equation contains the square of a variable (x^2), it is called a **quadratic equation.**

Solving Quadratic Equations by Factoring

A **quadratic equation** is an equation that can be written in the *standard form:*

$$ax^2 + bx + c = 0 \ (a \neq 0).$$

Whereas the highest power of the variable in a linear equation is 1, a quadratic equation must include the square of a variable. If the left side of a quadratic equation having the form $ax^2 + bx + c = 0$ can be factored, then the zero product rule allows you to solve the equation by setting each factor equal to 0.

To solve the quadratic equation $x^2 + 4x = 5$, follow these steps:

Step	Example
1. Write the equation in standard form.	1. $x^2 + 4x - 5 = 0$
2. Factor the quadratic polynomial.	2. $(x + 5)(x - 1) = 0$
3. Set each factor equal to 0.	3. $(x + 5 = 0)$ or $(x - 1 = 0)$
4. Solve each first-degree equation	4. $x = -5$ or $x = 1$
5. Write the solution set.	5. $\{-5, 1\}$

Each member of the solution set must be checked by substituting for x in the *original* equation.

$$\text{Let } x = -5.$$
$$\frac{x^2 + 4x}{(-5)^2 + 4(-5)} = 5$$
$$25 - 20$$
$$5 \overset{!}{=} 5 \checkmark$$

$$\text{Let } x = 1.$$
$$\frac{x^2 + 4x}{(1)^2 + 4(1)} = 5$$
$$1 + 4$$
$$5 \overset{!}{=} 5 \checkmark$$

When solving quadratic equations, keep in mind that:

- The quadratic equation must be expressed in standard form *before* you attempt to factor the quadratic polynomial.
- Every quadratic equation has *two* solutions. Each solution is called a **root** of the equation. The two roots may be equal.
- The solution set of a quadratic equation can be checked by verifying that each different root makes the *original* equation a true statement.
- Not every quadratic equation can be solved by factoring.

Examples

1. Solve for a: $a^2 + 6a + 9 = 0$.

Solution: $(a + 3)(a + 3) = 0$
 $(a + 3 = 0)$ or $(a + 3 = 0)$
  $a = -3$ or $a = -3$

The two roots are equal, so the root does not have to be written twice in the solution set.

The solution set is $\{-3\}$. The check is left for you.

2. Solve for a: $6a^2 + 18a + 12 = 0$.

Solution: Observe that 6 is a common factor of each term of the equation. Therefore the equation may be simplified *before* attempting to factor the quadratic polynomial by dividing each term of the equation by 6.

$$\frac{\overset{1}{\cancel{6}a^2}}{\cancel{6}} + \frac{\overset{3}{\cancel{18}a}}{\cancel{6}} + \frac{\overset{2}{\cancel{12}}}{\cancel{6}} = \frac{\overset{0}{\cancel{0}}}{\cancel{6}}$$
$$a^2 + 3a + 2 = 0$$
$$(a + 2)(a + 1) = 0$$
$$(a + 2 = 0) \quad \text{or} \quad (a + 1 = 0)$$
$$a = -2 \quad \text{or} \quad a = -1$$

The solution set is $\{-2, -1\}$. The check is left for you.

3. Solve for x: $2x^2 - x - 3 = 0$.

Solution: Factor the left side of the equation by replacing the middle term with two terms whose sum is $-x$. Choose the numerical coefficients of the two terms so that their product is $2(-3)$ or -6. Thus:

$$2x^2 - x - 3 = 0$$
$$2x^2 + \underbrace{2x - 3x}_{-x} - 3 = 0$$

Group the first and the
last pairs of terms together: $(2x^2 + 2x) + (-3x - 3) = 0$

Factor out $2x$ from the
first binomial and -3
from the second binomial: $2x(x + 1) - 3(x + 1) = 0$

Factor out the common
binomial factor: $(x + 1)(2x - 3) = 0$

Set each factor equal to 0
and solve the resulting
equations: $x + 1 = 0 \quad \text{or} \quad 2x - 3 = 0$
                        $x = -1 \qquad\qquad 2x = 3$
                                          $x = \frac{3}{2}$

The solution set is $\left\{-1, \frac{3}{2}\right\}$. The check is left for you.

4. If 2 is a root of the equation $x^2 + kx - 12 = 0$, find:
  (a) the value of k **(b)** the sum of the two roots

Solution: **(a)** Since 2 is a root of the given equation, let $x = 2$ and solve for k:

$$x^2 + kx \quad - 12 = 0$$
$$(2)^2 + k(2) - 12 = 0$$
$$4 + 2k \quad - 12 = 0$$
$$2k - 8 = 0$$
$$k = \frac{8}{2} = \mathbf{4}$$

(b) Replacing k with 4 in the original equation gives $x^2 + 4x - 12 = 0$. Solve this equation and then add the two roots.

$$x^2 + 4x - 12 = 0$$
$$(x - 2)(x + 6) = 0$$
$$x - 2 = 0 \quad \text{or} \quad x + 6 = 0$$
$$x = 2 \quad \text{or} \quad x = -6$$

Since $2 + (-6) = -4$, the sum of the two roots is **–4.**

5. Solve for n: $\dfrac{n-4}{2} = \dfrac{3n}{n+4}$.

Solution: Cross-multiply. Then write the quadratic equation in standard form.

$$(n - 4)(n + 4) = 2(3n)$$
$$n^2 - 16 = 6n$$
$$n^2 - 6n - 16 = 0$$
$$(n - 8)(n + 2) = 0$$
$$(n - 8 = 0) \quad \text{or} \quad (n + 2 = 0)$$
$$n = 8 \quad \text{or} \quad n = -2$$

The solution set is $\{-2, 8\}$. The check is left for you.

6. The length of a rectangular garden is twice its width. The garden is surrounded by a rectangular concrete walk having a uniform width of 4 feet. If the area of the garden and the walk is 330 square feet, what are the dimensions of the garden?

Solution: Let x = width of garden.
Then $2x$ = length of garden.
In the accompanying diagram the innermost rectangle represents the garden. Since the walk has a uniform width, the width of the larger (outer) rectangle is $4 + x + 4 = x + 8$. The length of the larger rectangle is $4 + 2x + 4 = 2x + 8$. The area of the larger rectangle is given as 330. Hence:

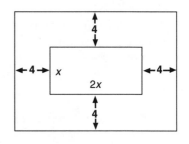

$$\text{Length} \times \text{Width} = \text{Area}$$
$$(2x + 8)(x + 8) = 330$$
$$2x^2 + 24x + 64 = 330$$
$$2x^2 + 24x + 64 - 330 = 0$$
$$2x^2 + 24x - 266 = 0$$
$$\frac{2x^2}{2} + \frac{24x}{2} - \frac{266}{2} = \frac{0}{2}$$
$$x^2 + 12x - 133 = 0$$
$$(x - 7)(x + 19) = 0$$
$$(x - 7 = 0) \text{ or } (x + 19 = 0)$$
$$x = 7 \quad \text{or} \quad x = -19$$

Reject -19 since the width must be a positive number.

The width of the garden is **7 feet** and the length is **14 feet.** The check is left for you.

Exercise Set 4.3

1–26. Find the solution set and check.

1. $x(x + 2) = 0$ **10.** $6 = t^2 - t$ **19.** $(x - 2)(x + 1) = 10$

2. $y^2 + 3y + 2 = 0$ **11.** $y^3 - 9y = 0$ **20.** $8x^2 + 18x = 5$

3. $x^2 + 14x + 49 = 0$ **12.** $y(y + 9) = 36$ **21.** $n^2 = 10(n + 300)$

4. $x^2 - 5x + 4 = 0$ **13.** $0 = 2a^2 + 10a + 8$ **22.** $b(b - 2) = b$

5. $x^2 - x = 12$ **14.** $8p^2 = 6p - p^2$ **23.** $2y^2 = 7y + 4$

6. $x^2 - 7x = 0$ **15.** $3t^2 + 14t = 5$ **24.** $5(x^2 - 2) + 23x = 0$

7. $q^2 - 6q = 27$ **16.** $2b^2 - 18 = 5b$ **25.** $(x + 3)^2 = 6x + 25$

8. $11n - n^2 = 0$ **17.** $9x^2 - 12x + 4 = 0$ **26.** $\dfrac{1}{x} - \dfrac{x-1}{14} = \dfrac{1}{7x}$

9. $2r^2 = 5r + 3$ **18.** $6t^2 = 7t + 3$

27–28. Solve for x and check.

27. $\dfrac{x+5}{x+1} = \dfrac{x-1}{4}$ **28.** $\dfrac{x-2}{x} = \dfrac{x+4}{3x}$

29. Find the perimeter of a right triangle whose legs have lengths represented by $x + 1$ and $3x$, and whose hypotenuse measures $5x - 7$.

30. If one of the roots of the equation $x^2 - x + q = 0$ is 3, find:
(a) the value of q **(b)** the product of the roots

31. For what value of b will the equation $bx^2 - bx - 2 = 0$ have 2 as a root?

32. For which of the following equations is the *product* of the roots equal to 4?
(1) $x^2 - 4 = 0$ (3) $2x^2 + 15x - 8 = 0$
(2) $3x^2 - 37x + 12 = 0$ (4) $x^2 - 3x - 4 = 0$

33. For what value(s) of x is the fraction $\dfrac{x-1}{x^2 - 2x - 3}$ *not* defined?

34. Which pair of equations have a root in common?

(1) $x^2 = 4$ and $\dfrac{x}{2} = 2$
(2) $x(x - 3) = 0$ and $x^2 + 2x - 3 = 0$
(3) $x^2 - 8x + 16 = 0$ and $x^2 - 5x + 4 = 0$
(4) $x^2 + x - 6 = 0$ and $x^2 - x - 6 = 0$

35–43. Solve algebraically.

35. The sum of the squares of two consecutive positive even integers is 52. Find the integers.

36. Find three consecutive positive, even integers such that the difference in the squares of the first and the third is 48.

37. The perimeter of a right triangle is 90. If the length of the shorter leg is 9, find the length of the hypotenuse.

38. If a side of a square is doubled and an adjacent side is diminished by 3, a rectangle is formed whose area is numerically greater than the area of the square by twice the length of the original side of the square. Find the dimensions of the original square.

39. The perimeter of a certain rectangle is 24 inches. If the length is doubled and the width is tripled, the area is increased by 160 square inches. Find the dimensions of the original rectangle.

40. A rectangular picture 30 centimeters wide and 50 centimeters long is surrounded by a frame having a uniform width. If the combined area of the picture and the frame is 2,016 square centimeters, what is the width of the frame?

41. A rectangular picture 24 inches by 32 inches is surrounded by a border of uniform width. If the area of the border is 528 square inches less than the area of the picture, find the width of the border.

42. The sum of the areas of a rectangle and a square is 68. If the length of the rectangle is twice its width, and the length of a side of the square exceeds the width of the rectangle by 2, find the width of the rectangle.

43. A rectangular piece of cardboard is twice as long as it is wide. From each of its four corners a square piece 3 inches on a side is cut out. The flaps on each side are then turned up to form a box that is open at the top. If the volume of the box is 168 cubic inches, find the original dimensions of the piece of cardboard.

44. Solve for the positive value of n: $\dfrac{3}{5} + \dfrac{n-2}{3} = \dfrac{14}{5n}$.

45. Solve for x and check: $\dfrac{1}{x} + \dfrac{1}{x-2} = \dfrac{x-1}{x}$.

4.4 SOLVING QUADRATIC EQUATIONS WITH IRRATIONAL ROOTS

KEY IDEAS

A quadratic equation that cannot be factored can be solved by expressing it as an equivalent equation that has the square of a variable term on one side of the equation and a number on the other side. Taking the square root of each side of this equation gives the two roots of the original quadratic equation.

Solving Quadratic Equations by Taking Square Roots

If the original quadratic equation has the form $ax^2 + c = k$, then you can find the two roots by solving for x^2, and then for x by taking the square root of each side of the equation.

Example

1. Solve for x: $3x^2 - 15 = 0$.

Solution:
$$3x^2 - 15 = 0$$
$$3x^2 = 15$$
$$\frac{3x^2}{3} = \frac{15}{3}$$
$$x^2 = 5$$

Take the square root of each side:
$$x = \pm\ \sqrt{5} \text{ or } \{-\sqrt{5}, \sqrt{5}\}$$

A quadratic equation that involves the square of a binomial and takes the general form $(x + a)^2 + c = 0$ can also be solved by taking square roots.

Example

2. Solve for x: $\qquad (x - 1)^2 - 3 = 0$.

Solution:
$$(x - 1)^2 - 3 = 0$$
$$(x - 1)^2 = 3$$

Take the square root of each side:
$$x - 1 = \pm\ \sqrt{3}$$
$$x = 1 \pm \sqrt{3} \text{ or } \{1 + \sqrt{3}, 1 - \sqrt{3}\}$$

Solving Quadratic Equations by Completing the Square

The quadratic equation $x^2 - 6x - 1 = 0$ cannot be factored. This quadratic equation can be solved, however, by completing the square. Follow these steps:

Step	Example
1. Write the original equation in the form $x^2 + bx = c$.	**1.** $x^2 - 6x = 1$
2. Find half the coefficient of x and square it.	**2.** $x^2 - 6x + \underline{?} = 1 + \underline{?}$ $\frac{1}{2}(-6) = -3$ $(-3)^2 = 9$
3. Add this number to each side of the original equation.	**3.** $x^2 - 6x + 9 = 1 + 9$
4. Write the trinomial as the square of a binomial.	**4.** $(x - 3)^2 = 10$
5. Take the square root of each side of the equation.	**5.** $x - 3 = \pm\sqrt{10}$
6. Solve the resulting equations and write the solution set.	**6.** $x = 3 \pm \sqrt{10}$ $\{3 + \sqrt{10}, 3 - \sqrt{10}\}$

Exercise Set 4.4

1–10. Solve each equation and express any irrational roots in simplest radical form.

1. $x^2 - 3 = 1$

2. $2y^2 - 14 = 0$

3. $\frac{w^2}{3} - 1 = 6$

4. $(x + 2)^2 = 5$

5. $19 - (2y - 3)^2 = 7$

6. $x^2 - 4x - 16 = 0$

7. $p^2 + 2p - 7 = 0$

8. $y^2 - 10y = 6$

9. $8t - 5 = t^2$

10. $x^2 + 7x + 5 = 0$

4.5 SOLVING QUADRATIC EQUATIONS BY FORMULA

KEY IDEAS

Starting with a linear equation of the form $ax + b = c$, you can solve for variable x in terms of constants a, b and c:

$$ax = c - b, \text{ which means } x = \frac{c - b}{a} \ (a \neq 0).$$

The resulting equation represents a general formula for solving linear equations having the form $ax + b = c$. For example, in the equation $2x + 3 = 11$, $a = 2$, $b = 3$, and $c = 11$, so that

$$x = \frac{c - b}{a} = \frac{11 - 3}{2} = \frac{8}{2} = 4.$$

Similarly, starting with a quadratic equation written in the standard form $ax^2 + bx + c = 0$ ($a \neq 0$), you can solve for variable x by using the method of completing the square. The resulting equation is called the **quadratic formula.**

Solving Quadratic Equations by Applying the Quadratic Formula

Any quadratic equation (including those that cannot be factored) that is put into the standard form $ax^2 + bx + c = 0$ can be solved by using the *quadratic formula:*

$$x = \frac{-b \pm \sqrt{b^2 - 4ac}}{2a} \ (a \neq 0)$$

For example, to solve the equation $3x^2 + 2x = 1$, follow these steps:

Step	Example
1. Put the equation into standard form.	**1.** $3x^2 + 2x \ \underline{-1} = 0$
2. Identify the values for a, b, and c.	**2.** $ax^2 + bx + c = 0$
	$a = 3$, $b = 2$, and $c = -1$

3. Write the quadratic formula, and replace the letters *a, b,* and *c* with their numerical values.	**3.** $x = \dfrac{-b \pm \sqrt{b^2 - 4ac}}{2a}$ $= \dfrac{-2 \pm \sqrt{(2)^2 - 4(3)(-1)}}{2(3)}$
4. Simplify.	**4.** $x = \dfrac{-2 \pm \sqrt{4 + 12}}{6}$ $= \dfrac{-2 \pm \sqrt{16}}{6}$ $x = \dfrac{-2 \pm 4}{6}$ $x = \dfrac{-2 + 4}{6}$ or $x = \dfrac{-2 - 4}{6}$ $x = \dfrac{2}{6}$ $\qquad x = -\dfrac{6}{6}$ $= \dfrac{1}{3}$ $\qquad = -1$
5. Write the solution set.	**5.** $\left\{\dfrac{1}{3}, -1\right\}$

In the preceding example the roots were rational, indicating that the original equation was factorable. In the next example the equation is *not* factorable, so its roots are *not* rational.

Example

Solve by formula: $x^2 + 8 = 7x$.

Solution:
Put the equation into standard form:

$$x^2 + 8 = 7x$$
$$x^2 - 7x + 8 = 0$$

Write the formula:

$$x = \frac{-b \pm \sqrt{b^2 - 4ac}}{2a}$$

Let $a = 1$, $b = -7$, and $c = 8$:

$$x = \frac{7 \pm \sqrt{(-7)^2 - 4(1)(8)}}{2(1)}$$

$$= \frac{7 \pm \sqrt{49 - 32}}{2}$$

$$= \frac{7 \pm \sqrt{17}}{2}$$

Write the solution set:

$$\left\{\frac{7 + \sqrt{17}}{2}, \frac{7 - \sqrt{17}}{2}\right\}$$

Selecting a Method of Solution

The quadratic formula can be used to find the roots of *any* quadratic equation that is written in standard form, including quadratic equations that are not factorable and have irrational roots. However, some types of quadratic equations may be solved more easily by using a previously learned method.

- Type I ($c = 0$). If the constant term of a quadratic equation is missing, solve the equation by factoring.

Example: Solve: $3t^2 - 7t = 0$.

$$t(3t - 7) = 0$$
$$(t = 0) \text{ or } (3t - 7 = 0)$$
$$t = 0 \quad \text{or} \quad t = \frac{7}{3}$$

The solution set is $\left\{0, \dfrac{7}{3}\right\}$.

- Type II ($b = 0$, $c \neq 0$). If the linear term is missing, solve the equation by taking the square root of each side of the equation.

Example: Solve: $4w^2 - 24 = 0$.

$$4w^2 = 24$$
$$w^2 = 6$$
$$w = \pm\sqrt{6}$$

The solution set is $\{\sqrt{6}, -\sqrt{6}\}$.

- Type III (a, b, and $c \neq 0$). If, after writing a quadratic equation in standard form, a quadratic trinomial appears on one side of the equation, try first to solve the equation by factoring.

Example: Solve: $3y^2 + 5y = 2y^2 + 14$.

$$3y^2 - 2y^2 + 5y - 14 = 0$$
$$y^2 + 5y - 14 = 0$$
$$(y + 7)(y - 2) = 0$$
$$(y + 7 = 0) \text{ or } (y - 2 = 0)$$
$$y = -7 \text{ or } y = 2$$

The solution set is $\{-7, 2\}$.

If the quadratic equation cannot be factored (or appears difficult to factor), solve the equation by using the quadratic formula.

Example: Solve: $2x + 4 = x^2$.
$$-x^2 + 2x + 4 = 0$$

97

$$x = \frac{-b \pm \sqrt{b^2 - 4ac}}{2a}$$

Let $a = -1$, $b = 2$, $c = 4$:

$$= \frac{-2 \pm \sqrt{(2)^2 - 4(-1)(4)}}{2(-1)}$$

$$= \frac{-2 \pm \sqrt{4 + 16}}{-2}$$

$$= \frac{-2 \pm \sqrt{20}}{-2}$$

Multiply numerator and denominator by -1:

$$= \frac{2 \mp \sqrt{20}}{2}$$

The solution set is $\left\{ \dfrac{2 + \sqrt{20}}{2}, \dfrac{2 - \sqrt{20}}{2} \right\}$.

Simplifying Irrational Roots

In the last example the roots $\dfrac{2 \pm \sqrt{20}}{2}$ may be expressed in *simplest form* by factoring the radicand 20 as the product of two positive integers, one of which is the highest perfect square factor of 20:

$$\frac{2 \pm \sqrt{20}}{2} = \frac{2 \pm \sqrt{4}\sqrt{5}}{2} = \frac{2 \pm 2\sqrt{5}}{2}$$

$$= \frac{2(1 \pm \sqrt{5})}{2} = \mathbf{1 \pm \sqrt{5}}$$

Exercise Set 4.5

1–24. Solve each equation by using the quadratic formula. Express irrational roots in simplest radical form.

1. $x^2 - 6x - 16 = 0$

2. $y^2 - 10y = 6$

3. $x(x + 4) = 3$

4. $n^2 + 8n - 3 = 0$

5. $0 = x^2 + 6x + 4$

6. $p^2 = 2p + 7$

7. $0 = x^2 + 3x - 10$

8. $8t - 5 = t^2$

9. $2x^2 - 10x + 5 = 0$

10. $3x^2 + 4 = 12x$

11. $4 - 7s = -2s^2$

12. $3t^2 + 9 = 2t^2 + 6t$

13. $2y^2 + 3(3y + 1) = 0$

14. $n(n - 8) = -7$

15. $2x + 5 = x^2$

16. $4x^2 = x + 3$

17. $6x^2 + 2 = 9x$

18. $5x^2 - 10x + 3 = 0$

19. $4x + 1 = 8x^2$

20. $3x(x - 2) = 5$

21. $\dfrac{h^2}{2} = 3h + 1$

22. $4x^2 + 36x = 63$

23. $3y^2 = y^2 + 3y + 8$

24. $10s - 6s^2 = 3$

25. In $\triangle ABC$, m $\angle C = 90$, BC exceeds the length of $\overline{AC}$ by 3, and AB exceeds the length of AC by 5. Find AC. [*Answer may be left in radical form.*]

26. The perimeter of a rectangle is 40, and the length of a diagonal is 16. Find the width of the rectangle. [*Answer may be left in radical form.*]

27–30. Solve each proportion for x. Express irrational roots in simplest radical form.

27. $\dfrac{3}{x-1} = \dfrac{x+1}{x}$

29. $\dfrac{1-x}{x-2} = \dfrac{4x}{1+x}$

28. $\dfrac{x+2}{2x-1} = \dfrac{2x+1}{x+3}$

30. $\dfrac{x-5}{3x-1} = \dfrac{x+2}{x-2}$

4.6 ANALYZING THE DISCRIMINANT

KEY IDEAS

Without actually solving a quadratic equation of the form $ax^2 + bx + c = 0$, the values of the coefficients a, b, and c can be used to provide information about the roots. The value of $b^2 - 4ac$ determines whether the two roots of a quadratic equation are real or not real, rational or irrational, equal or unequal.

Nature of the Roots

In the quadratic formula

$$x = \frac{-b \pm \sqrt{b^2 - 4ac}}{2a} \quad (a \neq 0),$$

$b^2 - 4ac$, the expression underneath the radical sign, is called the **discriminant**. The discriminant determines the *type* of roots. If the discriminant is a perfect square greater than 0, then the radical in the quadratic formula evaluates to an integer greater than 0, so that the roots are *rational* and *unequal;* if the discriminant is a positive number that is *not* a perfect square, then the roots must include a radical, so that the roots are *irrational* and *unequal.* If the discriminant is equal to 0, then the $\pm$ radical term vanishes and the two roots are *equal.*

If the discriminant is negative, the roots are *not real* because the square root of a negative number is not real. Numbers that arise from taking square roots of negative numbers are called **imaginary numbers**.

The accompanying table summarizes how the roots of a quadratic equation can be classified by looking at the discriminant.

CLASSIFYING ROOTS BY LOOKING AT THE DISCRIMINANT

Value of Discriminant	Type of Roots
1. $b^2 - 4ac < 0$	1. Not real (imaginary)
2. $b^2 - 4ac = 0$	2. Real, rational, and equal

3. $b^2 - 4ac > 0$ *and*
  (i) is *not* a perfect square
  (ii) is a perfect square
	3. Real, unequal, *and*
	  (i) irrational
	  (ii) rational

Examples

1. Find the discriminant and describe the nature of the roots of $3x^2 + 11x = 4$.

Solution: Write the equation in standard form:

$$3x^2 + 11x - 4 = 0; \quad \text{then } a = 3, b = 11, \text{ and } c = -4.$$

Next, evaluate the discriminant:

$$b^2 - 4ac = 11^2 - 4(3)(-4)$$
$$= 121 + 48$$
$$= \mathbf{169}$$

The discriminant 169 is a perfect square since $13 \times 13 = 169$. Therefore, the roots of the equation are **real, rational,** and **unequal.**

2. Find the positive value of k so that the roots of the equation $4x^2 + kx + 9 = 0$ are real and equal.

Solution: For the equation $4x^2 + kx + 9 = 0$, $a = 4$, $b = k$, and $c = 9$. If the roots are real and equal, then the discriminant must be equal to 0.

$$b^2 - 4ac = 0$$
$$k^2 - 4(4)(9) = 0$$
$$k^2 - 144 = 0$$
$$k^2 = 144$$
$$k = \pm \sqrt{144} = \pm 12$$

The positive value of k that makes the roots real and equal is **12.**

3. Find the largest integral value of k so that the roots of the equation $x^2 - 5x + k = 0$ are real.

Solution: For the equation $x^2 - 5x + k = 0$, $a = 1$, $b = -5$, and $c = k$. If the roots are real, then the discriminant must be greater than or equal to 0.

$$b^2 - 4ac \geq 0$$

$$(-5)^2 - 4(1)(k) \geq 0$$
$$25 - 4k \geq 0$$
$$-4k \geq -25$$
$$k \leq \frac{-25}{-4}$$
$$k \leq 6\frac{1}{4}$$

The largest integral value of k that makes the inequality true is **6.**

Exercise Set 4.6

1. If the discriminant of a quadratic equation with real coefficients is *not* negative, then the roots of the equation *must* be:
(1) rational   (2) irrational   (3) real   (4) not real

2. The roots of the equation $3x^2 + 5x + 2$ are:
(1) rational and unequal   (3) irrational
(2) rational and equal   (4) not real

3. The roots of the equation $x - 1 = x^2 - 2x + 1$ are:
(1) rational and unequal   (3) irrational
(2) rational and equal   (4) not real

4. The solution set of the equation $2x^2 + x = 3$ contains two:
(1) integers
(2) positive rational numbers
(3) nonintegral rational roots
(4) rational numbers, one positive and one negative

5. What value of k will make the roots of the equation $x^2 - 2kx + 16 = 0$ real, rational, and equal?
(1) $-2\sqrt{2}$ (2) 2   (3) $4\sqrt{2}$ (4) -4

6. For what value of c will the roots of the equation $x^2 + 6x + c = 0$ be equal?

7–10. For each equation, find the value of k that makes the roots real, rational, and equal.

7. $x^2 + kx + 25 = 0$ **9.** $9x^2 + k = 12x$

8. $9x^2 + 6x + k = 0$ **10.** $4x^2 - kx + 1 = 0$

11–14. For each equation, find the largest *integral value of k that makes the roots real.*

11. $x^2 - 4x + k = 0$ **13.** $2x^2 - 7x + k = 0$

12. $kx^2 - 9x + 3 = 0$ **14.** $kx^2 - 10x + k = 0$

15. What is the *smallest* integral value of k that makes the roots of the equation $3x^2 + 8x - k = 0$ real?

REGENTS TUNE-UP: CHAPTER 4

Each of the questions in this section has appeared on a previous Course II Regents Examination. Here is an opportunity for you to review the material in Chapter 4 and, at the same time, prepare for the Course II Regents Examination.

1. Solve for x: $\dfrac{x}{2} + \dfrac{x}{3} = 40$.

2. Solve for x: $\dfrac{1}{2} + \dfrac{5}{x-2} = 3$.

3. Solve for the positive value of x: $\dfrac{x-4}{5} = \dfrac{1}{x}$, $x \neq 0$.

4. Find the positive root of the equation $\dfrac{4}{x-1} = \dfrac{x+1}{12}$.

5. Solve for a: $\dfrac{a}{3} + \dfrac{5a}{12} = \dfrac{9}{4}$.

6. Which set contains all values of x for which the fraction $\dfrac{x+2}{x^2-49}$ is undefined?
(1) $\{0\}$ (2) $\{-2\}$ (3) $\{7\}$ (4) $\{7, -7\}$

7. An equation whose roots are 4 and -1 is:
(1) $x^2 + 3x + 4 = 0$ (3) $x^2 - 3x - 4 = 0$
(2) $x^2 - 3x + 4 = 0$ (4) $x^2 + 3x - 4 = 0$

8. What are the roots of the equation $2x^2 - 5x + 1 = 0$?
(1) $\dfrac{5 \pm \sqrt{17}}{4}$ (2) $\dfrac{-5 \pm \sqrt{21}}{4}$ (3) $\dfrac{5 \pm \sqrt{33}}{-4}$ (4) $\dfrac{-5 \pm \sqrt{23}}{-4}$

9. The solution for the quadratic equation $2x^2 - x - 14 = 0$ is
(1) $\dfrac{-1 \pm \sqrt{111}}{2}$ (2) $\dfrac{1 \pm \sqrt{111}}{4}$ (3) $\dfrac{1 \pm \sqrt{113}}{4}$ (4) $\dfrac{-1 \pm \sqrt{113}}{4}$

10. What is the sum of the roots of the equation $x^2 - 11x + 10 = 0$?
(1) 11   (2) 7   (3) 10   (4) -7

11. What is the product of the roots of the equation $x^2 - 2x - 15 = 0$?
(1) -15 (2) -2 (3) -8 (4) 30

12. (a) Factor and simplify: $\dfrac{2x+6}{x^2-9} \cdot \dfrac{x^2-3x}{10}$, $x \neq \pm 3$.

  (b) Combine: $\dfrac{6}{y} - \dfrac{5}{2y}$, $y \neq 0$.

(c) Solve for x: $\dfrac{2}{3} + \dfrac{x+7}{x} = 4,\ x \neq 0$.

13. (a) Express the quotient in simplest form:

$$\frac{x^2 - 36}{x^2 + 3x - 18} \div \frac{x^2 - 12x + 36}{x^2 - 6x}.$$

(b) Solve algebraically for x and check: $\dfrac{4}{x} - 1 = \dfrac{x+2}{x}$.

14. Answer both **(a)** and **(b)** for all values of x for which these expressions are defined.

(a) Solve for x and write the answer in simplest radical form:

$$\frac{1}{x} + \frac{1}{x+3} = 2.$$

(b) Express the following product in simplest form:

$$\frac{x^2 - 25}{2x - 2} \cdot \frac{x^2 + 4x - 5}{x^2 + 10x + 25}.$$

ANSWERS TO SELECTED EXERCISES: CHAPTER 4

Section 4.1

1. 1.1	**11.** –2	**21.** 12	**31.** 5	**41.** Width = 7,
3. –5	**13.** 2	**23.** 28	**33.** –5	length = 19
5. 1	**15.** 2	**25.** $-\frac{3}{2}$	**35.** 0.6	**43.** 9, 63
7. –3	**17.** 3	**27.** 8	**37.** 7	**45.** 20
9. 9	**19.** 18	**29.** $\frac{1}{2}$	**39.** 5	**47.** 12

Section 4.2

1. 10	**5.** 3	**9.** 5	**13.** 6
3. 3	**7.** 4	**11.** 2	

Section 4.3

1. $\{0, -2\}$	**15.** $\{-\frac{1}{3}, 5\}$	**29.** 30	**41.** 2 inches
3. $\{-7\}$	**17.** $\{\frac{2}{3}\}$	**31.** 1	**43.** Length = 20 inches,
5. $\{-3, 4\}$	**19.** $\{-3, 4\}$	**33.** $\{-1, 3\}$	width = 10 inches
7. $\{-3, 9\}$	**21.** $\{-50, 60\}$	**35.** 4, 6	**45.** $\{1, 4\}$
9. $\{-\frac{1}{2}, 3\}$	**23.** $\{-\frac{1}{2}, 4\}$	**37.** 41	
11. $\{0, -3, 3\}$	**25.** $\{-4, 4\}$	**39.** Length = 8 inches,	
13. $\{-4, -1\}$	**27.** $\{-3, 7\}$	width = 4 inches	

Section 4.4

1. ± 2

3. $\pm \sqrt{21}$

5. $\dfrac{3 \pm 2\sqrt{3}}{2}$

7. $-1 \pm 2\sqrt{2}$

9. $4 \pm \sqrt{11}$

Section 4.5

1. $-2, 8$

3. $-2 \pm \sqrt{7}$

5. $-3 \pm \sqrt{5}$

7. $-5, 2$

9. $\dfrac{5 \pm \sqrt{15}}{2}$

11. $\dfrac{7 \pm \sqrt{17}}{4}$

13. $\dfrac{-9 \pm \sqrt{57}}{4}$

15. $1 \pm \sqrt{6}$

17. $\dfrac{9 \pm \sqrt{33}}{12}$

19. $\dfrac{1 \pm \sqrt{6}}{4}$

21. $3 \pm \sqrt{11}$

23. $\dfrac{3 \pm \sqrt{73}}{4}$

25. $2 + 2\sqrt{5}$

27. $\dfrac{3 \pm \sqrt{13}}{2}$

29. $\dfrac{4 \pm \sqrt{21}}{5}$

Section 4.6

1. (3)

3. (1)

5. (4)

7. ± 10

9. 4

11. 4

13. 6

15. -5

Regents Tune-Up: Chapter 4

1. 48

3. 5

5. 3

7. (3)

9. (3)

11. (1)

13. (a) $\dfrac{x}{x - 3}$

(b) 1

GEOMETRIC CONCEPTS AND PROOFS

CHAPTER **5**

BASIC GEOMETRIC TERMS AND PROVING TRIANGLES CONGRUENT

5.1 BASIC GEOMETRIC TERMS AND CONCEPTS

KEY IDEAS

Proofs of statements in logic are based on reasoning *deductively.* In a deductive proof, a statement is proved in a step-by-step fashion using a set of accepted premises and facts. Similarly, statements in geometry, called **theorems,** are proved deductively using a given set of premises and:
- fundamental assumptions called **postulates;**
- undefined and defined terms;
- previously proved theorems.

Undefined and Defined Terms

The "first" terms of geometry are *point, line,* and *plane.* They can be described but cannot be defined using previously defined words. A **point** indicates position but has no physical dimensions. A **line** is a continuous set of points that extends indefinitely in two opposite directions. A **plane** is a flat surface that extends indefinitely in all directions.

From your work in Course I you should already be familiar with these terms: *line segment, ray, opposite rays,* and *angle.* You should also know that the measure of an **acute angle** is less than 90, the measure of a **right angle** equals 90, and the measure of an **obtuse angle** falls between 90 and 180. Here are some additional terms that you should already know:

- **Collinear points** are points that lie on the same straight line. In the accompanying diagram, points *A, B,* and *C* are collinear.

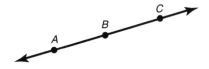

- A point P is **between** points A and B if:
    (1) points A, P, and B are collinear; and
    (2) $AP + PB = AB$.
  In the accompanying diagram, point P is between points A and B.

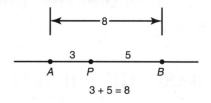

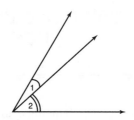

- **Adjacent angles** are two angles that have the same vertex, have a common side, and do *not* overlap. In the accompanying diagram, $\angle 1$ and $\angle 2$ are adjacent angles.

Congruent Angles and Segments

Angles or line segments that can be made to coincide are said to be *congruent*. Thus,

- Two angles are **congruent** if they have the same degree measure. If $m\angle A = 60$ and $m\angle B = 60$, then $\angle A \cong \angle B$; this is read as "Angle A is congruent to angle B."
- Two line segments are **congruent** if they have the same length. For example, if $AB = 10$ inches and $CD = 10$ inches, then $\overline{AB} \cong \overline{CD}$; this is read as "Line segment AB is congruent to line segment CD."

Midpoint and Segment Bisector

The **midpoint** of a line segment is the point on the segment that divides the segment into two shorter segments that have the same length. If, in the accompanying diagram, M is the midpoint of $\overline{AB}$, you may conclude that:

- $AM = MB$, or $\overline{AM} \cong \overline{MB}$.
- $AM = \frac{1}{2} AB$.
- $BM = \frac{1}{2} AB$.

Note: Matching vertical bars drawn through segments indicate that the segments are congruent.

A line, line segment, or ray is a **segment bisector** if it contains the midpoint of a segment through which it passes. In the accompanying diagram, line m is a bisector of $\overline{AB}$ since it passes through the midpoint M of $\overline{AB}$. A line segment can have more than one bisector.

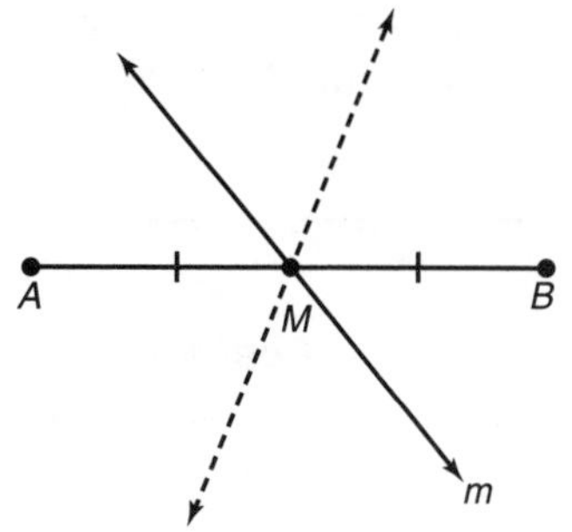

Angle Bisector

An **angle bisector** is a line (or line segment or ray) that divides an angle into two smaller angles that have equal degree measures. In the accompanying diagram, $\overrightarrow{BD}$ is the bisector of $\angle ABC$ if $m\angle ABD = m\angle CBD$. An angle has exactly one bisector.

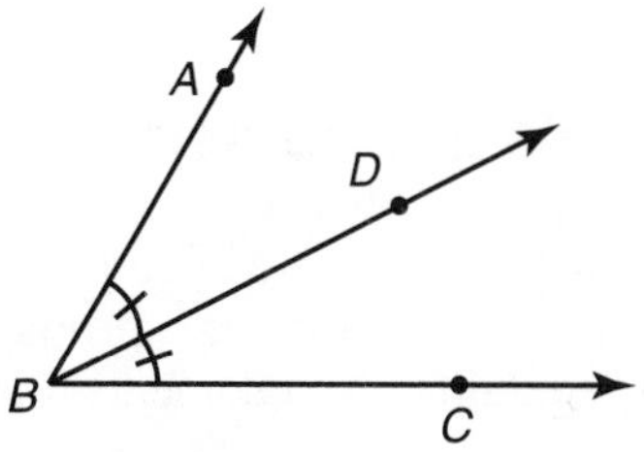

Note: Matching arcs, each with a dash through it, indicate that the angles have the same degree measure.

Properties of Equality and Congruence

The reflexive, symmetric, and transitive properties in geometry are summarized in the accompanying table.

EQUALITY AND CONGRUENCE PROPERTIES

Property	Relation Expressed in Words	Example
Reflexive	Any thing is equal (congruent) to itself.	$m\angle A = m\angle A$, $\overline{RS} \cong \overline{RS}$.
Symmetric	The members on either side of an equal sign (congruence symbol) may be interchanged.	If $m\angle A = m\angle B$, then $m\angle B = m\angle A$.
Transitive	If two quantities are equal (congruent) to the same quantity, then they are equal (congruent) to each other.	If $\overline{AB} \cong \overline{BC}$ and $\overline{XY} \cong \overline{BC}$, then $\overline{AB} \cong \overline{XY}$.

Postulates and Theorems

A **theorem** is a generalization that can be proved to be true. A familiar theorem that was proved informally in Course I is as follows: *The sum of the measures of the angles of any triangle is 180.* Not everything can be proved, however, since

107

there must be some basic assumptions, or postulates, that are needed as a beginning. A **postulate** (or axiom) is a statement that is accepted without proof.

MATH FACTS

> **Postulate:** Exactly one line can be drawn between two given points. (Two points *determine* a line.)

Proofs in Geometry

Geometric proofs are often presented in the statement-reason two-column format used in writing logic proofs. The "Reason" column of a geometric proof may contain only statements that fall into one of the following categories:

- The "Given" (the initial set of true premises).
- Postulates.
- Properties of equality and congruence.
- Definitions.
- Theorems that were previously proved.

Example

Given: $\angle A$ is a right angle,
$\quad\quad\;\;\angle B$ is a right angle.
Prove: $\angle A \cong B$.

Solution:

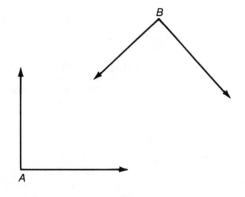

PROOF

Statement	Reason
1. $\angle A$ is a right angle, $\angle B$ is a right angle.	**1.** Given.
2. $m\angle A = 90$, $m\angle B = 90$	**2.** The measure of a right angle is 90.
3. $m\angle A = m\angle B$	**3.** Transitive property of equality.
4. $\angle A \cong \angle B$	**4.** If two angles are equal in measure, then they are congruent.

Angle Addition Postulate

In the accompanying diagram, $\overrightarrow{OP}$ lies in the interior of $\angle AOB$. The Angle Addition Postulate states that the measure of $\angle AOB$ is equal to the sum of the measures of the two adjacent angles that have $\overrightarrow{OP}$ as a common side; that is,

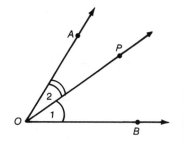

$$\mathrm{m}\angle AOB = \mathrm{m}\angle 1 + \mathrm{m}\angle 2.$$

Perpendicular Lines and Perpendicular Bisectors

Lines that meet at 90° angles are perpendicular.

Two lines are **perpendicular** if they intersect to form a right angle. If, in the accompanying diagram, line ℓ is perpendicular to line $m,$ we may write $\ell \perp m,$ where the symbol "$\perp$" is read as "is perpendicular to." A square box drawn at the point of intersection indicates that the lines are perpendicular.

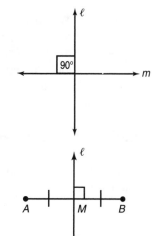

The **perpendicular bisector** of a segment is a line (or line segment or ray) that is perpendicular to the segment at its midpoint. In the accompanying diagram, line ℓ is the perpendicular bisector of AB since $\ell \perp \overline{AB}$ and $\overline{AM} \cong \overline{BM}$.

MATH FACTS

Postulate: Given a point and a line in a plane, there is exactly one line that contains the point and is perpendicular to the original line (see the accompanying diagram).

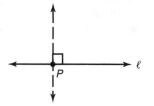

Point *P* is on line ℓ.

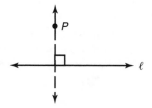

Point *P* is *not* on line ℓ.

Here are some theorems about right angles and perpendicular lines that you should know:

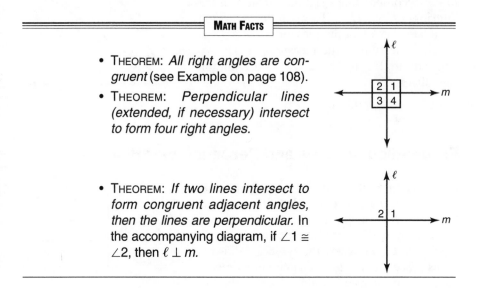

MATH FACTS

- THEOREM: *All right angles are congruent* (see Example on page 108).
- THEOREM: *Perpendicular lines (extended, if necessary) intersect to form four right angles.*

- THEOREM: *If two lines intersect to form congruent adjacent angles, then the lines are perpendicular.* In the accompanying diagram, if ∠1 ≅ ∠2, then ℓ ⊥ m.

Classifying Triangles

A triangle may be classified according to the number of congruent sides that it contains (see Figure 5.1).

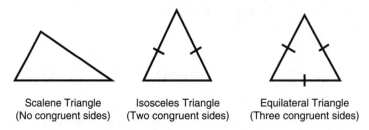

| Scalene Triangle | Isosceles Triangle | Equilateral Triangle |
| (No congruent sides) | (Two congruent sides) | (Three congruent sides) |

Figure 5.1 Triangles Classified by Number of Congruent Sides

A triangle may also be classified by the measure of its greatest angle. An **obtuse triangle** contains an obtuse angle. A **right triangle** contains a right angle, meaning that two sides of a right triangle, called *legs*, are perpendicular to each other; the side opposite the right angle is called the *hypotenuse*. An **acute triangle** contains three acute angles.

Median and Altitude

In every triangle a median and an altitude can be drawn from any vertex to the side opposite that vertex.

- A **median** of a triangle is a segment drawn from a vertex of a triangle to the midpoint of the opposite side.

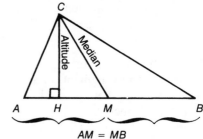

- An **altitude** of a triangle is a segment drawn from a vertex of a triangle perpendicular to the opposite side or, as in the accompanying diagram, to the opposite side extended.

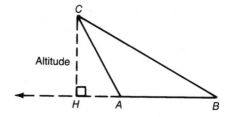

Distance

The term *distance* in geometry is always interpreted as the *shortest* path. In the figures accompanying the definitions below, the distance between points P and Q is the length of $\overline{PQ}$, while the distance between point P and line ℓ is the length of the perpendicular segment dropped from P to line ℓ.

- The **distance between two points** is the length of the segment determined by the two points.

- The **distance between a point and a line** is the length of the perpendicular segment drawn from the point to the line.

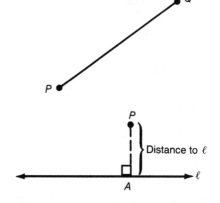

A point that is exactly the same distance from two other points is said to be **equidistant** from the two points. The midpoint of a segment, for example, is equidistant from the endpoints of the segment.

Exercise Set 5.1

1. In the accompanying diagram, point M is the midpoint of $\overline{RS}$. If $RM = 18$ and the length of $\overline{SM}$ is represented by $3x - 6$, find the value of x.

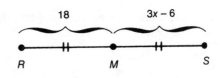

2. For the accompanying figure, state a pair of segments or angles that are congruent given that:
(a) $\overline{AL}$ bisects $\overline{BC}$.
(b) $\overline{BK}$ bisects $\angle ABC$.
(c) $\overline{BK}$ bisects $\overline{AL}$.
(d) $\overline{AL}$ bisects $\angle CAB$.

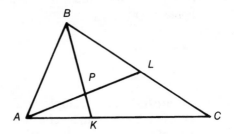

3–5. Justify the conclusion drawn in each case by identifying the property used to draw the conclusion as reflexive, transitive, or symmetric.

3. Given: $\overline{LM} \cong \overline{GH}$, $\overline{GH} \cong \overline{FV}$.
Conclusion: $\overline{LM} \cong \overline{FV}$.

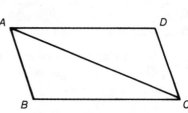

4. Given: Quadrilateral $ABCD$.
Conclusion: $\overline{AC} \cong \overline{AC}$.

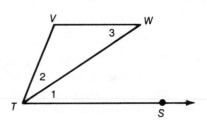

5. Given: $\overline{TW}$ bisects $\angle STV$, $\angle 1 \cong \angle 3$.
Conclusion: $\angle 2 \cong \angle 3$.

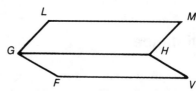

5.2 USING PROPERTIES OF EQUALITY IN PROOFS

KEY IDEAS

In solving equations, the addition, subtraction, multiplication, and division **properties of equality** are used. The **substitution principle** (a quantity may be substituted for its equal in any expression) is used in checking the roots of equations. These properties may also be applied to the measures of angles and segments.

Drawing Conclusions from Diagrams

Many proofs provide the "Given" (what you may assume to be true), the "Prove" (the conclusion that you have to demonstrate is true), and a diagram. In general, when looking at a diagram you may assume only that "obvious" properties, such as betweenness of points and collinearity of points, exist and that angles drawn as adjacent are, in fact, adjacent. Generally speaking, you may *not* assume just from looking at a diagram that segments or angles are congruent, or that lines are parallel or perpendicular.

Applying the Addition and Subtraction Properties of Equality

The examples that follow use the property that, if equals are added to (or subtracted from) equals, then the results are equal.

Examples

1. Given: $AD = FC$.
   Prove: $AC = FD$.

   Solution:

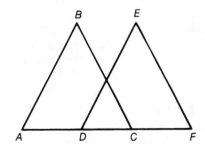

PROOF

Statement	Reason
1. $AD = FC$	1. Given.
2. $DC = DC$	2. Reflexive property of equality.
3. $AD + DC = FC + DC$	3. Addition property of equality.
4. $AC = FD$	4. Substitution principle.

2. Given: $\overline{WX} \perp \overline{XY}, \overline{ZY} \perp \overline{XY},$
$\quad\quad\quad$ m$\angle WXH = $ m$\angle ZYH.$
$\quad$ Prove: m$\angle 1 = $ m$\angle 2.$

Solution:

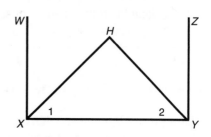

PROOF

Statement	Reason
1. $\overline{WX} \perp \overline{XY}, \overline{ZY} \perp \overline{XY}$	1. Given.
2. $\angle WXY$ is a right angle, $\angle ZYX$ is a right angle.	2. Perpendicular lines intersect to form right angles.
3. m$\angle WXY = $ m$\angle ZYX$	3. All right angles are equal in measure.
4. m$\angle WXH = $ m$\angle ZYH$	4. Given.
5. m$\angle WXY - $ m$\angle WXH$ $= $ m$\angle ZYX - $ m$\angle ZYH$	5. Subtraction property.
6. m$\angle 1 = $ m$\angle 2$	6. Substitution principle.

Applying the Multiplication Property of Equality

If each side of an equation is multiplied (or divided) by the same nonzero quantity, then the results are equal. In the special case when the multiplying factor is $\frac{1}{2}$, we say that "halves of equals are equal."

Example

3. Given: $AB = BC,$
$\quad\quad\quad$ E is the midpoint of $\overline{AB},$
$\quad\quad\quad$ F is the midpoint of $\overline{BC}.$
$\quad$ Prove: $AE = CF.$

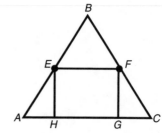

Solution:

PROOF

Statement	Reason
1. $AB = BC$	**1.** Given.
2. E is the midpoint of $\overline{AB}$, F is the midpoint of $\overline{BC}$.	**2.** Given.
3. $AE = \frac{1}{2}AB$ and $CF = \frac{1}{2}BC$	**3.** Definition of midpoint.
4. $AE = CF$	**4.** Halves of equals are equal.

Exercise Set 5.2

1. Given: $\overline{KB}$ bisects $\angle SBF$,
 $\overline{KB}$ bisects $\angle SKF$,
 $m\angle SKF = m\angle SBF$.
 Prove: $\angle 1 \cong \angle 2$.

2. Given: $m\angle TOB = m\angle WOM$.
 Prove: $m\angle TOM = m\angle WOB$.

3. Given: $\overline{TB} \cong \overline{WM}$.
 Prove: $\overline{TM} \cong \overline{WB}$.

4. Given: $BD = BE$, $DA = EC$.
 Prove: $AB = CB$.

5. Given: $\angle WXY$ is a right angle,
 $\angle ZYX$ is a right angle,
 $m\angle 1 = m\angle 2$.
 Prove: $m\angle 3 = m\angle 4$.

6. Given: $m\angle 1 = m\angle 2$,
 $m\angle 3 = m\angle 4$
 $m\angle H = m\angle WXY$.
 Prove: $m\angle H = m\angle ZYX$.

7. Given: $\angle WXY$ is a right angle,
 $\angle ZYX$ is a right angle,
 $\overline{XH}$ bisects $\angle WXY$,
 $\overline{YH}$ bisects $\angle ZYX$.
 Prove: $m\angle 1 = m\angle 2$.

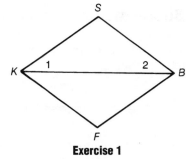

Exercise 1

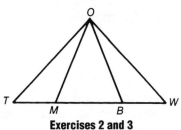

Exercises 2 and 3

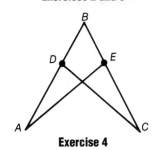

Exercise 4

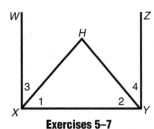

Exercises 5–7

5.3 SPECIAL PAIRS OF ANGLES

=== KEY IDEAS ===

Two angles are **supplementary** if the sum of their measures is 180, and are **complementary** if the sum of their measures is 90.

The pairs of nonadjacent angles formed when two lines intersect are called **vertical angles** and are congruent.

Supplementary and Complementary Angles

Two angles that are supplementary (or complementary) may or may not be adjacent angles.

=== MATH FACTS ===

- THEOREM: *If the exterior sides of two adjacent angles lie on a straight line, then the angles are supplementary.*

- THEOREM: *If the exterior sides of two adjacent angles are perpendicular, then the angles are complementary.*

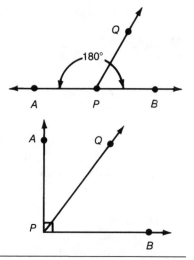

Examples

1. The measures of two complementary angles are in the ratio of 2 : 13. Find the measure of the smaller angle.

Solution: Let $2x$ = measure of smaller angle.
Then $13x$ = measure of larger angle.

$$2x + 13x = 90$$
$$15x = 90$$
$$\frac{15x}{15} = \frac{90}{15}$$
$$x = 6$$
$$2x = 2(6) = 12.$$

The measure of the smaller angle is **12.**

2. If the measure of an angle exceeds twice its supplement by 30, find the measure of the angle.

Solution: Let x = measure of angle.
Then $180 - x$ = measure of angle's supplement.

$$x = 2(180 - x) + 30$$
$$x = 360 - 2x + 30$$
$$x + 2x = 390$$
$$\frac{3x}{3} = \frac{390}{3}$$
$$x = \mathbf{130}$$

More Theorems on Supplementary and Complementary Angles

Suppose $m\angle C = 50$. If angles A and B are both complementary to $\angle C$, then each must have a measure of 40 and, therefore, must be congruent to the other. This observation suggests the following two theorems.

MATH FACTS

- THEOREM: *If two angles are* complementary *to the* same *angle (or to congruent angles), then they are congruent.*
- THEOREM: *If two angles are* supplementary *to the* same *angle (or to congruent angles), then they are congruent.*

Vertical Angles

Vertical angles are pairs of nonadjacent (opposite) angles formed when two lines intersect. In Figure 5.2, angles 1 and 3 are vertical angles and are congruent

117

since both are supplementary to $\angle 2$ (also $\angle 4$). Similarly, angles 2 and 4 are vertical angles and are congruent since both are supplementary to the same angle ($\angle 1$ and also $\angle 3$). This analysis provides an informal proof of the next theorem.

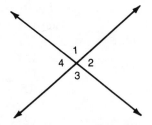

Figure 5.2 Vertical Angles

MATH FACTS

THEOREM: *Vertical angles are congruent and, therefore, are equal in measure.*

Examples

3. Given: $\overline{BD}$ bisects $\angle ABC$,
$\angle 3$ is complementary to $\angle 1$,
$\angle 4$ is complementary to $\angle 2$.
Prove: $\angle 3 \cong \angle 5$.

Solution:

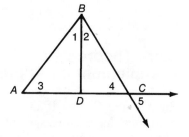

PROOF

Statement	Reason
1. $\overline{BD}$ bisects $\angle ABC$.	1. Given.
2. $\angle 1 \cong \angle 2$	2. Definition of angle bisector.
3. $\angle 3$ is complementary to $\angle 1$, $\angle 4$ is complementary to $\angle 2$.	3. Given.
4. $\angle 3 \cong \angle 4$	4. If two angles are complementary to congruent angles, then they are congruent.
5. $\angle 4 \cong \angle 5$	5. Vertical angles are congruent.
6. $\angle 3 \cong \angle 5$	6. Transitive property of congruence.

4. In the accompanying diagram, find the value of *y*.

Solution: Since vertical angles are equal in measure,

$$3y - 18 = 2y + 5$$
$$3y = 2y + 5 + 18$$
$$3y - 2y = 23$$
$$y = \mathbf{23}$$

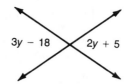

$3y - 18$ $2y + 5$

Exercise Set 5.3

1–5. For each of the following, find the value of x:

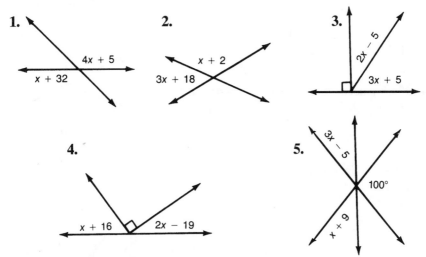

1.

$4x + 5$

$x + 32$

2.

$x + 2$

$3x + 18$

3.

$2x - 5$

$3x + 5$

4.

$x + 16$ $2x - 19$

5.

$3x - 5$

$100°$

$9x + 9$

6. If two angles are supplementary, find the measure of the *smaller* angle if the measures of the two angles are in the ratio of:
   (a) $1 : 8$ **(b)** $3 : 5$ **(c)** $3 : 1$ **(d)** $5 : 7$ **(e)** $7 : 11$

7. If two angles are complementary, find the measure of the *smaller* angle if the measures of the two angles are in the ratio of:
   (a) $2 : 3$ **(b)** $1 : 2$ **(c)** $4 : 5$ **(d)** $3 : 1$ **(e)** $1 : 5$

8. The measure of an angle exceeds three times its supplement by 4. Find the measure of the angle.

9. The measure of an angle exceeds three times the measure of its complement by 6. Find the measure of the angle.

10. The measure of an angle is 22 less than three times the measure of the complement of the angle. Find the measure of the angle.

11. The measure of the supplement of an angle is three times as great as the measure of the angle's complement. What is the measure of the angle?

12. Find the measure of an angle if it is 12 less than twice the measure of its complement.

13. The difference between the measures of an angle and its complement is 14. Find the measure of the *smaller* of the two angles.

14. The difference between the measures of an angle and its supplement is 22. Find the measure of the *smaller* of the two angles.

15. Find the value of x.

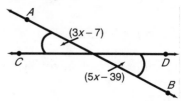

16. If $\overrightarrow{EF}$ bisects $\angle AED$, m $\angle AEC = x - 64$, and m$\angle DEB = 3x$, find m $\angle AEF$.

17. If $\overrightarrow{EF}$ bisects $\angle AED$, m$\angle CEB = 4x - 80$, and m$\angle DEF = x + 10$, find m$\angle AEC$.

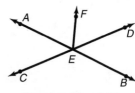

Exercises 16 and 17

18. Given: $\overline{BD}$ bisects $\angle ABC$.
　　 Prove: $\angle 1 \cong \angle 2$.

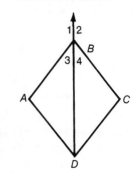

19. Given: $\angle 3$ is complementary to $\angle 1$,
　　　　　 $\angle 4$ is complementary to $\angle 2$.
　　 Prove: $\angle 3 \cong \angle 4$.

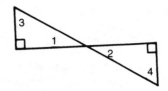

20. Given: $\overline{AB} \perp \overline{BD}, \overline{CD} \perp \overline{BD}$,
　　　　　 $\angle 1$ is complementary to $\angle 3$,
　　　　　 $\overline{BE}$ bisects $\angle ABD$.
　　 Prove: $\angle 2 \cong \angle 4$.

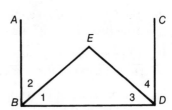

21. Given: $\overline{KL} \perp \overline{JM}$,
$\overline{KL}$ bisects $\angle PLQ$.
Prove: $\angle 1 \cong \angle 4$.

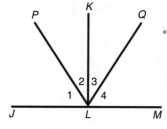

22. Given: $\overline{NW} \perp \overline{WT}, \overline{WB} \perp \overline{NT}$,
$\angle 4 \cong \angle 6$.
Prove: $\angle 2 \cong \angle 5$.

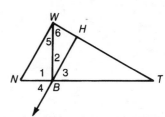

23. Given: $\overline{MT}$ bisects $\angle ETI$,
$\overline{KI} \perp \overline{TI}, \overline{KE} \perp \overline{TE}$,
$\angle 3 \cong \angle 1, \angle 5 \cong \angle 2$.
Prove: $\angle 4 \cong 6$.

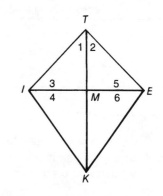

5.4 PROVING TRIANGLES CONGRUENT

KEY IDEAS

The size and shape of a triangle are determined by the measures of its six parts (three angles and three sides). In general, two polygons having the same number of sides are congruent if their vertices can be paired off so that corresponding angles are congruent and corresponding sides are congruent. If the polygons are triangles, it is sufficient to show that only *three* pairs of parts are congruent, provided that they are a particular set of congruent parts.

121

Congruent Triangles

If, in Figure 5.3, $\triangle ABC \cong \triangle RST$, then the vertices of the two triangles can be paired off so that three pairs of corresponding angles are congruent and three pairs of corresponding sides are congruent.

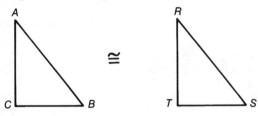

Figure 5.3 Congruent Triangles

Corresponding Angles	Corresponding Sides
$\angle A \cong \angle R$	$\overline{AB} \cong \overline{RS}$
$\angle B \cong \angle S$	$\overline{BC} \cong \overline{ST}$
$\angle C \cong \angle T$	$\overline{AC} \cong \overline{RT}$

Note that:

- Corresponding sides lie opposite corresponding angles.
- In naming pairs of congruent triangles, corresponding vertices are written in the same order.

$$\triangle ABC \quad \cong \quad \triangle RST$$

Here are some other ways in which this correspondence may be written:

$$\triangle CAB \cong \triangle TRS \qquad \triangle BAC \cong \triangle SRT \qquad \triangle CBA \cong \triangle TSR.$$

- Congruence of triangles satisfies the *reflexive, symmetric,* and *transitive* properties (see the table on page 107).

MATH FACTS

POSTULATES FOR PROVING TRIANGLES CONGRUENT

Here are some ways of proving that triangles are congruent:

- ***SSS* ≅ *SSS* Postulate:** Two triangles are congruent if the three sides of the first triangle are congruent to the corresponding parts of the second triangle.

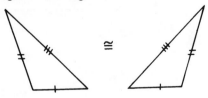

122

- **SAS ≅ SAS Postulate:**
  Two triangles are congruent if any two sides and the included angle of the first triangle are congruent to the corresponding parts of the second triangle.

- **ASA ≅ ASA Postulate:**
  Two triangles are congruent if any two angles and the included side of the first triangle are congruent to the corresponding parts of the second triangle.

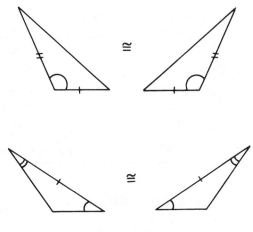

A Strategy for Proving Triangles Congruent

To prove that a pair of triangles are congruent, proceed as follows:

1. Mark off the diagram with:

- the "Given";
- common sides or angles, if any, that are parts of both triangles;
- congruent pairs of angles, if any, resulting from vertical angles or perpendicular lines.

2. Select the congruence method (for example, SSS, SAS, or ASA).

3. Write the formal proof.

Examples

1. Given: $\overline{AB} \cong \overline{BC}$,
$\overline{BD}$ bisects $\angle ABC$.
Prove: $\triangle ADB \cong \triangle CDB$.

Solution:
PLAN. Since $\overline{AB} \cong \overline{BC}$, $\angle ABD \cong \angle CBD$, and $\overline{BD}$ is a side of both triangles (note that on the diagram "×" is used to indicate that $\overline{BD}$ is congruent to itself), prove the triangles congruent by using the SAS postulate.

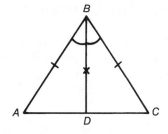

PROOF

Statement		Reason
1. $\overline{AB} \cong \overline{BC}$ *Side*		1. Given.
2. $\overline{BD}$ bisects $\angle ABC$.		2. Given.
3. $\angle ABD \cong \angle CBD$ *Angle*		3. A bisector divides an angle into two congruent angles.
4. $\overline{BD} \cong \overline{BD}$ *Side*		4. Reflexive property of congruence.
5. $\triangle ADB \cong \triangle CDB$		5. SAS postulate.

2. Given: $\overline{AD}$ bisects $\overline{BE}$,

$\angle B \cong \angle E$.

Prove: $\triangle ABC \cong \triangle DEC$.

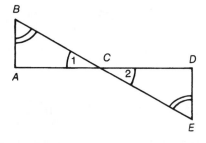

Solution:

PLAN. Since $\angle B \cong \angle E$, $\overline{BC} \cong \overline{EC}$, and $\angle 1 \cong \angle 2$ (vertical angles), prove the triangles congruent by using the ASA postulate.

PROOF

Statement		Reason
1. $\angle B \cong \angle E$ *Angle*		1. Given.
2. $\overline{AD}$ bisects $\overline{BE}$.		2. Given.
3. $\overline{BC} \cong \overline{EC}$ *Side*		3. A bisector divides a segment into two congruent segments.
4. $\angle 1 \cong \angle 2$ *Angle*		4. Vertical angles are congruent.
5. $\triangle ABC \cong \triangle DEC$		5. ASA postulate.

Proving Overlapping Triangles Congruent

Sometimes triangles are drawn so that one triangle overlaps the other. When this happens, examine the diagram closely in order to determine whether the same angle or the same side is contained in both triangles.

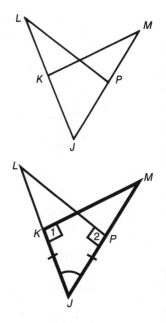

Example

3. Given: $\overline{MK} \perp \overline{JL}, \overline{LP} \perp \overline{JM},$
$\overline{JK} \cong \overline{JP}.$
Prove: $\triangle JMK \cong \triangle JLP.$

Solution: To help distinguish between the parts of the two triangles, outline the sides of one triangle with a thick, bold line (or, if handy, use a colored pencil). Notice that each triangle in the diagram has $\angle J$ as one of its angles.

PLAN. Since $\angle J \cong \angle J$ (*Angle*), $JK \cong JP$ (*Side*), and $\angle 1 \cong \angle 2$ (*Angle*), prove the triangles congruent by using the ASA postulate.

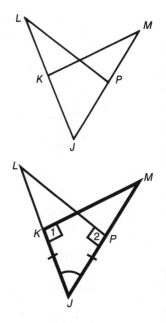

PROOF

Statement	Reason
1. $\overline{MK} \perp \overline{JL}, \overline{LP} \perp \overline{JM}$	1. Given.
2. Angles 1 and 2 are right angles.	2. Perpendicular lines intersect to form right angles.
3. $\angle 1 \cong \angle 2$ *Angle*	3. All right angles are congruent.
4. $\overline{JK} \cong \overline{JP}$ *Side*	4. Given.
5. $\angle J \cong \angle J$ *Angle*	5. Reflexive property of congruence.
6. $\triangle JMK \cong \triangle JLP$	6. ASA postulate.

Exercise Set 5.4

1. Given: C is the midpoint of $\overline{AD}$,
C is the midpoint of $\overline{BE}$.
Prove: $\triangle ABC \cong \triangle DEC.$

2. Given: $\overline{AB} \perp \overline{BE}, \overline{ED} \perp \overline{BE},$
$\overline{AD}$ bisects $\overline{BE}$.
Prove: $\triangle ABC \cong \triangle DEC.$

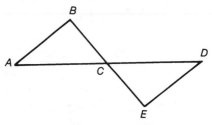

Exercises 1 and 2

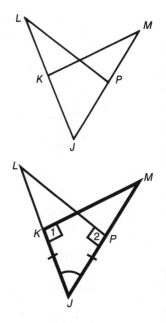
Unit Three **GEOMETRIC CONCEPTS AND PROOFS**

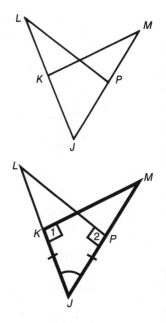

3. Given: $\overline{BD}$ is an altitude to side $\overline{AC}$,
$\overline{AE}$ is an altitude to side $\overline{BC}$,
$\overline{CE} \cong \overline{CD}$.
   Prove: $\triangle AEC \cong \triangle BDC$.

4. Given: $\overline{AB} \cong \overline{BC}$, $\angle A \cong \angle C$.
   Prove: $\triangle AEB \cong \triangle CDB$.

5. Given: $\overline{AE} \perp \overline{BC}$, $\overline{CD} \perp \overline{AB}$,
$\overline{BD} \cong \overline{BE}$.
   Prove: $\triangle ABE \cong \triangle CBD$.

6. Given: $\angle ABC \cong \angle DCB$,
$\angle 1 \cong \angle 2$,
$\overline{BE} \cong \overline{CE}$.
   Prove: $\triangle ABE \cong \triangle DCE$.

7. Given: $\overline{AB} \perp \overline{BE}$, $\overline{DC} \perp \overline{CE}$,
$\angle 1 \cong \angle 2$,
$\overline{AB} \cong \overline{DC}$
   Prove: $\triangle ABC \cong \triangle DCB$.

8. Given: $\overline{DE} \cong \overline{AE}$, $\overline{BE} \cong \overline{CE}$,
$\angle 1 \cong \angle 2$.
   Prove: $\triangle DBC \cong \triangle ACB$.

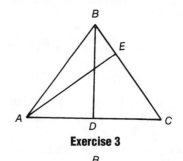

Exercise 3

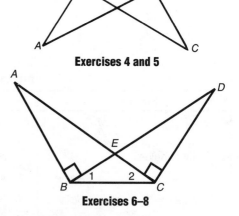

Exercises 4 and 5

Exercises 6–8

5.5 USING CONGRUENT TRIANGLES TO PROVE ANGLES AND SEGMENTS CONGRUENT AND LINES PERPENDICULAR; AAS AND HY-LEG THEOREMS

KEY IDEAS

If it can be demonstrated that two triangles are congruent, then the definition of congruent triangles permits you to conclude that any pair of corresponding angles or pair of corresponding sides are congruent. Congruent triangles can also be used to prove that two lines are perpendicular.

Proving Segments and Angles Congruent

To prove that a pair of segments or angles are congruent using congruent triangles, proceed by answering these questions:

1. What triangles contain these segments or angles as parts?

2. How can these triangles be proved congruent?

To illustrate, consider the following problem:

Given: $\overline{AC} \cong \overline{DB}$, $\overline{AB} \cong \overline{DC}$.
Prove: $\angle A \cong \angle D$.

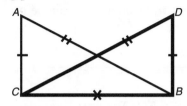

Angle A is an angle of $\triangle ABC$, while $\triangle DCB$ has $\angle D$ as one of its angles. If it is possible to prove that $\triangle ABC \cong \triangle DCB$, then it follows that $\angle A \cong \angle D$ since *corresponding parts of congruent triangles are congruent* (CPCTC). Here is a formal proof that uses the SSS postulate to show that the two triangles are congruent.

PROOF

Statement		Reason
1. $\overline{AC} \cong \overline{DB}$, *Side*		**1.** Given.
$\overline{AB} \cong \overline{DC}$ *Side*		
2. $\overline{BC} \cong \overline{BC}$ *Side*		**2.** Reflexive property of congruence.
3. $\triangle ABC \cong \triangle DCB$		**3.** SSS postulate.
4. $\angle A \cong \angle D$		**4.** CPCTC.

Example

1. Prove: If a point lies on the perpendicular bisector of a line segment, then it is equidistant from the endpoints of the line segment.

Solution: The "Given" is taken from the *if* clause of the statement to be proved, while the "Prove" is taken from the *then* clause.

Given: Line $\ell \perp \overline{AB}$ at M,
      $\overline{AM} \cong \overline{BM}$,
      point P is any point on ℓ,
      $\overline{AP}$ and $\overline{BP}$ are drawn.
Prove: $AP = BP$.

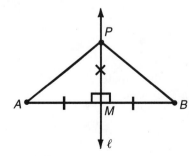

PLAN. Show that $\triangle AMP \cong \triangle BMP$ by SAS. By CPCTC, $\overline{AP} \cong \overline{BP}$. Therefore, $AP = BP$.

The formal proof is left for you to complete.

Additional Methods for Proving Triangles Congruent

Here are two theorems that can be used to prove that a pair of triangles are congruent.

==================== **MATH FACTS** ====================

- AAS $\cong$ AAS THEOREM: *Two triangles are congruent if two angles and a side opposite one of them in the first triangle are congruent to the corresponding parts of the second triangle.*
- HY-LEG $\cong$ HY-LEG THEOREM: *Two triangles are congruent if the hypotenuse and a leg of one right triangle are congruent to the corresponding parts of the second right triangle.* Note that this method applies only to *right* triangles.

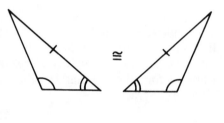

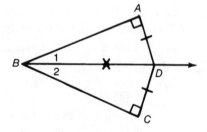

Examples

2. Given: $\overline{BA} \perp \overline{AD}, \overline{BC} \perp \overline{CD},$
$\overline{AD} \cong \overline{CD}.$
Prove: $\overline{BD}$ bisects $\angle ABC$.

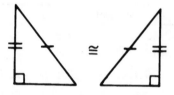

Solution:
PLAN. Show that $\angle 1 \cong \angle 2$ by proving that $\triangle BAD \cong \triangle BCD$, using the Hy-Leg Theorem.

PROOF

Statement	Reason
1. $\overline{BA} \perp \overline{AD}$, $\overline{BC} \perp \overline{CD}$	1. Given.
2. Triangles *BAD* and *BCD* are right triangles.	2. A triangle two of whose sides are perpendicular is a right triangle.
3. $\overline{BD} \cong \overline{BD}$ *Hyp*	3. Reflexive property of congruence.
4. $\overline{AD} \cong \overline{CD}$ *Leg*	4. Given.
5. $\triangle BAD \cong \triangle BCD$	5. Hy-Leg Theorem.
6. $\angle 1 \cong \angle 2$	6. CPCTC.
7. $\overrightarrow{BD}$ bisects $\angle ABC$.	7. A ray that divides an angle into two congruent angles bisects the angle.

3. Given: $\angle B \cong \angle C$,
$\overline{AH}$ is the altitude to side $\overline{BC}$.
Prove: $\overline{AB} \cong \overline{AC}$.

Solution:

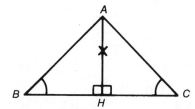

PLAN. Prove that $\triangle AHB \cong \triangle AHC$ by the AAS Theorem since $\angle B \cong \angle C$ (given), $\angle AHB \cong \angle AHC$ (an altitude forms right angles with the side to which it is drawn), and $\overline{AH} \cong \overline{AH}$ (reflexive property).

The formal proof is left for you to complete.

Proving Lines Perpendicular

If, in Figure 5.4, $\angle 1 \cong \angle 2$, then $\overline{BD} \perp \overline{AC}$. To prove that two lines are perpendicular using congruent triangles, proceed as follows:

1. Select a pair of adjacent angles formed by the two lines required to be proved perpendicular.

2. Prove that a pair of triangles that contain these angles are congruent.

3. Use CPCTC to conclude that the pair of adjacent angles are congruent.

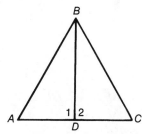

Figure 5.4 Proving Lines Are Perpendicular

4. State that the desired lines are perpendicular, giving, as a reason, "If two lines intersect to form congruent adjacent angles, then the lines are perpendicular." See Exercise 10 at the end of this section.

Exercise Set 5.5

1. Given: $\angle J \cong \angle M$,
$\overline{JK} \perp \overline{KL}, \overline{ML} \perp \overline{KL}$.
Prove: $\overline{JL} \cong \overline{MK}$.

2. Given: $\overline{JK} \perp \overline{KL}, \overline{ML} \perp \overline{KL}$,
$\overline{JL} \cong \overline{MK}$.
Prove: $\angle J \cong \angle M$.

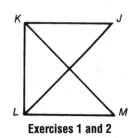

Exercises 1 and 2

3. Given: $\overline{JK} \cong \overline{PM}$,
$\overline{JK} \perp \overline{KM}, \overline{PM} \perp \overline{KM}$.
Prove: $\overline{KM}$ bisects $\overline{JP}$.

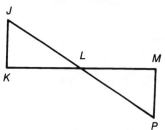

4. Given: $\overline{AB} \cong \overline{BC}$,
$\overline{BD}$ bisects $\angle ABC$.
Prove: $\triangle ADC$ is isosceles.

5. Given: $\triangle ADC$ is equilateral,
$\angle ADB \cong \angle CDB$
Prove: $\overline{BD}$ bisects $\angle ABC$.

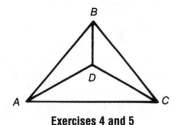

Exercises 4 and 5

6. Given: $\overline{AB} \perp \overline{BC}, \overline{AD} \perp \overline{DC}$,
$\angle 1 \cong \angle 2$.
Prove: $\overline{AC}$ bisects $\angle DAB$.

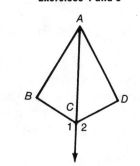

7. Given: $\overline{BE} \perp \overline{AC}, \overline{DF} \perp \overline{AC}$,
$\overline{AF} \cong \overline{CE}, \overline{BE} \cong \overline{DF}$,
Prove: $\overline{AB} \cong \overline{CD}$.

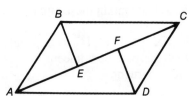

8. Given: $\overline{TL} \perp \overline{RS}$, $\overline{SW} \perp \overline{RT}$,
   $\overline{TL} \cong \overline{SW}$.
   Prove: $\overline{SL} \cong \overline{TW}$.

9. Given: $\overline{TL}$ is the altitude to $\overline{RS}$,
   $\overline{SW}$ is the altitude to $\overline{RT}$,
   $\overline{RS} \cong \overline{RT}$.
   Prove: $\overline{RW} \cong \overline{RL}$.

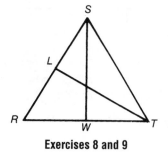

Exercises 8 and 9

10. Prove that the median drawn to the base of an isosceles triangle is perpendicular to the base.

5.6   THE ISOSCELES TRIANGLE

 KEY IDEAS

In an isosceles triangle, the congruent sides are called the **legs.** The angles that are opposite the legs are the **base angles,** and the side that they include is called the **base.** The angle opposite the base is the **vertex angle.**

In an isosceles triangle, the base angles have the same degree measure and are, therefore, congruent.

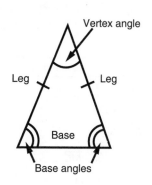

Congruent Sides Imply Congruent Angles

Congruent triangles can be used to prove that the base angles of an isosceles triangle are congruent. For example,

Given: $\overline{AB} \cong \overline{BC}$.

Prove: $\angle A \cong \angle C$.

Outline of Proof: In the accompanying diagram, the two triangles formed by drawing BD, the bisector of the vertex angle, are congruent by the SAS postulate since $\overline{AB} \cong \overline{BC}$ (given), $\angle 1 \cong \angle 2$, and $\overline{BD} \cong \overline{BD}$. Hence, $\angle A \cong \angle C$.

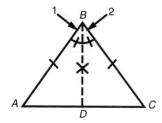

| MATH FACTS |

BASE ANGLES THEOREM: *If two sides of a triangle are congruent, then the angles opposite them are congruent.*

Example

1. Given: $\overline{SR} \cong \overline{ST}$,
$\overline{MP} \perp \overline{RS}, \overline{MQ} \perp \overline{ST}$,
M is the midpoint of $\overline{RT}$.
Prove: $\overline{MP} \cong \overline{MQ}$.

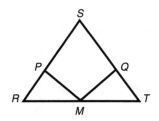

Solution:
PLAN. By the application of the Base Angles Theorem, $\angle R \cong \angle T$. Marking off the diagram suggests that triangles MPR and MQT may be proved congruent by using the AAS Theorem.

PROOF

Statement		Reason
1. $\overline{SR} \cong \overline{ST}$		1. Given.
2. $\angle R \cong \angle T$	Angle	2. If two sides of a triangle are congruent, then the angles opposite them are congruent.
3. $\overline{MP} \perp \overline{RS}, \overline{MQ} \perp \overline{ST}$		3. Given.
4. Angles MPR and MQT right angles.		4. Perpendicular lines intersect to form right angles.
5. $\angle MPR \cong \angle MQT$	Angle	5. All right angles are congruent.
6. M is the midpoint of $\overline{RT}$.		6. Given.
7. $\overline{RM} \cong \overline{TM}$	Side	7. A midpoint divides a segment into two congruent segments.
8. $\triangle MPR \cong \triangle MQT$		8. AAS Theorem.
9. $\overline{MP} \cong \overline{MQ}$		9. CPCTC.

Congruent Angles Imply Congruent Sides

Congruent triangles may be used to prove the *converse* of the Base Angles Theorem. For example,

Given: $\angle A \cong \angle C$.
Prove: $\overline{AB} \cong \overline{BC}$.
Outline of Proof: In the diagram, the two triangles formed by drawing the bisector of the vertex angle are congruent by AAS since $\angle A \cong \angle C$ (given), $\angle 1 \cong \angle 2$, and $\overline{BD} \cong \overline{BD}$. Hence, $\overline{AB} \cong \overline{BC}$.

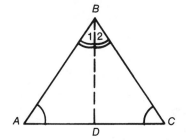

MATH FACTS

CONVERSE OF BASE ANGLES THEOREM: *If two angles of a triangle are congruent, then the sides opposite them are congruent.*

Example

2. Given: $\overline{CEA} \cong \overline{CDB}$,
    $\angle PAB \cong \angle PBA$.
   Prove: $\overline{PE} \cong \overline{PD}$.

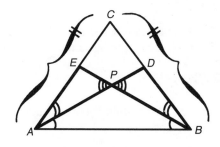

Solution:
PLAN. Show $\triangle EPA \cong \triangle DPB$ by the ASA postulate. Angles *EPA* and *DPB* are congruent since they are vertical angles. In $\triangle APB$, apply the converse of the Base Angles Theorem so that $\overline{AP} \cong \overline{BP}$. Use the subtraction property to obtain the other pair of corresponding congruent angles:

$m\angle CAB = m\angle CBA$ (Base Angles Theorem)
$-m\angle PAB = m\angle PBA$ (Given)

$\overline{}$

$m\angle EAP = m\angle DBP$

PROOF

Statement		Reason
1. $\angle EPA \cong \angle DPB$	*Angle*	1. Vertical angles are congruent.
2. $\angle PAB \cong \angle PBA$		2. Given.
3. $\overline{AP} \cong \overline{BP}$	*Side*	3. If two angles of a triangle are congruent, then the sides opposite them are congruent.
4. $\overline{CEA} \cong \overline{CDB}$		4. Given.
5. $\angle CAB \cong \angle CBA$		5. If two sides of a triangle are congruent, then the angles opposite them are congruent.
6. $m\angle CAB - m\angle PAB$ $= m\angle CBA - m\angle PBA$		6. Subtraction property of equality.
7. $\angle EAP \cong \angle DBP$	*Angle*	7. Substitution principle.
8. $\triangle EPA \cong \triangle DPB$		8. ASA postulate.
9. $\overline{PE} \cong \overline{PD}$		9. CPCTC.

Proving a Triangle Isosceles

To prove that a triangle is isosceles, show that *one* of the following statements is true:

- The triangle has a pair of congruent sides.
- The triangle has a pair of congruent angles.

Example

3. Prove that, if two altitudes of a triangle are congruent, then the triangle is isosceles.

Solution:
　　Given: $\overline{CD}$ is the altitude to $\overline{AB}$,
　　　　　 $\overline{AE}$ is the altitude to $\overline{BC}$,
　　　　　 $\overline{CD} \cong \overline{AE}$.
　　Prove: $\triangle ABC$ is isosceles.

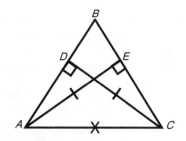

PLAN. Show that $\angle BAC \cong \angle BCA$ by proving $\triangle ADC \cong \triangle CEA$. Marking off the diagram suggests that the Hy-Leg method be used:

$$\overline{AC} \cong \overline{AC} \text{ (Hy)} \qquad \text{and} \qquad \overline{CD} \cong \overline{AE} \text{ (Leg)}$$

PROOF

Statement	Reason
1. $\overline{CD}$ is the altitude to $\overline{AB}$, $\overline{AE}$ is the altitude to $\overline{BC}$.	1. Given.
2. Triangles *ADC* and *CEA* are right triangles.	2. A triangle that contains a right angle is a right triangle. (***Note:*** This step consolidates several obvious steps.)
3. $\overline{CD} \cong \overline{AE}$ *Leg*	3. Given.
4. $\overline{AC} \cong \overline{AC}$ *Hy*	4. Reflexive property of congruence.
5. $\triangle ADC \cong \triangle CEA$	5. Hy-Leg Theorem.
6. $\angle BAC \cong \angle BCA$	6. CPCTC.
7. $\triangle ABC$ is isosceles.	7. A triangle that has a pair of congruent angles is isosceles.

Exercise Set 5.6

1. Given: $\angle 2 \cong \angle 4$,
$\angle BDA \cong \angle BDC$.
Prove: $\triangle ABC$ is isosceles.

2. Given: $\angle 1 \cong \angle 3$,
$\overline{AB} \cong \overline{BC}$.
Prove: $\triangle ADC$ is isosceles.

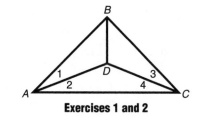

Exercises 1 and 2

3. Given: $\angle 1 \cong \angle 2$,
$\overline{AB} \cong \overline{BC}$,
F is the midpoint of $\overline{AB}$,
G is the midpoint of $\overline{BC}$.
Prove: $\overline{FD} \cong \overline{GE}$.

4. Given: $\angle 1 \cong \angle 2$,
$\overline{FD} \perp \overline{AC}$, $\overline{GE} \perp \overline{AC}$,
$\overline{AE} \cong \overline{CD}$.
Prove: $\triangle ABC$ is isosceles.

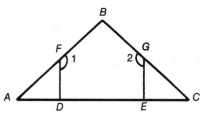

Exercises 3 and 4

5. Given: $\angle B \cong \angle C$,
$\overline{DB} \cong \overline{EC}$.
Prove: $\angle 1 \cong \angle 2$.

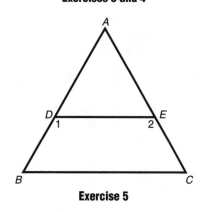

Exercise 5

135

6. Given: $\overline{AB} \cong \overline{BC}$, $\overline{AE} \cong \overline{CD}$.
   Prove: $\triangle DBE$ is isosceles.

7. Given: $\angle BDE \cong \angle BED$,
   $\angle ABE \cong \angle CBD$.
   Prove: $\triangle ABC$ is isosceles.

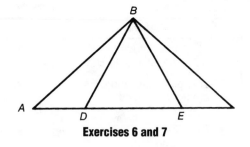

Exercises 6 and 7

8. Given: $\overline{DF} \cong \overline{CF}$, $\overline{AD} \cong \overline{FC}$,
   $\overline{BC} \cong \overline{ED}$.
   Prove: $\angle B \cong \angle E$.

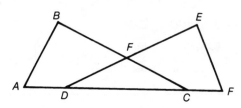

9. Given: $\overline{AB} \cong \overline{AC}$,
   $\overline{CE} \perp \overline{AB}$, $\overline{BD} \perp \overline{AC}$.
   Prove: $\overline{CE} \cong \overline{BD}$.

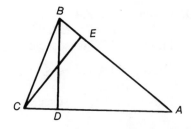

10. Given: $\overline{AB} \cong \overline{BC}$, $\overline{BE} \cong \overline{BF}$.
   Prove: $\triangle ADC$ is isosceles.

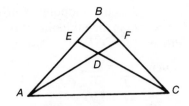

11. Given: $\overline{BE} \cong \overline{FC}$, $\overline{AF} \cong \overline{DE}$,
   $\overline{AF}$ and $\overline{DE}$ bisect
   each other at G.
   Prove: $\overline{AB} \cong \overline{DC}$.

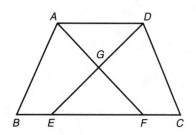

12. Given: D is the midpoint of
$\overline{BC}, \overline{ED} \cong \overline{FD}$,
$\angle EDC \cong \angle FDB$.
Prove: $\triangle ABC$ is isosceles.

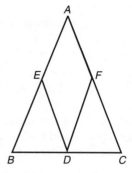

13. Prove that the medians drawn to the legs of an isosceles triangle are congruent.

14. Prove that, if two altitudes of a triangle are congruent, then the triangle is isosceles.

15. Prove that the bisectors of the base angles of an isosceles triangle are congruent.

16. Prove that, if the perpendicular bisector of a side of a triangle passes through the opposite vertex, then the triangle is isosceles.

5.7 PROOFS INVOLVING TWO PAIRS OF CONGRUENT TRIANGLES

KEY IDEAS

In some problems it may appear that there is not enough information in the "Given" to prove a pair of triangles congruent. Upon closer examination, however, it may be possible to prove a *different* pair of triangles congruent, and then use corresponding parts of these triangles to prove the desired pair of triangles congruent.

A mathematical proof may be presented in paragraph, rather than two-column, form.

Double-Congruence Proofs

In analyzing the example below, there does not appear to be enough information provided in the "Given" to prove that triangles *AED* and *CED* are congruent.

Given: $\overline{AB} \cong \overline{CB}$,

　　　　E is the midpoint of $\overline{AC}$.

Prove: $\triangle AED \cong \triangle CED$.

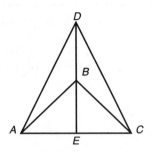

Therefore, look to prove a second pair of triangles (triangles AEB and CEB) congruent in order to obtain an additional pair of congruent parts (angles AED and CED) that can be used to prove the original pair of triangles (AED and CED) congruent.

When confronted by problems of this type, follow these steps:

Step	Example
1. Identify which additional pairs of angles or segments would have to be known to be congruent so that the desired pair of triangles could be proved congruent.	1. Based on the "Given," $\triangle AED$ could be proved congruent to $\triangle CED$ if it was known that angles AED and CED were congruent.
2. Look for a *different* pair of triangles that contain these parts and that you can prove congruent.	2. Triangles AEB and CEB contain these angles and can be proved congruent.
3. Prove the second pair of triangles congruent so that, by CPCTC, the needed pair of parts are congruent.	3. $\triangle AEB \cong \triangle CEB$ by the SSS postulate so that, by CPCTC, $\angle AED \cong \angle CED$.
4. Use this additional pair of congruent parts to help prove the original pair of triangles congruent.	4. $\triangle AED \cong \triangle CED$ by the SAS postulate.

The actual formal proof follows:

PROOF

Statement		Reason
Part I. To prove $\triangle AEB \cong \triangle CEB$:		
1. $\overline{AB} \cong \overline{CB}$	*Side*	1. Given.
2. E is the midpoint of $\overline{AC}$.		2. Given.
3. $\overline{AE} \cong \overline{CE}$	*Side*	3. A midpoint divides a segment into two congruent segments.
4. $\overline{BE} \cong \overline{BE}$		4. Reflexive property of congruence.
5. $\triangle AEB \cong \triangle CEB$		5. SSS postulate.

Part II. To prove △*AED* ≅ △*CED*:

6. ∠*AED* ≅ ∠*CED*	*Angle*	**6.** CPCTC.	
7. $\overline{DE}$ ≅ $\overline{DE}$	*Side*	**7.** Reflexive property of congruence.	
8. △*AED* ≅ △*CED*		**8.** SAS postulate.	

Proofs in Paragraph Form

A valid proof in mathematics may take several different forms. Although there is no standard format for a mathematical proof, the logic and correctness of the proof should be readily apparent. The following example presents a proof in paragraph rather than two-column form.

Example

Given: $\overline{AB}$ ≅ $\overline{AC}$, $\overline{BD}$ ≅ $\overline{CE}$, $\overline{BF}$ and $\overline{CG}$ are drawn perpendicular to $\overline{AD}$ and $\overline{AE}$, respectively.

Prove: $\overline{DF}$ ≅ $\overline{EG}$.

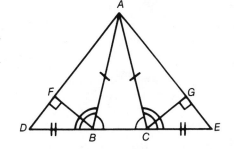

Solution:

PLAN. First prove △*ABD* ≅ △*ACE* in order to obtain an additional pair of congruent parts needed to prove that △*DFB* ≅ △*EGC*.

PROOF

Part I. △*ABD* ≅ △*ACE* by SAS since $\overline{AB}$ ≅ $\overline{AC}$, ∠*ABD* ≅ ∠*ACE* (supplements of the congruent base angles are congruent), and $\overline{BD}$ ≅ $\overline{CE}$. Therefore, ∠*D* ≅ ∠*B*.

Part II. △*DFB* = △*EGC* by AAS since ∠*D* ≅ ∠*B*, ∠*DFB* ≅ ∠*EGC* (right angles are congruent), and $\overline{BD}$ ≅ $\overline{CE}$. Therefore, $\overline{DF}$ ≅ $\overline{EG}$ by CPCTC.

Exercise Set 5.7

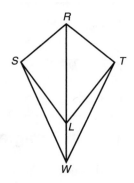

1. Given: $\overline{RS} \perp \overline{SL}$, $\overline{RT} \perp \overline{LT}$,
   $\overline{RS} \cong \overline{RT}$.
   Prove: **(a)** $\triangle RLS \cong \triangle RLT$.
   (b) $\overline{WL}$ bisects $\angle SWT$.

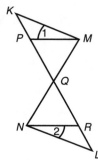

2. Given: $KPQRL$, MQN, $\overline{KM}$, $\overline{NL}$, $\overline{MP}$, $\overline{NR}$,
   $\overline{KL}$ and $\overline{MN}$ bisect each other at Q,
   $\angle 1 \cong \angle 2$.
   Prove: $\overline{PM} \cong \overline{NR}$.

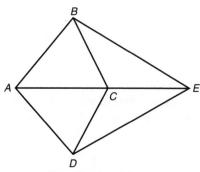

3. Given: $\overline{AB} \cong \overline{AD}$,
   $\overline{EA}$ bisects $\angle DAB$.
   Prove: $\triangle BCE \cong \triangle DCE$.

4. Given: $\overline{BE} \cong \overline{DE}$, $\overline{BC} \cong \overline{DC}$.
   Prove: $\overline{CA}$ bisects $\angle DAB$.

Exercises 3 and 4

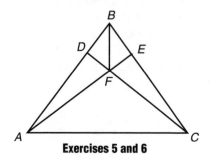

5. Given: $\angle FAC \cong \angle FCA$,
   $\overline{FD} \perp \overline{AB}$, $\overline{FE} \perp \overline{BC}$.
   Prove: $\overline{BF}$ bisects $\angle DBE$.

6. Given: $\overline{BD} \cong \overline{BE}$,
   $\overline{FD} \cong \overline{FE}$.
   Prove: $\triangle AFC$ is isosceles.

Exercises 5 and 6

7. Given: $\overline{AB} \perp \overline{BC}$, $\overline{DC} \perp \overline{BC}$,
   $\overline{DB}$ bisects $\angle ABC$,
   $\overline{AC}$ bisects $\angle DCB$,
Prove: $\overline{EA} \cong \overline{ED}$.

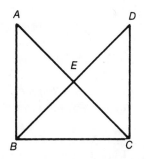

8. Given: $\overline{AE}$ and $\overline{DC}$ intersect at F,
   $\overline{DF} \cong \overline{EF}$,
   $\angle EFB \cong \angle DFB$.
Prove: $\triangle ABC$ is isosceles.

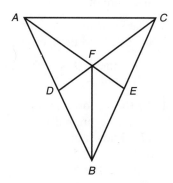

9. Given: $\overline{OR} \perp \overline{KG}$, $\overline{OL} \perp \overline{JG}$,
   $\overline{OK} \cong \overline{OJ}$.
Prove: $\overline{OG}$ bisects $\angle RGL$.

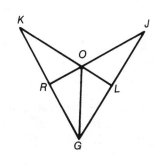

10. Given: $\overline{AE} \cong \overline{AF}$,
   $\angle 1 \cong \angle 4$, $\angle 2 \cong \angle 3$.
Prove: $\overline{AD} \cong \overline{AB}$.

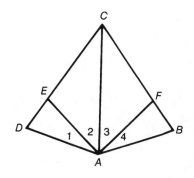

REGENTS TUNE-UP: CHAPTER 5

Each of the questions in this section has appeared on a previous Course II Regents Examination. Here is an opportunity for you to review the material in Chapter 5 and, at the same time, prepare for the Course II Regents Examination.

1. Two complementary angles have measures in the ratio 5 : 4. What is the measure of the *smaller* angle?

2. The measure of the supplement of ∠R is 60° more than twice the measure of ∠R. Find the measure of ∠R.

3. If median $\overline{AD}$ is perpendicular to side $\overline{BC}$ in $\triangle ABC$, then $\triangle ABC$ *must* be
(1) obtuse (2) right (3) scalene (4) isosceles

4. In the accompanying diagram, $\overline{ADB} \cong \overline{AEC}$. It can be proved that $\overline{CD} \cong \overline{BE}$ if what else is also known?
(1) ∠1 ≅ ∠2
(2) ∠3 ≅ ∠4
(3) ∠3 ≅ ∠5
(4) ∠4 ≅ ∠6

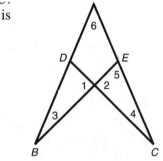

5. Given: $\overleftrightarrow{RPT}$ is a straight line, $\overline{RS} \cong \overline{RQ}$, $\overline{ST} \cong \overline{QT}$.
Prove: ∠SPT ≅ ∠QPT.

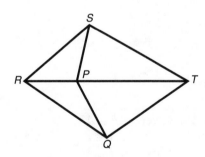

6. Given: $\overline{EG} \cong \overline{EH}$, $\overline{GD} \cong \overline{HF}$.
Prove: ∠1 ≅ ∠2.

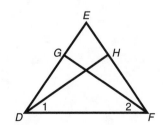

7. Given: $\overline{FG} \cong \overline{EG}$, $\angle EGC \cong \angle FGC$.
Prove: $\overline{AC} \cong \overline{BC}$.

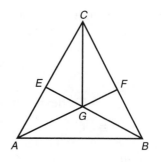

ANSWERS TO SELECTED EXERCISES: CHAPTER 5

Section 5.1
1. 8 **3.** Transitive property **5.** Transitive property

Section 5.2
1. (1) $\overline{KB}$ bisects angles *SBF* and *SKF* (Given); (2) $m\angle 1 = \frac{1}{2}m\angle SKF$, $m\angle 2 = \frac{1}{2}m\angle SBF$ (Definition of angle bisector); (3) $m\angle SKF = m\angle SBF$ (Given); (4) $m\angle 1 = m\angle 2$ (Halves of equals are equal); $\angle 1 \cong \angle 2$ (Definition of congruent angles).

3. (1) $\overline{TB} \cong \overline{WM}$ (Given); (2) $TB - MB = WM - MB$ (Subtraction property); (3) $TM = WB$ (Substitution); $\overline{TM} \cong \overline{WB}$ (Definition of congruent segments.

7. (1) Angles *WXY* and *ZYX* are right angles (Given); (2) $m\angle WXY = m\angle ZYX$ (All right angles are equal in measure); (3) $\overline{XH}$ bisects $\angle WXY$, and $\overline{YH}$ bisects $\angle ZYX$ (Given); (4) $m\angle 1 = \frac{1}{2}m\angle WXY$, $m\angle 2 = \frac{1}{2}m\angle ZYX$ (Definition of angle bisector); $m\angle 1 = m\angle 2$ (Halves of equals are equal).

Section 5.3
1. 9 **3.** 18 **5.** 19 **7. (a)** 36 **(c)** 40 **(e)** 15
9. 69 **11.** 45 **13.** 33 **15.** 16 **17.** 60

19. (1) $\angle 1 \cong \angle 2$ (Vertical angles are congruent); (2) $\angle 3$ is complementary to $\angle 1$, $\angle 4$ is complementary to $\angle 2$ (Given); (3) $\angle 3 \cong \angle 4$ (Complements of congruent angles are congruent).

23. (1) $\overline{MT}$ bisects $\angle ETI$ (Given); (2) $\angle 1 \cong \angle 2$ (Definition of angle bisector); (3) $\angle 3 \cong \angle 1$, $\angle 5 \cong \angle 2$ (Given); (4) $\angle 3 \cong \angle 5$ (Transitivity); (5) $\overline{KI} \perp \overline{TI}$, $\overline{KE} \perp \overline{TE}$ (Given); (6) $\angle 4$ is complementary to $\angle 3$, and $\angle 6$ is complementary to $\angle 5$ (Adjacent angles whose exterior sides form a right angle are complementary); (7) $\angle 4 \cong \angle 6$ (Complements of congruent angles are congruent).

Section 5.4
1. (1) *C* is the midpoint of $\overline{AD}$ and $\overline{BE}$ (Given); (2) $\overline{AC} \cong \overline{DC}$, $\overline{BC} \cong \overline{EC}$ (Definition of midpoint); (3) $\angle ACB \cong \angle DCE$ (Vertical angles are congruent); $\triangle ABC \cong \triangle DEC$ (SAS).

3. (1) $\overline{BD}$ and $\overline{AE}$ are altitudes (Given); (2) $\angle AEC \cong \angle BDC$ (Altitudes form right angles, and all right angles are congruent); (3) $\overline{CE} \cong \overline{CD}$ (Given); (4) $\angle C \cong \angle C$ (Reflexive property); (5) $\triangle AEC \cong \triangle BDC$ (ASA).

5. (1) $\overline{AE} \perp \overline{BC}$, $\overline{CD} \perp \overline{AB}$ (Given); (2) $\angle AEB \cong \angle CDB$ (Perpendicular lines form right angles, and all right angles are congruent); (3) $\overline{BD} \cong \overline{BE}$ (Given); (4) $\angle B \cong \angle B$ (Reflexive property); (5) $\triangle ABE \cong \triangle CBD$ (ASA).

7. (1) $\overline{AB} \cong \overline{DC}$, $\overline{AB} \perp \overline{BE}$, $\overline{DC} \perp \overline{CE}$, $m\angle 1 = m\angle 2$ (Given); (2) $m\angle ABE = m\angle DCE$ (Perpendicular lines form right angles, and all right angles are equal in measure); (3) $m\angle ABE + m\angle 1 = m\angle DCE + m\angle 2$ (Addition property); (4) $\angle ABC \cong \angle DCB$ (Substitution); (5) $\overline{BC} \cong \overline{BC}$ (Reflexive property); (6) $\triangle DBC \cong \triangle ACB$ (SAS).

Section 5.5
1. (1) $\angle J \cong \angle M$, $\overline{JK} \perp \overline{KL}$, $\overline{ML} \perp \overline{KL}$ (Given); (2) $\angle JKL \cong \angle MLK$ (Perpendicular lines form right angles, and all right angles are congruent); (3) $\overline{KL} \cong \overline{KL}$ (Reflexive property); (4) $\triangle JKL \cong \triangle MLK$ (AAS); (5) $\overline{JL} \cong \overline{MK}$ (CPCTC).

3. (1) $\overline{JK} \perp \overline{KM}$, $\overline{PM} \perp \overline{KM}$ (Given); (2) $\angle JKL \cong \angle PML$ (Perpendicular lines form right angles, and all right angles are congruent); (3) $\angle JLK \cong \angle PLM$ (Vertical angles are congruent); (4) $\overline{JK} \cong \overline{PM}$ (Given); (5) $\triangle JKL \cong \triangle PML$ (AAS); (6) $\overline{JL} \cong \overline{PL}$ (CPCTC); (7) $\overline{KM}$ bisects $\overline{JP}$ (Definition of bisector).

5. (1) $\triangle ADC$ is equilateral (Given); (2) $\overline{AD} \cong \overline{CD}$ (An equilateral triangle has three congruent sides); (3) $\angle ADB \cong \angle CDB$ (Given); (4) $\overline{BD} \cong \overline{BD}$ (Reflexive property); (5) $\triangle ADB \cong \triangle CDB$ (SAS); (6) $\angle ABD \cong \angle CBD$ (CPCTC); (7) $\overline{BD}$ bisects $\angle ABC$ (Definition of angle bisector).

9. (1) $\overline{TL}$ and $\overline{SW}$ are altitudes (Given); (2) $\angle SWR \cong \angle TLR$ (Altitudes form right angles, and all right angles are congruent); (3) $\angle R \cong \angle R$ (Reflexive property); (4) $\overline{RS} \cong \overline{RT}$ (Given); (5) $\triangle SWR \cong \triangle TLR$ (AAS); (6) $\overline{RW} \cong \overline{RL}$ (CPCTC).

Section 5.6
1. (1) $\angle 2 \cong \angle 4$ (Given); (2) $\overline{AD} \cong \overline{CD}$ (Converse of the Base Angles Theorem); (3) $\angle BDA \cong \angle BDC$ (Given); (4) $BD \cong BD$ (Reflexive property); (5) $\triangle ADB \cong \triangle CDB$ (SAS); (6) $\overline{AB} \cong \overline{CB}$ (CPCTC); (7) $\triangle ABC$ is isosceles (A triangle that has two congruent sides is isosceles).

3. (1) $\angle 1 \cong \angle 2$ (Given); (2) $\angle AFD \cong \angle CGE$ (Supplements of congruent angles are congruent); (3) $\overline{AB} \cong \overline{BC}$, and F and G are midpoints (Given); (4) $AF = \frac{1}{2}AB$, $CG = \frac{1}{2}BC$ (Definition of midpoint); (5) $\overline{AF} \cong \overline{CG}$ (Halves of congruent segments are congruent); (6) $\angle A \cong \angle C$ (Base Angles Theorem); (7) $\triangle AFD \cong \triangle CGE$ (ASA); (8) $\overline{FD} \cong \overline{GE}$ (CPCTC).

5. (1) $\angle B \cong \angle C$ (Given); (2) $AB = AC$ (Converse of the Base Angles Theorem); (3) $DB = EC$ (Given); (4) $AD = AE$ (Subtraction property);

144

(5) $\angle ADE \cong \angle AED$ (Base Angles Theorem); (6) $\angle 1 \cong \angle 2$ (Supplements of congruent angles are congruent).

7. (1) $\angle BDE \cong \angle BED$, $\angle ABE \cong \angle CBD$ (Given); (2) $\overline{BD} \cong \overline{BE}$ (Converse of the Base Angles Theorem); (3) $\angle ADB \cong \angle CEB$ (Supplements of congruent angles are congruent); (4) $\triangle ADB \cong \triangle CEB$ (ASA); (5) $\overline{AB} \cong \overline{BC}$ (CPCTC); (6) $\triangle ABC$ is isosceles (A triangle that has two congruent sides is isosceles).

9. (1) $\overline{AB} \cong \overline{BC}$ (Given); (2) $\angle EBC \cong \angle DCB$ (Base Angles Theorem); (3) $\overline{CE} \perp \overline{AB}$, $\overline{BD} \perp \overline{AC}$ (Given); (4) $\angle BEC \cong \angle CDB$ (Perpendicular lines form right angles, and all right angles are congruent); (5) $\overline{BC} \cong \overline{BC}$ (Reflexive property); (6) $\triangle BEC \cong \triangle CDB$ (AAS); (7) $\overline{CE} \cong \overline{BD}$ (CPCTC).

11. (1) $\overline{AF} \cong \overline{DE}$, $\overline{AF}$ and $\overline{DE}$ bisect each other at G (Given); (2) $EG = \frac{1}{2}DE$, $FG = \frac{1}{2}AF$ (Definition of bisector); (3) $\overline{EG} \cong \overline{FG}$ (Halves of congruent segments are congruent); (4) $\angle AFG \cong \angle DEF$ (Base Angles Theorem); (5) $BE = FC$ (Given); (6) $EF = EF$ (Reflexive property); (7) $BE + EF = FC + EC$ (Addition property); (8) $\overline{BF} \cong \overline{CE}$ (Substitution); (9) $\triangle AFB \cong \triangle DEC$ (SAS); (10) $\overline{AB} \cong \overline{DC}$ (CPCTC).

Section 5.7
1. (a) $\triangle RLS \cong \triangle RLT$ (Hyp-Leg). **(b)** (1) $\overline{SL} \cong \overline{TL}$ and $\angle SLR \cong \angle TLR$ (CPCTC); (2) $\angle SLW \cong \angle TLW$ (Supplements of congruent angles are congruent); (3) $\overline{LW} \cong \overline{LW}$ (Reflexive property); (4) $\triangle SLW \cong \triangle TLW$ (SAS); (5) $\angle SWL \cong \angle TWL$ (CPCTC); **(6)** $\overline{WL}$ bisects $\angle SWT$ (Definition of bisector).

3. (1) $\triangle ABC \cong \triangle ADC$ (SAS); (2) $\overline{BC} \cong \overline{DC}$ and $\angle ACB \cong \angle ACD$ (CPCTC); (3) $\angle BCE \cong \angle DCE$ (Supplements of congruent angles are congruent); (4) $\overline{CE} \cong \overline{CE}$ (Reflexive property); $\triangle BCE \cong \triangle DCE$ (SAS).

5. (1) $\triangle AFD \cong \triangle DFE$ (AAS); (2) $\overline{FD} \cong \overline{FE}$ (CPCTC); (3) $\overline{BF} \cong \overline{BF}$ (Reflexive property); (4) right triangle $FDB \cong$ right triangle FEB (Hyp-Leg); (5) $\angle FBD \cong \angle FEB$ (CPCTC); (6) $\overline{BF}$ bisects $\angle DBE$ (Definition of bisector).

Regents Tune-Up: Chapter 5
1. 40   **2.** 40   **3.** (4)   **4.** (2)

5. (1) $\triangle RST \cong \triangle RQT$ (SSS); (2) $\overline{ST} \cong \overline{QT}$ and $\angle STP \cong \angle QTP$ (CPCTC); (3) $\overline{TP} \cong \overline{TP}$ (Reflexive property); (4) $\triangle STP \cong \triangle QTP$ (SAS); (5) $\angle SPT \cong \angle QPT$ (CPCTC).

7. (1) $\triangle EGC \cong \triangle FGC$ (SAS); (2) $\angle AFC \cong \angle BEC$ and $\overline{FC} \cong \overline{EC}$ (CPCTC); (3) $\angle C \cong \angle C$ (Reflexive property); (4) $\triangle AFC \cong \triangle BEC$ (ASA); (5) $\overline{AC} \cong \overline{BC}$ (CPCTC).

CHAPTER 6

PARALLEL LINES AND TRIANGLES

6.1 PROPERTIES OF PARALLEL LINES

KEY IDEAS

Lines that lie in the same plane and never meet are called **parallel lines**. The symbol ‖ means "is parallel to," so that $\ell \parallel m$ is read as "Line ℓ is parallel to line m."

To identify parallel lines, mark them with arrowheads that point in the same direction. In the accompanying diagram, the corresponding pairs of arrowheads indicate that $\overline{AD} \parallel \overline{BC}$ and $\overline{AB} \parallel \overline{CD}$.

Angles Formed by Parallel Lines

A line that intersects two or more other lines in different points is called a **transversal**. If a transversal intersects *parallel* lines, each pair of angles that are formed are either congruent or supplementary.

If two parallel lines are cut by a transversal, then

- alternate interior angles are congruent;
- corresponding angles are congruent; and
- interior angles on the same side of the transversal are supplementary.

These relationships are summarized in the accompanying table.

PARALLEL LINE/ANGLE RELATIONSHIPS

Type of Angle Pair	Angle Relationship	Line ℓ ‖ Line m
Alternate interior angles	$\angle 3 \cong \angle 6$ and $\angle 4 \cong \angle 5$	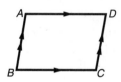
Corresponding angles	$\angle 1 \cong \angle 5$ and $\angle 3 \cong \angle 7$; $\angle 2 \cong \angle 6$ and $\angle 4 \cong \angle 8$	
Interior angles on the same side of the transversal	$m\angle 3 + m\angle 5 = 180$ and $m\angle 4 + m\angle 6 = 180$	

Examples

1. In the accompanying diagram, $\overleftrightarrow{AB} \parallel \overleftrightarrow{CD}$. If $m\angle AFG = 3x + 15$ and $m\angle FGD = 5x - 5$, find the value of x.

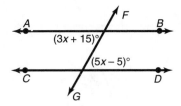

Solution: Since alternate interior angles formed by parallel lines are equal in measure:

$$m\angle AFG = m\angle FGD$$
$$3x + 15 = 5x - 5$$
$$5 + 15 = 5x - 3x$$
$$20 = 2x$$
$$\frac{20}{2} = \frac{2x}{2}$$
$$10 = x$$

The value of x is **10**.

2. In the accompanying diagram, $\overleftrightarrow{AB} \parallel \overleftrightarrow{CD}$ and $\overleftrightarrow{AC} \parallel \overleftrightarrow{BD}$. If $m\angle EAB = 65$ and $m\angle BDC = 3x + 7$, find the value of x.

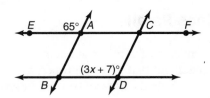

Solution: Since corresponding angles formed by parallel lines are equal in measure:

$m\angle DCA = m\angle EAB = 65$.

Since interior angles on the same side of the transversal are supplementary:

$$m\angle DCA + m\angle BDC = 180$$
$$65 + 3x + 7 = 180$$
$$3x + 72 = 180$$
$$3x = 108$$
$$x = \frac{108}{3} = 36$$

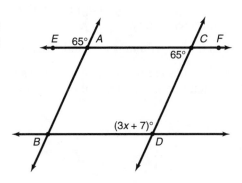

The value of x is **36**.

3. In the accompanying diagram, parallel lines $\overleftrightarrow{HE}$ and $\overleftrightarrow{AD}$ are cut by transversal $\overleftrightarrow{BF}$ at points G and C, respectively. If $m\angle HGF = 5n$ and $m\angle BCD = 2n + 66$, find the value of n.

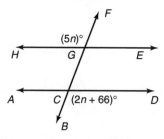

Solution: Since vertical angles are equal in measure,

$$m\angle EGC = m\angle FGH = 5n.$$

Angles EGC and BCD are corresponding angles and are equal in measure since lines $\overleftrightarrow{HE}$ and $\overleftrightarrow{AD}$ are parallel. Therefore,

$$m\angle EGC = m\angle BCD$$
$$5n = 2n + 66$$
$$5n - 2n = 66$$
$$\frac{3n}{3} = \frac{66}{3}$$
$$n = \mathbf{22}$$

Proving Lines Parallel

Although the converse of a true statement is not necessarily true, the converse of each statement that gives a property of parallel lines is true. These converses provide methods that can be used in proving lines parallel.

In a plane, two lines are parallel if:

- a pair of alternate interior angles are congruent; or
- a pair of corresponding angles are congruent; or
- a pair of interior angles on the same side of the transversal are supplementary.

In addition, you may conclude that, in a plane, two lines are parallel if:

- the lines are perpendicular to the same line (see Figure 6.1); or
- each line is parallel to the same line (see Figure 6.2).

If $\ell \perp p$ and $m \perp p$, then $\ell \parallel m$.

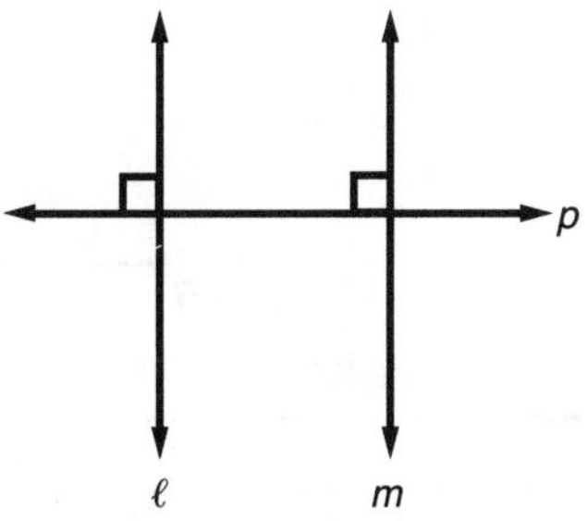

Figure 6.1   Lines Perpendicular to the Same Line

If $\ell \parallel p$ and $m \parallel p$, then $\ell \parallel m$.

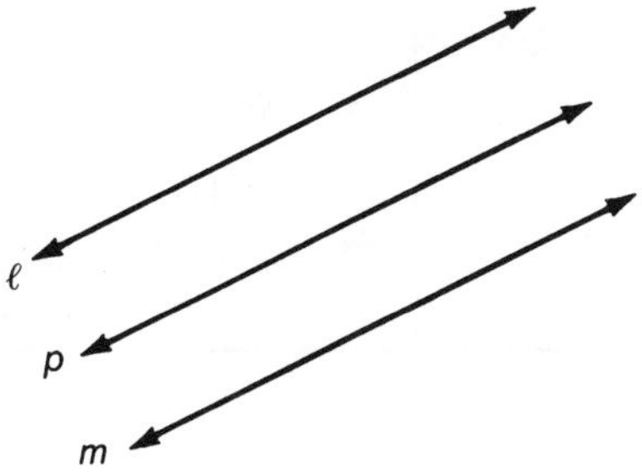

Figure 6.2   Lines Parallel to the Same Line

Examples

4. Given: $\overline{MP} \cong \overline{ST}, \overline{PL} \cong \overline{RT},$
     $\overline{MP} \parallel \overline{ST}.$
   Prove: $\overline{RS} \parallel \overline{LM}.$

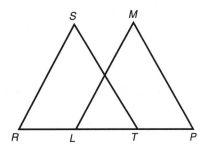

Solution:

PLAN. To prove a pair of line segments parallel, it is usually necessary to prove that an appropriate pair of angles are congruent.

Step 1. Look at the diagram. If $\overleftrightarrow{RS}$ is to be proved parallel to $\overleftrightarrow{LM}$, then it must be proved that $\angle SRT \cong \angle MLP$. This implies that the triangles that contain these angles must be proved congruent. Therefore, it is necessary to prove that $\triangle RST \cong \triangle LMP$.

Step 2. Mark off the diagram with the "Given."

Step 3. Use the SAS postulate.

Step 4. Write the proof.

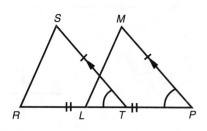

PROOF

Statement		Reason
1. $\overline{MP} \cong \overline{ST}$ *Side*		1. Given.
2. $\overline{MP} \parallel \overline{ST}$		2. Given.
3. $\angle MPL \cong \angle STR$ *Angle*		3. If two lines are parallel, then their corresponding angles are congruent.
4. $\overline{PL} \cong \overline{RT}$ *Side*		4. Given.
5. $\triangle RST \cong \triangle LMP$		5. SAS postulate.
6. $\angle SRT \cong \angle MLP$		6. CPCTC.
7. $\overline{RS} \parallel \overline{LM}$		7. Two lines are parallel if a pair of corresponding angles are congruent.

5. Given: $\triangle ABC$,
         $\overline{CM}$ is the median to $\overline{AB}$,
         $\overline{CM}$ is extended to point P
         so that $\overline{CM} \cong \overline{MP}$,
         $\overline{AP}$ is drawn.
   Prove: $\overline{AP} \parallel \overline{CB}$.

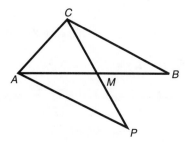

Solution: Mark off the diagram with the "Given":

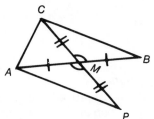

Consider the following proof in the paragraph form:

PROOF

Show $\triangle AMP \cong \triangle BMC$ by SAS. $\overline{BM} \cong \overline{AM}$ (a median divides a segment into two congruent segments), $\angle BMC \cong \angle AMP$ (vertical angles are congruent), and $\overline{CM} \cong \overline{MP}$ (given). Therefore, $\angle P \cong \angle BCM$ by CPCTC. It follows that $\overline{AP} \parallel \overline{CB}$ since two lines are parallel if a pair of alternate interior angles are congruent.

Exercise Set 6.1

1–9. Given that $\ell \parallel m$, find the value of x.

1.

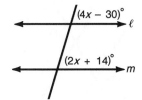

2.

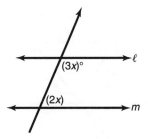

3.

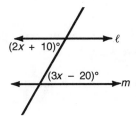

4.

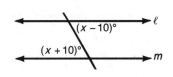

5.

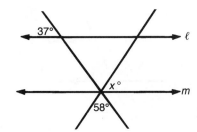

6.

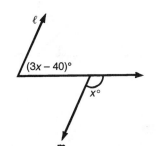

7.

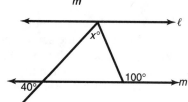

8.

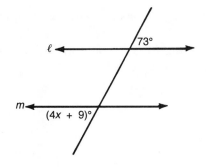

9.

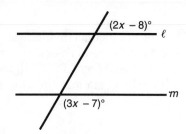

10. In each of the following, find the values of x and y if $\ell \parallel m$:

(a)

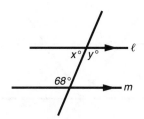

(b)

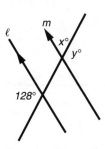

(c)

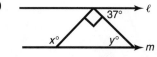

(d)

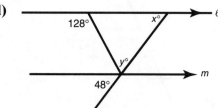

11. Two parallel lines are cut by a transversal. Find the measures of a pair of interior angles on the same side of the transversal if the angles:
   (a) are represented by $5x - 32$ and $x + 8$;
   (b) have measures such that the measure of one angle is four times the measure of the other.

12. In the accompanying diagram, $\overleftrightarrow{AB} \parallel \overleftrightarrow{CD}$ and $\overrightarrow{FG}$ bisects $\angle EFD$. If $m\angle EFG = x$ and $m\angle FEG = 4x$, find x.

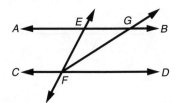

13. In the accompanying diagram, lines ℓ_1 and ℓ_2 are parallel and $m\angle 1 = 70$. What must the measure of $\angle 2$ be so that lines ℓ_3 and ℓ_4 will be parallel?

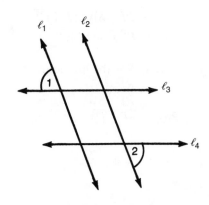

14. If, in the accompanying diagram, $L_1 \parallel L_2$ and $L_3 \parallel L_4$, then angle x is *not* always congruent to which angle?
   (1) a (2) b (3) c (4) d

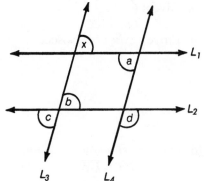

15. Given that lines p and q are parallel
   (a) Find x.
   (b) State whether line ℓ is parallel to line m.

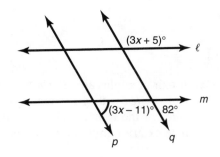

16. Given: $\overline{EF} \parallel \overline{AB}$, $\overline{ED} \parallel \overline{BC}$,
   $\overline{AD} \cong \overline{FC}$.
   Prove: $\overline{AB} \cong \overline{EF}$.

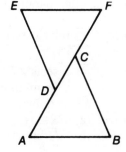

17. Given: $\overline{TW} \cong \overline{SP}$,

$\overline{RP} \parallel \overline{SW}, \overline{SP} \parallel \overline{TW}$.
Prove: $\overline{PS}$ bisects $\overline{RT}$.

18. Given: S is the midpoint of $\overline{RT}$,
$\overline{RP} \cong \overline{SW}$,
$\overline{RP} \parallel \overline{SW}$.
Prove: $\overline{SP} \parallel \overline{TW}$.

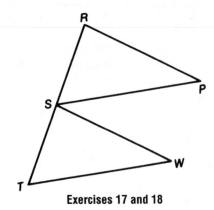

Exercises 17 and 18

19. Given: $\overline{QL} \cong \overline{QM}$,
$\overline{LM} \parallel \overline{PR}$.
Prove: $\triangle PQR$ is isosceles.

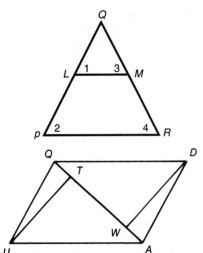

20. Given: $\overline{UT} \parallel \overline{DW}$,
$\overline{UT} \cong \overline{DW}, \overline{QW} \cong \overline{AT}$.
Prove: $\overline{UQ} \parallel \overline{AD}$.

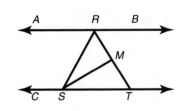

21. A pair of angles are *alternate exterior angles* if they are nonadjacent exterior angles that lie on opposite sides of the transversal. Prove that, if two lines are parallel, then alternate exterior angles are congruent.

22. Prove that, if one of two parallel lines is perpendicular to a third line, then the other parallel line is also perpendicular to the third line.

23. Given: $\overleftrightarrow{RS}$ intersects $\overleftrightarrow{ARB}$ and $\overleftrightarrow{CST}$,
$\overleftrightarrow{ARB} \parallel \overleftrightarrow{CST}$,
$\overrightarrow{RT}$ bisects $\angle BRS$,
M is the midpoint of $\overline{RT}$,
$\overline{SM}$ is drawn.
Prove: (a) $\overline{RS} \cong \overline{ST}$.
(b) $\overline{SM}$ bisects $\angle RST$.

24. Given: $\overline{AB} \parallel \overline{CD}$,
$\overline{AB} \cong \overline{CD}$, $\overline{AL} \cong \overline{CM}$.
Prove: $\angle CBL \cong \angle ADM$.

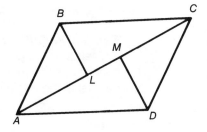

25. Given: $\overline{AB} \parallel \overline{GCD} \parallel \overline{FE}$ with
transversals $\overline{ACE}$ and $\overline{BCF}$,
$\overline{AC} \cong \overline{BC}$,
C is the midpoint of $\overline{GD}$.
Prove: $\overline{GF} \cong \overline{DE}$.

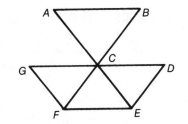

6.2 ANGLES OF A TRIANGLE

KEY IDEAS

In the accompanying diagram, can a line be drawn through B and parallel to $\overline{AC}$? Can a line be drawn from B to the midpoint of $\overline{AC}$? Can a line be drawn from B so that it is perpendicular to $\overline{AC}$?

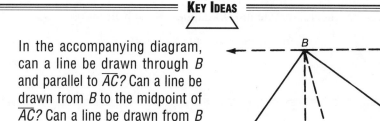

The answer to each of these questions is yes since in each case the line is determined. A line is **determined** if there exists exactly one line that can be drawn to satisfy a given condition or set of conditions.

The Parallel Postulate

Euclid, a Greek mathematician who lived in approximately 300 B.C., is credited with collecting and organizing the postulates and theorems that we study in plane geometry. The Parallel Postulate represents one of the fundamental assumptions made by Euclid.

Parallel Postulate: Through a given point *P,* not on a line, exactly one line may be drawn parallel to the original line.

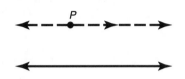

The Angles of a Triangle Theorem

According to the Parallel Postulate, a line may be drawn through one of the vertices of a triangle and parallel to the opposite side. In the accompanying diagram, line ℓ is drawn through *B* and parallel to $\overline{AC}$. Since angles 1, *B,* and 2 form a straight angle,

$$m\angle 1 + m\angle B + m\angle 2 = 180.$$

Angles 1 and *A* and angles 2 and *C* are equal in measure since parallel lines form congruent alternate interior angles. By substitution,

$$m\angle A + m\angle B + m\angle C = 180.$$

ANGLES OF A TRIANGLE THEOREM: *The sum of the measures of the angles of a triangle is 180.*

* A triangle may not have more than one right angle or more than one obtuse angle.

* If a triangle is equilateral, then it is also equiangular, so that each angle has a measure of 60.

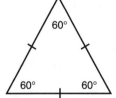

* If two angles of one triangle are congruent to two angles of another triangle, then the third pair of angles must be congruent.

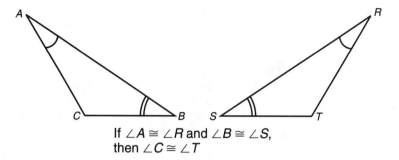

If $\angle A \cong \angle R$ and $\angle B \cong \angle S$,
then $\angle C \cong \angle T$

- The acute angles of a right triangle are complementary.

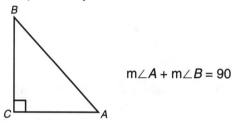

$m\angle A + m\angle B = 90$

Examples

1. The measures of the angles of a triangle are in the ratio of $2 : 3 : 5$. What is the measure of the smallest angle of the triangle?

Solution: Let $2x$ = measure of smallest angle of triangle.
Then $3x$ and $5x$ = measures of remaining angles.

$$2x + 3x + 5x = 180$$
$$10x = 180$$
$$\frac{10x}{10} = \frac{180}{10}$$
$$x = 18$$
$$2x = 2(18) = 36$$

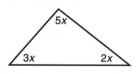

The measure of the smallest angle of the triangle is **36**.

2. In the accompanying diagram, $\overline{DE} \perp \overline{AC}$. If $m\angle ADB = 80$ and $m\angle CDE = 60$, what is $m\angle DAE$?

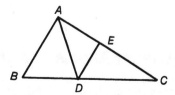

Solution: Since angles *ADB, ADE,* and *CDE* form a straight angle, the sum of their measures is 180. Hence

$$80 + m\angle ADE + 60 = 180$$
$$m\angle ADE = 180 - 140 = 40$$

In $\triangle ADE$,

$$m\angle DAE + m\angle ADE + m\angle AED = 180$$
$$m\angle DAE \quad\quad 40 \quad + \quad 90 \quad = 180$$
$$m\angle DAE + \quad\quad 130 \quad = 180$$
$$m\angle DAE = 180 - 130 = \mathbf{50}$$

3. In the accompanying diagram, $\overline{AD} \parallel \overline{EC}$, $\overline{DF} \parallel \overline{CB}$, $m\angle DAE = 34$, and $m\angle DFE = 57$. Find $m\angle ECB$.

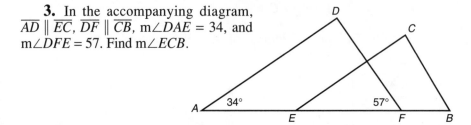

Solution: Since $\overline{AD} \parallel \overline{EC}$, transversal $\overline{AEFB}$ forms congruent corresponding angles, so that $m\angle CEB = m\angle DAE = 34$. Since $\overline{DF} \parallel \overline{CB}$, transversal $\overline{AEFB}$ forms congruent corresponding angles, so that $m\angle CBE = m\angle DFE = 57$. In $\triangle CEB$,

$$m\angle ECB + m\angle CEB + m\angle CBE = 180$$
$$m\angle ECB + \quad 34 \quad + \quad 57 \quad = 180$$
$$m\angle ECB + \quad\quad 91 \quad\quad = 180$$
$$m\angle ECB = 180 - 91 = \mathbf{89}$$

4. The degree measure of a base angle of an isosceles triangle exceeds twice the degree measure of the vertex angle by 15. Find the measure of the vertex angle.

Solution: Let x = measure of vertex angle.
Then $2x + 15$ = measure of a base angle.
$$(2x + 15) + (2x + 15) + x = 180$$
$$5x + 30 = 180$$
$$5x = 180 - 30$$
$$x = \frac{150}{5} = \mathbf{30}$$

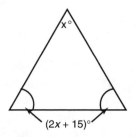

Exterior Angles of a Triangle

At each vertex of a triangle an *exterior* angle of the triangle may be formed by extending one of the sides of the triangle. Notice in Figure 6.3 that each pair of adjacent angles consisting of an exterior and interior angle of the triangle are supplementary. For example,

(1) $m\angle 1 + c = 180$.

Also note that:

(2) $(a + b) + c = 180$.

Comparing the left sides of equations (1) and (2) leads to the conclusion that

$$m\angle 1 = a + b.$$

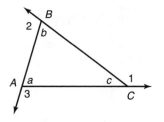

Figure 6.3 Exterior Angles of a Triangle

=== **MATH FACTS** ===

EXTERIOR ANGLE OF A TRIANGLE THEOREM. *The measure of an exterior angle of a triangle is equal to the sum of the measures of the two nonadjacent interior angles of the triangle.*

Examples:

5. For each of the accompanying diagrams, find the value of x.

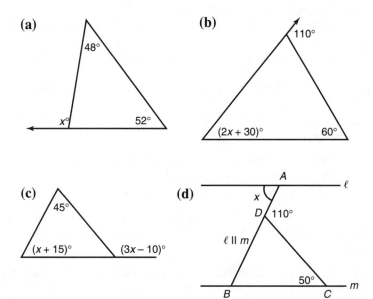

159

Solutions:

(a) $x = 48 + 52 = \mathbf{100}$

(b) $110 = 2x + 30 + 60$
$110 = 2x + 90$
$20 = 2x$
$x = \mathbf{10}$

(c) $3x - 10 = (x + 15) + 45$
$3x - 10 = x + 60$
$3x = x + 70$
$2x = 70$
$x = \mathbf{35}$

(d) Since $m\angle DBC = x$,
$x + 50 = 110$
$x = \mathbf{60}$

6. If the measure of an exterior angle formed by extending the base of an isosceles triangle is 112, what is the degree measure of the vertex angle?

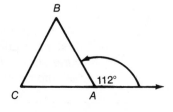

Solution: $m\angle A = 180 - 112 = 68$
Therefore $m\angle C$ must also equal 68.
$68 + 68 + m\angle B = 180$
$136 + m\angle B = 180$
$m\angle B = 180 - 136 = \mathbf{44}$

Exercise Set 6.2

1. Find the measure of the vertex angle of an isosceles triangle if:
   (a) the measure of a base angle is 43.
   (b) the measure of an exterior angle formed by extending the base is 117
   (c) the measure of the vertex angle is three times the measure of a base angle
   (d) the measure of the vertex angle exceeds the measure of a base angle by 15
   (e) the measure of a base angle exceeds the measure of the vertex angle by 15

2. Find the measure of the *smallest* angle of a triangle if the measures of the three angles of the triangle are in the ratio:
   (a) $1 : 2 : 6$ **(b)** $2 : 3 : 10$ **(c)** $1 : 1 : 2$ **(d)** $3 : 4 : 5$ **(e)** $2 : 7 : 7$

3. In the right triangle *ABC*, the measure of acute angle *A* exceeds twice the measure of $\angle B$ by 27. Find the measure of the *smallest* angle of the triangle.

4. When a ray bisects an angle of an equiangular triangle, what type of angle does the ray always form with the opposite side of the triangle?
   (1) acute   (2) right   (3) obtuse   (4) straight

160

5. For each of the following, the measures of the angles of $\triangle ABC$ are represented in terms of x. Find the value of $x,$ and classify the triangle as acute, right, or obtuse.

(a) $m\angle A = 3x + 8$
$m\angle B = x + 10$
$m\angle C = 5x$

(b) $m\angle A = x + 24$
$m\angle B = 4x + 17$
$m\angle C = 2x - 15$

(c) $m\angle A = 3x - 5$
$m\angle B = x + 14$
$m\angle C = 2x - 9$

6. In $\triangle ABC,$ $\overline{BD} \perp \overline{AC}.$ If $m\angle A = 72$ and $m\angle ABC = 54,$ find $m\angle CBD.$

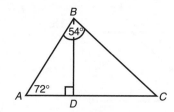

7. Given that $l \parallel m,$ $m\angle 2 = 110,$ and $m\angle 6 = 70,$ find each remaining numbered angle.

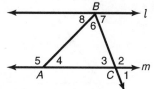

8–32. In each of the following, find the value of x:

8.

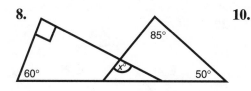

10.

$\overline{AB} \parallel \overline{DE}$

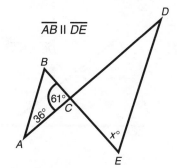

9.

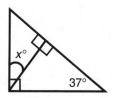

11.

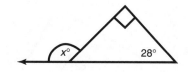

161

12.

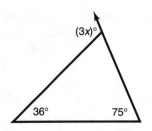

17.

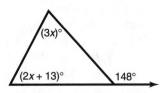

13.

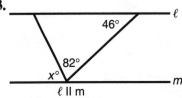

18.

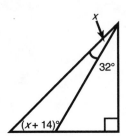

14.

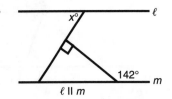

19.

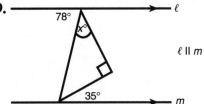

15.

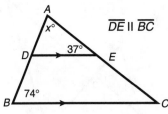

20.

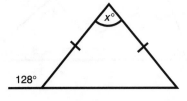

16.

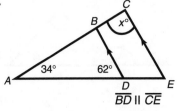

21.

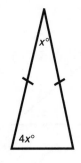

162

22.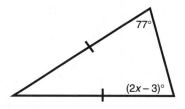

23.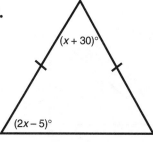

24.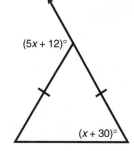

25.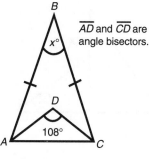

$\overline{AD}$ and $\overline{CD}$ are angle bisectors.

26.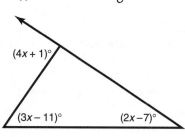

27.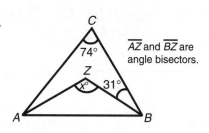

$\overline{AZ}$ and $\overline{BZ}$ are angle bisectors.

28–29. In each case, find the value of x.

28.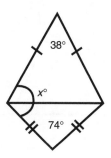

29.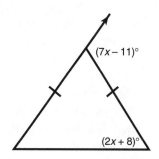

30.

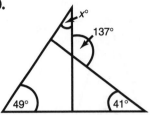

31.

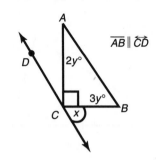

$\overleftrightarrow{AB} \parallel \overleftrightarrow{CD}$

32. Given: $\overline{EHF}$,
   $\overline{HK}$ intersects $\overline{FG}$ at R,
   $\overline{FG} \perp \overline{EGK}$,
   $\angle E \cong \angle K$.
   Prove: $\triangle HFR$ is isosceles.

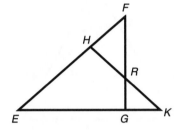

6.3   INEQUALITY RELATIONSHIPS IN A TRIANGLE

KEY IDEAS

In any triangle, the following are true:
- The length of each side is less than the sum of the lengths of the other two sides. In $\triangle ABC$,

$$c < a + b, \quad b < a + c, \quad \text{and} \quad a < b + c.$$

- The longest side is opposite the largest angle, and the shortest side is opposite the smallest angle. In $\triangle ABC$, $\overline{AB}$ is the longest side and $\overline{BC}$ is the shortest side.
- The measure of an exterior angle at any vertex is greater than the measure of either nonadjacent interior angle. In $\triangle ABC$,

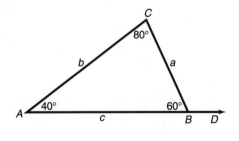

$$m\angle CBD > m\angle A \quad \text{and} \quad m\angle CBD > m\angle C.$$

Triangle Inequality Relationship

To determine whether a set of three positive numbers can represent the lengths of the sides of a triangle, verify that *each* number of the set is less than the sum of the other two.

Examples

1. Which of the following sets of numbers *cannot* represent the lengths of the sides of a triangle?
    (1) $\{9, 40, 41\}$ (2) $\{7, 7, 3\}$ (3) $\{4, 5, 1\}$ (4) $\{6, 6, 6\}$

Solution: The correct answer is **choice (3).** Although $4 < 5 + 1$ and $1 < 4 + 5$, 5 is *not* less than $4 + 1$.

2. If the lengths of two sides of an isosceles triangle are 3 and 7, what *must* be the length of the third side?

Solution: Since an isosceles triangle must have two sides of equal length, the length of the remaining side is either 3 or 7. The length of this side cannot be 3 since 7 is *not* less than $3 + 3$. Since $3 < 7 + 7$ and $7 < 3 + 7$, the length of the third side is **7.**

Noncongruent Sides Imply Noncongruent Angles

Here are three examples that illustrate inequality relationships in a triangle.

Examples

3. In $\triangle ABC$, $AB = 3$, $BC = 5$, and $AC = 7$. What is:
(a) the largest angle of the triangle?
(b) the smallest angle of the triangle?

Solutions: **(a)** $\angle B$ is the largest angle since it is opposite $\overline{AC}$, the longest side of $\triangle ABC$.
          (b) $\angle C$ is the smallest angle since it is opposite $\overline{AB}$, the shortest side of $\triangle ABC$.

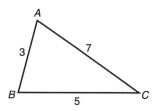

4. The measure of base angle R of isosceles triangle RST is 50. What is the longest side of the triangle?

Solution: First find the measures of the other two angles of the triangle. Since $\angle R$ = 50, $\angle T = 50$ and $\angle S = 180 - 100 = 80$. $\overline{RT}$ is the longest side since it lies opposite the largest angle ($\angle S$).

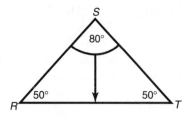

5. Given: $\overline{BD}$ bisects $\angle ABC$.
Prove: $AB > AD$.

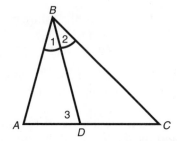

Solution:
PLAN. To prove $AB > AD$, first establish that m$\angle 3$ (the angle opposite $\overline{AB}$) is greater than m$\angle 1$ (the angle opposite $\overline{AD}$).

PROOF

Statement	Reason
1. m$\angle 3 >$ m$\angle 2$	1. The measure of an exterior angle of a triangle is greater than the measure of either nonadjacent interior angle.
2. $\overline{BD}$ bisects $\angle ABC$.	2. Given.
3. m$\angle 1 =$ m$\angle 2$	3. A bisector divides an angle into two angles having the same measure.
4. m$\angle 3 >$ m$\angle 1$	4. Substitution property of inequalities.
5. $AB > AD$	5. If two angles of a triangle are not equal in measure, then the sides opposite are not equal and the longer side is opposite the larger angle.

Exercise Set 6.3

1. In $\triangle ABC$, m$\angle A = 50$ and m$\angle B = 60$. Which is the *longest* side of the triangle?

2. In $\triangle ABC$, m$\angle A = 30$ and the measure of the exterior angle at B is 120. Which is the *longest* side of the triangle?

3. In right triangle ABC, altitude $\overline{CD}$ is drawn to hypotenuse $\overline{AB}$. Which is the *longest* side of $\triangle CDB$?

4. In $\triangle ABC$, m$\angle B = 120$, m$\angle A = 55$, and D is the point on $\overline{AC}$ such that $\overline{BD}$ bisects $\angle ABC$. Which is the *longest* side of $\triangle ABD$?

5. An exterior angle formed at vertex angle J of isosceles triangle JKL by extending leg $\overline{LJ}$ has a degree measure of 115. Which is the *longest* side of the triangle?

6. In $\triangle ABC$, $BC > AB$ and $AC < AB$. Which is the *longest* side of the triangle?

7. In $\triangle RST$, $m\angle R < m\angle T$ and $m\angle S > m\angle T$. Which is the *longest* side of the triangle?

8. In $\triangle ABC$, $AB > AC$ and $BC > AC$. Name the *smallest* angle of $\triangle ABC$.

9. In $\triangle RST$, $ST > RT$ and $RT > RS$.
   (a) If one of the angles of the triangle is obtuse, which angle of the triangle *must* it be?
   (b) If the measure of one of the angles of the triangle is 60, which angle of the triangle *must* it be?

10. Determine whether each of the following sets of numbers can represent the lengths of the sides of a triangle.
    (a) $\{8, 17, 15\}$ (b) $\left\{\frac{1}{2}, \frac{1}{3}, \frac{1}{6}\right\}$ (c) $\{1, 1, 3\}$ (d) $\{6, 6, 7\}$

11. In $\triangle ABC$, D is a point on $\overline{AC}$ such that $\overline{BD}$ bisects $\angle ABC$. If $m\angle ABC = 60$ and $m\angle C = 70$, then:
    (1) $AD > AB$ (2) $BD > BC$ (3) $AD > BD$ (4) $AB > AD$

12. In $\triangle ABC$, $CB > CA$, D is a point on $\overline{AC}$, and E is a point on $\overline{BC}$ such that $\overline{CE} \cong \overline{CD}$. Which statement is *always* true?
    (1) $m\angle CDE > m\angle A$
    (2) $m\angle B > m\angle CED$
    (3) $EB > AD$
    (4) $EB = AD$

13. In isosceles triangle ABC, $\overline{AC} \cong \overline{BC}$ and D is a point lying between A and B on base $\overline{AB}$. If $\overline{CD}$ is drawn, then which of the following is true?
    (1) $AC > CD$
    (2) $CD > AC$
    (3) $m\angle A > m\angle ADC$
    (4) $m\angle B > m\angle BDC$

14. In the accompanying diagram, parallel lines $\overleftrightarrow{AB}$ and $\overleftrightarrow{CD}$ are cut by transversal $\overleftrightarrow{AC}$. Segments $\overline{BC}$ and $\overline{AD}$ intersect at E, and $m\angle BAC < m\angle ACD$. If $\overline{CB}$ bisects $\angle ACD$ and $\overline{AD}$ bisects $\angle BAC$, then which statement is true?
    (1) $AC = AB$ (3) $AE < CE$
    (2) $AD < CD$ (4) $m\angle DAC > m\angle BCD$

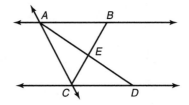

167

15. Given: $\overline{AB} \cong \overline{CB}$.
Prove: $AB > BD$.

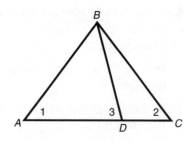

16. Given: $m\angle 1 = m\angle 2$.
Prove: $AD > ED$.

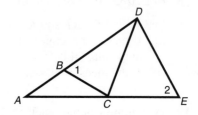

17. Given: Triangles AEC and ABC.
Prove: $m\angle 4 > m\angle AEC$.

18. Given: $AC > BC$.
Prove: $AD > BD$.

19. Given: $AD > BD$,
$\overline{AD}$ bisects $\angle BAC$.
Prove: $AC > DC$.

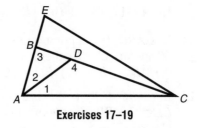

Exercises 17–19

20. Given: $\overline{AC} \cong \overline{BC}$, $\overline{AD} \cong \overline{BD}$,
Prove: **(a)** $\angle CAD \cong \angle CBD$.
(b) $AD > DE$.

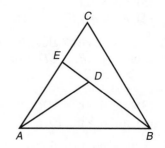

6.4 PROVING STATEMENTS INDIRECTLY

 KEY IDEAS

A statement is proved *directly* by showing in step-by-step fashion that it can be obtained from a given set of premises. The logic and geometric proofs presented so far have been *direct* proofs.

Sometimes, however, it is easier to prove a statement *indirectly* by assuming it is false and then showing that this assumption leads to a contradiction of a known fact. Reaching a contradiction means that the assumption was not correct, so the original statement must be true.

Indirect Method of Geometric Proof

To prove a statement *indirectly,* proceed as follows:

1. Assume the statement in the "Prove" is *not* true.
2. Show that this assumption contradicts a known fact.
3. Conclude that the statement in the "Prove" is true.

Consider this proof:
Given: $\triangle ABC$;
    $\angle C$ is obtuse.
Prove: $\angle A$ is *not* obtuse.

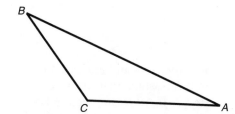

Solution: Prove "$\angle A$ is *not* obtuse" by following these steps:

PROOF

Step	Example
1. Assume the opposite of the statement to be proved.	1. Assume $\angle A$ is obtuse.
2. Show that the statement assumed to be true in Step 1 contradicts a premise or a known fact.	2. Since $\angle C$ is given as obtuse, the sum of the measures of the angles of $\triangle ABC$ will be greater than 180 if it is assumed $\angle A$ is obtuse. This contradicts the Angles of a Triangle Theorem, which states that the sum of the measures of the angles of any triangle is 180.
3. Conclude that the statement to be proved is true.	3. Thus, $\angle A$ is *not* obtuse.

Examples

1. Given: $\overline{TW} \perp \overline{RS}$,
$\angle 1 \not\cong \angle 2$.

Prove: $\overline{TW}$ is *not* the median to side $\overline{RS}$.

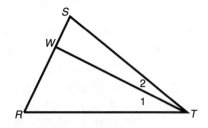

Solution: Use an indirect method of proof.

Step 1. Assume that $\overline{TW}$ is the median to side $\overline{RS}$.

Step 2. Hence, $\overline{WR} \cong \overline{WS}$ and triangles *TWS* and *TWR* are congruent by SAS $\cong$ SAS. By CPCTC, $\angle 1 \cong \angle 2$. But this contradicts the second premise.

Step 3. The conclusion $\overline{TW}$ is *not* the median to side $\overline{RS}$ is true since its negation leads to a contradiction and must therefore be false.

2. Given: $\overline{AB} \cong \overline{DB}$

Prove: $\overline{AB} \not\cong \overline{BC}$.

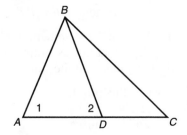

Solution: Use an indirect proof.

Step 1. Assume that $\overline{AB} \cong \overline{BC}$.

Step 2. If $\overline{AB} \cong \overline{BC}$, then $\angle 1 \cong \angle C$. Since $\overline{AB} \cong \overline{DB}$, $\angle 1 \cong \angle 2$. By the transitive property, $\angle 2 \cong \angle C$. But this contradicts the theorem that states that the measure of an exterior angle of a triangle ($\angle 2$) is greater than the measure of either nonadjacent interior angle ($\angle C$).

Step 3. $\overline{AB} \not\cong \overline{BC}$ is true since its negation leads to a contradiction.

Indirect Reasoning and Logic

Indirect proofs are based on the Law of Contrapositive Inference. In an indirect proof, a statement of the form "If p, then q" is proved by showing that $\sim q$ implies $\sim p$ ($\sim q \rightarrow \sim p$) and then concluding that its contrapositive is also true.

Exercise Set 6.4

1. If indirect reasoning is used to prove $a > b$, which assumption must be proved false?
(1) $a < b$ (2) $a \leq b$ (3) $a = b$ (4) $a \geq b$

2. If indirect reasoning is used to prove the theorem *"If two lines form a pair of congruent corresponding angles, then the lines are parallel,"* which assumption must be proved false?
(1) The corresponding angles are congruent.
(2) The corresponding angles are not congruent.
(3) The lines intersect.
(4) The lines do not intersect.

3. Given: $\angle 1 \cong \angle 3$.
Prove: $\angle 1 \not\cong \angle 2$.

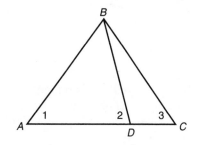

4. Given: $\angle 1 \cong \angle 2$.
Prove: $\overline{AB} \not\cong \overline{BC}$.

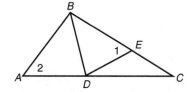

5. Given: $\overline{RS} \cong \overline{TS}$.
Prove: $\overline{RW} \not\cong \overline{WL}$.

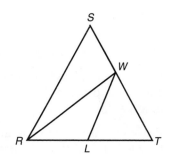

6. Given: △*ABC* is *not* isosceles,
∠*ADB* ≅ ∠*CDB*,
∠*ADC* is obtuse.
Prove: △*ADC* is *not* isosceles.

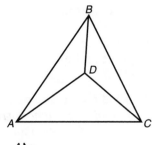

7. Given: *AC* > *AB*,
$\overline{DE}$ ≅ $\overline{CE}$.
Prove: $\overline{AB}$ is *not* parallel to $\overline{DE}$.

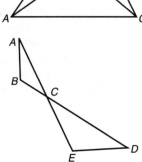

8. Given: △*ABC* is scalene,
$\overline{BD}$ bisects ∠*ABC*.
Prove: $\overline{BD}$ is *not* perpendicular to $\overline{AC}$.

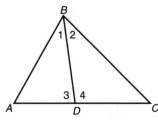

9. Given: $\overline{BC}$ ∥ $\overline{AD}$,
△*ABC* is *not* isosceles.
Prove: $\overline{AC}$ does *not* bisect ∠*BAD*.

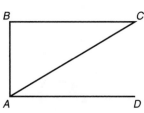

10–13. In each case, write an indirect proof.

10. Prove that the length of the line segment drawn from any vertex of an equilateral triangle to a point on the opposite side is less than the length of any side of the triangle.

11. Prove that, if the vertex angle of an isosceles triangle is obtuse, then the base is longer than either leg.

12. Prove that the shortest distance from a point to a line is the length of the perpendicular segment from the point to the line.

13. Prove that, if two lines form a pair of congruent corresponding angles, then the lines are parallel.

Each of the questions in this section has appeared on a previous Course II Regents Examination. Here is an opportunity for you to review the material in Chapter 6 and, at the same time, prepare for the Course II Regents Examination.

1. In an isosceles triangle, the ratio of the measure of the vertex angle to the measure of a base angle is 1 : 4. Find the measure of the vertex angle.

2. In the accompanying diagram, $\overleftrightarrow{WX} \parallel \overleftrightarrow{YZ}$; $\overleftrightarrow{AB}$ and $\overleftrightarrow{CD}$ intersect $\overleftrightarrow{WX}$ at E and $\overleftrightarrow{YZ}$ at F and G, respectively. If $m\angle CEW = m\angle BEX = 50$, find $m\angle EGF$.

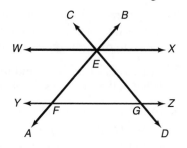

3. In the accompanying diagram of $\triangle ABC$, side $\overline{AB}$ is extended to D. If $m\angle ACB = x + 30$, $m\angle CAB = 2x + 10$, and $m\angle CBD = 4x + 30$, what is the value of x?

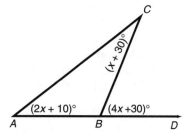

4. In the accompanying diagram, $\overline{ABC} \parallel \overline{DE}$, $m\angle FDE = 25$, $m\angle DFE = 130$, and $m\angle ABD = x$. What is the value of x?

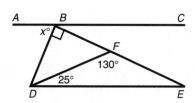

5. In the accompanying diagram of $\triangle ABC$, $\overline{DE} \perp \overline{AC}$, $m\angle BDA = 70$, and $m\angle EDC = 40$. What is the measure of $\angle DAC$?

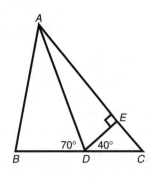

6. Two parallel lines are cut by a transversal. Two interior angles on the same side of the transversal are represented by $2x$ and $30 + x$. What is the measure of the *smaller* angle?

7. In $\triangle ABC$, $m\angle C = 55$ and $m\angle C > m\angle B$. What is the *longest* side of the triangle?

8. In the accompanying diagram, $\overleftrightarrow{AB}$ intersects $\overleftrightarrow{PQ}$ and $\overleftrightarrow{RS}$ at C and D, respectively. If $\overleftrightarrow{PQ} \parallel \overleftrightarrow{RS}$, $m\angle RDB = 2x - 10$, and $m\angle QCA = 3x - 65$, find x.

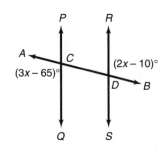

9. In $\triangle ABC$, $m\angle A = 41$, $m\angle B = 2x - 37$, and $m\angle C = 3x - 29$. Which side of the triangle is the *shortest* side?

10. In the accompanying diagram, $\overleftrightarrow{AB}$ is parallel to $\overleftrightarrow{CD}$, and $\overleftrightarrow{EF}$ is a transversal. If $m\angle BEF = 2x + 60$ and $m\angle DFE = 3x + 20$, what is $m\angle BEF$?

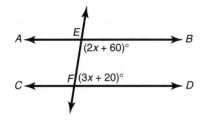

(1) 100   (2) 20   (3) 140   (4) 40

11. In $\triangle ABC$, $AB = 10$ and $BC = 5$. Which expression can be true?
(1) $AC = 5$ (2) $AC = 20$ (3) $AC < 5$ (4) $AC > 5$

12. Two angles of a triangle have degree measures of $55°$ and $65°$. Which *cannot* be a degree measure of an exterior angle of the triangle?
(1) $115°$ (2) $120°$ (3) $125°$ (4) $130°$

13. If the sum of the measures of two angles of a triangle is equal to the measure of the third angle, the triangle must be:
  (1) acute   (2) right   (3) obtuse   (4) scalene

14. In the accompanying diagram, $\overline{AFB} \parallel \overline{CDE}$. If $\overline{FD}$ bisects $\angle CFB$, which statement is true?
  (1) $\angle w \cong \angle y$ (2) $\angle y \cong \angle z$ (3) $\angle w \cong \angle z$ (4) $\angle x \cong \angle y$

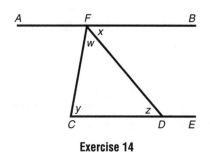
Exercise 14

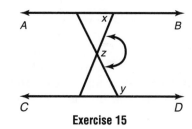
Exercise 15

15. In the accompanying diagram, $\overleftrightarrow{AB} \parallel \overleftrightarrow{CD}$, $m\angle x = 68$, and $m\angle y = 117$. What is the measure of $\angle z$?
  (1) 131   (2) 117   (3) 112   (4) 49

16. Triangle ABC is equilateral, and D is any point on $\overline{AB}$. Which of the following is *always* a correct conclusion?
  (1) $m\angle A > m\angle ADC$ (3) $CD > DB$
  (2) $m\angle B > m\angle BDC$ (4) $DB > CD$

17. In $\triangle ABC$, $m\angle B = 120$, $m\angle A = 55$, and D is a point on $\overline{AC}$ such that $\overline{BD}$ bisects $\angle ABC$. Which is the *longest* side of $\triangle ABD$?
  (1) $\overline{AB}$ (2) $\overline{AD}$ (3) $\overline{BD}$ (4) $\overline{DC}$

18. Which set of numbers *cannot* be the lengths of the sides of a triangle?
  (1) $\{2, 3, 4\}$ (2) $\{3, 5, 8\}$ (3) $\{6, 9, 10\}$ (4) $\{7, 8, 9\}$

ANSWERS TO SELECTED EXERCISES: CHAPTER 6

Section 6.1
1. 22   **9.** 39   **15. (a)** 31
3. 30   **11. (a)** 34, 146   **(b)** Line ℓ is *not* parallel to line m.
5. 85   **(b)** 36, 144
7. 60   **13.** 70

17. (1) $\overline{RP} \parallel \overline{SW}$, $\overline{SP} \parallel \overline{TW}$ (Given); (2) $\angle R \cong \angle TSW$, $\angle RSP \cong \angle T$ (If two lines are parallel, corresponding angles are congruent); (3) $\overline{TW} \cong \overline{SP}$ (Given); (4) $\triangle RSP \cong \triangle STW$ (AAS); (5) $\overline{RS} \cong \overline{TS}$ (CPCTC), so $\overline{PS}$ bisects $\overline{RT}$.

19. (1) $\overline{QL} \cong \overline{QM}$ (Given); (2) $\angle 1 \cong \angle 2$ (Base Angles Theorem); (3) $\overline{LM} \parallel \overline{PR}$ (Given); (4) $\angle 1 \cong \angle 2$ and $\angle 3 \cong \angle 4$ (If two lines are parallel, then corresponding angles are congruent); (5) $\angle 2 \cong \angle 4$ (Transitivity); (6) $\overline{QR} \cong \overline{QP}$ (Converse of Base Angles Theorem); (7) $\triangle PQR$ is isosceles (A triangle that contains two congruent sides is isosceles).

23. (a) (1) $\overline{RT}$ bisects $\angle BRS$ (Given); (2) $\angle BRM \cong \angle SRM$ (Definition of angle bisector); (3) $\overleftrightarrow{ARB} \parallel \overleftrightarrow{CST}$ (Given); (4) $\angle T \cong \angle BRM$ (If two lines are parallel, alternate interior angles are congruent); (5) $\angle SRM \cong \angle T$ (Transitivity); (6) $\overline{RS} \cong \overline{ST}$ (Converse of Base Angles Theorem). **(b)** (7) M is the midpoint of $\overline{RT}$ (Given); (8) $\overline{RM} \cong \overline{TM}$ (Definition of midpoint); (9) $\overline{SM} \cong \overline{SM}$ (Reflexive property); (10) $\triangle SRM \cong \triangle STM$ (SSS); (11) $\angle RSM \cong \angle TSM$ (CPCTC); (12) $\overline{SM}$ bisects $\angle RST$ (Definition of angle bisector).

Section 6.2

1. (a) 94
   (b) 108
   (e) 50
3. 21
5. (a) $x = 18$ right
   (c) $x = 30$ acute

9. 37
11. 118
13. 52
15. 79
17. 27
19. 47

21. 20
23. 32
25. 36
27. 127
29. 9
31. 54

Section 6.3

1. $\overline{AB}$
3. $\overline{BC}$

5. $\overline{LK}$
7. $\overline{RT}$

9. (a) $\angle R$
   (b) $\angle S$

11. (4)
13. (2)

15. $m\angle 1 = m\angle 2$, and $m\angle 3 > m\angle 2$. By substitution, $m\angle 3 > m\angle 1$, implying $AB > BD$.

17. $m\angle 4 > m\angle 3$, and $m\angle 3 > m\angle AEC$. Hence, $m\angle 4 > m\angle AEC$.

19. Since $AD > BD$, $m\angle 3 > m\angle 2$, $m\angle 1 = m\angle 2$, and, by substitution $m\angle 3 > m\angle 1$. But $m\angle 4 > m\angle 3$. Hence, $m\angle 4 > m\angle 1$, implying $AC > DC$

Section 6.4

1. (2)
2. (3)

3. Assume $m\angle 1 = m\angle 2$. Then $m\angle 2 > m\angle 3$. By substitution, $m\angle 1 > m\angle 3$. But this contradicts the "Given." Hence, $\angle 1 \not\cong \angle 2$.

5. Assume $\overline{RW} \cong \overline{WL}$. Then $m\angle WRL = m\angle WLR$ and $m\angle WLR > m\angle T$. By substitution, $m\angle WRL > m\angle T$. Since $m\angle SRT > m\angle WRL$, $m\angle SRT > m\angle T$, implying $TS > RS$. But this contradicts the "Given." Hence, $\overline{RW} \not\cong \overline{WL}$.

7. Assume $\overline{AB} \parallel \overline{DE}$. Then $\angle B \cong \angle D$. Since $\overline{DE} \cong \overline{CE}$, $\angle D \cong \angle DCE$. By transitivity, $\angle B \cong \angle DCE$. Since $\angle ACB \cong \angle DCE$, $\angle B \cong \angle ACB$, implying $\overline{AC} \cong \overline{AB}$. But this contradicts the "Given" ($AC > AB$). Hence $\overline{AB}$ is *not* parallel to $\overline{DE}$.

9. Assume $\overline{AC}$ bisects $\angle BAD$. Then $\angle BAC \cong \angle DAC$. Since $\overline{BC} \parallel \overline{AD}$, $\angle DAC \cong \angle BCA$. By transitivity, $\angle BAC \cong \angle BCA$, so $\triangle ABC$ is isosceles. But this contradicts the "Given." Hence, $\overline{AC}$ does *not* bisect $\angle BAD$.

Regents Tune-Up: Chapter 6

1. 20	**7.** *BC*	**13.** (2)
3. 10	**9.** *BC*	**15.** (1)
5. 20	**11.** (4)	**17.** (2)

## CHAPTER 7

SPECIAL QUADRILATERALS AND POLYGONS

7.1 PARALLELOGRAMS AND THEIR PROPERTIES

=== KEY IDEAS ===

A **parallelogram** is a special quadrilateral in which both pairs of opposite sides are parallel.

Angles of a Parallelogram

The notation $\square ABCD$ is read as "parallelogram $ABCD$." In a parallelogram (Figure 7.1):

- The sum of the measures of the angles is 360.

  $a + b + c + d = 360$

- Consecutive angles are supplementary.

  $a + b = 180$ and
  $b + c = 180$
  $c + d = 180$ and
  $a + d = 180$

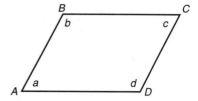

- Opposite angles are congruent.

  $\angle A \cong \angle C$ and $\angle B \cong \angle D$

Figure 7.1 Angles of a Parallelogram

Sides and Diagonals of a Parallelogram

In a parallelogram (Figure 7.2):

- Opposite sides are parallel.

  $\overline{AB} \parallel \overline{DC}$ and $\overline{AD} \parallel \overline{BC}$

- Opposite sides are congruent.
  $\overline{AB} \cong \overline{DC}$ and $\overline{AD} \cong \overline{BC}$
- Diagonals bisect each other.
  $\overline{AE} \cong \overline{EC}$ and $\overline{DE} \cong \overline{EB}$

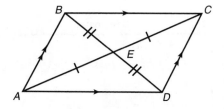

Figure 7.2 Sides and Diagonals of a Parallelogram

Examples

1. In $\square ABCD$, $m\angle B = 5x - 43$ and $m\angle D = 2x - 7$. Find the value of x.

Solution: Angles B and D are opposite angles of a parallelogram and are, therefore, congruent. Hence,

$$m\angle B = m\angle D$$
$$5x - 43 = 2x - 7$$
$$5x = 2x - 7 + 43$$
$$5x = 2x + 36$$
$$5x - 2x = 36$$
$$\frac{3x}{3} = \frac{36}{3}$$
$$x = \mathbf{12}$$

2. Given: $\square ABCD$,
         E is the midpoint of $\overline{AD}$,
         F is the midpoint of $\overline{BC}$.
  Prove: G is the midpoint of $\overline{EF}$.

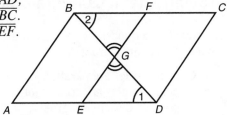

Solution:
PLAN. Show that $\triangle DGE \cong \triangle BGF$ by the AAS Theorem.

179

PROOF

Statement		Reason
1. $\square ABCD$		1. Given.
2. $\angle DGE \cong \angle BGF$	Angle	2. Vertical angles are congruent.
3. $\overline{AD} \parallel \overline{BC}$		3. Opposite sides of a parallelogram are parallel.
4. $\angle 1 \cong \angle 2$	Angle	4. If two lines are parallel, then alternate interior angles are congruent.
5. $AD = BC$		5. Opposite sides of a parallelogram are equal in length.
6. E is the midpoint of $\overline{AD}$, F is the midpoint of $\overline{BC}$.		6. Given.
7. $DE = 1\ AD,\ BF = 1\ BC$		7. Definition of midpoint.
8. $DE = BF$		8. Halves of equals are equal.
9. $\overline{DE} \cong \overline{BF}$	Side	9. Segments having equal lengths are congruent.
10. $\triangle DGE \cong \triangle BGF$		10. AAS Theorem.
11. $\overline{EG} \cong \overline{FG}$		11. CPCTC.
12. G is the midpoint of $\overline{EF}$.		12. Definition of midpoint.

Proving That a Quadrilateral Is a Parallelogram

To prove that a quadrilateral is a parallelogram, show that any *one* of the following statements is true:

- Opposite sides are parallel.
- Opposite angles are congruent.
- Opposite sides are congruent.
- Diagonals bisect each other.
- One pair of sides are both parallel and congruent.

Examples

3. Given: $\square ABCD$,
$\overline{BE} \perp \overline{AC}, \overline{DF} \perp \overline{AC}.$
Prove: $BEDF$ is a parallelogram.

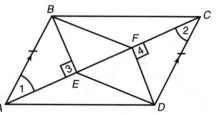

Solution:

PLAN. Prove that $\overline{BE}$ and $\overline{DF}$ are both parallel and congruent, so that quadrilateral *BEDF* is a parallelogram.

PROOF

Statement	Reason
1. $\overline{BE} \perp \overline{AC}$, $\overline{DF} \perp \overline{AC}$	1. Given.
2. $\overline{BE} \parallel \overline{DF}$	2. If two lines are perpendicular to the same line, they are parallel.
3. $\square ABCD$	3. Given.
4. $\overline{AB} \parallel \overline{DC}$	4. Opposite sides of a parallelogram are parallel.
5. $\angle 1 \cong \angle 2$ *Angle*	5. If two lines are parallel, then alternate interior angles are congruent.
6. Angles 3 and 4 are right angles.	6. Perpendicular lines intersect to form right angles.
7. $\angle 3 \cong \angle 4$ *Angle*	7. All right angles are congruent.
8. $\overline{AB} \cong \overline{DC}$ *Side*	8. Opposite sides of a parallelogram are congruent.
9. $\triangle AEB \cong \triangle CFD$	9. AAS Theorem.
10. $\overline{BE} \cong \overline{DF}$	10. CPCTC.
11. Quadrilateral *BEDF* is a parallelogram.	11. If one pair of sides of a quadrilateral are both parallel and congruent, then the quadrilateral is a parallelogram.

4. Prove that parallel lines are always the same distance apart.

Given: $\square ABCD$,
   $\ell \parallel m$,
   points *A* and *B*
   are on line ℓ,
   $\overline{AD} \perp$ line *m*,
   $\overline{BC} \perp$ line *m*.
Prove: $AD = BC$.

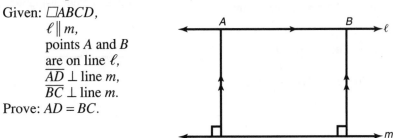

Solution:

PLAN. Prove that *ABCD* is a parallelogram.

PROOF

$\overline{AD} \parallel \overline{BC}$ since two lines that are perpendicular to the same line are parallel. Hence, the opposite sides of quadrilateral $ABCD$ are parallel. Since $ABCD$ is a parallelogram, $AD = BC$.

Exercise Set 7.1

1. In $\square MATH$, the measure of $\angle T$ exceeds the measure of $\angle H$ by 30. Find the measure of each angle of the parallelogram.

2. In $\square TRIG$, $m\angle R = 2x + 19$ and $m\angle G = 4x - 17$. Find the measure of each angle of the parallelogram.

3. In $\square RSTW$, diagonals $\overline{RT}$ and $\overline{SW}$ intersect at point A. If $SA = x - 13$ and $AW = 2x - 37$, find SW.

4. In the accompanying figure, $ABCD$ is a parallelogram. If $EB = AB$ and $m\angle CBE = 57$, what is the value of x?

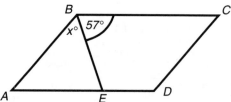

5 and 6. In each case, find the value of x.

5.

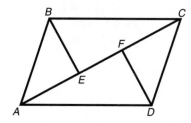

ABCD is a parallelogram.

6.

ABCD is a parallelogram.

7. Given: $\square ABCD$,
   $\overline{AE} \cong \overline{CF}$.
   Prove: $\angle ABE \cong \angle CDF$.

8. Given: $\square ABCD$,
$\overline{EF} \cong \overline{HG}$.
Prove: $\overline{AF} \cong \overline{CG}$.

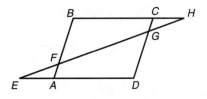

9. Given: $\square ABCD$,
B is the midpoint of $\overline{AE}$.
Prove: $\overline{EF} \cong \overline{FD}$.

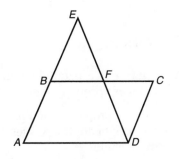

10. Given: $ABCD$ is a parallelogram,
$AD > DC$.
Prove: $m\angle BAC > m\angle DAC$.

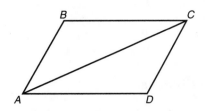

11. Given: $ABCD$ is a parallelogram,
$\overline{BR}$ bisects $\angle ABC$,
$\overline{DS}$ bisects $\angle CDA$.
Prove: $BRDS$ is a parallelogram.

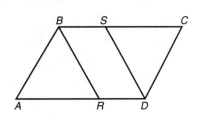

12. Given: $\square BMDL$,
$\overline{AL} \cong \overline{CM}$.
Prove: $ABCD$ is a parallelogram.

13. Given: $\square ABCD$,
$\angle ABL \cong \angle CDM$.
Prove: $BLDM$ is a parallelogram.

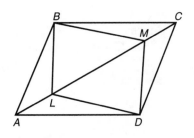

Exercises 12 and 13

7.2   SPECIAL PARALLELOGRAMS

$$\overset{\wedge}{\underset{\diagdown}{=\!\!\!=\!\!\!=}} \text{ KEY IDEAS } \overset{}{=\!\!\!=\!\!\!=}$$

A parallelogram may be equiangular, equilateral, or both equiangular and equilateral.

Rectangle

A **rectangle** is a parallelogram with four right angles. A rectangle (Figure 7.3) has these properties:

- All the properties of a parallelogram.
- Four right angles. Angles A, B, C, and D are right angles.
- Congruent diagonals. $\overline{AC} \cong \overline{BD}$.

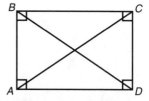

Figure 7.3 Rectangle

Examples

1. In rectangle $ABCD$, diagonals $\overline{AC}$ and $\overline{BD}$ intersect at point E. If $AE = 2x - 9$ and $CE = x + 7$, find BD.

Solution: Since the diagonals of a rectangle bisect each other,

$$AE = CE$$
$$2x - 9 = x + 7$$
$$2x = x + 16$$
$$2x - x = 16$$
$$x = 16$$

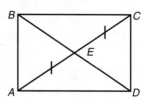

Hence $CE = x + 7 = 16 + 7 = 23$.   Also, $AE = 23$.   Therefore, $AC = 23 + 23 = 46$. Since the diagonals of a rectangle are congruent,

$$BD = AC = \mathbf{46}.$$

2. Given: Rectangle *ABCD*,
$\overline{EF} \cong \overline{EG}$.
Prove: $\overline{AG} \cong \overline{DF}$.

Solution:

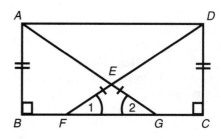

PLAN. Prove $\triangle ABG \cong \triangle DCF$ by $AAS \cong AAS$.

PROOF

Statement	Reason
1. Rectangle *ABCD*	**1.** Given.
2. Angles *B* and *C* are right angles.	**2.** A rectangle contains four right angles.
3. $\angle B \cong \angle C$ *Angle*	**3.** All right angles are congruent.
4. $\overline{EF} \cong \overline{EG}$	**4.** Given.
5. $\angle 1 \cong \angle 2$ *Angle*	**5.** If two sides of a triangle are congruent, the angles opposite these sides are congruent.
6. $\overline{AB} \cong \overline{CD}$ *Side*	**6.** Opposite sides of a rectangle are congruent.
7. $\triangle ABG \cong \triangle DCF$	**7.** $AAS \cong AAS$.
8. $\overline{AG} \cong \overline{DF}$	**8.** Corresponding sides of congruent triangles are congruent.

Rhombus

A **rhombus** is a parallelogram with four congruent sides. A rhombus (Figures 7.4 and 7.5) has these properties:

- All the properties of a parallelogram.
- Four congruent sides.
  $\overline{AB} \cong \overline{BC} \cong \overline{CD} \cong \overline{DA}$

Figure 7.4 Sides of a Rhombus

185

- Diagonals that bisect opposite pairs of angles.

$\angle 1 \cong \angle 2$ and $\angle 3 \cong \angle 4$
$\angle 5 \cong \angle 6$ and $\angle 7 \cong \angle 8$

- Diagonals that are perpendicular to (and bisect) each other.

$\overline{AC} \perp \overline{BD}$

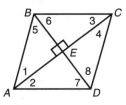

Figure 7.5 Diagonals of a Rhombus

Examples

3. Given that *ABCD* is a rhombus and m$\angle 1 = 40$, find the measure of each of the following angles:

   (a) $\angle 2$ **(b)** $\angle 3$ **(c)** $\angle ADC$

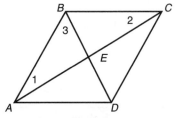

Solutions: (a) Triangle *ABC* is isosceles since $\overline{AB} \cong \overline{BC}$. Hence, the base angles of the triangle must be congruent:

$$m\angle 1 = m\angle 2 = \mathbf{40}.$$

(b) In $\triangle AEB$, $\angle AEB$ is a right angle since the diagonals of a rhombus are perpendicular to each other. Since the sum of the measures of the angles of a triangle is 180, the measure of $\angle 3$ must be **50**.

(c) Since the diagonals of a rhombus bisect the angles of the rhombus, if m$\angle 3 = 50$, then m$\angle ABC = 100$. Since opposite angles of a rhombus are equal in measure, m$\angle ADC$ must also equal **100**.

4. The perimeter of rhombus *ABCD* is 20, and the measure of angle *A* is 60. Find the length of the *shorter* diagonal.

Solution: A rhombus is equilateral, so the length of each side is equal to $\frac{20}{4}$ or 5. Since consecutive angles of a rhombus are supplementary, m$\angle B = $ m$\angle D = 120$. The shorter diagonal is $\overline{BD}$ since it lies opposite a 60° angle, while $\overline{AC}$ is the longer diagonal since it lies opposite a 120° angle. Diagonal $\overline{BD}$ bisects angles *B* and *D*, so $\triangle ABD$ is equiangular; this means that it is also equilateral.

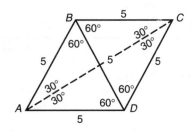

Hence, $BD = AB = AD = \mathbf{5}$.

Square

A **square** is a rectangle with four congruent sides. A square can also be defined as a rhombus with four congruent angles. A square (Figure 7.6) has these special properties:

- All the properties of a parallelogram.
- All the properties of a rectangle.
- All the properties of a rhombus.

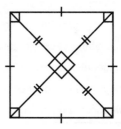

Figure 7.6 Square

Proving That a Quadrilateral Is a Special Parallelogram

Methods for proving that a quadrilateral is a special type of parallelogram are based on the *converses* of the statements that give the definitions and properties of these figures.

To prove that a quadrilateral is a rectangle, show that the quadrilateral is a parallelogram with *one* of the following properties:

- A right angle.
- Congruent diagonals.

To prove that a quadrilateral is a rhombus, show that the quadrilateral:

- has four congruent sides; or
- is a parallelogram with a pair of congruent adjacent sides; or
- is a parallelogram with perpendicular diagonals; or
- is a parallelogram in which each diagonal bisects a pair of opposite angles of the quadrilateral.

To prove that a quadrilateral is a square, show that the quadrilateral is:

- a rectangle with a pair of congruent adjacent sides; or
- a rhombus with a right angle.

┤ **MATH FACTS** ├

SUMMARY OF PROPERTIES OF THE RECTANGLE, RHOMBUS, AND SQUARE

Property	Rectangle	Rhombus	Square
1. All the properties of a parallelogram?	Yes	Yes	Yes
2. Equiangular (4 right angles)?	Yes	No	Yes
3. Equilateral (4 congruent sides)?	No	Yes	Yes
4. Diagonals congruent?	Yes	No	Yes
5. Diagonals bisect opposite angles?	No	Yes	Yes
6. Diagonals perpendicular?	No	Yes	Yes

Exercise Set 7.2

1. In rhombus *RSTW*, diagonal $\overline{RT}$ is drawn. If m∠*RST* = 108, find m∠*SRT*.

2. Given: Rectangle *ABCD*,
         M is the midpoint of $\overline{BC}$.
   Prove: △*AMD* is isosceles.

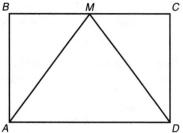

3. Given: Rectangle *ABCD*,
         $\overline{BE} \cong \overline{CE}$.
   Prove: $\overline{AF} \cong \overline{DG}$.

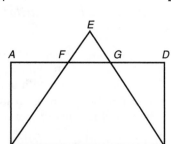

4. Given: Rhombus *ABCD*,
         $\overline{BL} \cong \overline{CM}, \overline{AL} \cong \overline{BM}$.
   Prove: *ABCD* is a square.

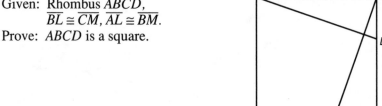

5. Given: $\square ABCD$,
  $m\angle 2 > m\angle 1$.
Prove: $\square ABCD$ is *not* a rectangle.

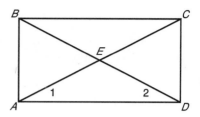

6. Given: Rhombus $ABCD$.
Prove: $\triangle ASC$ is isosceles.

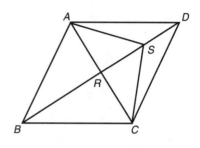

7. Given: Square $ABCD$,
  $\angle 1 \cong \angle 2$.
Prove: $\overline{BE} \cong \overline{DF}$.

8. Given: Rectangle $ABCD$
  $\angle 1 \cong \angle 2$, $\angle BEF \cong \angle DFE$.
Prove: $ABCD$ is a square.

9. Given: Rectangle $ABCD$
  $\overline{BE} \cong \overline{DF}$, $\angle CEF \cong \angle CFE$.
Prove: **(a)** $ABCD$ is a square.
  (b) $\triangle EAF$ is isosceles.

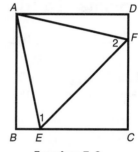

Exercises 7–9

7.3 MIDPOINT THEOREMS

KEY IDEAS

The special properties of parallelograms may be used to prove theorems about segments drawn to the midpoints of the sides of a triangle.

Median Drawn to the Hypotenuse of a Right Triangle

In the accompanying rectangle, since M is the midpoint of $\overline{AC}$,

$$AM = \tfrac{1}{2} AC.$$

Also, since the diagonals of a rectangle are congruent,

189

$$AM = \tfrac{1}{2}BD.$$

In right triangle BAD, $\overline{AM}$ represents the median to hypotenuse $\overline{BD}$.

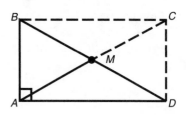

MEDIAN-HYPOTENUSE THEOREM. *The length of the median drawn to the hypotenuse of a right triangle is one-half of the length of the hypotenuse.*

Midpoints of a Triangle

In the accompanying figure, if D and E are midpoints of $\overline{AB}$ and $\overline{BC}$, respectively, then

$$\overline{DE} \parallel \overline{AC} \quad \text{and} \quad DE = \tfrac{1}{2}AC.$$

See Exercise 4 at the end of this section.

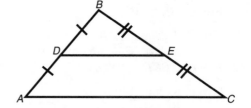

MIDPOINTS OF A TRIANGLE THEOREM. *The line segment connecting the midpoints of two sides of a triangle is parallel to the third side and its length is one-half the length of the third side.*

Perimeter Theorem

If the midpoints of the three sides of a triangle are connected, then another triangle is formed. The length of each side of the new triangle is one-half the length of a side of the original triangle. In the accompanying diagram, points

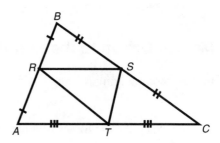

R, S, and *T* are the midpoints of $\overline{AB}$, $\overline{BC}$, and $\overline{AC}$, respectively. Thus, the perimeter of $\triangle RST$ is one-half the perimeter of $\triangle ABC$.

=== **MATH FACTS** ===

> PERIMETER THEOREM. *The perimeter of the triangle formed by joining the midpoints of three sides of a triangle is one-half the perimeter of the original triangle.*

Example

Find the perimeter of the triangle formed by joining the midpoints of the sides of a triangle whose sides measure 5, 12, and 13.

Solution: The perimeter of the original triangle is 30 (5 + 12 + 13). The perimeter of the triangle formed by joining the midpoints of the sides of this triangle is one-half of 30 or **15**.

Exercise Set 7.3

1. The length of the median drawn to the hypotenuse of a right triangle is represented by the expression $3x - 7$, while the hypotenuse is represented by $5x - 4$. Find the length of the median.

2. The lengths of the sides of a triangle are 9, 40, and 41. Find the perimeter of the triangle formed by joining the midpoints of the sides.

3. In $\triangle RST$, *E* is the midpoint of $\overline{RS}$ and *F* is the midpoint of $\overline{ST}$. If $EF = 5y - 1$ and $RT = 7y + 10$, find the length of $\overline{EF}$ and of $\overline{RT}$.

4. Given: *D* is the midpoint of $\overline{AB}$,
   E is the midpoint of $\overline{BC}$,
   $\overline{DE}$ is extended so that $\overline{DE} \cong \overline{EF}$,
   $\overline{CF}$ is drawn.

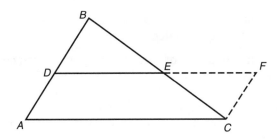

Prove: **(a)** $\triangle BED \cong \triangle CEF$.
     (b) $\overline{AD} \cong \overline{CF}$.
     (c) Quadrilateral $ADFC$ is a parallelogram.
     (d) $\overline{DE} \parallel \overline{AC}$ and $DE = \frac{1}{2}AC$.

5. Given: $\overline{DE} \cong \overline{DF}$,
           points D, E, and F are midpoints of
           $\overline{AC}$, $\overline{AB}$, and $\overline{BC}$, respectively.
  Prove: $\triangle ABC$ is isosceles.

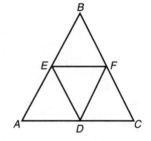

6. Given: $\square RSTW$,
           in $\triangle WST$, B and C are midpoints of $\overline{SW}$ and $\overline{ST}$, respectively.
  Prove: $WACT$ is a parallelogram.

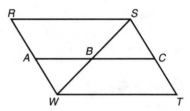

7. Given: $ABCD$ is a rhombus,
           E, F, G, H are midpoints
           of $\overline{AX}$, $\overline{BX}$, $\overline{CX}$, and $\overline{DX}$,
           respectively.
  Prove: $EFGH$ is a rhombus.

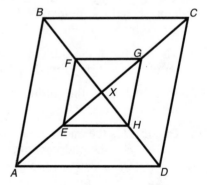

8. Prove that, if the midpoints of the sides of a rectangle are joined consecutively, the resulting quadrilateral is a rhombus.

9. Prove that, if the midpoints of a quadrilateral are joined consecutively, a parallelogram is formed.

7.4 PROPERTIES OF TRAPEZOIDS

KEY IDEAS

A **trapezoid** is *not* a parallelogram since a trapezoid is a quadrilateral that has exactly *one* pair of parallel sides, called *bases.* The nonparallel sides of a trapezoid are called *legs.* If points L and M are the midpoints of legs $\overline{AB}$ and $\overline{DC}$, then $\overline{LM}$ is called the *median* of the trapezoid. If the legs are congruent ($\overline{AB} \cong \overline{DC}$), then the trapezoid is *isosceles.*

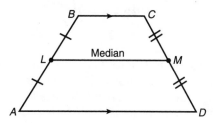

Properties of Trapezoids

Unlike a parallelogram, a trapezoid has one and only one pair of parallel sides. An *isosceles trapezoid* (Figure 7.7) has these additional properties:

- The legs are congruent.

  $AB \cong DC$

- The upper and lower base angles are congruent.

  $\angle A \cong \angle D$ and $\angle B \cong \angle C$

- The diagonals are congruent.

  $\overline{AC} \cong \overline{DB}$

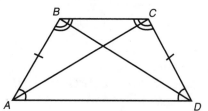

Figure 7.7 Isosceles Trapezoid

MATH FACTS

SUMMARY OF PROPERTIES OF DIAGONALS OF SPECIAL QUADRILATERALS

Special Quadrilateral	Diagonals Are Always		Diagonals Always Bisect	
	Congruent	Perpendicular	Each Other	Vertex Angles
Parallelogram	No	No	Yes	No
Rectangle	Yes	No	Yes	No
Rhombus	No	Yes	Yes	Yes
Square	Yes	Yes	Yes	Yes
Trapezoid	No	No	No	No
Isosceles Trapezoid	Yes	No	No	No

Examples

1. In the accompanying diagram of isosceles trapezoid $ABCD$, $\overline{AB} \parallel \overline{DC}$ and diagonals $\overline{DB}$ and $\overline{AC}$ intersect at E. Which statement is *not* true?

(1) $\overline{AC} \cong \overline{BD}$
(2) $\angle CDB \cong \angle DBA$
(3) $\triangle ADC \cong \triangle ABC$
(4) $\triangle CBA \cong \triangle DAB$

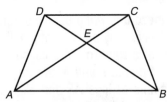

Solution: Choice (1) is true since the diagonals of an isosceles trapezoid are congruent. Choice (2) is true since $\overline{AB} \parallel \overline{DC}$, and therefore alternate interior angles are congruent. Choice (4) is true since $\overline{AD} \cong \overline{BC}$, $\angle DAB \cong \angle CBA$ (base angles of an isosceles trapezoid are congruent), and $\overline{AB} \cong \overline{AB}$, so that the triangles are congruent by the SAS postulate. **Choice (3)** is *not* true.

2. Given: Isosceles trapezoid
with $\overline{BC} \parallel \overline{AD}$,
$\overline{GP} \perp \overline{AB}$, $\overline{EQ} \perp \overline{CD}$,
P and Q are midpoints
of $\overline{AB}$ and $\overline{CD}$,
respectively.
Prove: $\overline{GP} \cong \overline{EQ}$.

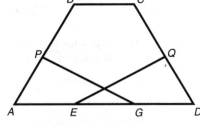

Solution:
PLAN: Prove $\triangle APG \cong \triangle EQD$ by
$ASA \cong ASA$.

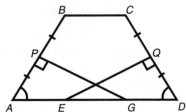

PROOF

Statement	Reason
1. Isosceles trapezoid with $\overline{BC} \parallel \overline{AD}$.	1. Given.
2. $\angle A \cong \angle D$ *Angle*	2. Base angles of an isosceles trapezoid are congruent.
3. P and Q are midpoints of $\overline{AB}$ and $\overline{CD}$, respectively.	3. Given.
4. $AP = \frac{1}{2}AB$ and $DQ = \frac{1}{2}DC$	4. Definition of midpoint.
5. $AB = DC$	5. The legs of an isosceles trapezoid are congruent and, as a result, have the same length.

194

6. $AP = DQ$		6. Halves of equals are equal.
7. $\overline{AP} \cong \overline{DQ}$	*Side*	7. Line segments that are equal in length are congruent.
8. $\overline{GP} \perp \overline{AB}$ and $\overline{EQ} \perp \overline{CD}$		8. Given.
9. $\angle APG$ and $\angle DQE$ are right angles.		9. Perpendicular lines intersect to form right angles.
10. $\angle APG \cong \angle DQE$	*Angle*	10. All right angles are congruent.
11. $\triangle APG \cong \triangle EQD$		11. $ASA \cong ASA$.
12. $\overline{GP} \cong \overline{EQ}$		12. Corresponding sides of congruent triangles are congruent.

Altitudes and Median of a Trapezoid

An **altitude** of a trapezoid is any segment drawn from one base perpendicular to the other base. The **median** of a trapezoid is the segment joining the midpoints of its legs. In Figure 7.8, $\overleftrightarrow{BX}$ and $\overleftrightarrow{CY}$ are altitudes; in Figure 7.9, $\overline{LM}$ is a median. It can be proved that:

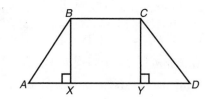

Figure 7.8 Altitudes of a Trapezoid

and
$$\overline{LM} \parallel \overline{AD} \parallel \overline{BC}$$
$$LM = \tfrac{1}{2}(AD + BC).$$

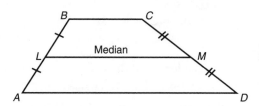

Figure 7.9 Median of a Trapezoid

MATH FACTS

MEDIAN OF A TRAPEZOID THEOREM. *The median of a trapezoid is parallel to the bases, and its length is one-half the sum of the lengths of the bases.*

195

To prove this theorem, it is necessary to draw line segment $\overline{BM}$ and extend it so that it meets the extension of line segment $\overline{AD}$.

$\overline{LM}$ is a line segment joining the midpoints of two sides of $\triangle ABE$. Hence,

$\overline{LM} \parallel \overline{ADE}$ and

$LM = \frac{1}{2}(AD + DE)$.

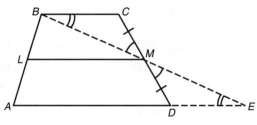

Triangles BMC and EMD are congruent by ASA, so $DE = BC$. By substitution,

$LM = \frac{1}{2}(AD + BC)$.

Examples

3. In trapezoid $ABCD$, $\overline{BC} \parallel \overline{AD}$ and $\overline{RS}$ is the median.
(a) If $AD = 13$ and $BC = 7$, find RS.
(b) If $BC = 6$ and $RS = 11$, find AD.

Solutions: **(a)** $RS = \frac{1}{2}(13 + 7) = \frac{1}{2}(20) = \textbf{10}$

(b) If median $= \frac{1}{2}$(sum of bases), then

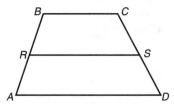

Sum of bases $= 2 \times$ median
$$AD + 6 = 2 \times 11$$
$$AD + 6 = 22$$
$$AD = 22 - 6 = \textbf{16}$$

4. The length of the lower base of a trapezoid is three times the length of the upper base. If the median has a 24-inch length, find the lengths of the bases.

Solution: Let $a = $ length of upper base.
Then $3a = $ length of lower base.

Since sum of bases $= 2 \times$ median,
$$a + 3a = 2 \times 24$$
$$4a = 48$$
$$a = \frac{48}{4} = 12$$
$$3a = 36$$

The length of the upper base is **12 inches**, and the length of the lower base is **36 inches**.

Proving That a Quadrilateral Is a Trapezoid

To prove that a quadrilateral is a trapezoid, show that *both* of the following statements are true:

- One pair of sides is parallel.
- One pair of sides is *not* parallel.

Proving That a Trapezoid Is Isosceles

To prove that a trapezoid is an isosceles trapezoid, show that *one* of the following statements is true:

- The legs are congruent.
- The lower (or upper) base angles are congruent.
- The diagonals are congruent.

Example

5. Given: Trapezoid *ABCD*,
  $\overline{BC} \parallel \overline{AD}$,
  $\overline{EB} \cong \overline{EC}$.

Prove: *ABCD* is an isosceles
  trapezoid.

Solution:
PLAN. Show that $\angle A \cong \angle D$.

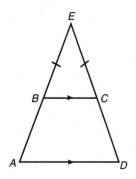

PROOF

Statement	Reason
1. Trapezoid *ABCD* with $\overline{BC} \parallel \overline{AD}$, $\overline{EB} \cong \overline{EC}$	**1.** Given.
2. $\angle EBC \cong \angle ECB$	**2.** If two sides of a triangle ($\triangle EBC$) are congruent, then the angles opposite these sides are congruent.
3. $\angle A \cong \angle EBC$, $\angle D \cong \angle ECB$	**3.** If two lines are parallel, then corresponding angles are congruent.
4. $\angle A \cong \angle D$	**4.** Transitive property.
5. *ABCD* is an isosceles trapezoid.	**5.** If a trapezoid has a pair of congruent base angles, then it is an isosceles trapezoid.

Exercise Set 7.4

1. In a trapezoid *BYTE*, $\overline{BE} \parallel \overline{YT}$ and median $\overline{LM}$ is drawn.

    (a) *LM* = 35. If the length of *BE* exceeds the length of $\overline{YT}$ by 14, find the lengths of the bases.

    (b) If $YT = x + 9$, $LM = x + 15$, and $BE = 2x - 5$, find the lengths of $\overline{YT}$, $\overline{LM}$, and $\overline{BE}$.

2. Given: Trapezoid *ABCD*,
        $\overline{AD} \parallel \overline{BC}$,
        $\overline{BE}$ and $\overline{CF}$ are
        altitudes drawn to $\overline{AD}$,
        $\overline{AE} \cong \overline{DF}$.

    Prove: Trapezoid *ABCD* is
        isosceles.

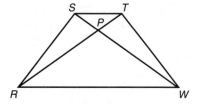

3. Given: Isosceles trapezoid *RSTW*.
    Prove: $\triangle RPW$ is isosceles.

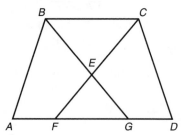

4. Given: Trapezoid *ABCD*,
        $\overline{EF} \cong \overline{EG}$, $\overline{AF} \cong \overline{DG}$,
        $\overline{BG} \cong \overline{CF}$.

    Prove: Trapezoid *ABCD* is isosceles.

5. Given: Trapezoid *ABCD* with median $\overline{LM}$,
        P is the midpoint of $\overline{AD}$,
        $\overline{LP} \cong \overline{MP}$.

    Prove: Trapezoid *ABCD* is isosceles.

6. Given: Isosceles trapezoid *ABCD*,
        $\angle BAK \cong \angle BKA$.

    Prove: *BKDC* is a parallelogram.

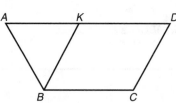

7.5 ANGLES OF A POLYGON

KEY IDEAS

Each point of a polygon at which two sides intersect is called a **vertex** of the polygon.

At each vertex there is an interior angle of the polygon. If the polygon has n sides, the sum S of the measures of these n interior angles is given by the formula

$$S = (n - 2) \cdot 180.$$

Regular Polygons

If each side of a polygon has the same length, the polygon is **equilateral**. If each angle of a polygon has the same measure, the polygon is **equiangular**. A polygon that is both equilateral *and* equiangular is called a **regular polygon**.

Angles of a Quadrilateral and a Polygon

In Figure 7.10, $\overline{BD}$ is a diagonal. A **diagonal** of a polygon is a line segment joining two nonconsecutive vertices of the polygon. Notice that $\overline{BD}$ divides quadrilateral $ABCD$ into two triangles the sum of whose angles is the same as the sum of all the angles of the polygon. Thus, the sum of the measures of the four angles of the quadrilateral is equal to 2×180 or 360.

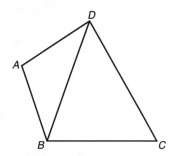

Figure 7.10 Diagonal of a Polygon

MATH FACTS

A polygon having n sides can be separated into $n - 2$ nonoverlapping triangles so that the sum S of the measures of the angles of a polygon having n sides is given by the formula

$$S = (n - 2) \cdot 180.$$

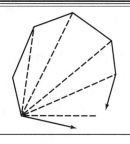

Examples

1. The measures of the angles of a quadrilateral are in the ratio of $1:2:3:4$. Find the measure of the *largest* angle of the quadrilateral.

Solution: Let x = measure of *smallest* angle of quadrilateral.
Then $2x$, $3x$, and $4x$ represent the measures of the remaining angles of the quadrilateral.

$$x + 2x + 3x + 4x = 360$$
$$10x = 360$$
$$x = \frac{360}{10} = 36$$
$$4x = 4(36) = 144$$

The measure of the largest angle of the quadrilateral is **144**.

2. (a) Find the sum of the measures of the angles of a hexagon.
(b) If the hexagon is a regular, find the measure of each interior angle.

Solutions: **(a)** A hexagon has six sides. $S = (n - 2) \cdot 180$
$$= (6 - 2) \cdot 180$$
$$= 4 \cdot 180$$
$$= \mathbf{720}$$

(b) A regular polygon is equiangular, so the measure of each angle can be found by dividing the sum of the angle measures by 6 (the number of interior angles of the regular hexagon).

$$\text{Measure of each angle} = \frac{\text{Sum of measures of angles}}{\text{Number of angles}}$$
$$= \frac{720}{6} = \mathbf{120}$$

3. If the sum of the measures of the angles of a polygon is 900, determine the number of sides.

Solution:
$$900 = 180(n - 2)$$
$$\frac{900}{180} = n - 2$$
$$5 = n - 2$$
$$n = \mathbf{7}$$

Exterior Angles of a Polygon

At each vertex of a polygon, an *exterior* angle may be formed by extending one of the sides of the polygon so that the interior and exterior angles at that vertex are supplementary. In Figure 7.11, angles 1, 2, 3, and 4 are exterior angles and the sum of their measures is 360.

In general:

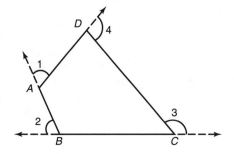

Figure 7.11 Exterior Angles of a Polygon

==== **MATH FACTS** ====

EXTERIOR ANGLES OF POLYGONS

- The sum of the measures of the exterior angles of a polygon having any number of sides (one exterior angle at each vertex) is 360.
- If a regular polygon has n sides, then the measure of each exterior angle is $\dfrac{360}{n}$.

Examples

4. Find the measure of each interior angle and each exterior angle of a regular decagon.

Solution: A decagon has 10 sides.

Method 1	Method 2
$\begin{aligned} \text{Sum} &= 180(n-2) \\ &= 180(10-2) \\ &= 180(8) \\ &= 1{,}440 \end{aligned}$	First determine the measure of an exterior angle: $$\text{Exterior angle} = \frac{360}{10} = \mathbf{36}$$
Since there are 10 interior angles, each of which is identical in measure, $$\text{Interior angle} = \frac{1{,}440}{10} = \mathbf{144}$$ Since interior and exterior angles are supplementary, $$\text{Exterior angle} = 180 - 144 = \mathbf{36}$$	Since an interior angle and an adjacent exterior angle are supplementary, $$\text{Interior angle} = 180 - 36 = \mathbf{144}$$

5. The measure of each interior angle of a regular polygon is 150. Find the number of sides.

Solution: Use a method similar to the approach illustrated in Method 2 of Example 4. Since the measure of each interior angle is 150, the measure of an exterior angle is $180 - 150$, or 30. Therefore,

$$30 = \frac{360}{n}$$

$$n = \frac{360}{30} = \mathbf{12}$$

Exercise Set 7.5

1–4. Find the sum of the measures of the interior angles of a polygon having the given number, n, of sides.

1. $n = 5$ **2.** $n = 6$ **3.** $n = 9$ **4.** $n = 13$

5–7. Find the number of sides of a polygon for which the sum, S, of the measures of its interior angles is given.

5. $S = 1,800$ **6.** $S = 2,700$ **7.** $S = 2,160$

8. If the measures of three interior angles of a quadrilateral are 42, 75, and 118, what is the measure of the other interior angle?

9. If the measures of four interior angles of a pentagon are 116, 138, 94, and 88, what is the measure of the other interior angle?

10. If the measures of five interior angles of a hexagon are 95, 154, 80, 145, and 76, what is the measure of the other interior angle?

11–14. Find the measure of each interior angle of a regular polygon having the given number, n, of sides.

11. $n = 5$ **12.** $n = 8$ **13.** $n = 15$ **14.** $n = 24$

15. Find the number of sides of a regular polygon if the measure of an interior angle is 162.

16. Find the number of sides of a regular polygon if the measure of an interior angle is 140.

17. Find the number of sides in a regular polygon in which the measure of an interior angle is three times the measure of an exterior angle.

18. Find the number of sides in a regular polygon in which the measure of an interior angle exceeds six times the measure of an exterior angle by 12.

19. For which type of polygon is the measure of an interior angle always equal to the measure of an exterior angle?
(1) equilateral triangle   (3) rhombus
(2) square   (4) hexagon

20. Which of the following *cannot* represent the measure of an exterior angle of a regular polygon?
(1) 72   (2) 15   (3) 27   (4) 45

REGENTS TUNE-UP: CHAPTER 7

Each of the questions in this section has appeared on a previous Course II Regents Examination. Here is an opportunity for you to review the material in Chapter 7 and, at the same time, prepare for the Course II Regents Examination.

---

1. In rectangle $ABCD$ with diagonals $\overline{AC}$ and $\overline{BD}$, $AC = 3x - 15$ and $BD = 7x - 55$. Find x.

2. In $\square ABCD$, $m\angle A = 3x - 40$ and $m\angle C = 7x - 100$. Find the numerical value of x.

3. In equilateral triangle ABC, $AB = 16$. Find the perimeter of the triangle formed by connecting the midpoints of the sides of $\triangle ABC$.

4. In rhombus $ABCD$, $m\angle BCD = 80$. Find $m\angle BDA$.

5. The measures of two consecutive angles of a parallelogram are in the ratio 3 : 7. Find the measure of an acute angle of the parallelogram.

6. In parallelogram $LMNO$, an exterior angle at vertex O measures $72°$. Find the measure, in degrees, of $\angle L$.

7. In the accompanying diagram of parallelogram $ABCD$, $\overline{DE}$ is perpendicular to diagonal $\overline{AC}$. If $m\angle BAC = 40$ and $m\angle ADE = 70$, find $m\angle B$.

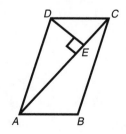

8. If the diagonals of a quadrilateral are perpendicular and *not* congruent, the quadrilateral may be:
(1) a rhombus   (3) a rectangle
(2) an isosceles trapezoid   (4) a square

9. An example of a quadrilateral whose diagonals are congruent but do not bisect each other is
(1) a square   (3) a rhombus
(2) an isosceles trapezoid   (4) a rectangle

10. A parallelogram *must* be a rectangle if the diagonals
(1) are congruent   (3) bisect the angles
(2) are perpendicular   (4) bisect each other

11. If the midpoints of the sides of a quadrilateral are joined consecutively, the resulting figure will *always* be a
(1) rhombus   (2) square   (3) rectangle   (4) parallelogram

12. Given four distinct quadrilaterals: square, rectangle, rhombus, and parallelogram. One is chosen at random. What is the probability that its diagonals are congruent?
(1) 1   (2) $\frac{1}{4}$ (3) $\frac{2}{4}$ (4) 0

13. The sum of the measures of the interior angles of a hexagon is
(1) 360   (2) 540   (3) 720   (4) 1280

14. In quadrilateral $ABCD$, if $\overline{AB} \cong \overline{DC}$ and $\overline{AD} \cong \overline{BC}$, then diagonals $\overline{AC}$ and $\overline{BD}$ must
(1) be perpendicular   (3) be congruent
(2) be parallel   (4) bisect each other

15. Let p represent "The diagonals are congruent," and let q represent "The diagonals are perpendicular." For which quadrilateral is $p \wedge \sim q$ true?
(1) parallelogram   (3) square
(2) rhombus   (4) rectangle

16. What is the sum of the measures of the exterior angles of a regular pentagon?
(1) 180   (2) 360   (3) 540   (4) 720

17. Given: Quadrilateral $ABCD$,
       diagonal $\overline{AEFC}$,
       $\overline{DE} \perp \overline{AC}, \overline{BF} \perp \overline{AC}$,
       $\overline{AE} \cong \overline{CF}, \overline{DE} \cong \overline{BF}$.
Prove: $ABCD$ is a parallelogram.

18. Given: Rhombus *ABCD, E* is
the midpoint of $\overline{DF}$.
Prove: $\overline{AD} \cong \overline{BF}$.

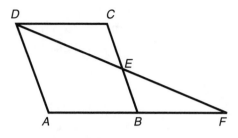

19. Given: Rectangle *ABCD,* $\overline{DF} \cong \overline{CE}$.
Prove: **(a)** $\triangle ADE \cong \triangle BCF$.
(b) $\angle 1 \cong \angle 2$.
(c) $\overline{GF} \cong \overline{GE}$.

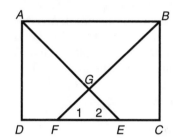

20. Given: Quadrilateral *ABCD,*
$\overline{FG} \cong \overline{EG}, \overline{AG} \cong \overline{CG},$
$\angle B \cong \angle D$.
Prove: **(a)** $\overline{BC} \cong \overline{DA}$.
(b) *ABCD* is a
parallelogram.

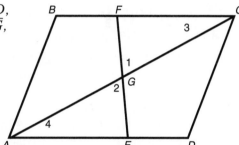

ANSWERS TO SELECTED EXERCISES: CHAPTER 7

Section 7.1
1. 75, 105, 75, 105   **3.** 22   **5.** 111
7. (1) $\overline{AE} \cong \overline{CF}$, *ABCD* is a parallelogram (Given); (2) $\overline{AB} \cong \overline{DC}$ and $\overline{AB} \parallel \overline{DC}$
(Opposite sides of a parallelogram are congruent and parallel); (3) $\angle BAE \cong$
$\angle DCF$ (If two lines are parallel, alternate interior angles are congruent); (4)
$\triangle BAE \cong \triangle DCF$ (SAS); (5) $\angle ABE \cong \angle CDF$ (CPCTC).
9. (1) *ABCD* is a parallelogram (Given); (2) $\overline{AB} \parallel \overline{DC}$ (Opposite sides of a
parallelogram are parallel); (3) $\angle E \cong \angle CDF$ (If two lines are parallel, alternate interior angles are congruent); (4) $\angle EFB \cong \angle DFC$ (Vertical angles are
congruent); (5) *B* is the midpoint of $\overline{AE}$ (Given); (6) $\overline{EB} \cong \overline{AB}$ (Definition of
midpoint); (7) $\overline{AB} \cong \overline{CD}$ (Opposite sides of a parallelogram are congruent);
(8) $\overline{EB} \cong \overline{CD}$ (Transitivity); (9) $\triangle BEF \cong \triangle CDF$ (AAS); (10) $\overline{EF} \cong \overline{FD}$
(CPCTC).

13. $\overline{AB} \cong \overline{CD}$ and $\overline{AB} \parallel \overline{CD}$, so $\angle BAL \cong \angle DCM$. $\triangle ALB \cong \triangle CMD$ (ASA). $\overline{BL} \cong \overline{DM}$ and $\angle ALB \cong \angle CMD$ (CPCTC). Taking supplements of congruent angles, $\angle BLM \cong \angle DML$ so that $\overline{BL} \parallel \overline{DM}$. Hence, $BLDM$ is a parallelogram.

Section 7.2
1. 36
3. $\angle EBC \cong \angle ECB$. Since $\overline{AD} \parallel \overline{BC}$, $\angle AFB \cong \angle EBC$ and $\angle DGC \cong \angle ECB$. By transitivity, $\angle AFB \cong \angle DGC$. $\angle A \cong \angle D$, and $\overline{AB} \cong \overline{DC}$, so $\triangle FAB \cong \triangle GDC$ (AAS). $\overline{AF} \cong \overline{DG}$ (CPCTC).
5. Use an indirect proof. Assume $ABCD$ is a rectangle. Then $\triangle BAD \cong \triangle CDA$ (SAS). $\angle 1 \cong \angle 2$ (CPCTC), contradicting the "Given."
7. (1) $ABCD$ is a square (Given); (2) $\angle B$ and $\angle D$ are right angles (A square contains four right angles); (3) $\overline{AB} \cong \overline{AD}$ (Adjacent sides of a square are congruent); $\angle 1 \cong \angle 2$ (Given); $\overline{AE} \cong \overline{AF}$ (Converse of the Base Angles Theorem); (6) $\triangle ABE \cong \triangle ADF$ (Hyp-Leg); (7) $\overline{BE} \cong \overline{DF}$ (CPCTC).

Section 7.3
1. 23   **3.** $EF = 19$, $RT = 38$
5. $DE = \frac{1}{2}BC$ and $DF = \frac{1}{2}AB$. Since $DE = DF$, then $\frac{1}{2}BC = \frac{1}{2}AB$ implies that $BC = AB$. Hence, $\triangle ABC$ is isosceles.

9. Given: Quadrilateral $ABCD$, P, Q, R, and
             S are the midpoints of $\overline{AB}$, $\overline{BC}$,
             $\overline{CD}$, and $\overline{AD}$, respectively.
   Prove: $PQRS$ is a parallelogram.
   PLAN. Show that $\overline{PS} \parallel \overline{QR}$ and $\overline{PS} \cong \overline{QR}$ by
             applying the Midpoints of a Triangle
             Theorem.

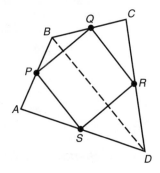

Section 7.4
1. (a) $YT = 28$, $BE = 42$ **(b)** $YT = 35$, $LM = 41$, $BE = 47$
3. Show $\triangle RSW \cong \triangle WTR$ by SAS. By CPCTC, $\angle TRW \cong \angle SWR$ so $\overline{RP} \cong \overline{WP}$ (Converse of the Base Angles Theorem), and $\triangle RPW$ is isosceles.
5. By the Base Angles Theorem, $\angle PLM \cong \angle PML$. Since $\overline{LM}$ is a median, $\overline{LM} \parallel \overline{AD}$, so $\angle PLM \cong \angle APL$ and $\angle PML \cong \angle DPM$. By transitivity, $\angle APL \cong \angle DPM$. Show $\triangle LAP \cong \triangle MDP$ by SAS. By CPCTC, $\angle A \cong \angle D$, implying trapezoid $ABCD$ is isosceles.

Section 7.5
1. 540   **7.** 14   **13.** 156   **19.** (2)
3. 1,260   **9.** 104   **15.** 20
5. 12   **11.** 108   **17.** 8

Regents Tune-Up: Chapter 7

1. 10   **5.** 54   **9.** (2)   **13.** (3)

3. 24   **7.** 120   **11.** (4)   **15.** (4)

17. PLAN: $\triangle AED \cong \triangle CFB$ by SAS. Then $AD \cong BC$ and $\angle EAD \cong \angle FCB$. Since alternate interior angles are congruent, $\overline{AD} \parallel \overline{BC}$. Since quadrilateral $ABCD$ has two sides that are both parallel and congruent, $ABCD$ is a parallelogram.

19. PLAN: **(a)** $\triangle ADE \cong \triangle BCF$ (SAS). **(b)** $\angle 1 \cong \angle 2$ (CPCTC). **(c)** $\overline{GF} = \overline{GE}$ (Converse of the Base Angles Theorem).

CHAPTER 8

SIMILAR AND RIGHT TRIANGLES

8.1 RATIO AND PROPORTIONS

KEY IDEAS

The **ratio** of two numbers a and b ($b \neq 0$) is the quotient of the numbers, and is written as

$$\frac{a}{b} \quad \text{or} \quad a : b \text{ (read as "} a \text{ is to } b \text{").}$$

A **proportion** is an equation that states that two ratios are equal. To *solve* a proportion for an unknown member, set the cross-products equal and solve the resulting equation.

$$\text{If} \quad \frac{a}{b} = \frac{c}{d}, \quad \text{then} \quad a \times d = b \times c,$$

where b and d cannot be equal to 0. The terms b and c are called the **means**, and the terms a and d are the **extremes**.

The Mean Proportional

In the proportion $\frac{4}{6} = \frac{6}{9}$, 6 is the *mean proportional* between 4 and 9. Whenever the means of a proportion are identical, the value that appears as the means is referred to as the **mean proportional** or **geometric mean** between the first and last terms (extremes) of the proportion.

Example

Find the mean proportional between each pair of extremes.
(a) 3 and 27   **(b)** 5 and 7

Solutions: **(a)** Let m = mean proportional between 3 and 27. Then

$$\frac{3}{m} = \frac{m}{27}$$
$$m^2 = 3(27) = 81$$
$$m = \pm \sqrt{81} = \pm \mathbf{9}.$$

(b) Let m = proportional between 5 and 7. Then

$$\frac{5}{m} = \frac{m}{7}$$
$$m^2 = 35$$
$$m = \pm \sqrt{35}.$$

Properties of Proportions

Here are some algebraic properties of proportions that show how the terms of a proportion can be manipulated so that an equivalent proportion results.

- **Property 1.** If the numerators and denominators of both members of a proportion are interchanged, then an equivalent proportion results.

$$\text{If } \frac{a}{b} = \frac{c}{d}, \text{ then } \frac{b}{a} = \frac{d}{c}$$

(provided that a, b, c, and d are nonzero numbers).

- **Property 2.** If either pair of opposite terms of a proportion are interchanged, then an equivalent proportion results.

$$\text{(a) If } \frac{a}{b} = \frac{c}{d}, \text{ then } \frac{d}{b} \diagdown \frac{c}{a}.$$

$$\text{(b) If } \frac{a}{b} = \frac{c}{d}, \text{ then } \frac{a}{c} \diagup \frac{b}{d}.$$

- **Property 3.** If the denominator is added to or subtracted from the numerator on each side of the proportion, then an equivalent proportion results.

$$\text{(a) If } \frac{a}{b} = \frac{c}{d}, \text{ then } \frac{a+b}{b} = \frac{c+d}{d}.$$

$$\text{(b) If } \frac{a}{b} = \frac{c}{d}, \text{ then } \frac{a-b}{b} = \frac{c-d}{d}.$$

- **Property 4.** If the product of two nonzero numbers equals the product of another pair of nonzero numbers, then a proportion may be formed by making the factors of one product the extremes, and making the factors of the other product the means. For example, if $R \times S = T \times W$, then a true proportion can be formed:

  - by making R and S the *extremes:* $\frac{R}{T} = \frac{W}{S}$; or
  - by making R and S the *means:* $\frac{T}{R} = \frac{S}{W}$.

Exercise Set 8.1

1. Find the measure of the largest angle of a triangle if the measures of its interior angles are in the ratio 3 : 5 : 7.

2. Find the measure of the vertex angle of an isosceles triangle if the measures of the vertex angle and a base angle have the ratio 4:3.

3. The measures of a pair of consecutive angles of a parallelogram have the ratio 5 : 7. Find the measure of each angle of the parallelogram.

4. Solve for x.

(a) $\dfrac{2}{6} = \dfrac{8}{x}$ (c) $\dfrac{2x-5}{3} = \dfrac{9}{4}$ (e) $\dfrac{3}{x} = \dfrac{x-4}{7}$

(b) $\dfrac{2}{x} = \dfrac{x}{50}$ (d) $\dfrac{4}{x+3} = \dfrac{1}{x-3}$ (f) $\dfrac{x+3}{x+7} = \dfrac{x-3}{3}$

5. Find the mean proportional between:
(a) 4 and 16 (b) $3e$ and $12e^3$ (c) $\frac{1}{2}$ and $\frac{1}{8}$ (d) 6 and 9

6. Determine whether each of the following pairs of ratios is in proportion:

(a) $\frac{1}{2}$ and $\frac{9}{18}$ (b) $\frac{12}{10}$ and $\frac{3}{5}$ (c) $\frac{4}{9}$ and $\frac{12}{36}$ (d) $\frac{15}{25}$ and $\frac{20}{12}$

8.2 COMPARING LENGTHS OF SIDES OF SIMILAR POLYGONS

KEY IDEAS

When a photograph is enlarged, the original and enlarged figures are **similar** since they have exactly the same shape. In making a blueprint, every object must be drawn to scale so that the figures in the blueprint are in proportion and are similar to their real-life counterparts.

Similar Polygons

Congruent polygons have the same shape *and* the same size, while similar figures have the same shape, but may differ in size. The triangles in Figure 8.1 are similar.

Notice that the lengths of corresponding sides of triangles I and II have the same ratio and are, therefore, in proportion:

$$\frac{\text{Side in } \triangle\text{I}}{\text{Side in } \triangle\text{II}} = \frac{3}{6} = \frac{4}{8} = \frac{5}{10} = \frac{1}{2} \text{ or } 1 : 2.$$

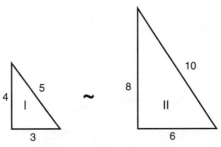

Figure 8.1 Similar Triangles

Two triangles (or any other two polygons having the same number of sides) are **similar** if both of the following conditions are met:

1. Corresponding angles have the same degree measure.
2. The lengths of corresponding sides are in proportion.

The symbol for similarity is ~. The notation $\triangle ABC \sim \triangle RST$ is read as "triangle *ABC is similar to* triangle *RST.*"

Also observe that the perimeters of two similar triangles have the same ratio as the lengths of a pair of corresponding sides:

$$\frac{\text{Perimeter of } \triangle \text{I}}{\text{Perimeter of } \triangle \text{II}} = \frac{3+4+5}{6+8+10} = \frac{12}{24} = \frac{1}{2} \text{ or } 1:2.$$

MATH FACTS

The perimeters of two similar triangles have the same ratio as the lengths of any pair of corresponding sides.

Examples

1. Quadrilateral *ABCD* is similar to quadrilateral *RSTW*. The lengths of the sides of quadrilateral *ABCD* are 6, 9, 12, and 18. If the length of the longest side of quadrilateral *RSTW* is 24, what is the length of its shortest side?

Solution: Let x = length of shortest side of quadrilateral *RSTW*. Since the lengths of corresponding sides of similar polygons must have the same ratio, the following proportion is true:

$$\frac{\text{Shortest side of quad } ABCD}{\text{Shortest side of quad } RSTW} = \frac{\text{Longest side of quad } ABCD}{\text{Longest side of quad } RSTW}$$

Substitute given values:	$\dfrac{6}{x} = \dfrac{18}{24}$
Write $\frac{18}{24}$ in lowest terms:	$\dfrac{6}{x} = \dfrac{3}{4}$
Cross-multiply:	$3x = 24$
	$x = \dfrac{24}{3} = 8$

The length of the shortest side of quadrilateral *RSTW* is **8**.

2. The longest side of a polygon exceeds twice the length of the longest side of a similar polygon by 3. If the ratio of the perimeters of the two polygons is 4 : 9, find the length of the longest side of each polygon.

Solution: Let x = length of longest side of smaller polygon.
Then $2x + 3$ = length of longest side of larger polygon.

$$\frac{\text{Perimeter of smaller polygon}}{\text{Perimeter of larger polygon}} = \frac{\text{Longest side of smaller polygon}}{\text{Longest side of larger polygon}}$$

Substitute given values:	$\dfrac{4}{9} = \dfrac{x}{2x + 3}$
Cross-multiply:	$9x = 4(2x + 3)$
	$\quad\ = 8x + 12$

$$9x - 8x = 12$$
$$x = 12$$
$$2x + 3 = 2(12) + 3 = 24 + 3 = 27$$

The length of the longest side of the smaller polygon is **12**, and the length of the longest side of the larger polygon is **27**.

Altitudes and Medians of Similar Triangles

The lengths of corresponding *altitudes,* the lengths of corresponding *medians,* and the *perimeters* of similar triangles (Figure 8.2) have the same ratio as the lengths of any pair of corresponding sides:

$$\frac{\text{Perimeter of } \triangle ABC}{\text{Perimeter of } \triangle RST} = \frac{BX}{SY} = \frac{BM}{SL} = \frac{AB}{RS} = \frac{BC}{ST} = \frac{AC}{RT}.$$

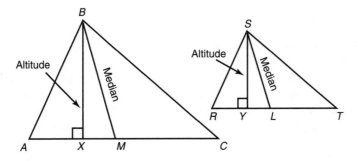

Figure 8.2 Altitudes and Medians in Similar Triangles

Example

3. Triangle $RST \sim \triangle KLM$. The length of altitude $\overline{SA}$ exceeds the length of altitude $\overline{LB}$ by 5. If $RT = 9$ and $KM = 6$, find the length of each altitude.

Solution: Let $x =$ length of altitude $\overline{LB}$.
Then $x + 5 =$ length of altitude $\overline{SA}$.

$$\frac{x+5}{x} = \frac{9}{6}$$
$$9x = 6(x + 5)$$
$$= 6x + 30$$
$$3x = 30$$
$$x = 10$$

Altitude $LB = x = \mathbf{10}$
Altitude $SA = x + 5 = \mathbf{15}$

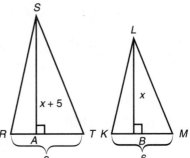

AA Theorem of Similarity

This theorem states that two *triangles* are similar if two angles of one triangle are congruent to two angles of the other triangle. In Figure 8.3, angles A and C in $\triangle BAC$ and corresponding angles R and T in $\triangle SRT$ are congruent, so the triangles are similar.

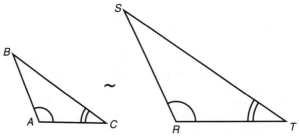

Figure 8.3 Congruent Angles in Similar Triangles

213

Examples

4. In the accompanying diagram, $\overline{AB} \perp \overline{BE}$ and $\overline{DE} \perp \overline{BE}$.

(a) State why $\triangle ABC \sim \triangle DEC$.

(b) Write a proportion that shows the relationship between the lengths of the corresponding sides of the two triangles.

(c) If $AB = 8$, $AC = 10$, and $DC = 25$, find DE.

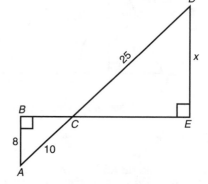

Solutions: **(a)** Two triangles are similar if two angles of one triangle are congruent to the corresponding angles in the other triangle. Since $\angle B \cong \angle E$ (all right angles are congruent) and $\angle BCA \cong \angle ECD$ (vertical angles are congruent), $\triangle ABC \sim \triangle DEC$.

(b) Since the lengths of corresponding sides of similar triangles are in proportion,

$$\frac{\text{Side of } \triangle ABC}{\text{Corresponding side of } \triangle DEC} = \frac{AB}{DE} = \frac{AC}{DC} = \frac{BC}{EC}.$$

(c) Let $DE = x$. Then

$$\frac{AB}{DE} = \frac{AC}{DC}$$
$$\frac{8}{x} = \frac{10}{25}$$
$$10x = 8(25)$$
$$= 200$$
$$x = \frac{200}{10} = 20$$

Thus, $DE = \mathbf{20}$.

Examples

5. A pole 10 feet high casts a 15-foot-long shadow on level ground. At the same time a man casts a shadow that is 9 feet in length. How tall is the man?

Solution: By assuming that the shadows are perpendicular to the pole and the man, you may use right triangles to represent these situations, where x represents the height of the man.

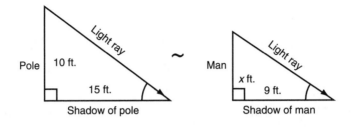

Pole 10 ft.

Light ray

15 ft.

Shadow of pole

~

Man

x ft.

Light ray

9 ft.

Shadow of man

Also assume that in each triangle the light rays make angles with the ground that have the same degree measure. Since all right angles have the same degree measure, the two right triangles are similar and the lengths of their sides are in proportion.

$$\frac{\text{Height of pole}}{\text{Height of man}} = \frac{\text{Shadow of pole}}{\text{Shadow of man}}$$

$$\frac{10}{x} = \frac{15}{9}$$

$$\frac{10}{x} = \frac{5}{3}$$

$$5x = 3(10)$$

$$x = \frac{30}{5} = 6$$

The man is **6 feet** tall.

6. In $\triangle RST$, line segment $\overline{EF}$ is parallel to side $\overline{RT}$ and intersects side $\overline{RS}$ at point E and side $\overline{TS}$ at point F.

(a) If $SE = 8$, $ER = 6$, and $FT = 15$, find SF.

(b) If $SE = 6$, $ER = 4$, and $FT = 6$, find ST.

(c) If $ER = 5$, $EF = 8$, and RT is 2 more than SE, find SE.

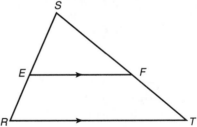

Solutions: Since $\overline{EF} \parallel \overline{RT}$, $\angle E \cong \angle R$ and $\angle F \cong \angle T$. Hence, $\triangle ESF \sim \triangle RST$.

(a) Let $SF = x$. Then $ST = x + 15$. Since the lengths of corresponding sides of similar triangles are in proportion,

$$\frac{SE}{SR} = \frac{SF}{ST}$$

$$\frac{8}{8+6} = \frac{x}{x+15}$$

$$\frac{8}{14} = \frac{x}{x+15}$$

215

$$14x = 8(x + 15)$$
$$= 8x + 120$$
$$6x = 120$$
$$x = \frac{120}{6} = 20$$

Hence, $SF = \textbf{20}$.

(b) Let $ST = x$. Then $SF = x - 6$. Since the lengths of corresponding sides of similar triangles are in proportion,

$$\frac{SE}{SR} = \frac{SF}{ST}$$
$$\frac{6}{6+4} = \frac{x-6}{x}$$
$$\frac{6}{10} = \frac{x-6}{x}$$
$$10(x-6) = 6x$$
$$10x - 60 = 6x$$
$$4x = 60$$
$$x = \frac{60}{4} = 15$$

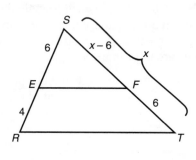

Hence, $ST = \textbf{15}$.

(c) Let $SE = x$. Then $RT = x + 2$. Since the lengths of corresponding sides of similar triangles are in proportion,

$$\frac{SE}{SR} = \frac{EF}{RT}$$
$$\frac{x}{x+5} = \frac{8}{x+2}$$
$$x(x+2) = 8(x+5)$$
$$x^2 + 2x = 8x + 40$$
$$x^2 - 6x - 40 = 0$$
$$(x-10)(x+4) = 0$$
$$x - 10 = 0 \text{ or } x + 4 = 0$$
$$x = 10 \text{ or } \quad x = -4$$

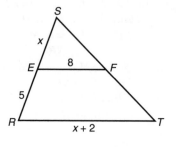

Reject $x = -4$ since x represents the length of a segment. Thus, $SE = \textbf{10}$.

Exercise Set 8.2

1. Triangle $GAL \sim \triangle SHE$. Name three pairs of congruent angles and three equal ratios.

2. The ratio of perimeters of two similar polygons is $3 : 5$. If the length of the shortest side of the smaller polygon is 24, find the length of the shortest side of the larger polygon.

3. Triangle $ZAP \sim \triangle MYX$. If $ZA = 3$, $AP = 12$, $ZP = 21$, and $YX = 20$, find the lengths of the remaining sides of $\triangle MYX$.

4. Quadrilateral $ABCD \sim$ quadrilateral $RSTW$. The lengths of the sides of quadrilateral $ABCD$ are $3, 6, 9$, and 15. If the length of the longest side of quadrilateral $RSTW$ is 20, find the perimeter of $RSTW$.

5. The length of the longest side of a polygon exceeds twice the length of the longest side of a similar polygon by 3. If the ratio of similitude of the polygons is $4 : 9$, find the length of the longest side of each polygon.

6. Triangle $RST \sim \triangle JKL$.
  (a) $\overline{RA}$ and $\overline{JB}$ are medians to sides $\overline{ST}$ and $\overline{KL}$, respectively. $RS = 10$ and $JK = 15$. If the length of $\overline{JB}$ exceeds the length of $\overline{RA}$ by 4, find the lengths of medians $\overline{JB}$ and $\overline{RA}$.
  (b) $\overline{SH}$ and $\overline{KO}$ are altitudes to sides $\overline{RT}$ and $\overline{JL}$, respectively. If $SH = 12$, $KO = 15$, $LK = 3x - 2$, and $TS = 2x + 1$, find the lengths of $\overline{LK}$ and $\overline{TS}$.
  (c) The perimeter of $\triangle RST$ is 25 and the perimeter of $\triangle JKL$ is 40. If $ST = 3x + 1$ and $KL = 4x + 4$, find the lengths of $\overline{ST}$ and $\overline{KL}$.
  (d) The ratio of perimeters of $\triangle RST$ and $\triangle JKL$ is $3 : x$. The length of altitude $\overline{SU}$ is $x - 4$, and the length of altitude $\overline{KV}$ is 15. Find the length of altitude $\overline{SU}$.

7. A person 5 feet tall is standing near a tree 30 feet high. If the person's shadow is 4 feet long, how many feet long is the shadow of the tree?

8. In the accompanying diagram, $\overline{DE} \parallel \overline{BC}$, $AD = 8$, $AB = 12$, and $EC = 5$. Find AE.

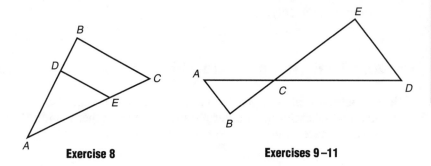

Exercise 8   **Exercises 9–11**

9–11. In the accompanying figure, $\overline{AB} \perp \overline{BE}$ and $\overline{DE} \perp \overline{BE}$.

9. If $AB = 4$, $BC = 2$, and $DE = 6$, find EC.

10. If $BC = 5$, $BE = 15$, and $AC = 3$, find DC.

11. If $AC = 8$, $DC = 12$, and $BE = 15$, find BC.

12. In $\triangle PRT$, K is a point on $\overline{TP}$ and G is a point on $\overline{TR}$ such that $\overline{KG} \parallel \overline{PR}$. If $TP = 20$, $KP = 4$, and $GR = 7$, find TG.

13. Given $\triangle ABC$, $\triangle DEF$, $\angle A \cong \angle D$, $\angle B \cong \angle E$, $AB = 4$, $DF = 6$, $DE = x$, and $AC = x + 5$.
    (a) Write an equation in terms of x that can be used to find DE.
    (b) Find DE.

14. In the accompanying diagram of $\triangle ABC$, D is a point on $\overline{AB}$, E is a point on $\overline{BC}$, and $\overline{DE} \parallel \overline{AC}$. If $BD = 5$, $DA = x + 2$, $BE = x + 4$, and $EC = 2x + 4$, find x.

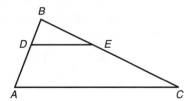

15. In right triangle ABC, $\angle C$ is a right angle. Point D is on leg $\overline{AC}$, and point E is on hypotenuse $\overline{AB}$ with $\overline{AD} \perp \overline{DE}$.
    (a) If $AD = 8$, $DE = 6$, $CD = 3x + 1$, and $BC = x + 13$, find the value of x.
    (b) If $BC = 20$, CD is 3 less than AD, and DE is 3 more than AD, find AD.

8.3 PROOFS INVOLVING SIMILAR TRIANGLES

KEY IDEAS

To prove that two triangles are similar, show that two angles of one triangle are congruent to two angles of the second triangle (AA Theorem of Similarity).

Proving That Triangles Are Similar

Unlike congruence proofs, proofs that use the AA Theorem of Similarity to prove that two triangles are similar require that *two*, rather than three, pairs of parts (in this case, angles) be proved congruent.

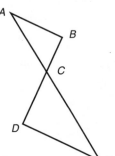

Example

    1. Given: $\overline{CB} \perp \overline{BA}$, $\overline{CD} \perp \overline{DE}$.
       Prove: $\triangle ABC \sim \triangle EDC$.

Solution:

PLAN. Use the AA theorem. The two triangles include right and vertical angles that yield two pairs of congruent angles.

PROOF

Statement	Reason
1. $\overline{CB} \perp \overline{BA}$, $\overline{CD} \perp \overline{DE}$	1. Given.
2. Angles ABC and EDC are right angles.	2. Perpendicular lines intersect to form right angles.
3. $\angle ABC \cong \angle EDC$ *Angle*	3. All right angles are congruent.
4. $\angle ACB \cong \angle ECD$ *Angle*	4. Vertical angles are congruent.
5. $\triangle ABC \sim \triangle EDC$	5. AA theorem.

Using Similar Triangles to Prove That Lengths of Segments Are in Proportion

To establish that the lengths of four segments are in proportion, first show that a pair of triangles that contain these segments as corresponding sides are similar. Then apply the reverse of the definition of similarity and conclude that the lengths of the segments are in proportion, using as a reason: *The lengths of corresponding sides of similar triangles are in proportion.*

Examples

2. Given: $\overline{AB} \parallel \overline{DE}$.

    Prove: $\dfrac{EC}{BC} = \dfrac{ED}{AB}$.

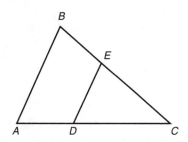

Solution:

PLAN. *Step 1.* Select the triangles that contain these segments as sides. Read across the proportion:

$$\triangle ECD$$
$$\frac{EC}{BC} = \frac{ED}{AB}$$
$$\triangle BCA$$

219

Step 2. Mark on the diagram the "Given" and all pairs of corresponding congruent angles.

Step 3. Write the proof.

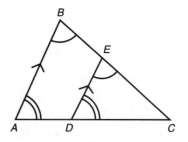

PROOF

Statement	Reason
1. $AB \parallel DE$	1. Given.
2. $\angle CED \cong \angle CBA$, *Angle* $\angle CDE \cong \angle CAB$ *Angle*	2. If two lines are parallel, then their corresponding angles are congruent.
3. $\triangle ECD \sim \triangle BCA$	3. AA theorem.
4. $\dfrac{EC}{BC} = \dfrac{ED}{AB}$	4. The lengths of corresponding sides of similar triangles are in proportion.

In this proof:

- If the original proportion in the "Prove" had been written as $\dfrac{EC}{ED} = \dfrac{BC}{AB}$, then reading *across* the proportion would *not* yield the vertices of the triangles to be proved similar. In that case, reading down each ratio would give the required triangles:

$$\left(\frac{EC}{ED}\right) = \left(\frac{BC}{AB}\right)$$
$$\longrightarrow \triangle ECD \sim \triangle BCA \longleftarrow$$

- Statement 3 establishes the following relationship: *A line intersecting two sides of a triangle and parallel to the third side forms a triangle similar to the original triangle.*

3. Given: $\overline{AC} \perp \overline{CB}, \overline{ED} \perp \overline{AB}$.
   Prove: $EB : AB = ED : AC$.

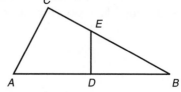

Solution:

PLAN. *Step 1.* Rewrite the proportion in the "Prove" in fractional form as $\dfrac{EB}{AB} = \dfrac{ED}{AC}$.

Step 2. Determine the pair of triangles that must be proved similar.

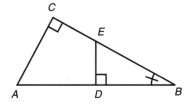

$$\triangle EBD$$
$$\frac{EB}{AB} = \frac{ED}{AC}$$
$$\triangle ABC$$

Step 3. Mark on the diagram the "Given" and all pairs of corresponding congruent angle pairs.

Step 4. Write the proof.

PROOF

Statement	Reason
1. $\overline{AC} \perp \overline{CB}$, $\overline{ED} \perp \overline{AB}$	1. Given.
2. Angles C and EDB are right angles.	2. Perpendicular lines intersect to form right angles.
3. $\angle C \cong \angle EDB$ *Angle*	3. All right angles are congruent.
4. $\angle B \cong \angle B$ *Angle*	4. Reflexive property of congruence.
5. $\triangle EBD \sim \triangle ABC$	5. AA theorem.
6. $EB{:}AB = ED{:}AC$	6. The lengths of corresponding sides of similar triangles are in proportion.

Using Similar Triangles to Prove That Products of Segment Lengths Are Equal

If $\frac{A}{B} = \frac{C}{D}$, then $A \times D = B \times C$. The reason is that in a proportion the product of the means equals the product of the extremes. Instead of generating a product from a proportion, it is sometimes necessary to be able to take a product and determine the related proportion that would yield that product.

Suppose that the lengths of four segments are related in such a way that

$$KM \times LB = LM \times KD.$$

What proportion gives this result when the products of its means and extremes are set equal to each other? A true proportion may be derived from the product by making a pair of terms appearing on the same side of the equal sign (say, *KM* and *LB*) the extremes. The pair of terms on the opposite side of the equal sign (*LM* and *KD*) then become the means:

$$\frac{KM}{LM} = \frac{KD}{LB}.$$

Note that an equivalent proportion results if *KM* and *LB* are made the means rather than the extremes.

This analysis will be useful in the example that follows.

Example

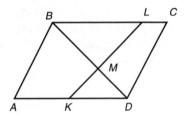

4. Given: *ABCD* is a parallelogram.
   Prove: $KM \times LB = LM \times KD.$

Solution:

PLAN. Analyze the solution to this type of problem by *working backward,* beginning with the "Prove."

Step 1. Express the product as an equivalent proportion (this was accomplished in the discussion that preceded this example).

$$\frac{KM}{LM} = \frac{KD}{LB}$$

Step 2. From the proportion (and, in some problems, in conjunction with the "Given"), determine the pair of triangles to be proved similar.

$$\triangle KMD$$
$$\frac{KM}{LM} = \frac{KD}{LB}$$
$$\triangle LMB$$

Step 3. Mark on the diagram the "Given," and decide how to show the triangles similar.
STRATEGY: Use the AA theorem.

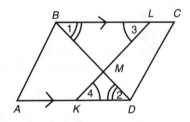

Step 4. Write the formal two-column proof. The steps in the proof should reflect the logic of this analysis, proceeding from step 4 back to step 1 (proving the triangles similar, forming the appropriate proportion, and, lastly, writing the product):

PROOF

Statement	Reason
1. $\square ABCD$	1. Given.
2. $\overline{AD} \parallel \overline{BC}$	2. Opposite sides of a parallelogram are parallel.
3. $\angle 1 \cong \angle 2$, $\angle 3 \cong \angle 4$	3. If two lines are parallel, then their alternate interior angles are congruent.
4. $\triangle KMD \sim \triangle LMB$	4. AA theorem.
5. $\dfrac{KM}{LM} = \dfrac{KD}{LB}$	5. The lengths of corresponding sides of similar triangles are in proportion.
6. $KM \times LB = LM \times KD$	6. In a proportion, the product of the means equals the product of the extremes.

In developing the plan for the proof in Example 4, suppose you formed the proportion

$$\frac{KM}{KD} = \frac{LM}{LB}.$$

Reading across the top (K-M-L), we do not find a set of letters that correspond to the vertices of a triangle. When this happens, read down rather than across. Reading down the first ration (K-M-D) gives the vertices of one of the desired triangles, and reading down the second ratio (L-M-B) gives the vertices of the other triangle.

SUMMARY

To prove that the products of the lengths of the sides of two triangles are equal, follow these steps:

Step 1. From the product, write a proportion by making one pair of factors the means and the other pair of factors the extremes.

Step 2. Use the proportion to identify the triangles that contain the desired segments as sides.

Step 3. Mark on the diagram the "Given," as well as any additional congruent parts resulting from vertical angles, right angles, congruent alternate interior angles, and so forth.

Step 4. Write the formal proof:

- Prove that the triangles are similar.
- Write the desired proportion, using as a reason: *Lengths of corresponding sides of similar triangles are in proportion.*
- Write the desired product, using as a reason: *In a proportion the product of the means equals the product of the extremes.*

Exercise Set 8.3

1. Given: $\overline{XW} \cong \overline{XY}$,
$\overline{HA} \perp \overline{WY}$, $\overline{KB} \perp \overline{WY}$
Prove: $\triangle HWA \sim \triangle KYB$.

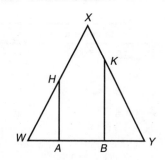

2. Given: $\triangle ABC$ with $\overline{AB} \cong \overline{BC}$.
Points D, E, and F are on $\overline{AB}$,
$\overline{BC}$, and $\overline{AC}$, respectively, so
that $\overline{ED} \perp \overline{DF}$, $\overline{DF} \perp \overline{AC}$, and
$\overline{FE} \perp \overline{BC}$.
Prove: **(a)** $\triangle FEC \sim \triangle EDF$.
(b) $\triangle EDF \sim \triangle DFA$.

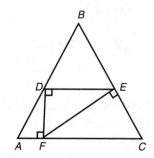

3. Given: Rectangle $DEFG$,
$\triangle ABC$ with a right angle at B,
$\overline{AEB}$, $\overline{BDC}$, $\overline{AFGC}$.
Prove: $\dfrac{AE}{ED} = \dfrac{EF}{BD}$.

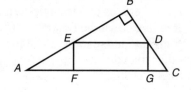

4. Given: $\overline{HW} \parallel \overline{TA}$, $\overline{HY} \parallel \overline{AX}$.
Prove: $\dfrac{AX}{HY} = \dfrac{AT}{HW}$.

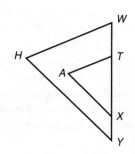

5. Given: $\overline{MN} \parallel \overline{AT}$,
$\angle 1 \cong \angle 2$.
Prove: $\dfrac{NT}{AT} = \dfrac{RN}{RT}$.

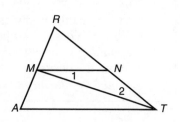

6. Given: $\triangle ABC$, $\overline{CD}$ is the altitude to $\overline{AB}$, $\overline{AR} \cong \overline{BR}$, $\overline{AR}$ intersects $\overline{CD}$ at E.

Prove: $AD \times DC = BD \times DE$.

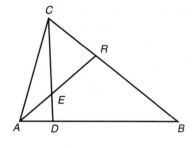

7. Given: $\overline{SR} \cong \overline{SQ}$, $\overline{RQ}$ bisects $\angle SRW$.

Prove: $\dfrac{SQ}{RW} = \dfrac{SP}{PW}$.

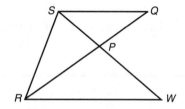

8. Given: Parallelogram $ABCD$, $\overline{AC}$ bisects $\angle FAB$, and $\overline{AG} \cong \overline{AE}$.

Prove: $\triangle AHG \sim \triangle CHD$.

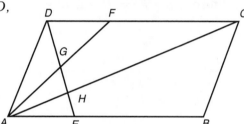

9. Given: $\overline{MC} \perp \overline{JK}$, $\overline{PM} \perp \overline{MQ}$, $\overline{TP} \cong \overline{TM}$.

Prove: $\dfrac{PM}{MC} = \dfrac{PQ}{MK}$.

10. Given: T is the midpoint of $\overline{PQ}$, $\overline{MP} \cong \overline{MQ}$, $\overline{JK} \parallel \overline{MQ}$.

Prove: $\dfrac{PM}{JK} = \dfrac{TQ}{JT}$.

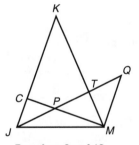

Exercises 9 and 10

11. Given: $\overline{EF}$ is the median of trapezoid $ABCD$.

Prove: $EI \times GH = IH \times EF$.

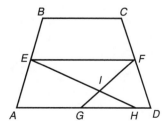

225

12. Given: $\overline{RS} \perp \overline{ST}$, $\overline{SW} \perp \overline{RT}$.
Prove: $(ST)^2 = TW \times RT$.

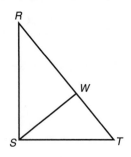

13. Given: $\overline{BH} \perp \overline{AC}$, $\overline{AF} \perp \overline{BC}$.
Prove: $BH : AF = BC : AC$.

14. Given: $\overline{AF}$ bisects $\angle BAC$,
$\overline{BH}$ bisects $\angle ABC$,
$\overline{BC} \cong \overline{AC}$.
Prove: $AH \times EF = BF \times EH$.

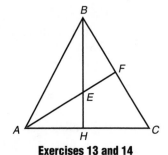

Exercises 13 and 14

15. Given: $\overline{XY} \parallel \overline{LK}$, $\overline{XZ} \parallel \overline{JK}$.
Prove: $JY \times ZL = XZ \times KZ$.

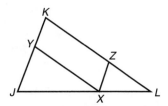

16. Given: $ABCD$ is a parallelogram,
$\overline{CB}$ is extended through B to E,
$\overline{DE}$ is drawn intersecting $\overline{AB}$ at F.
(a) Prove: $\dfrac{EB}{DA} = \dfrac{BF}{AF}$.
(b) If $EF = 6$, DF is 5 less
than EB, and AD is 3
less than EB, find EB.

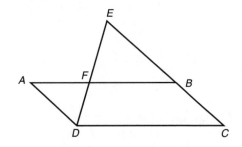

17. Given: Quadrilateral $ABCD$,
$\overline{AB} \perp \overline{BC}$, $\overline{AB} \perp \overline{AD}$,
$\overline{AC} \perp \overline{CD}$.
Prove: $BC \times AD = (AC)^2$.

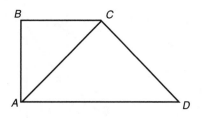

18. Given: $\triangle ABC$ with $\overline{CDA}$, $\overline{CEB}$, $\overline{AFB}$,
$\overline{DE} \parallel \overline{AB}$, $\overline{EF} \parallel \overline{AC}$,
$\overline{CF}$ intersects $\overline{DE}$ at G.
Prove: **(a)** $\triangle CAF \sim \triangle FEG$.
(b) $DG \times GF = EG \times GC$.

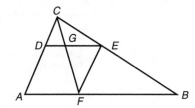

19. Given: $\triangle ABC$ with $\overline{ABE}$, $\overline{ADC}$,
$\overline{BD}$ bisects $\angle ABC$,
$\overline{EC} \parallel \overline{BD}$.
Prove: **(a)** $\dfrac{AD}{DC} = \dfrac{AB}{BE}$.

(b) If $AD = 6$, $DC = 9$, AB is represented by x, and BE is represented by $x + 4$, find x.

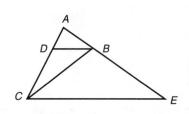

8.4 PROPORTIONS IN A RIGHT TRIANGLE

KEY IDEAS

In the accompanying right triangle, $\overline{CD}$ is the altitude to
hypotenuse $\overline{AB}$. $\overline{CD}$ separates
right triangle ABC into similar
triangles such that:

$$\frac{x}{b} = \frac{b}{c}, \quad \frac{y}{a} = \frac{a}{c}, \quad \frac{x}{h} = \frac{h}{y}.$$

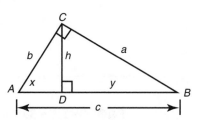

Mean Proportion Altitude Theorem

This theorem states that the altitude to the hypotenuse of a right triangle divides the triangle into two smaller right triangles that are similar to each other.

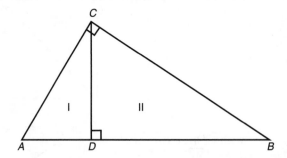

Figure 8.4 Similar Triangles Formed by an Altitude Drawn to the Hypotenuse of a Right Triangle

In Figure 8.4, $\triangle$I ~ $\triangle$II. Since the lengths of corresponding sides of similar triangles are in proportion,

$$\frac{\text{Hypotenuse segment}}{\text{Altitude}} = \frac{\text{Altitude}}{\text{Other hypotenuse segment}}$$

$$\frac{AD}{CD} = \frac{CD}{BD}.$$

Mean Proportion Leg Theorem

This theorem states that the altitude to the hypotenuse of a right triangle divides the triangle into two smaller right triangles each of which is similar to the original triangle. In Figure 8.4, $\triangle$I ~ $\triangle ACB$ and $\triangle$II ~ $\triangle ACB$. For each pair of similar triangles

$$\frac{\text{Segment next to leg}}{\text{Leg}} = \frac{\text{Leg}}{\text{Whole hypotenuse}},$$

$$\frac{AD}{AC} = \frac{AC}{AB} \quad \text{and} \quad \frac{BD}{BC} = \frac{BC}{AB},$$

| MATH FACTS |

PROPORTIONS IN A RIGHT TRIANGLE

If in a right triangle the altitude is drawn to the hypotenuse, then:

- either leg is the mean proportional between the hypotenuse and the segment of the hypotenuse adjacent to that leg, and
- the altitude is the mean proportional between the two segments of the hypotenuse.

Examples

1. In each case, find the value of x.

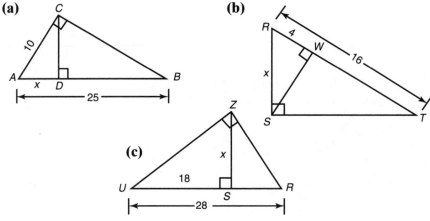

(a)

(b)

(c)

Solutions: **(a)** $\dfrac{AD}{AC} = \dfrac{AC}{AB}$ $\left(\dfrac{\text{Hyp segment}}{\text{Leg}} = \dfrac{\text{Leg}}{\text{Hyp}}\right)$

$$\frac{x}{10} = \frac{10}{25}$$

$$25x = 100$$

$$x = \frac{100}{25} = \mathbf{4}$$

(b) $\dfrac{RW}{RS} = \dfrac{RS}{RT}$ $\left(\dfrac{\text{Hyp segment}}{\text{Leg}} = \dfrac{\text{Leg}}{\text{Hyp}}\right)$

$$\frac{4}{x} = \frac{x}{16}$$

$$x^2 = 64$$

$$x = \sqrt{64} = \mathbf{8}$$

(c) $\dfrac{US}{ZS} = \dfrac{ZS}{RS}$ $\left(\dfrac{\text{Hyp segment 1}}{\text{Altitude}} = \dfrac{\text{Altitude}}{\text{Hyp segment 2}}\right)$

$$\frac{18}{x} = \frac{x}{8} \qquad \text{NOTE: } RS = 26 - 18 = 8$$

$$x^2 = 144$$

$$x = \sqrt{144} = \mathbf{12}$$

2. In right triangle JKL, $\angle K$ is the right angle. Altitude $\overline{KH}$ is drawn in such a way that the length of $\overline{JH}$ exceeds the length of $\overline{HL}$ by 5. If $KH = 6$, find the length of the hypotenuse.

Solution: Let x = length of $\overline{LH}$.
Then $x + 5$ = length of $\overline{JH}$.

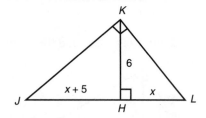

$$\frac{x}{6} = \frac{6}{x+5} \quad \left(\frac{\text{Hyp segment 1}}{\text{Altitude}} = \frac{\text{Altitude}}{\text{Hyp segment 2}}\right)$$

$x(x + 5) = 36$

$x^2 + 5x = 36$

$x^2 + 5x - 36 = 36 - 36$

$x^2 + 5x - 36 = 0$

$(x + 9)(x - 4) = 0$

$x + 9 = 0$ or $x - 4 = 0$

$\quad x = -9 \qquad\qquad x = 4$

(Reject since a $LH = x = 4$
length cannot be a $JH = x + 5 = 9$
negative number.)

JL (hypotenuse length) $= 4 + 9 =$ **13**.

Exercise Set 8.4

1–3. In each case, find the value of r, s, and t. (Answers may be left in radical form.)

1.

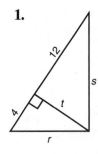

2.

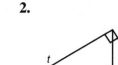

3.

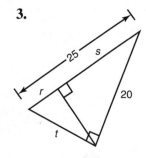

4–9. In right triangle JKL, ∠K is the right angle and $\overline{KH} \perp \overline{JL}$.

4. If $JH = 4$ and $HL = 16$, find KH.   **8.** If $JK = 14$, $HL = 21$, find JH.

5. If $JH = 5$ and $HL = 4$, find KL.   **9.** If $KH = 12$, $JL = 40$, find JK
                                                            (assume $\overline{JK}$ is the shorter leg of
6. If $JH = 8$, $JL = 20$, find KH.   right triangle JKL).

7. If $KL = 18$, $JL = 27$, find JK.

10. The altitude drawn to the hypotenuse of a right triangle divides the hypotenuse into segments such that their lengths are in the ratio of 1 : 4. If the length of the altitude is 8, find the length of:
   (a) each segment of the hypotenuse
   (b) the longer leg of the triangle

11. The altitude drawn to the hypotenuse of a right triangle divides the hypotenuse into segments of lengths 2 and 8. Find the length of the altitude.

12. In right triangle ABC, altitude $\overline{CD}$ is drawn to the hypotenuse. If $AD = 4$ and $DB = 5$, find AC.

13. If the altitude drawn to the hypotenuse of a right triangle has length 8, the lengths of the segments of the hypotenuse may be
   (1) 4 and 16   (2) 2 and 4   (3) 3 and 5   (4) 32 and 32

14. In $\triangle ABC$, m$\angle C = 90$ and $\overline{CD}$ is the altitude to hypotenuse $\overline{AB}$.
   (a) If $CD = 12$ and $AD = 6$, find the length of $\overline{DB}$.
   (b) If $AD = 5$ and $DB = 15$, find the length of $\overline{AC}$.

15–19. In each case, solve algebraically.

15. In right triangle ABC, $\overline{CD}$ is the altitude to hypotenuse $\overline{AB}$. If $CD = 12$, $AD = x$, and BD is 7 more than AD, find x.

16. In right triangle ABC, altitude $\overline{CD}$ is drawn to hypotenuse $\overline{AB}$. If $AC = 4$ and DB is 4 more than the length of $\overline{AD}$, find AD.

17. In right triangle RST, altitude $\overline{TP}$ is drawn to hypotenuse $\overline{RS}$. If $TP = 6$ and RP is 9 less than PS, find the length of hypotenuse $\overline{RS}$.

18. In right triangle ABC, altitude $\overline{CD}$ is drawn to hypotenuse $\overline{AB}$. If AB is four times as large as AD and AC is 3 more than AD, find the length of $\overline{AD}$.

19. In right triangle ABC, altitude $\overline{CD}$ is drawn to hypotenuse $\overline{AB}$. If AD is 12 and DB is 3 less than the altitude, find the length of $\overline{CD}$.

8.5 THE PYTHAGOREAN THEOREM

KEY IDEAS

The Pythagorean theorem states that the lengths of the sides of a *right* triangle satisfy the following relationship:

$$(\text{Leg}_1)^2 + (\text{Leg}_2)^2 = (\text{Hypotenuse})^2,$$
$$a^2 + b^2 = c^2.$$

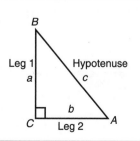

Applying the Pythagorean Theorem

When the lengths of any two sides of a right triangle are known, the Pythagorean relationship provides a way of determining the length of the remaining side.

Examples

1. For each right triangle, find the value of x.

(a)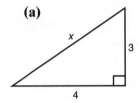

(b)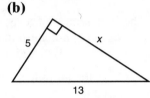

(c)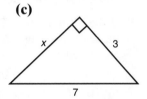

Solutions:

(a) $3^2 + 4^2 = x^2$
$9 + 16 = x$
$25 = x^2$
$\sqrt{x^2} = \pm \sqrt{25}$
$x = 5$

(b) $x^2 + 5^2 = 13^2$
$x^2 + 25 = 169$
$x^2 = 169 - 25$
$\sqrt{x^2} = \pm \sqrt{144}$
$x = 12$

(c) $x^2 + 3^2 = 7^2$
$x^2 + 9 = 49$
$x^2 = 49 - 9$
$\sqrt{x^2} = \pm \sqrt{40}$
$x = \sqrt{40}$
$= \sqrt{4} \cdot \sqrt{10}$
$= 2\sqrt{10}$

In each of these examples, the negative value of x is discarded since the length of a side of a triangle cannot be negative.

2. If the length of a diagonal of a square is 10, what is the length of a side of the square?

Solution: Let $x =$ length of a side of the square.

A diagonal of a square (or rectangle) is a line segment that connects any two nonconsecutive corners (called **vertices**) of the figure, thus forming two right triangles.

Apply the Pythagorean relationship in right triangle ABC:

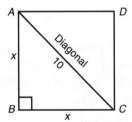

$x^2 + x^2 = 10^2$
$2x^2 = 100$
$x^2 = \dfrac{100}{2}$
$x = \sqrt{50} = \sqrt{25}\sqrt{2} = 5\sqrt{2}$

3. The perimeter of a right triangle is 60. If the length of the hypotenuse is 26, find the length of the shorter leg of the triangle.

Solution: The sum of the lengths of the legs = $60 - 26 = 34$.

$$\text{Let } x = \text{length of shorter leg.}$$
$$\text{Then } 34 - x = \text{length of remaining leg.}$$
$$x^2 + (34 - x)^2 = 26^2$$
$$x^2 + x^2 - 68x + 1156 = 676$$
$$2x^2 - 68x + 1156 - 676 = 0$$
$$2x^2 - 68x + 480 = 0$$
$$\frac{2x^2}{2} - \frac{68x}{2} + \frac{480}{2} = \frac{0}{2}$$
$$x^2 - 34x + 240 = 0$$
$$(x - 10)(x - 24) = 0$$
$$(x - 10 = 0) \text{ or } (x - 24 = 0)$$
$$x = 10 \text{ or } \qquad x = 24$$

The length of the shorter leg of the right triangle is **10**.

Pythagorean Triples

A **Pythagorean triple** is a set of positive integers $\{a, b, c\}$ that satisfy the equation $a^2 + b^2 = c^2$. There are many Pythagorean triples. The sets

$$\{3, 4, 5\} \quad \text{and} \quad \{5, 12, 13\} \quad \text{and} \quad \{8, 15, 17\}$$

are commonly encountered Pythagorean triples. Observe that:

$3^2 + 4^2 = 5^2$	$5^2 + 12^2 = 13^2$	$8^2 + 15^2 = 17^2$
$9 + 16 \mid 25$	$25 + 144 \mid 169$	$64 + 225 \mid 289$
$25 = 25\checkmark$	$169 = 169\checkmark$	$289 = 289\checkmark$

Whole-number multiples of any Pythagorean triple also comprise a Pythagorean triple. For example, if each member of the set $\{3, 4, 5\}$ is multiplied by 2, the set $\{6, 8, 10\}$ that is obtained is also a Pythagorean triple since $6^2 + 8^2 = 10^2$ ($36 + 64 = 100$). If each member of the set $\{3, 4, 5\}$ is multiplied by 3, the set $\{9, 12, 15\}$, which is also a Pythagorean triple since $9^2 + 12^2 = 15^2$ ($81 + 144 = 225$), is obtained.

Examples

4. Which of the following is *not* a Pythagorean triple?
    (1) $\{9, 40, 41\}$ (2) $\{15, 20, 25\}$ (3) $\{8, 12, 17\}$ (4) $\{10, 24, 26\}$

Solution: Choice (1) represents a Pythagorean triple since

$$9^2 + 40^2 = 41^2$$
$$81 + 1600 \mid 1681$$
$$1681 = 1681.\checkmark$$

Choice (2) is a multiple of $\{3, 4, 5\}$ where each element is multiplied by 5. Choice (4) is a multiple of $\{5, 12, 13\}$ where each element is multiplied by 2. In choice (3) you can easily verify that $8^2 + 12^2 \neq 17^2$, so $\{8, 12, 17\}$ is *not* a Pythagorean triple.

The correct answer is **choice (3)**.

5. The perimeter of an isosceles triangle is 36, and the length of the base is 10. Find the length of the altitude drawn to the base.

Solution: The sum of the lengths of the legs $= 36 - 10$, or 26, so that the length of each leg is 13. The altitude drawn to the base of an isosceles triangle bisects the base so that a 5-12-13 right triangle is formed.

The length of the altitude drawn to the base is **12**.

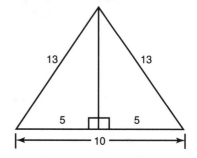

6. The lengths of the diagonals of a rhombus are 18 and 24. Find the length of a side of the rhombus.

Solution: Recall that the diagonals of a rhombus bisect each other and intersect at right angles.

The lengths of the sides of $\triangle AED$ form a multiple of a 3-4-5 right triangle. Each member of the triple is multiplied by 3. Hence, the length of the hypotenuse is $3 \cdot 5$, or 15.

Side $\overline{AD}$ of the rhombus has a length of **15**.

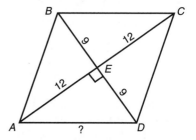

7. Each leg of an isosceles trapezoid has a length of 17. The lengths of its bases are 9 and 39. Find the length of an altitude.

Solution: Drop two altitudes, one from each of the upper vertices.

Quadrilateral $BEFC$ is a rectangle (since $\overline{BE}$ and $\overline{CF}$ are congruent, are parallel, and intersect $\overline{AD}$ at right angles). Hence $BC = EF = 9$. Since right triangle $AEB \cong$ right triangle DFC, $AE = DF = 15$. Triangle AEB is an 8-15-17 right triangle, where 17 is the length of the hypotenuse. The length of an altitude is **8**.

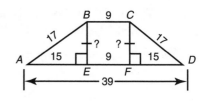

Converse of the Pythagorean Relationship

If the lengths of the sides of a triangle satisfy the Pythagorean relationship, then the triangle is a right triangle.

Example

8. The lengths of the sides of a triangle are 2, $\sqrt{5}$, and 3. Determine whether the triangle is a right triangle.

Solution:
$$2^2 + (\sqrt{5})^2 \overset{?}{=} 3^2$$
$$\begin{array}{c|c} 4+5 & 9 \\ & 9 = 9 \checkmark \end{array}$$

Therefore the **triangle is a right triangle**.

Exercise Set 8.5

1–4. In each case, find the value of x. Whenever appropriate, answers may be left in radical form.)

1. 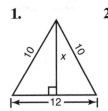   **2.** 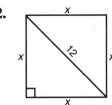   **3.** 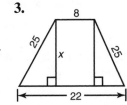   **4.**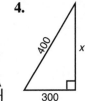

5. If the lengths of the diagonals of a rhombus are 12 and 16, find the perimeter of the rhombus.

6. If the perimeter of a rhombus is 164 and the length of the longer diagonal is 80, find the length of the shorter diagonal.

7. Find the length of the altitude drawn to a side of an equilateral triangle whose perimeter is 30.

8. The length of the base of an isosceles triangle is 14. If the length of the altitude drawn to the base is 5, find the length of each of the legs of the triangle.

9. In a right triangle, one leg has length 7 and the hypotenuse has length 10. What is the length, in radical form, of the other leg?

10. Find the length of a diagonal of a rectangle whose length is 9 and whose width is 12.

11. The length of the hypotenuse of a right triangle exceeds the length of the longer leg by 1. If the length of the shorter leg is 7, find the length of the longer leg.

12. Find the length of a diagonal of a square whose perimeter is 16.

13. If the hypotenuse of an isosceles right triangle is 12, find the length of each leg.

14. Determine whether the set $\{3, \sqrt{7}, \text{and } 4\}$ can represent the lengths of the sides of a right triangle.

15. In isosceles triangle ABC, $\overline{AB} \cong \overline{BC}$, and $\overline{BD}$ is the altitude to base $\overline{AC}$. If $BD = x$, $AB = 2x - 1$, and $AC = 2x + 2$, find the length of $\overline{BD}$.

16. In right triangle ABC, $BC = x$, $AC = 8 - x$, and hypotenuse $AB = 6$. Find x. (*Answer may be left in radical form.*)

8.6 SPECIAL RIGHT TRIANGLE RELATIONSHIPS

KEY IDEAS

If the measures of the acute angles of a right triangle are 30 and 60, or 45 and 45, then special relationships exist between the lengths of the sides of the right triangle.

30°-60° Right Triangle Relationships

In a 30°-60° right triangle (Figure 8.5) the following relationships hold:

- The length of the *shorter* leg (the side opposite the 30° angle) is one-half the length of the hypotenuse:

$$AD = \tfrac{1}{2}AB.$$

- The length of the *longer* leg (the side opposite the 60° angle) is one-half the length of the hypotenuse multiplied by $\sqrt{3}$:

$$BD = \tfrac{1}{2}AB \cdot \sqrt{3}.$$

- The length of the *longer* leg is equal to the length of the shorter leg multiplied by $\sqrt{3}$:

$$BD = AD \cdot \sqrt{3}.$$

Figure 8.5 30°-60° Right Triangle

Examples

1. In parallelogram *RSTW*, m∠*R* = 30 and *RS* = 12. Find the length of an altitude.

Solution: Altitude $SH = \frac{1}{2}(12) = \mathbf{6}$.

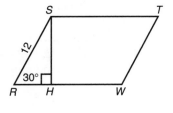

2. In △*JKL*, m∠*K* = 120 and *JK* = 10. Find the length of the altitude drawn from vertex *J* to side $\overline{LK}$ (extended if necessary).

Solution: Since ∠*K* is obtuse, the altitude falls in the exterior of the triangle, intersecting the extension of $\overline{LK}$, say at point *H*. Triangle *JHK* is a 30°-60° right triangle. Hence,

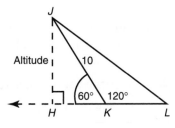

$$JH = \frac{1}{2} \cdot 10 \cdot \sqrt{3} = 5\sqrt{3}.$$

The length of the altitude from vertex *J* to side $\overline{LK}$ is **5√3**.

45°-45° Right Triangle Relationships

In a 45°-45° (isosceles) right triangle (Figure 8.6) the following relationships hold:

- The lengths of the *legs* are equal:

  $$AC = BC.$$

- The length of the *hypotenuse* is equal to the length of either leg multiplied by √2:

  $$AB = AC \cdot \sqrt{2} \text{ or } AB = BC \cdot \sqrt{2}.$$

- The length of either *leg* is equal to one-half the length of the hypotenuse multiplied by √2:

  $$AC \text{ (or } BC) = \frac{1}{2} AB \cdot \sqrt{2}.$$

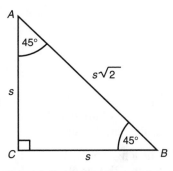

Figure 8.6 45°-45° Right Triangle

Example

3. In isosceles trapezoid *ABCD*, the measure of a lower base angle is 45 and the length of upper base $\overline{BC}$ is 5. If the length of an altitude is 7, find the lengths of the legs, $\overline{AB}$ and $\overline{DC}$.

Solution: Drop altitudes from *B* and *C,* forming two congruent 45°-45° right triangles. $AE = BE = 7$. Also, $FD = 7$. $AB = AE \cdot \sqrt{2} = 7\sqrt{2}$. The length of each leg is $\mathbf{7\sqrt{2}}$.

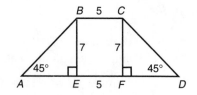

Exercise Set 8.6

1. The measure of the vertex angle of an isosceles triangle is 120, and the length of each leg is 8. Find the length of:
   (a) the altitude drawn to the base   **(b)** the base

2. If the perimeter of a square is 24, find the length of a diagonal.

3. If the length of a diagonal of a square is 18, find the perimeter of the square.

4. Find the length of the altitude drawn to side $\overline{AC}$ of $\triangle ABC$ if $AB = 8$, $AC = 14$, and m$\angle A$ equals:
   (a) 30   **(b)** 120   **(c)** 135

5. The lengths of the bases of an isosceles trapezoid are 9 and 25. Find the length of the altitude and of each of the legs if the measure of each lower base angle is:
   (a) 30   **(b)** 45   **(c)** 60

6. Find the values of *x, y,* and *z.*

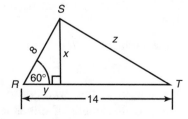

7. The lengths of two adjacent sides of a parallelogram are 6 and 14. If the measure of an included angle is 60, find the length of the shorter diagonal of the parallelogram.

8. The length of each side of a rhombus is 10, and the measure of an angle of the rhombus is 60. Find the length of the longer diagonal of the rhombus.

9. Find the length of a diagonal of a square whose area is:
   (a) 16   **(b)** 25   **(c)** $9x^2$

10. Find the area of an equilateral triangle whose perimeter is:
    (a) 24   **(b)** 30   **(c)** equal to the perimeter of a square of area 81

8.7 AREA FORMULAS

KEY IDEAS

Sometimes it is necessary to apply a special right triangle relationship in order to find the length of a segment needed to determine the area of a special quadrilateral or triangle.

Some Area Formulas

Table 8.1 summarizes area formulas for some special quadrilaterals and triangles.

TABLE 8.1 AREA FORMULAS

Figure	Area =
1. Rectangle	Base × Height
2. Square	Side × Side
3. Parallelogram	Base × Height
4. Triangle	$\frac{1}{2}$ × Base × Height
5. Equilateral triangle	$\frac{1}{4}$ × (Side)^2 × $\sqrt{3}$
6. Trapezoid	$\frac{1}{2}$ × Altitude × Sum of bases
7. Rhombus (or square)	$\frac{1}{2}$ × Diagonal$_1$ × Diagonal$_2$

Examples

1. Find the area of a rectangle whose diagonal is 10 and whose base is 8.

Solution: The height (width) is 6 since $\triangle ABD$ is a 6-8-10 right triangle. Therefore,

$$\text{Area} = \text{Base} \times \text{Height}$$
$$= 8 \times 6 = \textbf{48.}$$

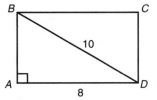

2. The lengths of a pair of adjacent sides of a parallelogram are 6 and 10 centimeters. If the measure of their included angle is 30, find the area of the parallelogram.

Solution: In parallelogram *ABCD*, altitude *BH* = 3 since the length of the side opposite a 30° angle in a 30°-60° right triangle is one-half the length of the hypotenuse (side $\overline{AB}$).

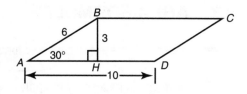

Area of parallelogram *ABCD* = *BH*
$$= AD \cdot BH$$
$$= 10 \cdot 3 = \textbf{30 cm}^2$$

3. In the accompanying figure, *ABCD* is a trapezoid with $\overline{AB} \parallel \overline{CD}$, $\overline{BA} \perp \overline{AD}$, $\overline{CD} \perp \overline{AD}$, *AB* = 10, *BC* = 17, and *AD* = 15. Find the area of trapezoid *ABCD*.

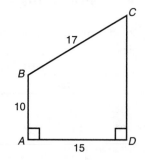

Solution: First find the length of base $\overline{CD}$ by drawing altitude $\overline{BH}$ to $\overline{CD}$. Since parallel lines are everywhere equidistant, *BH* = *AD* = 15. The lengths of the sides of right triangle *BHC* form an 8-15-17 Pythagorean triple, where *CH* = 8. Thus, *CD* = *CH* + *HD* = 8 + 10 = 18.

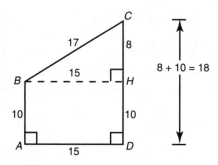

Area of trap *ABCD* = $\frac{1}{2}$ × Altitude × Sum of bases
$$= \frac{1}{2}(BH)(AB + CD)$$
$$= \frac{1}{2}(15)(10 + 18)$$
$$= \frac{1}{2}(15)(28)$$
$$= \frac{1}{2}(420) = \textbf{210}$$

4. Find the area of an isosceles trapezoid the length of whose bases are 8 and 20 and whose lower base angle has a measure of 45.

Solution: Since $\overline{BH}$ is the side opposite the 45° angle in a 45°-45° right triangle, $BH = AH = 6$.

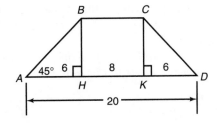

Area of isosceles trap $ABCD = \frac{1}{2} \times$ Altitude $\times$ Sum of bases

$$= \frac{1}{2} BH(AD + BC)$$

$$= \frac{1}{2}(6)(20 + 8)$$

$$= 3(28) = \mathbf{84}$$

5. The length of the longer diagonal of a rhombus is 24, and the length of a side is 13. Find the area of the rhombus.

Solution: As the accompanying diagram illustrates, the triangle that contains one-half of the length of the shorter diagonal is a 5-12-13 right triangle, so the length of the shorter diagonal is 2×5, or 10.

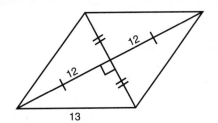

Area of rhombus $= \frac{1}{2} \times$ Diagonal$_1 \times$ Diagonal$_2$

$$= \frac{1}{2}(10 \times 24)$$

$$= \frac{1}{2}(240) = \mathbf{120}$$

Exercise Set 8.7

1. Find the area of each of the following:
   (a) a rectangle whose base is 6 and whose diagonal is 10
   (b) a square whose diagonal is 8
   (c) a parallelogram having two adjacent sides of 12 and 15 centimeters and an included angle of measure 60 (answer may be left in radical form)

2. Find the dimensions of each of the following:
   (a) a rectangle whose area is 75 and whose base and altitude are in the ratio of 3 : 1

(b) a rectangle that has an area of 135 and whose base is represented
by $x + 2$ and whose altitude is represented by $2x + 1$

*3–11. In each case, find the area of the figure shown. (Whenever appropriate,
answers may be left in radical form.)*

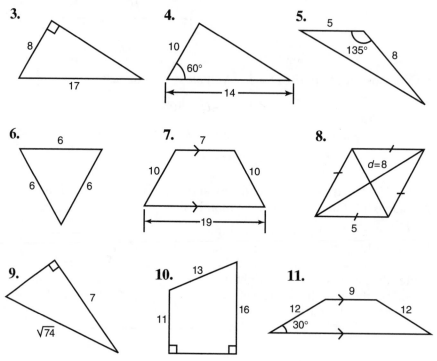

3.   8   17

4.   10   60°   14

5.   5   135°   8

6.   6   6   6

7.   7   10   10   19

8. $d=8$ 5

9.   7 $\sqrt{74}$

10.   13   11   16

11.   9   12   30°   12

12. Find the length of the shorter diagonal of a rhombus if:
   (a) the length of the longer diagonal is 15 and the area is 90
   (b) the lengths of the diagonals are in the ratio of 2:3, and the area of
   the rhombus is 147

13. Find the length of an altitude of a trapezoid if:
   (a) its area is 72 and the sum of the lengths of the bases is 36
   (b) its area is 80 and the length of its median is 16
   (c) the sum of the lengths of the bases is numerically equal to one-third
   of the area of the trapezoid

14. Find the area of a rhombus if its perimeter is 68 and the length of one of
its diagonals is 16.

15. Find the area of a triangle if the lengths of a pair of adjacent sides are 6
and 14 and the measure of the included angle is:
   (a) 90   **(b)** 30   **(c)** 120 *(Leave answer in radical form.)*

16. The area of a rhombus is 40, and the length of one of its diagonals is 8. Find the length of the other diagonal.

17. The length of base $\overline{AB}$ of $\triangle ABC$ and the length of a side of a square are each 8. If the area of the triangle is equal to the area of the square, find the length of the altitude drawn to $\overline{AB}$.

18. In $\triangle ABC$, m$\angle C = 90$, m$\angle A = 30$, and $AB = 12$. What is the length of $\overline{AC}$?

19. The lengths of two adjacent sides of a parallelogram are 10 and 8, and the measure of the included angle is 30. What is the area of the parallelogram?

20. If the lengths of the bases of an isosceles trapezoid are 16 and 10, and each leg makes an angle of $45°$ with the longer base, find the area of the trapezoid.

21. In a trapezoid, the length of one base is five times the length of the other base. The height of the trapezoid is 1 less than the length of the shorter base. If the area of the trapezoid is 90, find the length of the *shorter* base. [*Only an algebraic solution will be accepted.*]

22. In the accompanying figure, $ABCD$ is a trapezoid with $\overline{CD} \parallel \overline{AB}$. Triangles AOD, DOC, and COB are equilateral, $\overline{OE} \perp \overline{CD}$, and $OA = 6$. (*Answers may be left in radical form.*)
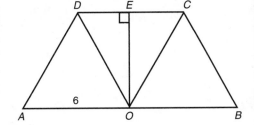
   (a) Find OE.
   (b) Find the area of $\triangle DOC$.
   (c) Find the area of trapezoid $ABCD$.
   (d) Find the area of trapezoid $OECB$.

8.8 TRIGONOMETRY OF THE RIGHT TRIANGLE

KEY IDEAS

For the accompanying figure, since $\triangle ABC \sim \triangle ADE \sim \triangle AFG$, the following extended proportion may be written:

$$\frac{BC}{AB} = \frac{DE}{AD} = \frac{FG}{AF} = \frac{\text{Length of leg opposite } \angle A}{\text{Length of hypotenuse}}$$

For any given acute angle, this ratio is the same regardless of the size of the right triangle. It will be convenient to refer to this

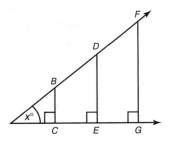

type of ratio by a special name—the *sine ratio*. The **sine** of an acute angle of a right triangle is the ratio formed by taking the length of the leg opposite the angle and dividing it by the length of the hypotenuse. In a similar fashion, other ratios may also be formed, with each being given a special name.

Definitions of Trigonometric Ratios

A **trigonometric ratio** is the ratio of the lengths of a pair of sides of a right triangle selected with respect to a given angle of the triangle (Figure 8.7). Three commonly formed trigonometric ratios are called *sine, cosine,* and *tangent:*

$$\text{Sine of } \angle A = \frac{\text{Length of leg opposite } \angle A}{\text{Length of hypotenuse}} = \frac{BC}{AB};$$

$$\text{Cosine of } \angle A = \frac{\text{Length of leg adjacent to } \angle A}{\text{Length of hypotenuse}} = \frac{AC}{AB};$$

$$\text{Tangent of } \angle A = \frac{\text{Length of leg opposite } \angle A}{\text{Length of leg adjacent to } \angle A} = \frac{BC}{AC}.$$

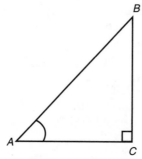

Figure 8.7 Right Triangle

When working with the trigonometric ratios, keep in mind the following:

- Sine, cosine, and tangent may be abbreviated as *sin, cos,* and *tan,* respectively.
- The trigonometric ratios may be taken with respect to either of the acute angles of the triangle:

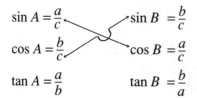

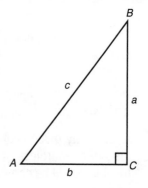

- Since sin A and cos B are both equal to $\frac{a}{c}$, they are equal to each other. Similarly, cos A and sin B are equal since both are equal to $\frac{b}{c}$. Since angles A and B are complementary, the sine of an angle is equal to the cosine of the angle's complement. For example, sin 60° = cos 30°.
- The definitions of the three trigonometric ratios should be memorized.

Examples

1. In right triangle ABC, $\angle C$ is the right angle. If $AC = 4$ and $BC = 3$, find the value of each of the following:
   (a) tan A **(b)** sin A **(c)** cos A

Solutions: Since $\triangle ABC$ is a 3-4-5 right triangle, $AB = 5$.

(a) $\tan A = \dfrac{\text{Leg opposite } \angle A}{\text{Leg adjacent } \angle A} = \dfrac{3}{4} = \mathbf{0.75}$

(b) $\sin A = \dfrac{\text{Leg opposite } \angle A}{\text{Hypotenuse}} = \dfrac{3}{5} = \mathbf{0.6}$

(c) $\cos A = \dfrac{\text{Leg adjacent to } \angle A}{\text{Hypotenuse}} = \dfrac{4}{5} = \mathbf{0.8}$

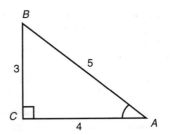

2. Find the value of x if sin $2x = $ cos $3x$.

Solution: If angles A and B are complementary, sin $A = $ cos B. Therefore,

$$2x + 3x = 90$$
$$5x = 90$$
$$x = \frac{90}{5} = \mathbf{18}$$

Evaluating Trigonometric Functions Using a Calculator

A scientific calculator can be used to find the value of the sine, cosine, and tangent of a given angle. When you first turn on your calculator, the unit of angle measurement is set to DEGrees. If you do not see DEG in small type in the display window, press the [DRG] key until DEG is displayed.

To evaluate a trigonometric function of $n°$, enter n and then press the appropriate trigonometric function key. Most scientific calculators will display a decimal value with at least eight-place decimal accuracy, so you will usually need to round off the answer that appears in the display window. As a general practice, round off answers correct to four decimal places.

Example: To evaluate sin 57° correct to *four decimal places,* follow these steps:

Step 1. Enter 57.

Step 2. Press the [SIN] key.

Step 3. Round off the value that appears in the display window. Since 0.8386706 will appear, sin 57° = 0.8387 correct to *four decimal places.*

Not all calculators work in the same way. For example, some scientific calculators require that you first press the [SIN] key, enter 57, and then press the [=] key.

Finding Angle Measures Using a Calculator

Most scientific calculators have either an INVerse function key, a 2nd function key, or a SHIFT key that allows you to find the degree measure of an angle when the value of a trigonometric function of that angle is known.

Example: If tan x = 2.197, the degree measure of angle x correct to the *nearest degree* can be obtained by proceeding as follows:

Step 1. Enter 2.197.

Step 2. Press the [INV] or [2nd] key or [SHIFT] key.

Step 3. Press the [TAN] key.

Step 4. Round off the value that appears in the display window to the nearest degree. Since 65.526579 will appear, angle x, correct to the *nearest degree,* is 66°.

If the procedure outlined above does not work with your calculator, try steps 2 and 3 first, then enter the angle and press the [=] key. For example, if your calculator has a [SHIFT] key, follow this sequence:

$$[SHIFT] \rightarrow [TAN] \rightarrow [2.197] \rightarrow [=].$$

Examples

3. Find the value of each of the following:
(a) tan 27°   **(b)** sin 64°   **(c)** cos 35°

Solutions: **(a) 0.5095**   **(b) 0.8988**   **(c) 0.8192**

4. Find the degree measure of angle x.
(a) sin x = 0.7071   **(b)** tan x = 0.6009   **(c)** cos x = 0.7986

Solutions: **(a)** x = 45°   **(b)** x = 31°   **(c)** x = 37°

5. Find the degree measure of $\angle A$ correct to the *nearest degree.*
(a) tan A = 0.7413   **(c)** sin A = 0.6599
(b) cos A = 0.8854   **(d)** tan A = 2.2500

Solution: **(a)** A = 37°   **(b)** A = 28°   **(c)** A = 41°   **(d)** A = 66°.

6. Find the value of *x* correct to the *nearest tenth*.

(a)   **(b)**

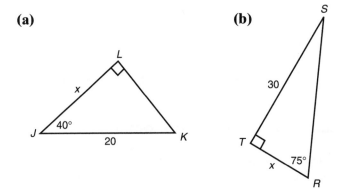

Solutions: **(a)** *Step 1*. Decide which trigonometric ratio to use, and then write the corresponding equation:

$$\cos J = \frac{\text{Leg adjacent to } \angle J}{\text{Hypotenuse}}$$

$$\cos 40° = \frac{x}{20}.$$

Step 2. Evaluate cos 40° using a scientific calculator. Since cos 40° = 0.7660,

$$0.7660 = \frac{x}{20}.$$

Step 3. Solve the equation. It may help to think of the equation as a proportion:

$$\frac{0.7660}{1} = \frac{x}{20}.$$

Solve by cross-multiplying:

$$x = 20(0.7660) = 15.32.$$

Step 4. Round off your answer to the desired accuracy. In this example you are asked to express the answer correct to the nearest tenth. Hence,

$$x = \textbf{15.3}.$$

(b) Since the problem involves both legs of the right triangle, use the tangent ratio:

$$\tan R = \frac{\text{Leg opposite } \angle R}{\text{Leg adjacent to } \angle R}$$

$$\tan 75° = \frac{30}{x}$$

$$x = \frac{30}{\tan 75°}$$
$$= \frac{30}{3.7321}$$
$$= 30 \div 3.7321$$
$$= 8.038$$
$$= \textbf{8.0} \text{ (correct to the \textit{nearest tenth})}$$

Indirect Measurement and Trigonometry

A trigonometric ratio may be used to arrive at the measure of a part of a right triangle that may be difficult, if not impossible, to calculate by direct measurement.

Example

7. A plane takes off from a runway, and climbs while maintaining a constant angle with the ground. When the plane has traveled 1,000 meters, its altitude is 290 meters. Find, correct to the *nearest degree,* the angle at which the plane has risen with respect to the horizontal ground.

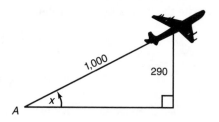

Solution: To find the value of ∠*x*, first determine the appropriate trigonometric ratio. The sine ratio relates the three quantities under consideration:

$$\sin x = \frac{\text{Leg opposite } \angle A}{\text{Hypotenuse}}$$
$$= \frac{290}{1,000} = 0.2900.$$

Using a scientific calculator, you find that ∠*x* = **17°**.

Angles of Elevation and Depression

The angles formed by an observer's line of vision and a horizontal line are sometimes referred to by special names. The **angle of elevation** represents the angle through which an observer must *raise* his or her line of sight with respect to a horizontal line in order to see an object. For example, if to see a bird in flight John must raise his line of sight 35° with respect to the horizontal ground, then the angle of elevation of the bird is 35°.

If in order to view an object the observer must *lower* his or her line of sight with respect to a horizontal line, the angle thus formed is called the

angle of depression. For example, if a pilot of an airplane in flight must lower her line of sight 23° to spot a landmark on the ground, then the angle of depression of the landmark is 23°. As Figure 8.8 illustrates:

- The angle of elevation *e* is an angle of a right triangle that has the line of sight as its hypotenuse, while the angle of depression *d* falls outside this triangle.
- The angle of elevation and the angle of depression are numerically equal (*e* = *d*) since they are alternate interior angles formed by parallel (horizontal) lines and a transversal (the line of sight).

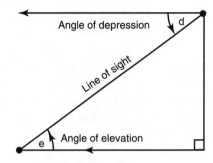

Figure 8.8 Angles of Elevation and Depression

Examples

8. A man standing 30 feet from a flagpole observes the angle of elevation of its top to be 48°. Find the height of the flagpole, correct to the *nearest tenth* of a foot.

Solution: Step 1. Draw a right triangle and label it with the given information.

Step 2. Decide which trigonometric ratio to use, and then write the corresponding equation:

$$\tan 48° = \frac{x \text{ (leg opposite angle)}}{30 \text{ (leg adjacent to angle)}}.$$

Step 3. Replace tan 48° by its value, obtained by using a scientific calculator, and then solve for *x:*

$$1.1106 = \frac{x}{30}$$
$$x = 30(1.1106) = 33.318$$
$$= \mathbf{33.3} \text{ (correct to the *nearest tenth* of a foot).}$$

9. An airplane pilot observes the angle of depression of a point on a landing field to be 28°. If the plane's altitude at this moment is 900 meters, find the distance from the pilot to the observed point on the landing field, correct to the *nearest meter*.

Solution: Step 1. Draw a right triangle, and label it with the given information. Use the fact that the angle of elevation and the angle of depression are numerically equal.

Step 2. Decide which trigonometric ratio to use and then write the corresponding equation:

$$\sin 28° = \frac{900 \text{ (leg opposite angle)}}{x \text{ (hypotenuse)}}.$$

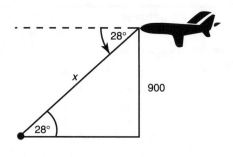

Step 3. Note that in this case forming a ratio in which the variable is in the denominator is unavoidable. Replace sin 28° by its value obtained using a scientific calculator, and then solve for *x:*

$$0.4695 = \frac{900}{x}$$

$$x = \frac{900}{0.4695} = 1916.93$$

$$= \mathbf{1917} \text{ (correct to the } \textit{nearest meter)}$$

Using Trigonometry to Solve Geometry Problems

Sometimes trigonometry is needed to calculate the measures of parts of geometric figures.

Examples

10. The lengths of two adjacent sides of a triangle are 10 and 16. If their included angle measures 39°, find the area of the triangle, correct to the *nearest square unit.*

Solution: Draw the altitude to the side whose length is 16. In the right triangle formed, use the sine ratio to find the length of the altitude.

$$\sin 39° = \frac{h}{10}$$

$$0.6293 = \frac{h}{10}$$

$$h = 10(0.6293) = 6.293 \text{ or } 6.3 \text{ to the } \textit{nearest tenth}$$

$$\text{Area} = \tfrac{1}{2} \text{ (Base} \times \text{Height)}$$

$$= \tfrac{1}{2} (16 \times 6.3)$$

$$= \tfrac{1}{2} (100.8)$$

$$= 50.4$$

$$= \mathbf{50} \text{ (correct to the } \textit{nearest square unit)}$$

11. In rhombus $ABCD$, $AC = 40$ and $m\angle DAB = 72$.

(a) Find the length of diagonal DB to the *nearest tenth*.

(b) Find the area of rhombus $ABCD$ to the *nearest integer*.

(c) Find the length of a side of rhombus $ABCD$ to the *nearest integer*.

Solutions: The following properties of a rhombus are needed in order to make use of right triangle trigonometry:

- The diagonals of a rhombus bisect the angles at the vertices they connect, so

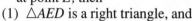

$$m\angle EAD = \tfrac{1}{2}m\angle DAB = \tfrac{1}{2}(72) = 36.$$

- The diagonals of a rhombus are the perpendicular bisectors of each other. Therefore, if diagonals $\overline{AC}$ and $\overline{BD}$ intersect at point E, then

(1) $\triangle AED$ is a right triangle, and

(2) $AE = \tfrac{1}{2}AC = \tfrac{1}{2}(40) = 20.$

(a) To find DB, first find DE, using the tangent ratio in right triangle AED.

$$\tan \angle EAD = \frac{\text{Leg opposite } \angle EAD}{\text{Leg adjacent to } \angle EAD}$$

$$\tan 36° = \frac{DE}{AE}$$

$$0.7265 = \frac{DE}{20}$$

$$0.7265 \times 20 = DE$$

$$14.53 = DE$$

$$DB = 2 \times DE = 2 \times 14.53 = 29.06$$

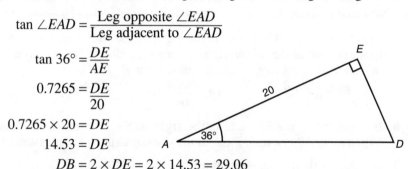

Diagonal $DB = \mathbf{29.1}$ (correct to the *nearest tenth*).

(b) The area of a rhombus is equal to one-half the product of the lengths of its diagonals.

$$\text{Area of } ABCD = \tfrac{1}{2}(AC)(DB) = \tfrac{1}{2}(40)(29.1)$$

$$= (20)(29.1)$$

Area of rhombus $ABCD = \mathbf{582}$ (correct to the *nearest integer*).

(c) To find AD, use the cosine ratio:

$$\cos \angle EAD = \frac{\text{Leg adjacent to } \angle EAD}{\text{Hypotenuse}} = \frac{AE}{AD}$$

$$\cos 36° = \frac{20}{AD}$$

$$AD = \frac{20}{\cos 36°} = \frac{20}{0.8090} = 24.69$$

Side $AD = 25$ (correct to the *nearest integer*).

Exercise Set 8.8

A. Problems Involving Trigonometric Definitions and Relationships

1. In each case, find the degree measure of angle x.
   (a) $\sin x = \cos (x + 28)$ (c) $\sin (2x + 17) = \cos (x + 13)$
   (b) $\cos 4x = \sin 18°$ (d) $\cos (5x + 12) = \sin (2x - 13)$

2. Express the value of each of the following *in radical form:*
   (a) $\sin 45°$ (c) $\sin 60°$ (e) $\tan 30°$
   (b) $\cos 45°$ (d) $\cos 30°$ (f) $\tan 60°$

3. In right triangle ABC, $\angle C$ is the right angle, $AB = 25$, and $AC = 24$. Find the values of the sine, cosine, and tangent of the *smallest* angle of the triangle.

4. In right triangle RST, $\angle T$ is the right angle. If $\sin R = \dfrac{9}{41}$, find the values of $\cos R$ and $\tan R$.

5. In right triangle ABC, $\angle C$ is the right angle, $BC = 6$, and $AB = 10$. Express each of the following as a single fraction in lowest terms:
   (a) $\sin A + \cos A$ (c) $\sin A + \cos B$
   (b) $\tan A + \tan B$ (d) $\dfrac{\sin A}{\cos A}$

6. In right triangle ABC, $\angle C$ is the right angle. The ratio of leg AC to hypotenuse AB is 4 to 5. Find, to the *nearest degree,* the measure of $\angle B$.

7. As shown in the accompanying diagram, a 25-foot ladder leans against the side of a house. The base of the ladder is 12 feet from the house on level ground.
   (a) Find, to the *nearest degree,* the measure of the angle that the ladder makes with the ground.
   (b) Find, to the *nearest foot,* the distance from the top of the ladder to the ground.

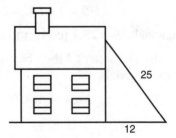

8. As shown in the accompanying diagram, a kite is flying at the end of a 200-meter straight string. If the string makes an angle of 68° with the ground, how high, to the *nearest meter,* is the kite?

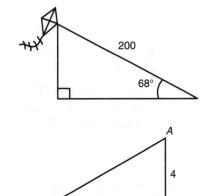

9. In right triangle *ABC,* ∠*C* is the right angle, *AC* = 4, and *BC* = 7.
   (a) Find, to the *nearest degree,* the measure of ∠*B.*
   (b) Find, to the *nearest integer,* the length of $\overline{AB}$.

B. Problems Involving Angles of Elevation and Depression

10. At noon, a tree having a height of 10 feet casts a shadow 15 feet in length. Find, to the *nearest degree,* the angle of elevation of the sun at this time.

11. Find, to the *nearest foot,* the height of a building that casts a shadow of 80 feet when the angle of elevation of the sun is 42°.

12. A man observes the angle of depression from the top of a cliff overlooking the ocean to a ship to be 37°. If at this moment the ship is 1,000 meters from the foot of the cliff, find, to the *nearest meter,* the height of the cliff.

13. When the altitude of a plane is 800 meters, the pilot spots a target at a distance of 1,200 meters. At what angle of depression does the pilot observe the target?

14. Find, to the *nearest degree,* the angle of elevation of the sun when a man 6 feet tall casts a shadow 4 feet long.

15. At an angle of depression of 42°, an airplane pilot is able to view a target that is at a distance of 1,000 meters from the pilot. Find, to the *nearest 10 meters,* the altitude of the plane.

C. Problems Involving Geometric Figures

16. The lengths of a pair of adjacent sides of a rectangle are 10 and 16. Find, to the *nearest degree,* the angle a diagonal makes with the longer side.

17. The lengths of two adjacent sides of a parallelogram are 8 and 12, and the measure of their included angle is 42. Find, to the *nearest square unit,* the area of the parallelogram.

18. Find, to the *nearest square unit,* the area of a triangle if the lengths of two adjacent sides are 7 and 12 and the measure of the included angle is 58°.

19. The lengths of diagonals of a rhombus are 12 and 16. Find, to the *nearest degree,* the measures of the four angles of the rhombus.

20. Given: Rhombus *ABCD* with diagonals $\overline{BD}$ and $\overline{AC}$ intersecting at *E, AB* = 13, *BD* = 10.

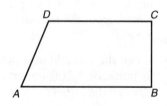

Find:
(a) *AC*
(b) area of rhombus *ABCD*
(c) m ∠*EAB,* to the *nearest degree*

21. The length of each leg of an isosceles triangle is 20. If each leg makes an angle of 50° with the base, find:
(a) the length of the base, to the *nearest tenth*
(b) the area of the triangle, to the *nearest square unit*

22. The measure of the vertex angle of an isosceles triangle is 72. If the length of the altitude drawn to the base is 10, find:
(a) the length of the base, to the *nearest tenth*
(b) the area of the triangle, to the *nearest square unit*
(c) the length of a leg, to the *nearest tenth*

23. In the accompanying diagram, quadrilateral *ABCD* is a trapezoid with $\overline{AB} \parallel \overline{CD}$, m∠*A* = 67, m∠*B* = 90, *DC* = 12, and *AD* = 8.

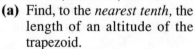

(a) Find, to the *nearest tenth,* the length of an altitude of the trapezoid.
(b) Find, to the *nearest integer,* the length of $\overline{AB}$.
(c) Find, to the *nearest integer,* the area of the trapezoid.

24. In the accompanying figure, *ABCD* is a trapezoid. If *AB* = 14, *BC* = 10, and m∠*BCD* = 38, find:
(a) *AD,* to the *nearest tenth*
(b) *CD,* to the *nearest tenth*
(c) the area of trapezoid *ABCD,* to the *nearest square unit*

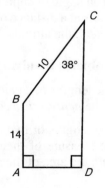

254

REGENTS TUNE-UP: CHAPTER 8

Each of the questions in this section has appeared on a previous Course II Regents Examination. Here is an opportunity for you to review the material in Chapter 8 and, at the same time, prepare for the Course II Regents Examination.

1. Find, in radical form, the length of a diagonal of a square if the perimeter of the square is 20.

2. In $\triangle ABC$, D is a point on $\overline{AB}$ and E is a point on $\overline{AC}$ such that $\overline{DE} \parallel \overline{BC}$. If $AD = 4$, $DB = 2$, and $AC = 9$, find AE.

3. What is the length of a side of a square whose diagonal measures $3\sqrt{2}$?

4. In right triangle ABC, hypotenuse $AB = 10$. The altitude drawn from C to $\overline{AB}$ intersects $\overline{AB}$ at D. If $AD = 2$, find CD.

5. A rhombus has a side of length 10 and one diagonal of length 16. Find the length of the other diagonal.

6. In right triangle QRS, $m\angle Q = 90$, $RS = 13$, and $RQ = 5$. Find the area of $\triangle QRS$.

7. If point A is 6 meters due east of point C and point B is 8 meters due north of point C, find the distance, in meters, between A and B.

8. An angle is picked at random. What is the probability that the cosine of that angle is greater than 1?

9. Find the positive root of the equation $\dfrac{4}{x-1} = \dfrac{x+1}{12}$.

10. Two triangles are similar. The lengths of the sides of the smaller triangle are 4, 6, and 8, and the perimeter of the larger triangle is 27. Find the length of the *shortest* side of the larger triangle.

11. In $\triangle ABC$, point D is on $\overline{AC}$ and point E is on $\overline{BC}$ such that $\overline{DE} \parallel \overline{AB}$, $DE = 4$, $CD = 6$, and $DA = 3$. Find AB.

12. The length of a side of an equilateral triangle is 10. What is the length, in radical form, of an altitude of the triangle?

13. In right triangle ABC, altitude $\overline{CD}$ is drawn to hypotenuse $\overline{AB}$. If $AD = 4$ and $DB = 5$, find AC.

14. Find, to the nearest foot, the height of a tree that casts a 12-foot shadow when the angle of elevation of the sun is $38°$.

15. In the accompanying diagram of trapezoid $ABCD$, $CB = 6$, m$\angle A =$ 45, m$\angle B = 90$, and base $DC = 2$. Find the length of base $\overline{AB}$.

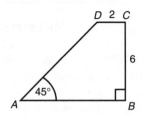

16. The vertex angle of an isosceles triangle measures $56°$, and each leg measures 8. Find the area of the triangle to the *nearest tenth*.

17. In the accompanying diagram of right triangle ABC, $AC = 12$, $AB = 13$, and $BC = 5$. What is the value of $\sin A - \cos A$?

(1) $\dfrac{7}{13}$ (3) $\dfrac{17}{13}$

(2) $-\dfrac{7}{13}$ (4) $-\dfrac{17}{13}$

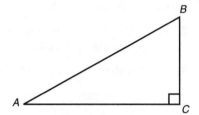

18. In $\triangle ABC$, altitude $\overline{AD}$ is drawn to base $\overline{BC}$. If $AD = 12$, $AB = 15$, and $AC = 13$, what is BC?

(1) 5 (3) 14

(2) 9 (4) 42

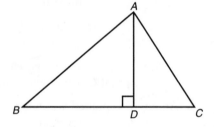

19. In the accompanying diagram, $\overline{AB}$ and $\overline{CD}$ intersect at point E so that $\overline{AC}$ is parallel to $\overline{DB}$. If $AC = 3$, $DB = 4$, and $AB = 14$, what is AE?

(1) 19 (3) 8

(2) 10.5 (4) 6

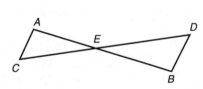

20. In the accompanying diagram, $\triangle RST$ is the right triangle and $\overline{SP}$ is the altitude to hypotenuse $\overline{RT}$. If $SP = 6$ and the lengths of $\overline{RP}$ and $\overline{PT}$ are in the ratio 1 : 4, what is the length of $\overline{RP}$?

(1) 12 (3) 3

(2) 15 (4) 9

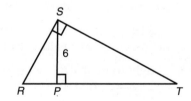

21. If the altitude drawn to the hypotenuse of a right triangle has length 10, the lengths of the segments of the hypotenuse may be:
(1) 5 and 20   (2) 2 and 5   (3) 3 and 7   (4) 50 and 50

22–23. Solve each problem algebraically.

22. In right triangle ABC, $\overline{CD}$ is the altitude drawn to hypotenuse $\overline{AB}$. The length of $\overline{DB}$ is 5 units longer than the length of $\overline{AD}$. If $CD = 3$, find the length, in radical form, of $\overline{AD}$.

23. In $\triangle ABC$, D is a point on $\overline{AB}$ and E is a point on $\overline{AC}$ such that $\overline{DE} \parallel \overline{BC}$. If $AD = 2$, $DB = x - 1$, $AE = x$, and $EC = x + 2$, find AE.

24. (a) In the accompanying diagram, a tree 15 meters high casts a shadow 10 meters long. What is the angle of elevation of the sun to the *nearest degree?*

(b) Right triangle DEF has the right angle at F, $\angle D = 50°$, and $EF = 8$. Find DF to the *nearest integer.*

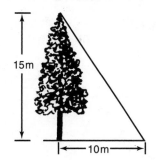

25. In the accompanying figure of right trapezoid $ABCD$, $AB = 10$, $DC = 18$, $m\angle C = 49$, and $\overline{BE} \perp \overline{DEC}$.
(a) Find BE to the *nearest integer.*
(b) Find the area of $ABCD$ to the *nearest integer.*
(c) Find BC to the *nearest integer.*
(d) If a dart is thrown at random and lands in trapezoid $ABCD$, what is the probability that the dart will also land in rectangle $ABED?$

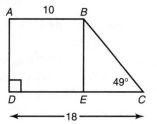

26. In the accompanying diagram of isosceles triangle ABC, $\overline{AB} \cong \overline{CB}$ and the length of altitude BD is 2 more than the length of AD. The area of isosceles triangle ABC is 10.
(a) Find the length of $\overline{AD}$ to the *nearest tenth.*
(b) Using the answer from part **a**, find the length of $\overline{AB}$ to the *nearest tenth.*

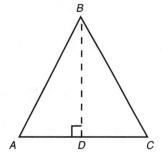

27. Given: V is a point on $\overline{ST}$ such
that $\overline{RVW}$ bisects $\angle SRT$,
$\overline{TW} \cong \overline{TV}$.
Prove: $RW \times SV = RV \times TW$.

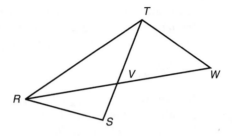

ANSWERS TO SELECTED EXERCISES: CHAPTER 8

Section 8.1
1. 84   **3.** 75, 105, 75, 105   **5. (a)** 8   **(b)** $6e^2$ **(c)** $\frac{1}{4}$ **(d)** $\sqrt{54}$

Section 8.2
2. 40   **5.** 12, 27   **9.** 3   **13. (a)** $\dfrac{4}{x+5} = \dfrac{x}{6}$ **15. (a)** 5
4. 60   **7.** 24   **11.** 6   **(b)** 3   **(b)** 9

Section 8.3
1. That $\angle W \cong \angle Y$ and right $\angle HAW \cong$ right $\angle KBY$ implies $\triangle HWA \sim \triangle KYB$.

4. Show $\triangle TAX \sim \triangle WHY$. $\angle W \cong \angle ATX$ and $\angle Y \cong \angle AXT$ since $\parallel$ line segments have congruent corresponding angles.

5. Show $\triangle RMN \sim \triangle RAT$. $\angle RMN \cong \angle A$ and $\angle RNM \cong \angle T$. Write $\dfrac{MN}{AT} = \dfrac{RN}{RT}$. By the converse of the Base Angles Theorem, $NT = MN$. Substitute NT for MN in the proportion.

7. Show $\triangle SQP \sim \triangle WRP$. $\angle SPQ \cong \angle WPR$ (Angle). Since $\overline{SR} \cong \overline{SQ}$, $\angle SRQ \cong \angle SQR$. $\angle SRQ \cong \angle WRP$ (Definition of angle bisector). By transitivity, $\angle SQR \cong \angle WRP$ (Angle).

9. Show $\triangle PMQ \sim \triangle MKC$. Right $\angle MCK \cong$ right $\angle PMQ$. Since $\overline{TP} \cong \overline{TM}$, $\angle TPM \cong \angle TMP$.

10. Show $\triangle PMT \sim \triangle JKT$. Since $\overline{MP} \cong \overline{MQ}$, $\angle MPQ \cong \angle MQP$. Since $\overline{JK} \parallel \overline{MQ}$, $\angle J \cong \angle MQP$ so that, by transitivity, $\angle J \cong \angle MPQ$ (Angle). $\angle K \cong \angle QMT$ (Congruent alternate interior angles). $\angle QMT \cong \angle PMT$ (since $\triangle MTP \cong \triangle MTQ$ by SSS). By transitivity, $\angle K \cong \angle PMT$ (Angle). Write the proportion $\dfrac{PM}{JK} = \dfrac{PT}{JT}$. Substitute TQ for PT (see the "Given") in the proportion.

14. Show $\triangle AEH \sim \triangle BEF$. $\angle BEF \cong \angle HEA$ and $\angle EAH \cong \angle EBF$ (Halves of equals are equal).

15. First prove the proportion $\dfrac{JY}{XZ} = \dfrac{YX}{ZL}$ by proving $\triangle JYX \sim \triangle XZL$. To prove these triangles similar, show $\angle JYX \cong \angle XZL$ and $\angle J \cong \angle ZXL$. Since $KYXZ$ is a parallelogram, $KZ = YX$, so $\dfrac{JY}{XZ} = \dfrac{YX}{ZL} = \dfrac{KZ}{ZL}$. In the proportion $\dfrac{JY}{XZ} = \dfrac{KZ}{ZL}$, cross-multiplying gives the desired product.

Section 8.4
1. $r = 8, s = \sqrt{192}, t = \sqrt{48}$ **9.** $\sqrt{160}$ **15.** 9
3. $r = 16, s = 9, t = 15$ **11.** 4 **17.** 15
5. 6 **13.** (1) **19.** 6

Section 8.5
1. 8 **5.** 40 **9.** $\sqrt{51}$ **11.** 24 **15.** 3
3. $6\sqrt{2}$ **7.** $5\sqrt{3}$ **10.** 15 **13.** $6\sqrt{2}$ **16.** $4 \pm \sqrt{2}$

Section 8.6
1. (a) 4 **(b)** $8\sqrt{3}$ **7.** $\sqrt{148}$
3. $36\sqrt{2}$ **9. (a)** $4\sqrt{2}$
5. (a) altitude $= \dfrac{8}{\sqrt{3}}$, leg $= \dfrac{16}{\sqrt{3}}$ **(c)** $3x\sqrt{2}$

  (b) altitude $= 8$, leg $= 8\sqrt{2}$ **10. (a)** $16\sqrt{3}$
  (c) altitude $= 8\sqrt{3}$, leg $= 16$ **(c)** $36\sqrt{3}$

Section 8.7
1. (a) 24 **7.** 104 **17.** 16
  (b) 32 **9.** 17.5 **19.** 40
  (c) $90\sqrt{3}$ **21.** 6
3. 60 **11.** $54 + \dfrac{36}{\sqrt{3}}$ **22. (a)** $3\sqrt{3}$ **(c)** $27\sqrt{3}$
5. $10\sqrt{2}$ **(b)** $9\sqrt{3}$ **(d)** $13.5\sqrt{3}$
  13. (a) 4 **(b)** 5 **(c)** 6
  15. (a) 42 **(b)** 21 **(c)** $21\sqrt{3}$

Section 8.8
1. (a) 62 **(c)** 20 **9. (a)** 30° **19.** 74°, 106°, 74°, 106°
3. $\sin A = \dfrac{7}{25}, \cos A = \dfrac{24}{25},$ **(b)** 8 **21. (a)** 25.7
  11. 72 **(b)** 197
  $\tan A = \dfrac{7}{24}$ **13.** 42° **23. (a)** 7.4
  15. 670 **(b)** 15
5. (a) $\dfrac{7}{5}$ **(c)** $\dfrac{6}{5}$ **17.** 64 **(c)** 100

  (b) $\dfrac{25}{12}$ **(d)** $\dfrac{3}{4}$
7. (a) 61° **(b)** 22

Regents Tune-Up: Chapter 8

1. $5\sqrt{2}$

3. 3

5. 12

7. 10

9. 7

11. 6

13. 6

15. 8

17. (2)

19. (4)

21. (1)

22. $\dfrac{-5 + \sqrt{61}}{2}$

24. (a) 56°

    (b) 7

26. (a) 2.3

    (b) 4.9

27. Rewrite the product as $\dfrac{RW}{RV} = \dfrac{TW}{SV}$. Prove $\triangle RSV \sim \triangle RTW$. Since RVW bisects $\angle SRT$ (Given), $\angle SRV \cong \angle TRW$ (Angle). Since $\overline{TW} \cong \overline{TV}$ (Given), $\angle TVW = \angle W$. Also, $\angle RVS \cong \angle TVW$ (vertical angles are congruent). By transitivity, $\angle RVS \cong \angle W$ (Angle). Hence, $\triangle RSV \sim \triangle RTW$ by the AA Theorem of Similarity.

Unit Four ANALYTIC GEOMETRY

CHAPTER 9

COORDINATE GEOMETRY

9.1 COORDINATES AND AREA

=== **KEY IDEAS** ===

A **coordinate plane** may be created by drawing a horizontal number line called the **x-axis** and a vertical number line called the **y-axis**. The x-axis and the y-axis are sometimes referred to as the **coordinate axes**, and their point of intersection is the **origin**. The process of locating a point or a series of points in the coordinate plane is called **graphing**.

Coordinates can be used to find the area of a triangle or a quadrilateral whose vertices are given.

Graphing Ordered Pairs

Each point in the coordinate plane is located (see Figure 9.1) by using an ordered pair of numbers of the form (x, y), in which the first number of the pair is the x-coordinate, and the second number is the y-coordinate. The x-coordinate, sometimes called the **abscissa**, tells the number of units the point is located to the right $(x > 0)$ or to the left $(x < 0)$ of the origin. The y-coordinate, sometimes called the **ordinate**, indicates the number of units the point is located above $(y > 0)$ or below $(y < 0)$ the origin. For example, to graph point $(3, 5)$, start at the origin, move 3 units to the right, and then 5 units up.

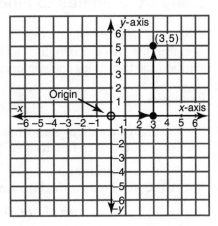

Figure 9.1 Graphing Ordered Pairs

The Four Quadrants

The coordinate axes divide the plane into four regions called **quadrants**. As shown in Figure 9.2, the quadrants are numbered in counterclockwise order, beginning at the upper right and using Roman numerals. Notice that points $A(2, 3)$, $B(-4, 5)$, $C(-3, -6)$, and $D(3, -3)$ lie in different quadrants. The signs of the x- and y-coordinates of a point determine the quadrant in which the point lies.

Coordinates	Location of Point
$(+,+)$	Quadrant I
$(-,+)$	Quadrant II
$(-,-)$	Quadrant III
$(+,-)$	Quadrant IV

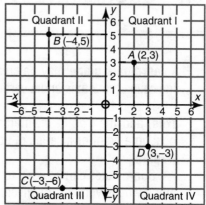

Figure 9.2 The Four Quadrants

Using Coordinates to Find Area

If one side of a triangle or special quadrilateral is parallel to a coordinate axis, then the area of the figure can be determined by drawing an altitude to that side and then using the appropriate area formula.

Examples

1. Graph a parallelogram whose vertices are $A(2, 2)$, $B(5, 6)$, $C(13, 6)$, and $D(10, 2)$, and then find its area.

Solution: In the accompanying graph, altitude $\overline{BH}$ has been drawn to base $\overline{AD}$. Count boxes to find the lengths of these segments.

$$
\begin{aligned}
\text{Area of } ABCD &= bh \\
&= (AD)(BH) \\
&= (8)(4) \\
&= \textbf{32 square units}
\end{aligned}
$$

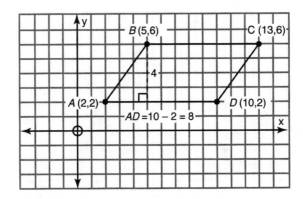

2. Graph a trapezoid whose vertices are $A(-4, 0)$, $B(-4, 3)$, $C(0, 6)$, and $D(0, 0)$, and then find its area.

Solution: In the accompanying graph, $\overline{AB}$ and $\overline{CD}$ are the bases of trapezoid $ABCD$. $\overline{AD}$ may be considered an altitude since it is perpendicular to both bases.

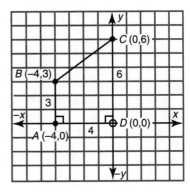

Area of trap $ABCD = \frac{1}{2}h(b_1 + b_2)$

$$= \frac{1}{2}(AD)(AB + CD)$$

$$= \frac{1}{2}(4)(3 + 6)$$

$$= 2(9)$$

$$= \textbf{18 square units}$$

Using Subtraction to Find Area

Example 3 illustrates a method that can be used to find the area of a quadrilateral or the area of a triangle that does not have a vertical or horizontal side.

Example

3. Find the area of the quadrilateral whose vertices are $A(-2, 2)$, $B(2, 5)$, $C(8, 1)$, and $D(-1, -2)$.

Solution: Circumscribe a rectangle about quadrilateral $ABCD$ by drawing intersecting horizontal and vertical segments through the vertices of the quadrilateral as shown in the accompanying diagram.

The area of quadrilateral $ABCD$ is calculated *indirectly* as follows:

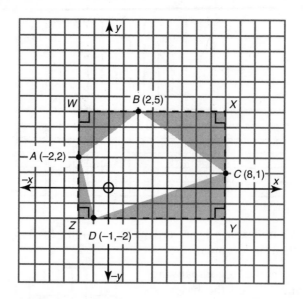

Step 1. Find the area of the rectangle.

$$\text{Area rect } WXYZ = (ZY)(YX) = (10)(7) = 70$$

Step 2. Find the sum of the areas of the right triangles in the four corners of the rectangle. Keep in mind that the area of a right triangle is equal to one-half the product of the lengths of the legs of the triangle.

$$\text{Sum} = \text{Area rt } \triangle BWA = \tfrac{1}{2}(BW)(WA) = \tfrac{1}{2}(4)(3) = 6$$
$$+ \text{Area rt } \triangle BXC = \tfrac{1}{2}(BX)(XC) = \tfrac{1}{2}(6)(4) = 12$$
$$+ \text{Area rt } \triangle DYC = \tfrac{1}{2}(DY)(YC) = \tfrac{1}{2}(9)(3) = 13.5$$
$$+ \text{Area rt } \triangle DZA = \tfrac{1}{2}(DZ)(ZA) = \tfrac{1}{2}(1)(4) = 2$$
$$\overline{\text{Sum of } \triangle \text{ areas} = 33.5}$$

Step 3. Subtract the sum of the areas of the right triangles from the area of the rectangle.

$$
\begin{aligned}
\text{Area quad } ABCD &= \text{Area rect } WXYZ - \text{Sum of areas of right triangles} \\
&= \quad\quad 70 \quad\quad - \quad\quad\quad 33.5 \\
&= \textbf{36.5}
\end{aligned}
$$

Exercise Set 9.1

1. The vertices of $\triangle ABC$ are $A(-4, 0)$, $B(2, 4)$, and $C(4, 0)$. What is the area of the triangle?
  (1) 8 (2) 16 (3) 32 (4) 64

2. The coordinates of the vertices of rectangle $ABCD$ are $A(2, 2)$, $B(2, 6)$, $C(8, 6)$, and $D(8, 2)$. The area of rectangle $ABCD$ is:
(1) 16   (2) 24   (3) 36   (4) 48

3. Find the areas of the triangles whose vertices are:
(a) $A(0, 5)$, $B(6, 0)$, $C(0, 0)$
(b) $A(-4, 0)$, $B(0, 0)$, $C(0, -9)$
(c) $A(2, 2)$, $B(2, 7)$, $C(5, 2)$
(d) $X(-3, 0)$, $Y(0, 8)$, $Z(3, 0)$
(e) $R(-3, 3)$, $S(4, 9)$, $T(9, 5)$
(f) $J(-5, 2)$, $K(-3, 6)$, $L(3, 1)$

4. Given the triangle determined by points $A(1, 4)$, $B(1, 1)$ and $C(x, 1)$, find x if the area of $\triangle ABC$ is 6.

5. The rectangle whose vertices are $A(0, 0)$, $B(0, 5)$, $C(h, k)$, and $D(8, 0)$ lies in the first quadrant.
(a) What are the values of h and k?
(b) What is the area of rectangle $ABCD$?

6. Find the area of the parallelogram whose vertices are:
(a) $A(2, 3)$, $B(5, 9)$, $C(13, 9)$, $D(10, 3)$
(b) $A(-4, -2)$, $B(-2, 6)$, $C(10, 6)$, $D(8, -2)$

7. Find the area of the trapezoid whose vertices are:
(a) $A(0, 0)$, $B(0, 5)$, $C(7, 11)$, $D(7, 0)$
(b) $A(-3, 0)$, $B(-3, 2)$, $C(5, 6)$, $D(5, 0)$
(c) $A(0, 0)$, $B(-2, -6)$, $C(9, -6)$, $D(7, 0)$
(d) $T(-4, -4)$, $R(-1, 5)$, $A(6, 5)$, $P(9, -4)$

8. Find the area of the hexagon whose vertices are $A(4, 5)$, $B(7, 0)$, $C(4, -5)$, $D(-4, -5)$, $E(-7, 0)$, and $F(-4, 5)$.

9. Find the area of the quadrilateral whose vertices are $A(-4, -2)$, $B(0, 5)$, $C(9, 3)$, and $D(7, -4)$.

10. Find the area of the quadrilateral whose vertices are $M(-4, 2)$, $A(0, 5)$, $T(3, 3)$, and $H(1, -5)$.

11. Find the area of pentagon $ABCD$, whose vertices are $A(-2, -5)$, $B(-2, 2)$, $C(2, 4)$, $D(5, 2)$, and $E(5, -3)$.

12. Given the parallelogram whose vertices are $M(-3, 2)$, $A(4, 8)$, $T(15, 5)$, and $H(8, -1)$:
(a) find the area of parallelogram $MATH$.
(b) find the area of $\triangle AMH$.

9.2 MIDPOINT AND DISTANCE FORMULAS

If the coordinates of the endpoints of $\overline{AB}$ are $A(x_1, y_1)$ and $B(x_2, y_2)$, then:

- the coordinates of the **midpoint** of $\overline{AB}$ are $\left(\dfrac{x_1 + x_2}{2}, \dfrac{y_1 + y_2}{2}\right)$;

- the **length** of $\overline{AB}$ (or the **distance** between points A and B) may be found by using the formula

$$AB = \sqrt{(x_2 - x_1)^2 + (y_2 - y_1)^2}.$$

Using the Midpoint Formula

Figure 9.3 illustrates that the x- and y-coordinates of the midpoint of a line segment are equal to the *averages* of the corresponding coordinates of the endpoints of the segment.

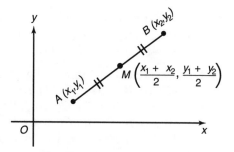

Figure 9.3 The Midpoint Formula

Examples

1. What are the coordinates of the center of a circle that has a diameter whose endpoints are (4, 9) and (−10, 1)?

Solution: The center of a circle is located at the midpoint of any diameter of the circle. Let $(x_1, y_1) = (4, 9)$ and $(x_2, y_2) = (-10, 1)$.

$$\overline{x} = \frac{x_1 + x_2}{2} \qquad \text{and} \qquad \overline{y} = \frac{y_1 + y_2}{2}$$

$$= \frac{4 + (-10)}{2} = \frac{-6}{2} \qquad\qquad = \frac{9 + 1}{2} = \frac{10}{2}$$

$$= -3 \qquad\qquad\qquad\qquad = 5$$

The coordinates of the center of the circle are **(−3, 5)**.

2. If the midpoint of a line segment is (7, −1) and the coordinates of one endpoint are (5, 4), what are the coordinates of the other endpoint?

Solution: Let (x, y) represent the coordinates of the unknown endpoint. Then

$$7 = \frac{5+x}{2} \qquad \text{and} \qquad -1 = \frac{4+y}{2}.$$

Multiply each side of each equation by 2:

$$2 \cdot 7 = 2\left(\frac{5+x}{2}\right) \qquad \text{and} \qquad 2(-1) = 2\left(\frac{4+y}{2}\right)$$
$$14 = 5 + x \qquad\qquad\qquad -2 = 4 + y$$
$$9 = x \qquad\qquad\qquad\qquad -6 = y$$

The coordinates of the other endpoint are **(9, –6)**.

Using the Distance Formula

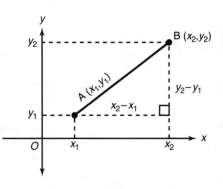

Figure 9.4 illustrates that points $A(x_1, y_1)$ and $B(x_2, y_2)$ determine a right triangle whose legs have lengths of $|x_2 - x_1|$ and $|y_2 - y_1|$. The length of the hypotenuse of this right triangle represents the distance between the two points and, using the Pythagorean theorem, is given by the expression

$$\sqrt{(x_2 - x_1)^2 + (y_2 - y_1)^2}.$$

Since each difference is squared, the order in which the coordinates are subtracted does *not* matter.

Examples

3. Point $(-2, 4)$ is on a circle whose center is at $(1, 0)$. Find the length of the radius of the circle.

Solution: Use the distance formula to find the length of the segment joining points $(-2, 4)$ and $(1, 0)$. Let $(x_1, y_1) = (-2, 4)$ and $(x_2, y_2) = (1, 0)$.

$$\begin{aligned}
\text{Radius length} &= \sqrt{(x_2 - x_1)^2 + (y_2 - y_1)^2} \\
&= \sqrt{[1 - (-2)]^2 + (0 - 4)^2} \\
&= \sqrt{(1 + 2)^2 + (-4)^2} \\
&= \sqrt{9 + 16} \\
&= \sqrt{25} \\
&= \mathbf{5}
\end{aligned}$$

4. The coordinates of vertices of quadrilateral $ABCD$ are $A(-3, 0)$ $B(4, 7)$, $C(9, 2)$, and $D(2, -5)$. Prove that:

    (a) $ABCD$ is a parallelogram   **(b)** $ABCD$ is a rectangle

Solutions: **(a)** If the diagonals of a quadrilateral have the same midpoint, they bisect each other and the quadrilateral is a parallelogram.

To find the midpoint of $\overline{AC}$: Let $(x_1, y_1) = A(-3, 0)$, and $(x_2, y_2) = C(9, 2)$.

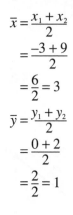

$$\bar{x} = \frac{x_1 + x_2}{2}$$

$$= \frac{-3 + 9}{2}$$

$$= \frac{6}{2} = 3$$

$$\bar{y} = \frac{y_1 + y_2}{2}$$

$$= \frac{0 + 2}{2}$$

$$= \frac{2}{2} = 1$$

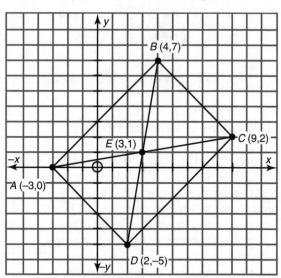

The midpoint of $\overline{AC}$ is $(3,1)$.

To find the midpoint of $\overline{BD}$: Let $(x_1, y_1) = B(4, 7)$, and $(x_2, y_2) = D(2, -5)$.

$$\bar{x} = \frac{x_1 + x_2}{2} \qquad\qquad \bar{y} = \frac{y_1 + y_2}{2}$$

$$= \frac{4 + 2}{2} = \frac{6}{2} = 3 \qquad\qquad = \frac{7 + (-5)}{2} = \frac{2}{2} = 1$$

The midpoint of $\overline{BD}$ is $(3,1)$.

Since the diagonals have the same midpoint, they bisect each other and **$ABCD$ is a parallelogram**.

(b) If the diagonals of a parallelogram have the same length, then the parallelogram is a rectangle.

To find AC: Let $(x_1, y_1) = A(-3, 0)$, and $(x_2, y_2) = C(9, 2)$.

$$AC = \sqrt{(x_2 - x_1)^2 + (y_2 - y_1)^2}$$

$$= \sqrt{[9 - (-3)]^2 + (2 - 0)^2}$$

$$= \sqrt{12^2 + 2^2}$$

$$= \sqrt{144 + 4}$$

$$= \sqrt{148}$$

To find BD: Let $(x_1, y_1) = B(4, 7)$, and $(x_2, y_2) = D(2, -5)$.

$$BD = \sqrt{(x_2 - x_1)^2 + (y_2 - y_1)^2}$$

$$= \sqrt{(2 - 4)^2 + (-5 - 7)^2}$$

$$= \sqrt{(-2)^2 + (-12)^2}$$

$$= \sqrt{4 + 144}$$

$$= \sqrt{148}$$

Since $AC = BD = \sqrt{148}$, the diagonals of parallelogram $ABCD$ have the same length. Therefore, parallelogram **$ABCD$ is a rectangle**.

5. The coordinates of the vertices of a triangle are $A(-3, 7)$, $B(2, -2)$, and $C(11, 3)$.
(a) Show that $\triangle ABC$ is an isosceles right triangle.
(b) Find the area of $\triangle ABC$.

Solutions: (a) Use the distance formula to find the length of each side of the triangle.

$$AC = \sqrt{[11 - (-3)]^2 + (3 - 7)^2} = \sqrt{14^2 + (-4)^2} = \sqrt{212}$$
$$AB = \sqrt{[2 - (-3)]^2 + (-2 - 7)^2} = \sqrt{5^2 + (-9)^2} = \sqrt{106}$$
$$BC = \sqrt{(11 - 2)^2 + [3 - (-2)]^2} = \sqrt{9^2 + 5^2} = \sqrt{106}$$

To prove that $\triangle ABC$ is a right triangle, show that the lengths of its sides satisfy the Pythagorean relationship.

$$\begin{array}{c|c} (AC)^2 \overset{?}{=} (AB)^2 & + (BC)^2 \\ (\sqrt{212})^2 & (\sqrt{106})^2 + (\sqrt{106})^2 \\ 212 & 106 + 106 \\ 212 & = 212 \checkmark \end{array}$$

Since the square of the length of the longest side of $\triangle ABC$ is equal to the sum of the squares of the lengths of the other two sides, $\triangle ABC$ is a right triangle. Since $AB = BC$, $\triangle ABC$ **is an isosceles right triangle**.
(b) The area of a right triangle is equal to one-half the product of the lengths of its legs.

$$\text{Area of } \triangle ABC = \tfrac{1}{2} \times (\sqrt{106}) \times (\sqrt{106})$$
$$= \tfrac{1}{2} \times 106 = \textbf{53 square units}$$

6. The coordinates of the vertices of $\triangle RST$ are $R(9, 8)$, $S(-2, 5)$, and $T(4, -1)$. Find the length of the median drawn from R to $\overline{ST}$.

Solution: Step 1. Since the median to $\overline{ST}$ intersects $\overline{ST}$ at its midpoint, you must first find the coordinates of the midpoint $M(\bar{x}, \bar{y})$ of $\overline{ST}$. Let $(x_1, y_1) = (-2, 5)$, and $(x_2, y_2) = (4, -1)$.

$$\bar{x} = \frac{x_1 + x_2}{2} \quad \text{and} \quad \bar{y} = \frac{y_1 + y_2}{2}$$
$$= \frac{-2 + 4}{2} \qquad\qquad = \frac{5 + (-1)}{2}$$
$$= \frac{2}{2} = 1 \qquad\qquad = \frac{4}{2} = 2$$

The coordinates of M are $(1, 2)$.

Step 2. Find the length of the segment joining $R(9, 8)$ and $M(1, 2)$.

$$RM = \sqrt{(9-1)^2 + (8-2)^2}$$
$$= \sqrt{(8)^2 + (6)^2}$$
$$= \sqrt{64 + 36}$$
$$= \sqrt{100} = \mathbf{10}$$

7. The coordinates of the vertices of parallelogram *PQRS* are $P(0, -4)$, $Q(x, y)$, $R(2, 4)$, and $S(5, -1)$.

(a) Find the numerical coordinates of point Q.

(b) Prove that *PQRS* is a rhombus.

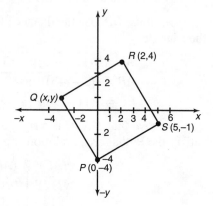

Solutions: **(a)** Use the midpoint formula to find the coordinates of the midpoint of each diagonal.

$$\text{Midpoint of } \overline{PR} = \left(\frac{0+2}{2}, \frac{-4+4}{2}\right) = \left(\frac{2}{2}, \frac{0}{2}\right) = (1, 0)$$
$$\text{Midpoint of } \overline{QS} = \left(\frac{x+5}{2}, \frac{y+(-1)}{2}\right) = \left(\frac{x+5}{2}, \frac{y-1}{2}\right)$$

Since the diagonals of a parallelogram bisect each other, diagonal $\overline{PR}$ and diagonal $\overline{QS}$ must have the same midpoint. Thus,

$$\frac{x+5}{2} = 1 \quad \text{and} \quad \frac{y-1}{2} = 0$$
$$x + 5 = 2 \qquad\qquad y - 1 = 0$$
$$x = -3 \qquad\qquad\quad y = 1$$

Hence, the coordinates of point Q are **(-3, 1)**.

(b) Use the distance formula to find the lengths of any pair of adjacent sides of parallelogram *PQRS*.

$$PQ = \sqrt{(x_2 - x_1)^2 + (y_2 - y_1)^2}$$
$$= \sqrt{(-3-0)^2 + (1-(-4))^2}$$
$$= \sqrt{(-3)^2 + (1+4)^2}$$
$$= \sqrt{9+25}$$
$$= \sqrt{34}$$

$$QR = \sqrt{(x_2 - x_1)^2 + (y_2 - y_1)^2}$$
$$= \sqrt{(2-(-3))^2 + (4-1)^2}$$
$$= \sqrt{(2+3)^2 + (3)^2}$$
$$= \sqrt{25+9}$$
$$= \sqrt{34}$$

Since opposite sides of a parallelogram have the same length, $PQ = RS = \sqrt{34}$ and $QR = PS = \sqrt{34}$. Thus, **parallelogram *PQRS* is a rhombus** since all four sides have the same length.

Lengths of Horizontal and Vertical Segments

Two points that have the same x- (or y-) coordinate determine a vertical (or horizontal) line segment. The distance between two points that determine a horizontal or vertical segment may be calculated either by using the distance formula or, more simply, by finding the positive difference of the *unequal* coordinates of the points by subtracting the smaller x- (or y-) coordinate from the larger x- (or y-) coordinate.

As illustrated in Figure 9.5, points $A(1, 3)$ and $B(5, 3)$ determine a horizontal segment since they have the same y-coordinate. Using the distance formula gives

$$AB = \sqrt{(5-1)^2 + (3-3)^2}$$
$$= \sqrt{4^2 + 0}$$
$$= \sqrt{16} = 4$$

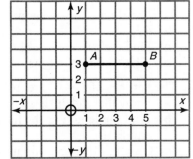

Figure 9.5 Determining the Length of a Horizontal Segment

The simpler method for determining the length of $\overline{AB}$ is to subtract the smaller x-coordinate from the larger x-coordinate: $AB = 5 - 1 = 4$.

Example

7. Find the distance between points $(2, -1)$ and $(2, 4)$.

Solution: Since the two points have the same x-coordinate, the two points determine a vertical line segment whose length is found by subtracting the smaller y-coordinate from the larger y-coordinate.

The length of the segment is $4 - (-1) = 4 + 1 = 5$.

Exercise Set 9.2

1. The coordinates of two vertices of an equilateral triangle are $(-a, 0)$, and $(a, 0)$. Express in terms of a the coordinates of the third vertex of the triangle.

2. Line segment $\overline{AB}$ has midpoint M. If the coordinates of A are $(-3, 2)$ and the coordinates of M are $(-1, 5)$, what are the coordinates of B?
(1) $(1, 10)$ (2) $(1, 8)$ (3) $(0, 7)$ (4) $(-5, 8)$

3. The length of the line segment connecting the points whose coordinates are $(3, -1)$ and $(6, 5)$ is:
(1) $\sqrt{45}$ (2) 5 (3) 3 (4) $\sqrt{97}$

4. The coordinates of the endpoints of the base of an isosceles triangle are (2, 1) and (8, 1). The coordinates of the vertex of this triangle may be:
(1) (1, 5) (2) (2, 5) (3) (2, –6) (4) (5, –6)

5. If $A(2, –1)$ and $B(6, 5)$ are the endpoints of a diameter of a circle, find the coordinates of the center of the circle.

6. What is the length of a radius of a circle whose center is at the origin and that passes through point (–8, 15)?

7. The coordinates of the endpoints of a diameter of a circle are (–1, 7) and (9, –17).
(a) Find the coordinates of the center of the circle.
(b) Find the length of the radius of the circle.

8. The vertices of $\triangle ABC$ are $A(2, 7)$, $B(8, 9)$, and $C(6, 3)$.
(a) Show that $\triangle ABC$ is an isosceles triangle.
(b) Find the length of the median drawn to the base of isosceles triangle ABC.
(c) Graph $\triangle ABC$ and find its area.

9. The coordinates of the vertices of parallelogram $ABCD$ are $A(2, 1)$, $B(4, 3)$, $C(10, 3)$, and $D(x, 1)$. What is the value of x?

10. Show that quadrilateral $QRST$, with coordinates $Q(–5, 2)$, $R(7, 6)$, $S(8, 3)$, and $T(–4, –1)$, is a rectangle, and state a reason for your conclusion.

11. Show that quadrilateral $ABCD$, with vertices $A(–2, 8)$, $B(–4, 2)$, $C(8, 6)$, and $D(4, 10)$, is *not* a parallelogram.

12. The vertices of parallelogram $ABCD$ are $A(–3, 1)$, $B(2, 6)$, $C(x, y)$, and $D(4, 0)$.
(a) Find the numerical coordinates of point C.
(b) Prove that parallelogram $ABCD$ is a rhombus.

13. The vertices of $\triangle ABC$ are $A(5, 7)$, $B(11, –1)$, and $C(3, 3)$.
(a) Prove that $\triangle ABC$ is a right triangle.
(b) Show that the length of the median drawn to the hypotenuse is one-half the length of the hypotenuse.

14–17. In each case, do the following:
(a) Show that $\triangle ABC$ is a right triangle.
(b) Find the area of $\triangle ABC$.

14. $A(2, 3)$, $B(6, 0)$, $C(12, 8)$

15. $A(2, 0)$, $B(11, 8)$, $C(6, 10)$

16. $A(–1, –2)$, $B(3, 1)$, $C(0, 5)$

17. $A(–1, –1)$, $B(1, –2)$, $C(3, 2)$

18. Given: $\triangle ABC$ with vertices $A(2, 1)$, $B(10, 7)$, and $C(4, 10)$.
    (a) Find the area of $\triangle ABC$.
    (b) Find the length of side $\overline{AB}$.
    (c) Using the answers from parts (a) and (b), find the length of the altitude drawn from C to $\overline{AB}$.

19. The vertices of $\triangle ABC$ are $A(4, 4)$, $B(12, 10)$, and $C(6, 13)$.
    (a) Show that $\triangle ABC$ is *not* equilateral.
    (b) Find the area of $\triangle ABC$.

9.3 SLOPE OF A LINE

=== **KEY IDEAS** ===

If you think of a line in the coordinate plane as a hill, then the **slope** of the line is a number that represents its steepness. The steeper a non-vertical line, the greater is the absolute value of its slope. The slope of a vertical line is undefined, and the slope of a horizontal line is 0.

Slope relationships can be used to demonstrate special properties of triangles and quadrilaterals.

Defining Slope

An **oblique line** is a line that is *not* parallel to a coordinate axis. Figure 9.6 illustrates that, when moving between two points on an oblique line, there is a change in vertical and horizontal distances. The change in the vertical distance between two points is measured by the difference in their y-coordinates, while the change in the horizontal distance is measured by the difference in their x-coordinates. In general, the slope of the line that contains points (x_1, y_1) and (x_2, y_2) is defined as a ratio:

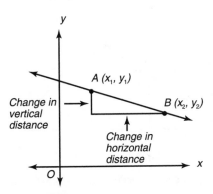

Figure 9.6 Slope of a Line

$$\textbf{Slope} = \frac{\textbf{Change in } y\textbf{-coordinates}}{\textbf{Change in } x\textbf{-coordinates}} = \frac{y_2 - y_1}{x_2 - x_1}.$$

When calculating the differences in the numerator and the denominator of the slope fraction, the x- and y-coordinates of the *same* point must be in the *same* position, either both first or both second.

273

Example

1. What is the slope of the line that passes through points $(1, -2)$ and $(4, 7)$?

Solution: Let $(x_1, y) = (1, -2)$, and $(x_2, y_2) = (4, 7)$.

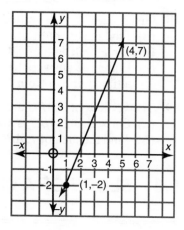

$$\text{Slope} = \frac{y_2 - y_1}{x_2 - x_1}$$

$$= \frac{7 - (-2)}{4 - 1}$$

$$= \frac{7 + 2}{3} = \frac{9}{3} = 3$$

When using the slope formula in Example 1, either of the two given points may be considered the "second" point. For example, the same answer could be obtained by letting $(x_1, y_1) = (4, 7)$ and $(x_2, y_2) = (1, -2)$.

Positive Versus Negative Slope

The slope of an oblique line may be either a positive or a negative number. Figure 9.7 illustrates that, as x increases:

- If the line rises, then its slope m is positive.
- If the line falls, then its slope m is negative.

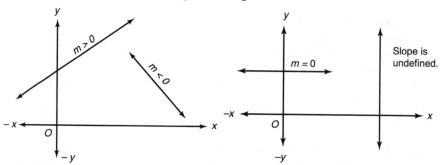

Figure 9.7 Positive and Negative Slopes   **Figure 9.8** Slopes of Horizontal and Vertical Lines

Slopes of Horizontal and Vertical Lines

On a horizontal line there is no change in y, and on a vertical line there is no change in x. Therefore, as shown in Figure 9.8:

- The slope m of a horizontal line is 0.
- The slope m of a vertical line is *not* defined.

Slopes of Parallel Lines

You can tell whether two nonvertical lines are parallel by comparing their slopes.

- If two nonvertical lines have the same slope, the lines are parallel.
- If two nonvertical lines are parallel, the lines have the same slope.

Example

2. The coordinates of the vertices of quadrilateral $ABCD$ are $A(-2, 0)$, $B(10, 3)$, $C(5, 7)$, and $D(1, 6)$. Prove that $ABCD$ is a trapezoid.

Solution: A quadrilateral is a trapezoid if it has exactly one pair of parallel sides. Find and then compare the slopes of the four sides.

$$\text{Slope of } \overline{AB} = \frac{3 - 0}{10 - (-2)} = \frac{3}{12} = \frac{1}{4}$$

$$\text{Slope of } \overline{BC} = \frac{7 - 3}{5 - 10} = \frac{4}{-5} = \frac{-4}{5}$$

$$\text{Slope of } \overline{CD} = \frac{6 - 7}{1 - 5} = \frac{-1}{-4} = \frac{1}{4}$$

$$\text{Slope of } \overline{AD} = \frac{6 - 0}{1 - (-2)} = \frac{6}{3} = 2$$

Side $\overline{AB}$ is parallel to $\overline{CD}$ since their slopes are equal. Sides $\overline{BC}$ and $\overline{AD}$ are *not* parallel since their slopes are *not* equal.

Therefore, **quadrilateral $ABCD$ is a trapezoid** with parallel bases $\overline{AB}$ and $\overline{CD}$.

Slopes of Perpendicular Lines

Pairs of numbers like $\frac{2}{3}$ and $-\frac{3}{2}$ are *negative reciprocals* since their product is -1. If $\frac{2}{3}$ and $-\frac{3}{2}$ represent the slopes of two lines, then these lines are perpendicular. In general:

- If two nonvertical lines have slopes that are negative reciprocals, then the lines are perpendicular.
- If two nonvertical lines are perpendicular, then the slopes of the lines are negative reciprocals.

Example

3. The coordinates of the vertices of $\triangle PQR$ are $P(-1, -1)$, $Q(1, -2)$, and $R(3, 2)$. Prove that $\triangle PQR$ is a right triangle.

Solution: A triangle contains a right angle if two of its sides are perpendicular. Find and then compare the slopes of sides $\overline{PQ}$, $\overline{PR}$, and $\overline{QR}$.

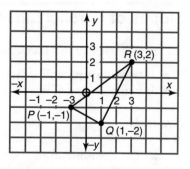

Slope of $\overline{PQ} = \dfrac{-2-(-1)}{1-(-1)} = \dfrac{-2+1}{1+1} = \dfrac{-1}{2}$

Slope of $\overline{PR} = \dfrac{2-(-1)}{3-(-1)} = \dfrac{2+1}{3+1} = \dfrac{3}{4}$

Slope of $\overline{QR} = \dfrac{2-(-2)}{3-1} = \dfrac{2+2}{2} = \dfrac{4}{2} = \dfrac{2}{1}$

Since the slopes of $\overline{PQ}$ and $\overline{QR}$ are negative reciprocals, $\overline{PQ} \perp \overline{QR}$. Therefore $\angle PQR$ is a right angle, and $\triangle PQR$ **is a right triangle**.

In Example 3, instead of using slope, you could use the distance formula to find the length of each side of the triangle and then show that these lengths satisfy the Pythagorean relationship, $(PR)^2 = (PQ)^2 + (QR)^2$.

Determining Whether Points Are on the Same Line

Collinear points are points that lie on the same line. Three or more points are collinear if and only if the slope calculated using any two pairs of points is always the same.

Example

4. Point $C(x, 14)$ lies on the same line as $A(6, -1)$ and $B(2, 5)$. Without graphing, find the value of x.

Solution: Since points A, B, and C are collinear, the slope of $\overline{AB}$ is the same as the slope of $\overline{BC}$.

$$\text{Slope of } \overline{AB} = \text{Slope of } \overline{BC}$$
$$\frac{5-(-1)}{2-6} = \frac{14-5}{x-2}$$
$$\frac{6}{-4} = \frac{9}{x-2}$$
$$6(x-2) = -36$$
$$6x - 12 = -36$$
$$x = \frac{-24}{6} = \mathbf{-4}$$

Summary of Methods for Proving That a Figure Is a Special Triangle or Quadrilateral

Slope relationships provide additional methods for proving that a triangle or quadrilateral has a special property.

- *To prove that a triangle is a right triangle:*
  1. use the distance formula to find the length of each side of the triangle. Then show that the square of the length of the longest side of the triangle is equal to the sum of the squares of the lengths of the other two sides; or
  2. use the slope formula to show that a pair of adjacent sides of the triangle are perpendicular and, as a result, form a right angle.

- *To prove that a quadrilateral is a parallelogram:*
  1. use the midpoint formula to show that the diagonals bisect each other; or
  2. use the slope formula to show that both pairs of opposite sides are parallel; or
  3. use the slope and distance formulas to show that the same pair of sides are parallel and have the same length.

- *To prove that a quadrilateral is a rectangle:*
  1. show that the quadrilateral is a parallelogram that contains a right angle. Use the slope formula to show that opposite pairs of sides are parallel and a pair of adjacent sides are perpendicular; or
  2. show that the quadrilateral is a parallelogram in which the diagonals have the same length. Use the midpoint formula to show that the diagonals bisect each other, and the distance formula to show that the diagonals are equal in length.

- *To prove that a quadrilateral is a rhombus:*
  1. use the distance formula to show that the quadrilateral is equilateral; or
  2. use the slope formula to show that the opposite sides are parallel and the diagonals are perpendicular.

- *To prove that a quadrilateral is a square:*
  1. show that the quadrilateral is a rhombus that contains a right angle. Use the distance formula to show that the quadrilateral is equilateral, and the slope formula to show that a pair of adjacent sides are perpendicular; or
  2. show that the quadrilateral is a rectangle with an adjacent pair of sides that have the same length. Use the midpoint and distance formulas to show that the diagonals bisect each other and have the same length. Then use the distance formula to show that a pair of adjacent sides are equal in length; or

277

3. use the midpoint, distance, and slope formulas to show that the diagonals of the quadrilateral bisect each other, have the same length, and are perpendicular.

- *To prove that a quadrilateral is a trapezoid:*
  use the slope formula to show that one pair of sides are parallel *and* the other pair of sides are *not* parallel.

- *To prove that a triangle or a trapezoid is isosceles:*
  1. use the distance formula to show that two sides of the triangle are congruent;
  2. use the distance formula to show that the two nonparallel sides, or the diagonals, of the trapezoid are congruent.

Example

5. The coordinates of the vertices of quadrilateral *MATH* are $M(-2, -1)$, $A(1, 6)$, $T(8, 3)$, and $H(5, -4)$. Prove that *MATH* is a square.

Solution: A quadrilateral is a square if it is equilateral and contains a right angle.

Step 1. Use the distance formula

$$\sqrt{(x_2 - x_1)^2 + (y_2 - y_1)^2}$$

to show that *MATH* has four sides with the same length.

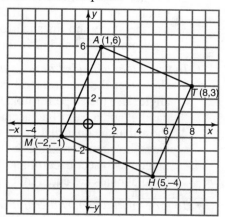

$$
\begin{aligned}
MA &= \sqrt{(-2-1)^2 + (-1-6)^2} \\
&= \sqrt{(-3)^2 \quad + \quad (-7)^2} \\
&= \sqrt{9 \quad\quad + \quad 49} \\
&= \sqrt{58}
\end{aligned}
$$

$$
\begin{aligned}
TH &= \sqrt{(5-8)^2 + (-4-3)^2} \\
&= \sqrt{(-3)^2 \quad + \quad (-7)^2} \\
&= \sqrt{9 \quad\quad + \quad 49} \\
&= \sqrt{58}
\end{aligned}
$$

$$
\begin{aligned}
AT &= \sqrt{(8-1)^2 + (3-6)^2} \\
&= \sqrt{(7)^2 \quad + \quad (-3)^2} \\
&= \sqrt{49 \quad + \quad 9} \\
&= \sqrt{58}
\end{aligned}
$$

$$
\begin{aligned}
MH &= \sqrt{(-2-5)^1 + (-1-(-4))^2} \\
&= \sqrt{(-7)^2 \quad + \quad (-1+4)^2} \\
&= \sqrt{49 \quad\quad + \quad 9} \\
&= \sqrt{58}
\end{aligned}
$$

Since $MA = AT = TH = MH = \sqrt{58}$, quadrilateral *MATH* is equilateral and, as a result, is a rhombus.

Step 2. MATH has all the properties of a parallelogram. If *MATH* contains one right angle, then the remaining three angles must also be right angles. Use the slope formula to show that any pair of adjacent sides are perpendicular and that, as a result, *MATH* contains a right angle. Find and then compare the slopes of $\overline{MA}$ and $\overline{AT}$.

$$\text{Slope of } \overline{MA} = \frac{-2-1}{-1-6} = \frac{-3}{-7} = \frac{3}{7}$$

$$\text{Slope of } \overline{AT} = \frac{8-1}{3-6} = \frac{7}{-3} = -\frac{7}{3}$$

The fractions $\frac{3}{7}$ and $-\frac{7}{3}$ are negative reciprocals. Hence, $\overline{MA} \perp \overline{AT}$, so $\angle A$ is a right angle.

Therefore, **quadrilateral *MATH* is a square** since it is equilateral and contains a right angle.

Exercise Set 9.3

1. Quadrilateral *ABCD* is a parallelogram. Given that the slope of $\overline{AB}$ is $\frac{3}{4}$, find:
   (a) the slope of $\overline{DC}$
   (b) the slope of $\overline{BC}$ if *ABCD* is a rectangle
   (c) the slope of $\overline{BD}$ if *ABCD* is a rhombus and the slope of $\overline{AC}$ is $\frac{7}{6}$

2. In parallelogram *ABCD*, the coordinates of *A* are (2, 3) and the coordinates of *B* are (4, 8). The slope of $\overline{CD}$ is:
   (1) $\frac{2}{5}$ (2) $-\frac{2}{5}$ (3) $\frac{5}{2}$ (4) $-\frac{5}{2}$

3. In each of the following cases, determine whether $\overline{AB}$ is parallel to $\overline{CD}$, perpendicular to $\overline{CD}$, or neither.
   (a) $A(1, 5), B(-1, 9); C(2, 6), D(1, 8)$
   (b) $A(-2, 7), B(1, 4); C(-8, 3), D(-7, 4)$
   (c) $A(1, -5), B(-4, 5); C(0, -7), D(4, 9)$
   (d) $A(-3, 6), B(1, 1); C(-7, 3), D(1, -7)$
   (e) $A(3, 5), B(7, 6); C(-2, 1), D(9, 5)$
   (f) $A(-1, -2), B(-1, 5); C(3, 4), D(-2, 4)$

4. The slope of $\overleftrightarrow{AB}$ is $\frac{3}{5}$, and the slope of $\overleftrightarrow{CD}$ is $\frac{9}{k}$. Find the value of k if:

   (a) $\overleftrightarrow{AB} \parallel \overleftrightarrow{CD}$ **(b)** $\overleftrightarrow{AB} \perp \overleftrightarrow{CD}$

5. The coordinates of the vertices of parallelogram *ABCD* are $A(0, 0)$, $B(5, 0)$, $C(8, 1)$, and $D(x, 1)$. Find the value of x.

6. The coordinates of the vertices of parallelogram *ABCD* are $A(1, y)$, $B(4, 10)$, $C(12, 10)$, and $D(9, 4)$. Find the value of y.

7. Which pair of points will determine a line parallel to the *y*-axis?
   (1) (1, 1) and (2, 3)   (3) (2, 3) and (2, 5)
   (2) (1, 1) and (3, 3)   (4) (2, 5) and (4, 5)

8. Which pair of points will determine a line parallel to the *x*-axis?
   (1) (1, 3) and (–2, 3)   (3) (1, 3) and (1, –1)
   (2) (1, –1) and (–1, 1)   (4) (1, 1) and (–3, –3)

9. The point whose coordinates are (4, –2) lies on a line whose slope is $\frac{3}{2}$. The coordinates of another point on this line may be:
   (1) (1, 0)   (2) (2, 1)   (3) (6, 1)   (4) (7, 0)

10. The line joining $A(-2, 0)$ and $B(10, 3)$ is parallel to the line joining $C(5, 7)$ and $D(1, k)$. Find the value of k.

11. Determine whether point C lies on line $\overleftrightarrow{AB}$.
   (a) $A(-4, -5), B(0, -2), C(8, 4)$ **(c)** $A(1, 2), B(5, 8), C(-3, -4)$
   (b) $A(-3, 2), B(4, 2), C(-5, 2)$ **(d)** $A(2, 1), B(10, 7), C(-4, -6)$

12. The coordinates of the vertices of quadrilateral $ABCD$ are $A(2, 0), B(10, 2), C(6, 7),$ and $D(2, 6)$. Prove that $ABCD$ is a trapezoid.

13. The coordinates of the vertices of trapezoid $ABCD$ are $A(1, 5), B(7, k), C(2, -4),$ and $D(-7, -1)$. If $\overline{AB}$ and $\overline{DC}$ are the bases of the trapezoid, find the value of k.

14. In trapezoid $ABCD$ with bases $\overline{AD}$ and $\overline{BC}$, the coordinates of the vertices are $A(3, 1), B(1, 7), C(4, 9),$ and $D(k, 5)$. Find the value of k.

15. The coordinates of the vertices of rectangle $ABCD$ are $A(-8, -1), B(4, 3), C(5, 0),$ and $D(-7, k)$. Find the value of k.

16. Parallelogram $ABCD$ has vertices $A(2, -1), B(8, 1),$ and $D(4, k)$. The slope of $\overline{AD}$ is equal to 2.
   (a) Find k.   **(b)** Find the coordinates of C.

17. The vertices of a triangle are $P(1, 2), Q(-3, 6),$ and $R(4, 8)$.
   (a) Find the slope of $\overline{PR}$.
   (b) A line through Q is parallel to $\overline{PR}$. If this line contains point $(x, 14)$, find the value of x.

18. If $E(5, h)$ is a point on the line joining $A(0, 1)$ and $B(-2, -1)$, what is the value of $h?$

19. Given points $A(-2, 3), B(1, 0), C(7, 6),$ and $D(0, 5)$.
   (a) Prove that quadrilateral $ABCD$ is a trapezoid.
   (b) Prove that quadrilateral $ABCD$ is *not* an isosceles trapezoid.
   (c) If diagonal $\overline{AC}$ is drawn, prove that $\triangle ABC$ is a right triangle.
   (d) If points $B, E(h, k),$ and C are collinear, find the values of h and k such that points $A, B, E,$ and D are the vertices of a square.

20. The coordinates of the vertices of quadrilateral *ABCD* are *A*(3, 0), *B*(7, 0), *C*(7, 11), and *D*(3, 8).
  (a) Prove that *ABCD* is a trapezoid.
  (b) Using graph paper, draw the trapezoid.
  (c) Find the area of the trapezoid.
  (d) Find the perimeter of the trapezoid.

21. Given points *A*(1, −1), *B*(5, 7), *C*(0, 4), and *D*(3, *k*).
  (a) Find the slope of $\overline{AB}$.
  (b) Find *k* if: (1) $\overline{AB} \parallel \overline{CD}$ (2) $\overline{AB} \perp \overline{CD}$

22. The coordinates of the vertices of △*ABC* are *A*(1, 2), *B*(5, 4), and *C*(3, 8).
  (a) Find the coordinates of midpoint *D* of side $\overline{AC}$ and the coordinates of midpoint *E* of side $\overline{BC}$.
  (b) Show that $\overline{DE} \parallel \overline{AB}$.
  (c) Find the slope of the median to side $\overline{BC}$.
  (d) Find the slope of the altitude to side $\overline{AC}$.

23. Quadrilateral *ABCD* has coordinates *A*(−2, 3), *B*(4, 6), *C*(3, 2), and *D*(−3, −1). Show that:
  (a) the opposite sides are parallel
  (b) the diagonals are *not* perpendicular

24. The vertices of △*ABC* are *A*(1, 1), *B*(10, 4), and *C*(7, 7).
  (a) Find the slope of $\overleftrightarrow{AB}$.
  (b) If *D*(7, *k*) is a point on $\overleftrightarrow{AB}$, find *k*.
  (c) Find the slope of the altitude from *C* to $\overline{AB}$.
  (d) Show by means of slope that △*ABC* is a right triangle.

25. The coordinates of the vertices of △*ABC* are *A*(6, 2), *B*(−4, 4), and *C*(−2, −4).
  (a) Find the coordinates of midpoint *D* of side $\overline{AB}$ and the coordinates of midpoint *E* of side $\overline{BC}$.
  (b) Show that $\overline{DE} \parallel \overline{AC}$.
  (c) Show that $DE = \frac{1}{2} AC$.

26. The vertices of △*ABC* are *A*(−1, 2), *B*(7, 0), and *C*(1, −6).
  (a) Show that point *D*(4, −3) is on $\overline{BC}$.
  (b) Show that $\overline{AD}$ is the perpendicular bisector of $\overline{BC}$.
  (c) Show that △*ABC* is an isosceles triangle.

27. The vertices of quadrilateral *KLMN* are *K*(2, 3), *L*(7, 3), *M*(4, 7), and *N*(−1, 7). Prove that *KLMN* is a rhombus.

28. Quadrilateral *ABCD* has vertices *A*(−1, 0), *B*(3, 3), *C*(6, −1), and *D*(2, −4). Prove that *ABCD* is a square.

29. Quadrilateral *TRAP* has vertices *T*(0, 0), *R*(0, 5), *A*(9, 8), and *P*(12, 4). Prove that *TRAP* is an isosceles trapezoid.

9.4 EQUATIONS OF LINES

KEY IDEAS

The numerical relationship between the x- and y-coordinates of each point on a line is the same and can be expressed as an *equation*. For example, if the sum of the x- and y-coordinates of every point on a certain line is 5, then an equation of this line is $x + y = 5$.

An equation of a line may be written in more than one way. For example, the equation $x + y = 5$ may also be written as $y = -x + 5$.

Slope-Intercept Form

When an equation of a nonvertical line is written in the form

$$y = mx + b,$$

the equation is said to be in **slope-intercept form** since the graph of this equation is a line that has a slope of m and intersects the y-axis at b.

Examples

1. Line p is parallel to the line $y + 4x = 3$, and line q is perpendicular to the line $y + 4x = 3$.
 (a) What is the slope of line p?
 (b) What is the slope of line q?

Solutions: Write the equation of the given line in $y = mx + b$ form: $y = -4x + 3$. The slope of the line is $m = -4$.
 (a) Since parallel lines have the same slope, the slope of line p is **–4**.
 (b) Since perpendicular lines have slopes that are negative reciprocals, the slope of line q is $\frac{1}{4}$.

2. The line whose equation is $y - 3x = b$ passes through point $A(2, 5)$.
 (a) Find the slope of the line.
 (b) Find the y-intercept of the line.

Solutions: **(a)** To find the slope, put the equation of the line in $y = mx + b$ form. The equation $y - 3x = b$ may be written as $y = 3x + b$, which means that the slope of the line is **3**.
 (b) In the equation $y = 3x + b$, b represents the y-intercept of the line. Since point A lies on the line, its coordinates must satisfy the equation. To find the value of b, replace x by 2 and y by 5 in the original equation.

$$y - 3x = b$$
$$5 - 3 \cdot 2 = b$$
$$5 - 6 = b$$
$$-1 = b$$

The y-intercept is **–1**.

Writing an Equation of a Line: Slope-Intercept Form

If a line has a slope of 2 ($m = 2$) and a y-intercept of 5 ($b = 5$), then an equation of the line may be written by replacing m and b in $y = mx + b$ with their numerical values: $y = 2x + 5$.

Example

3. Write an equation of the line whose y-intercept is 1 and that is perpendicular to the line $y = \frac{1}{2}x - 4$.

Solution: The slope of the given line is $\frac{1}{2}$. Since the lines are perpendicular, the slope m of the desired line is the negative reciprocal of $\frac{1}{2}$, which is –2. An equation of the required line is **$y = -2x + 1$**.

Writing an Equation of a Line: Point-Slope Form

If the slope m of a line and the coordinates of a point $P(a, b)$ on the line are known, then an equation of the line may be written by using the point-slope form:

$$y - b = m(x - a).$$

Examples

4. Write an equation of a line that is parallel to the line $y + 2x = 5$ and passes through point $(1, 4)$.

Solution: Since the lines are parallel, the slope m of the desired line is equal to the slope of the line $y + 2x = 5$. The line $y + 2x = 5$ may be written in the slope-intercept form as $y = -2x + 5$. Therefore, its slope is –2, so $m = -2$.

Method 1 (Slope-Intercept Form)	Method 2 (Point-Slope Form)
Find b by replacing m by -2, x by 1, and y by 4: $$y = mx + b$$ $$4 = -2(1) + b$$ $$4 = -2 + b$$ $$6 = b$$ Therefore, $y = -2x + 6$	Since $(a, b) = (1, 4)$, replace m by -2, a by 1, and b by 4: $$y - b = m(x - a)$$ $$y - 4 = -2(x - 1)$$

The slope-intercept and point-slope forms of an equation of a line are equivalent. For example, the equation $y - 4 = -2(x - 1)$ may be expressed in $y = mx + b$ form as follows:

$$y - 4 = -2(x - 1)$$
$$= -2x + 2$$
$$y = -2x + 2 + 4$$
$$y = -2x + 6$$

5. Write an equation of the line that passes through the origin and is perpendicular to the line whose equation is $y = 3x - 6$.

Solution: The slope of the line whose equation is $y = 3x - 6$ is 3, so the slope m of a perpendicular line is $-\frac{1}{3}$ (the negative reciprocal of 3). Since the required line passes through the origin, $(a, b) = (0, 0)$. Therefore,

$$y - b = m(x - a)$$
$$y - 0 = -\frac{1}{3}(x - 0)$$

or

$$y = -\frac{1}{3}x.$$

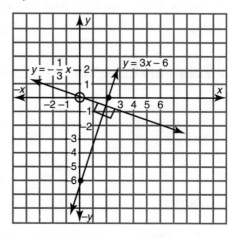

6. The vertices of $\triangle ABC$ are $A(-3, -1)$, $B(1, 11)$, and $C(8, -3)$.

(a) Find an equation of the line that can be drawn through A and parallel to $\overline{BC}$.

(b) Find an equation of the line that contains points B and C.

(c) Find an equation of the altitude from A to side $\overline{BC}$.

(d) If the altitude from A to side $\overline{BC}$ intersects $\overline{BC}$ at D (x,y), use the answers from parts (b) and (c) to find the numerical coordinates of point D.

Solutions:

(a) To write an equation of the line that can be drawn through A and parallel to $\overline{BC}$, use the point-slope form $y - b = m\,(x - a)$, where m is the slope of $\overline{BC}$ and (a, b) are the coordinates of point A:

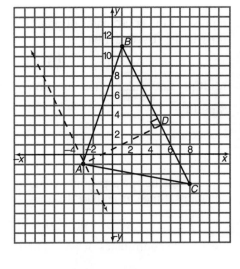

$$m = \frac{-3 - 11}{8 - 1} = \frac{-14}{7} = -2.$$

Let $(a, b) = (-3, -1)$. Then

$$y - b = m\,(x - a)$$
$$y - (-1) = -2(x - (-3))$$
$$y + 1 = -2(x + 3)$$
$$= -2x - 6$$
$$\boldsymbol{y = -2x - 7.}$$

(b) To write an equation of the line that contains points B and C, use the point-slope form $y - b = m\,(x - a)$, where m is the slope of $\overline{BC}$ and (a, b) are the coordinates of either point B or point C. From part (a), $m = -2$. Let $(a, b) = B(1, 11)$. Then

$$y - b = m\,(x - a)$$
$$y - 11 = -2(x - 1)$$
$$= -2x + 2$$
$$\boldsymbol{y = -2x + 13.}$$

(c) To write an equation of the altitude from A to side $\overline{BC}$ use the point-slope form $y - b = m\,(x - a)$, where m is the slope of the altitude and (a, b) are the coordinates of point A. Since an altitude is perpendicular to the side to which it is drawn and the slope of $\overline{BC}$ is -2, $m = \frac{1}{2}$. Let $(a, b) = (-3, -1)$. Then

$$y - b = m\,(x - a)$$
$$y - (-1) = \frac{1}{2}(x - (-3))$$
$$y + 1 = \frac{1}{2}(x + 3)$$
$$= \frac{1}{2}x + \frac{3}{2}$$
$$\boldsymbol{y = \frac{1}{2}x + \frac{1}{2}.}$$

(d) If the altitude from A to side $\overline{BC}$ intersects $\overline{BC}$ at $D\,(x, y)$, then the coordinates of point D must satisfy the equations for lines BC and AD at the same time. Thus, the solution of the system

$$y = -2x + 13$$
$$y = \frac{1}{2}x + \frac{1}{2}$$

represents the coordinates of point D. To solve this system, substitute $\frac{1}{2}x + \frac{1}{2}$ for y in the first equation:

$$\frac{1}{2}x + \frac{1}{2} = -2x + 13$$

Multiply both sides of the equation by 2: $\quad 2\left(\frac{1}{2}x\right) + 2\left(\frac{1}{2}\right) = 2(-2x) + 2(13)$

Simplify: $\hspace{8cm} x + 1 = -4x + 26$

Isolate x: $\hspace{8.5cm} 5x = 25$

$$x = \frac{25}{5} = 5$$

To find the corresponding value of y, replace x by 5 in either of the original equations. Since, from part (b), $y = -2x + 13$,

$$y = -2(5) + 13 = -10 + 13 = 3.$$

Hence, the coordinates of point D are **(5, 3)**.

Equations of Vertical and Horizontal Lines

In Figure 9.9 the equation $x = a$ defines a vertical line that, extended if necessary, intersects the x-axis at a. Each point on a vertical line $x = a$ has an x-coordinate of a.

Similarly, in Figure 9.9 the equation $y = b$ defines a horizontal line that, extended if necessary, intersects the y-axis at b. Each point on a horizontal line $y = b$ has a y-coordinate of b.

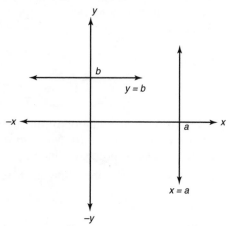

Figure 9.9 Equations of Vertical and Horizontal Lines

Example

7. Write an equation of a line that passes through point $(-3, 5)$ and is parallel to the:

(a) x-axis   (b) y-axis

Solutions: **(a)** As shown in the accompanying diagram, a line parallel to the x-axis is a horizontal line, so its equation takes the general form $y = b$. Since the line passes through $(-3, 5)$, $b = 5$.

An equation of the line is **$y = 5$**.

(b) Similarly, a line parallel to the *y*-axis is vertical, so its equation takes the form $x = a$. Since the line passes through $(-3, 5)$, $a = -3$.

An equation of the line is **$x = -3$**.

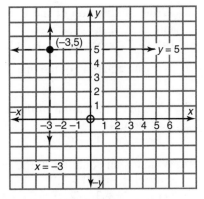

Here is a summary of some different forms of an equation of a line.

General Form of Equation	Comments
y = mx + b	m = slope of line; b = y-intercept
y − b = m(x − a)	Use when the slope m of the line and the coordinates (a, b) of a point on the line are known. Also use when two points on the line are given, after first using their coordinates to calculate m.
x = a	Vertical line (parallel to y-axis) that intersects the x-axis at a.
y = b	Horizontal line (parallel to x-axis) that intersects the y-axis at b.

Exercise Set 9.4

1. Find the slope of a line that is parallel to the given line.
   (a) $y = 2x + 5$ **(b)** $y - 3 = x$ **(c)** $2x + y = 8$ **(d)** $3x + 4y = 12$

2. Find the slope of a line that is perpendicular to the given line.
   (a) $y = 3x - 1$ **(b)** $y = \frac{3}{5}x + 2$ **(c)** $x - 4y = 9$ **(d)** $3y + 4x = 12$

3. Which line is parallel to the line $y = 2x + 4$?
   (1) $y = 2x + 6$ (2) $y = 4 - 2x$ (3) $y = 4x - 2$ (4) $2y = x - 2$

4. Write an equation of the line that is parallel to the given line and passes through the given point.
   (a) $y = 2x - 1$; $(-4, 0)$ **(c)** $2y - 1 = 6x$; $(0, -3)$
   (b) $y - 4x = 2$; $(2, -5)$ **(d)** $3x - 2y = 6$; $(-2, 1)$

5. Write an equation of the line that is perpendicular to the given line and passes through the given point.
   (a) $y = -\frac{1}{2}x + 3$; $(0, 4)$ **(c)** $y + x = 5$; $(-7, 3)$
   (b) $y = 3x + 1$; $(-6, 2)$ **(d)** $3y + 2x = 12$; $(3, -4)$

287

6. Write an equation of the line that contains the given point and has a y-intercept of b.
   (a) $(-2, 4); b = -2$ **(b)** $(1, -3); b = 5$ **(c)** $(3, 7); b = -2$

7. Write an equation of the line that has an x-intercept of -3 and a y-intercept of 4.

8. Which is an equation of the line that passes through point $(0, 2)$ and has a slope of 4?
   (1) $x = 2y - 4$ (2) $y = 2x + 4$ (3) $4x + y = 2$ (4) $y = 4x + 2$

9. Which is an equation of the line that is parallel to $y = 2x - 8$ and passes through point $(0, -3)$?
   (1) $y = 2x + 3$ (2) $y = 2x - 3$ (3) $y = -\frac{1}{2}x + 3$ (4) $y = -\frac{1}{2}x - 3$

10. Write an equation of the line that passes through point $A(-4, 3)$ and is parallel to the line $2y - x = 3$.

11. Write an equation of the line that passes through point $B(3, 1)$ and is perpendicular to the line $3y + 2x = 15$.

12. Write an equation of the line that contains point $(-5, 2)$ and is parallel to:
    (a) the x-axis   **(b)** the y-axis   **(c)** the line $y + x = 3$

13. Write an equation of the line that contains point $(4, -1)$ and is perpendicular to:
    (a) the x-axis   **(b)** the y-axis   **(c)** the line $y - 2x = 3$

14. Write an equation of the line that passes through the two given points.
    (a) $(-2, 7)$ and $(4, 7)$ **(c)** $(1, -3)$ and $(-1, 5)$
    (b) $(-5, 8)$ and $(-5, -3)$ **(d)** $(2, -2)$ and $(-4, 4)$

15. Which is an equation of the line that passes through points $(1, 3)$ and $(-1, 1)$?
    (1) $x = 1$ (2) $y = 2x + 1$ (3) $y = x + 2$ (4) $y = 3$

16. The vertices of $\triangle ABC$ are $A(0, 6)$, $B(-8, 0)$ and $C(0, 0)$. Write an equation of the line that passes through one of the vertices of the triangle and is parallel to:
    (a) $\overline{AC}$ **(b)** $\overline{BC}$ **(c)** $\overline{AB}$

17. Write an equation of the perpendicular bisector of the segment that joins points $(3, -7)$ and $(5, 1)$.

18. The coordinates of the vertices of $\triangle ABC$ are $A(-3, -4)$, $B(-1, 7)$, and $C(3, 5)$.
    (a) Write an equation of the line drawn through B and parallel to $\overline{AC}$.
    (b) Write an equation of the altitude drawn from C to side $\overline{AB}$.
    (c) Write an equation of the median drawn from A to side $\overline{BC}$.
    (d) Using graph paper, find the area of $\triangle ABC$.

19. The coordinates of the vertices of △ABC are $A(1, 2)$, $B(7, 0)$, and $C(3, -2)$.
   (a) Show that △ABC is an isosceles triangle.
   (b) Write an equation of the altitude drawn from vertex C to the base of the triangle.
   (c) Write an equation of the median drawn from vertex C to the base of the triangle.
   (d) Prove that △ABC is a right triangle.

20. The vertices of parallelogram $STWU$ are $S(1, 1)$, $T(-2, 3)$, $W(0, b)$, and $U(3, -5)$.
   (a) Find the slope of $\overline{ST}$.
   (b) Express the slope of $\overline{UW}$ in terms of b.
   (c) Find the value of b.
   (d) Write an equation of the line passing through point S and perpendicular to $\overline{ST}$.

21. Given: points $A(1, -1)$, $B(5, 7)$, $C(0, 4)$, and $D(3, k)$.
   (a) Find the slope of $\overleftrightarrow{AB}$.
   (b) Express the slope of $\overleftrightarrow{CD}$ in terms of k.
   (c) If $\overleftrightarrow{AB} \parallel \overleftrightarrow{CD}$, find k.
   (d) Write an equation of $\overleftrightarrow{CD}$.

22. The vertices of △PQR are $P(1, 2)$, $Q(-3, 6)$, and $R(4, 8)$.
   (a) Find the coordinates of S, the midpoint of $\overline{PQ}$.
   (b) Express, in radical form, the length of median $\overline{RS}$.
   (c) Find the slope of $\overline{PR}$.
   (d) A line through point Q is parallel to $\overline{PR}$. If this line passes through point $(x, 14)$, find the value of x.

9.5 TRANSFORMATIONS IN THE COORDINATE PLANE

KEY IDEAS

The process of moving each point of a figure according to some given rule is called a **transformation**. Each point of the new figure corresponds to exactly one point of the original figure and is called the **image** of that point. Sometimes the image of a point P is designated as point P', which is read as "P prime."

Reflections, translations, and *dilations* are special types of transformations; each uses a different rule for locating images of points of the figure that are undergoing the transformation.

Reflections in a Line

A **reflection** in a line may be thought of as the mirror image of a point or set of points with respect to a *line of symmetry* that serves as the "mirror." As illustrated in Figure 9.10, the image of a point P is determined in such a way that the line of symmetry (line ℓ) is the perpendicular bisector of the segment ($\overline{PP'}$) determined by the original point (P) and its image (P').

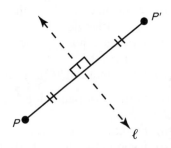

Figure 9.10 Reflections of a Point in a Line

MATH FACTS

RULES FOR REFLECTIONS IN LINES

- The reflection of point (a, b) in the x-axis is point $(a, -b)$.
- The reflection of point (a, b) in the y-axis is point $(-a, b)$.
- The reflection of point (a, b) in the line whose equation is $y = x$ is point (b, a).

In each case the line of reflection (x-axis, y-axis, and line $y = x$) is the perpendicular bisector of the line segment whose endpoints are the original point (a, b) and its image under the reflection.

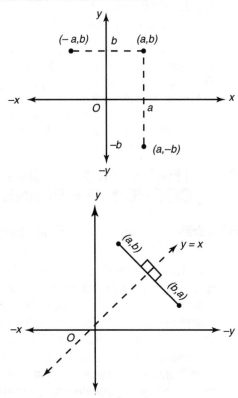

Example

1. The coordinates of the vertices of $\triangle ABC$ are $A(0, 1)$, $B(3, 4)$, and $C(5, 2)$. Determine the coordinates of the vertices of the image of $\triangle ABC$ under a reflection in the:

    (a) x-axis   **(b)** y-axis   **(c)** line $y = x$

Solutions: **(a)** In general, under a reflection in the x-axis, $P(a, b) \rightarrow P'(a, -b)$.

    Therefore, $A(0, 1) \rightarrow \boldsymbol{A\,'(0, -1)}$,
                   $B(3, 4) \rightarrow \boldsymbol{B'(3, -4)}$,
                   $C(5, 2) \rightarrow \boldsymbol{C'(5, -2)}$.

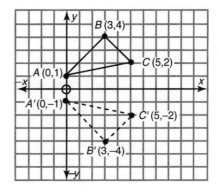

(b) In general, under a reflection in the y-axis, $P(a, b) \rightarrow P'(-a, b)$.

    Therefore, $A(0, 1) \rightarrow \boldsymbol{A\,'(0, 1)}$,
                   $B(3, 4) \rightarrow \boldsymbol{B'(-3, 4)}$,
                   $C(5, 2) \rightarrow \boldsymbol{A\,'(-5, 2)}$.

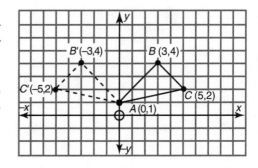

(c) In general, under a reflection in the line $y = x$, $P(a, b) \rightarrow P'(b, a)$.

    Therefore, $A(0, 1) \rightarrow \boldsymbol{A\,'(1, 0)}$,
                   $B(3, 4) \rightarrow \boldsymbol{B'(4, 3)}$,
                   $C(5, 2) \rightarrow \boldsymbol{A\,'(2, 5)}$.

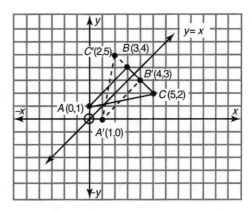

Reflections in a Point

If point P' is the image of point P under a reflection in point A, then A is the midpoint of $\overline{PP'}$. A point and its image under a reflection in the origin must have coordinates that have the same absolute value but are opposite in sign, so that the average of the x-coordinates and the average of the y-coordinates are each 0.

MATH FACTS

RULES FOR REFLECTIONS IN POINTS

- The reflection of point $P(a, b)$ in the origin $(0, 0)$ is point $P'(-a, -b)$. (See the accompanying diagram.)

- In general, the reflection of point P in point A is the point P' that makes A the midpoint of $\overline{PP'}$.

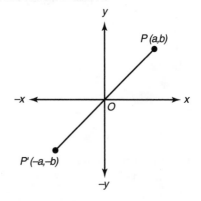

Example

2. Point $R(6, 1)$ is reflected in point $P(1, 2)$. What are the coordinates of the image of R under this reflection?

Solution: Point $P(1, 2)$ is the midpoint of the segment joining $R(6, 1)$ and its image $R'(x, y)$. Therefore,

$$1 = \frac{6 + x}{2} \quad \text{and} \quad 2 = \frac{1 + y}{2}$$
$$2 = 6 + x \qquad\qquad 4 = 1 + y$$
$$-4 = x \qquad\qquad\quad 3 = y$$

The coordinates of the image of $R(6, 1)$ are **(–4, 3)**.

Translations

A **translation** may be thought of as a "slide" of a figure in a plane in which the image of each point of the figure is moved the same distance in the horizontal

(x) direction and the same distance in the vertical (y) direction. The image of a figure that is translated is congruent to the original figure.

MATH FACTS

RULE FOR TRANSLATIONS

The image of a point $P(x, y)$ that is translated h units in the horizontal direction and k units in the vertical direction is point $P'(x + h, y + k)$. The accompanying diagram illustrates a translation in which both h and k are positive numbers.

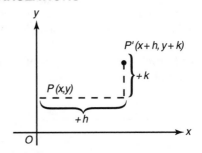

- If $h > 0$, the translation shifts the figure horizontally to the right; if $h < 0$, the figure is shifted horizontally to the left.
- If $k > 0$, the translation shifts the figure vertically up; if $k < 0$, the figure is shifted vertically down.

Example

3. The coordinates of the vertices of $\triangle ABC$ are $A(2, -3)$, $B(0, 4)$, and $C(-1, 5)$. If the image of point A under a translation is point $A'(0, 0)$, find the coordinates of the images of points B and C under this translation.

Solution: In general, after a translation of h units in the horizontal direction and k units in the vertical direction, the image of $P(x, y)$ is $P'(x + h, y + k)$. Since

$$A(2, -3) \rightarrow A'(2 + h, -3 + k) = A'(0, 0),$$

it follows that

$$
\begin{aligned}
2 + h &= 0 \quad \text{and} \quad h = -2, \\
-3 + k &= 0 \quad \text{and} \quad k = 3.
\end{aligned}
$$

Therefore,

$$
\begin{aligned}
B(0, 4) &\rightarrow B'(0 + [-2], 4 + 3) = B'(-2, 7), \\
C(-1, 5) &\rightarrow C'(-1 + [-2], 5 + 3) = C'(-3, 8).
\end{aligned}
$$

The coordinates of point B' are **(–2, 7)**, and the coordinates of point C' are **(–3, 8)**.

Dilations

Reflections, translations, and rotations produce figures that are *congruent* to the original figures, since under these transformations the lengths of the sides and the measures of the angles of the figures remain the same. A **dilation** is a transformation that produces a figure that is *similar* to the original figure. After a dilation the original figure may be enlarged or reduced with respect to a given point of reference, called the *center of dilation*. The scale factor by which the original figure is enlarged or reduced is called the *constant of dilation*. For example, if two triangles are similar and their ratio of similitude is 2, then the larger triangle may be thought of as a dilation of the smaller triangle with a constant of dilation equal to 2.

MATH FACTS

RULE FOR DILATIONS

The image of $P(x, y)$ under a dilation with respect to the origin is $P'(cx, cy)$, where c is the constant of dilation. The accompanying figure illustrates a dilation in which $c > 1$, so that $OP' > OP$.

- If $c > 1$, the dilation produces a figure that is larger than the original figure.
- If $0 < c < 1$, the dilation produces a figure that is smaller than the original figure.
- If $c = 1$, the dilation produces a figure that is congruent to the original figure.

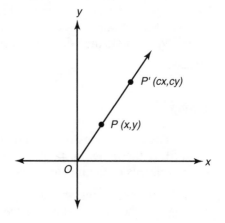

Example

4. After a dilation with respect to the origin, the image of point $A(2, 3)$ is $A'(4, 6)$. What are the coordinates of the image of $B(1, 5)$ after the same dilation?

Solution: The constant of dilation is 2 since

$$A(2, 3) \rightarrow A'(2 \cdot 2, 2 \cdot 3) = A'(4, 6).$$

Therefore, after the same dilation the x- and y-coordinates of point B are each multiplied by 2:

$$B(1, 5) \rightarrow B'(2 \cdot 1, 2 \cdot 5) = B'(2, 10).$$

The coordinates of point B' are **(2, 10)**.

Exercise Set 9.5

1. Point $(-4, -1)$ is reflected in point P. If the coordinates of its image are $(2, -3)$, what are the coordinates of point P?

2. The image of $(-2, 1)$ under a translation is $(1, 0)$. What are the coordinates of the image of $(2, 3)$ under the same translation?

3. Which of the following transformations does *not* produce an image that is congruent to the original figure?
   (1) Point reflection   (2) Dilation   (3) Translation   (4) Line reflection

4. After a dilation, $(4, -2)$ is the image of $(2, -1)$. What are the coordinates of the image of $(-6, 0)$ after the same dilation?

5. Under a translation the image of the origin is point $(5, -3)$. What is the image of point $(3, 2)$ under the same translation?

6. The image of $A(2, 2)$ under a reflection in point P is $A'(-3, 5)$. What are the coordinates of the image of $B(4, -2)$ under a reflection in point P?

7. Verify that (b, a) is the image of (a, b) under a reflection in the line $y = x$ by showing that the line $y = x$ is the perpendicular bisector of the line segment determined by (a, b) and (b, a).

8. Given hexagon $ABCDEF$ with coordinates $A(2, 2)$, $B(4, 0)$, $C(2, -2)$, $D(-2, -2)$, $E(-4, 0)$, $F(-2, 2)$, write the coordinates of the image of the given point after the transformation described.
   (a) The image of point A after a reflection in the line $y = -x$
   (b) The image of point F after a reflection in the y-axis
   (c) The image of point B after a reflection in the origin
   (d) The image of point D after the transformation $(x, y) \rightarrow (x + 6, y + 2)$

9. **(a)** On graph paper, draw and label $\triangle ABC$ whose coordinates are $A(2, 1)$, $B(6, 4)$, $C(8, 1)$.
   (b) Graph and state the coordinates of $\triangle A'B'C'$, the reflection of $\triangle ABC$ in the x-axis.
   (c) Graph and state the coordinates of $\triangle A''B''C''$, the image of $\triangle A'B'C'$ after applying the translation rule $(x, y) \rightarrow (x - 6, y - 2)$.

10. Given points $A(3, 0)$ and $B(-4, 6)$, write the coordinates of the images of points A and B after each transformation described.
    (a) The images of points A and B after a reflection in the line $y = x$

(b) The images of points A and B after a reflection in the origin

(c) The images of points A and B after a dilation with respect to the origin such that $(x, y) \rightarrow (\frac{1}{2}x, \frac{1}{2}y)$

11. Given $A(3, 3)$, answer the following questions:

(a) In a reflection in point P, the image of A is $(2, 1)$. What are the coordinates of the image of $(4, -3)$ in a reflection in point P?

(b) In a dilation with respect to the origin, the image of A is $(2, 2)$. What are the coordinates of the image of $(6, 9)$ under the same dilation?

(c) Under a translation, the image of A is $(0, 2)$. What are the coordinates of the image of $(5, -1)$ under the same translation?

12. Given $A(8, 5)$ and $B(6, 1)$ and transformations T, R, and S as described below:

$$T: (x, y) \rightarrow (x + 1, y - 5)$$
$$R: (x, y) \rightarrow (y, x)$$
$$S: (x, y) \rightarrow (-x, y)$$

(a) Graph $\overline{AB}$ and its image $\overline{A'B'}$ after transformation T.

(b) Graph $\overline{A''B''}$, the image of $\overline{AB}$ after transformation R.

(c) Graph $\overline{A'''B'''}$, the image of $\overline{AB}$ after transformation S.

(d) Compare the slopes of the pairs of segments listed below, and indicate whether these slopes are *equal, reciprocals, additive inverses,* or *negative reciprocals.*

(1) $\overline{AB}$ and $\overline{A'B'}$ (2) $\overline{AB}$ and $\overline{A''B''}$ (3) $\overline{AB}$ and $\overline{A'''B'''}$

9.6 COORDINATE PROOFS USING GENERAL COORDINATES

KEY IDEAS

A theorem or property about a figure can be proved by placing a representative figure in the coordinate plane with variables and zeros used as general coordinates instead of specific nonzero numbers. The slope, midpoint, or distance formula is then applied to the general coordinates to show that the figure has the desired property.

Positioning Figures Using General Coordinates

Since a figure may be reflected, rotated, or translated without changing its size or shape, there are infinitely many ways in which a given type of polygon can be placed in the coordinate plane. Here are two general guidelines for positioning a polygon in the coordinate plane so that the calculations needed to prove a theorem about the figure are simplified.

1. Position the polygon so that the coordinates of its vertices can be represented by using a minimum number of different letters and a maximum number of zeros. Typically, this means that the polygon should be placed in the coordinate plane in such a way that the origin is one of the vertices of the polygon, and at least one of the sides of the polygon coincides with a coordinate axis.

2. Consider the defining characteristics of the given polygon when positioning it. For example, a right triangle is usually positioned so that its two legs coincide with the coordinate axes, thus forming a right angle at the origin. In Figure 9.11 two adjacent sides of a square are positioned so that they coincide with the coordinate axes, while opposite sides are drawn as horizontal and vertical segments with the coordinates of the vertices chosen so that

$AB = BC = CD = DA = a$ units.

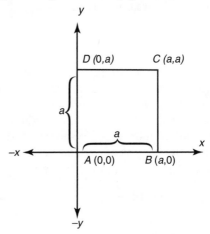

Figure 9.11 Positioning a Square

Examples

1. Quadrilateral $QRST$ has vertices $Q(a, b)$, $R(0,0)$, $S(c, 0)$, and $T(a + c, b)$. Prove that $QRST$ is a parallelogram.

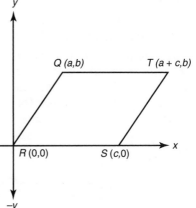

Solution: Quadrilateral $QRST$ is a parallelogram if its diagonals have the same midpoint and, therefore, bisect each other.

Step 1. Find the midpoint of the segment joining $R(0, 0)$ and $T(a + c, b)$.

$$\bar{x} = \frac{0 + (a + c)}{2} = \frac{a + c}{2},$$
$$\bar{y} = \frac{0 + b}{2} = \frac{b}{2}$$

The midpoint of diagonal $\overline{RT}$ is $\left(\frac{a + c}{2}, \frac{b}{2}\right)$.

Step 2. Find the midpoint of the segment joining $Q(a, b)$ and $S(c, 0)$.

$$\bar{x} = \frac{a + c}{2}, \qquad \bar{y} = \frac{b + 0}{2} = \frac{b}{2}.$$

The midpoint of diagonal $\overline{QS}$ is $\left(\dfrac{a + c}{2}, \dfrac{b}{2}\right)$.

Conclusion: Since diagonals $\overline{RT}$ and $\overline{QS}$ have the same midpoint, they bisect each other and **quadrilateral $QRST$ is a parallelogram**.

2. Using methods of coordinate geometry, prove that the diagonals of a rectangle are congruent.

Solution: In the accompanying diagram, the rectangle is positioned so that one of the vertices coincides with the origin and a pair of adjacent sides coincide with the coordinate axes. To show that $\overline{AC} \cong \overline{BD}$, find the lengths of $\overline{AC}$ and $\overline{BD}$ by applying the distance formula, $\sqrt{(x_2 - x_1)^2 + (y_2 - y_1)^2}$:

$$AC = \sqrt{(a - 0)^2 + (b - 0)^2} \qquad\qquad BD = \sqrt{(0 - a)^2 + (b - 0)^2}$$
$$\quad\; = \sqrt{a^2 + b^2} \qquad\qquad\qquad\qquad\;\; = \sqrt{a^2 + b^2}$$

Conclusion: Since the lengths of diagonals $\overline{AC}$ and $\overline{BD}$ are both equal to $\sqrt{a^2 + b^2}$, $\boldsymbol{\overline{AC} \cong \overline{BD}}$.

3. Prove that the line segment joining the midpoints of two sides of a triangle is parallel to the third side of the triangle.

Solution: In the accompanying diagram, the choice of coordinates of $2a$, $2b$, and $2c$ simplifies the calculations since it eliminates fractions for the coordinates of the vertices of the midpoints of sides $\overline{AB}$ and $\overline{BC}$:

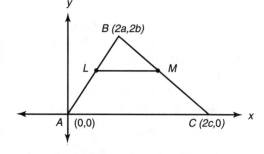

$$L(x, y) = L\left(\frac{0 + 2a}{2}, \frac{0 + 2b}{2}\right) = L\left(\frac{2a}{2}, \frac{2b}{2}\right) = L(a, b)$$

$$M(x, y) = M\left(\frac{2a + 2c}{2}, \frac{2b + 0}{2}\right) = M\left(\frac{2(a + c)}{2}, \frac{2b}{2}\right) = M(a + c, b)$$

$$\text{Slope of } \overline{LM} = \frac{y_2 - y_1}{x_2 - x_1} = \frac{b - b}{a + c - c} = \frac{0}{a} = 0$$

$$\text{Slope of } \overline{AC} = \frac{y_2 - y_1}{x_2 - x_1} = \frac{0 - 0}{2c - 0} = \frac{0}{2c} = 0$$

Conclusion: Since line segment $\overline{LM}$ and side $\overline{AC}$ have the same slope, **they are parallel**.

Exercise Set 9.6

1. The coordinates of two vertices of an equilateral triangle are $(-a, 0)$ and $(a, 0)$. Express in terms of a the coordinates of the third vertex of the triangle.

2. The coordinates of the vertices of square $ABCD$ are $A(0, 0)$, $B(0, t)$, $C(x, y)$, and $D(t, 0)$.
   (a) Express the coordinates of C in terms of t.
   (b) Prove that the diagonals of square $ABCD$ are congruent.
   (c) Prove that the diagonals of square $ABCD$ are perpendicular.

3. Using the methods of coordinate geometry, prove that the length of the line segment joining the midpoints of two sides of a triangle is one-half the length of the third side of the triangle.

4. The coordinates of the vertices of right triangle ABC are $A(0, 2a)$, $B(2b, 0)$, and $C(0, 0)$. Using the methods of coordinate geometry, prove that:
   (a) the length of the median drawn to the hypotenuse of the triangle is one-half the length of the hypotenuse
   (b) the midpoint of the hypotenuse is equidistant from the three vertices of the right triangle

5. The coordinates of the vertices of quadrilateral $ABCD$ are $A(0, 0)$, $B(a, b)$, $C(c, b)$, and $D(a + c, 0)$. Prove that $ABCD$ is an isosceles trapezoid.

6. The coordinates of the vertices of quadrilateral $MATH$ are $M(0, 0)$, $A(r, t)$, $T(s, t)$, and $H(s - r, 0)$. Prove that:
   (a) quadrilateral $MATH$ is a parallelogram
   (b) the diagonals of quadrilateral $MATH$ are *not necessarily* perpendicular
   (c) the diagonals of quadrilateral $MATH$ are *not necessarily* congruent

7. The coordinates of the vertices of parallelogram $ABCD$ are $A(0, 0)$, $B(b, y)$, $C(a + b, y)$, and $D(a, 0)$.
   (a) If $ABCD$ is a rhombus, express y in terms of a and b.
   (b) If $ABCD$ is a rhombus, prove that its diagonals are perpendicular.

8. The vertices of an isosceles trapezoid with bases $\overline{BC}$ and $\overline{AD}$ are $A(0, 0)$, $B(b, c)$, $C(h, k)$, and $D(a, 0)$
   (a) Express h and k in terms of a, b, and/or c.
   (b) Use the methods of coordinate geometry to prove that the diagonals of an isosceles trapezoid are congruent.

299

REGENTS TUNE-UP: CHAPTER 9

Each of the questions in this section has appeared on a previous Course II Regents Examination. Here is an opportunity for you to review the material in Chapter 9 and, at the same time, prepare for the Course II Regents Examination.

---

1. What are the coordinates of A', the image of point $A(-5, 1)$ after a reflection in the *y*-axis?

2. What is the slope of the line that passes through points $(4, 9)$ and $(-1, 12)$?

3. Find the distance between the points whose coordinates are $(2, 7)$ and $(8, -1)$.

4. The coordinates of the vertices of parallelogram $ABCD$ are $A(2, 1)$, $B(4, 3)$, $C(10, 3)$, $D(x, 1)$. What is the value of x?

5. Write an equation of the line that passes through point $(2, 7)$ and has a slope of 4.

6. Find, to the *nearest tenth*, the distance between two points whose coordinates are $(-2, 5)$ and $(3, -4)$.

7. The endpoints of $\overline{AB}$ are $A(x, 3)$ and $B(4, 7)$. If the coordinates of the midpoint M of $\overline{AB}$ are $(-1, 5)$, find x.

8. Write an equation of the line that passes through points $(2, 1)$ and $(6, 3)$.

9. The line that passes through points $(-2, 3)$ and $(5, y)$ has a slope of $\frac{4}{7}$. Find y.

10. What is the image of $(4, -3)$ after a reflection in the *x*-axis?

11. If point $(k, 2)$ is on the line whose equation is $2x + 3y = 4$, what is the value of k?

12. The slope of $\overleftrightarrow{RU}$ is $\frac{3}{5}$. If $\overleftrightarrow{RU} \parallel \overleftrightarrow{ST}$ and the slope of $\overleftrightarrow{ST}$ is $\frac{x-6}{x}$, what is the value of x?

13. If line ℓ is perpendicular to line m and the slope of line ℓ is undefined, what is the slope of line m?
    (1) 1   (2) $\frac{1}{2}$ (3) 0   (4) –1

14. A translation moves $A(2, 3)$ onto $A'(4, 8)$. What are the coordinates of B', the image of $B(4, 6)$, under the same translation?
    (1) (12, 18)   (2) (6, 8)   (3) (8, 12)   (4) (6, 11)

15. Which point is closest to the origin?
    (1) (5, 12)   (2) (6, 8)   (3) (10, 4)   (4) (0, 11)

16. If the endpoints of a diameter of a circle are $(2, -1)$ and $(4, 0)$, what are the coordinates of the center of the circle?

(1) $(6, -1)$ (2) $\left(3, -\frac{1}{2}\right)$ (3) $\left(3, \frac{1}{2}\right)$ (4) $(2, -1)$

17. The graph of the equation $x - 3y = 6$ is parallel to the graph of

(1) $y = -3x + 7$ (2) $y = -\frac{1}{3}x + 5$ (3) $y = 3x - 8$ (4) $y = \frac{1}{3}x + 8$

18. The graph of which equation is perpendicular to the graph of $y = \frac{1}{2}x + 3$?

(1) $y = -\frac{1}{2}x + 5$ (2) $2y = x + 3$ (3) $y = 2x + 5$ (4) $y = -2x + 3$

19. Which is an equation of the line that is parallel to $y = 2x - 8$ and passes through point $(0, -3)$?

(1) $y = 2x + 3$ (2) $y = 2x - 3$ (3) $y = -\frac{1}{2}x + 3$ (4) $y = -\frac{1}{2}x - 3$

20. Given points $A(-4, -2)$, $B(16, 8)$, and $C(8, 4)$, which statement is true?
(1) $A, B,$ and C are vertices of a triangle.
(2) $\overline{AB}$ is perpendicular to $\overline{BC}$.
(3) $A, B,$ and C are collinear.
(4) $\angle ACB$ is an acute angle.

21. Under the translation that maps $(3, -4)$ onto its image $(1, 0)$, what is the image of any point (x, y)?
(1) $(x + 2, y + 4)$ (3) $(x + 2, y - 4)$
(2) $(x - 2, y - 4)$ (4) $(x - 2, y + 4)$

22. Which is an equation of the line that is parallel to $y = 3x - 5$ and has the same y-intercept as $y = -2x + 7$?
(1) $y = 3x - 2$ (2) $y = -2x - 5$ (3) $y = 3x + 7$ (4) $y = -2x - 7$

23. If points $(3, 2)$ and $(x, -5)$ lie on a line whose slope is $-\frac{7}{2}$, then x equals
(1) 5 (2) 6 (3) $\frac{15}{7}$ (4) 4

24. Line segment $\overline{AB}$ has midpoint M. If the coordinates of A are $(2, 3)$ and the coordinates of M are $(-1, 0)$, what are the coordinates of B?
(1) $(1, 3)$ (3) $(-4, -3)$
(2) $\left(\frac{1}{2}, \frac{3}{2}\right)$ (4) $(-4, 6)$

25. Given points $A(0, 0)$, $B(3, 2)$, and $C(-2, 3)$, which statement is true?
(1) $\overline{AB}$ is parallel to $\overline{AC}$.
(2) $\overline{AB}$ is perpendicular to $\overline{AC}$.
(3) AB is greater than BC.
(4) $\overline{BC}$ is perpendicular to $\overline{CA}$.

26. Given points $A(2, 2)$ and $B(6, 3)$:
   (a) Find the coordinates of A', the image of A after a dilation of constant 4 with respect to the origin.

(b) Write the equation of line $\overleftrightarrow{AA}'$

(c) Find the coordinates of B', the image of B after a reflection in line $\overleftrightarrow{AA}'$.

(d) Show that $ABA'B'$ is *not* a parallelogram.

27. The vertices of $\triangle ABC$ are $A(5, 8)$, $B(-3, 4)$, and $C(0, -2)$.
  (a) Using coordinate geometry, show that $\triangle ABC$ is:
    (1) *not* isosceles   (2) a right triangle
  (b) Find the area of $\triangle ABC$.

28. The vertices of $\triangle ABC$ are $A(7, 1)$, $B(6, 7)$, and $C(11, 3)$.
  (a) Find the area of $\triangle ABC$.
  (b) Find, in radical form, the length of the median from B to $\overline{AC}$.

29. Quadrilateral $JAME$ has vertices $J(2, -2)$, $A(8, -1)$, $M(9, 3)$, and $E(3, 2)$.
  (a) Prove that $JAME$ is a parallelogram.
  (b) Prove that $JAME$ is *not* a rectangle.

30. Quadrilateral $PQRS$ has vertices $P(-3, -4)$, $Q(9, 5)$, $R(-1, 10)$, and $S(-5, 7)$. Prove that $PQRS$ is an isosceles trapezoid.

31. The coordinates of $\triangle ABC$ are $A(0, 0)$, $B(2, 6)$, and $C(4, 2)$. Using coordinate geometry, prove that, if the midpoints of sides $\overline{AB}$ and $\overline{AC}$ are joined, the segment formed is parallel to the third side and equal to one-half the length of the third side.

32. The coordinates of the endpoints of line segment AB are $A(4, 1)$ and $B(5, 4)$.
  (a) Graph $\overline{AB}$
  (b) Graph $\overline{A'B'}$, the image of $\overline{AB}$, after a reflection over the line $y = x$.
  (c) Graph $\overline{A''B''}$, the image of $\overline{A'B'}$, after the transformation $(x, y) \rightarrow (x - 5, y - 5)$.
  (d) Graph $\overline{A'''B'''}$, the image of $\overline{A''B''}$, after a reflection through the origin.
  (e) Write a translation rule that will make $\overline{B'''A'''}$ the image of $\overline{A'B'}$.

33. Quadrilateral $JAKE$ has coordinates $J(0, 3a)$, $A(3a, 3a)$, $K(4a, 0)$, $E(-a, 0)$. Prove by coordinate geometry that $JAKE$ is an isosceles trapezoid.

ANSWERS TO SELECTED EXERCISES: CHAPTER 9

Section 9.1

1. (2)

3. (c) 7.5
  (e) 26

5. (a) (8, 5)
7. (a) 45
  (b) 32

(b) 40
(c) 54
(d) 90

9. 76
11. 49

Section 9.2

1. $(3, 4)$

3. (1)

5. $(4, 2)$

7. (a) $(4, -5)$
   (b) 13

9. 8

11. Midpoint of $\overline{AC} = (3,7)$
and midpoint of $\overline{BD} = (0,6)$.
Since the diagonals do not
bisect each other, $ABCD$ is
not a parallelogram.

15. 29

17. 5

19. (b) 30

Section 9.3

1. (a) $\frac{3}{4}$
  (b) $-\frac{4}{3}$
  (c) $-\frac{6}{7}$

5. 3

7. (3)

9. (4)

13. 3

15. -4

17. (a) 2
   (b) -7

21. (a) 2 **(b)** (1) 10
    (2) $\frac{5}{2}$

24. (a) $\frac{1}{3}$ **(b)** 3 **(c)** -3

Section 9.4

1. (a) 2 **(b)** 1
  (c) $-\frac{3}{4}$

3. (1)

5. (a) $y = 2x + 4$
  (c) $y = x + 10$

7. $y = \frac{4}{3}x + 4$

9. (2)

11. $y = \frac{3}{2}x - \frac{7}{2}$

13. (a) $x = 4$
   (b) $y = -1$
   (c) $y = -\frac{1}{2}x + 1$

15. (3)

17. $y = -\frac{1}{4}x - 2$

19. (b) $y = 3x - 11$
   (c) $y = 3x - 11$

21. (a) 2
   (b) $\dfrac{k-4}{3}$
   (c) 10
   (d) $y = 2x + 4$

Section 9.5

1. $(-1, -2)$

2. $(5, 2)$

3. (2)

4. $(-12, 0)$

5. $(8, -1)$

6. $(-5, 9)$

8. (a) $(-2, 2)$ **(c)** $(-4, 0)$
  (b) $(-2, -2)$ **(d)** $(4, 0)$

Section 9.6

1. $\left(0, \sqrt{3a}\right)$ or $\left(0, -\sqrt{3a}\right)$

2. (a) $C(t, t)$

Regents Tune-Up: Chapter 9

1. $(-5, -1)$

3. 10

5. $y = 4x - 1$

7. -6

9. 7

11. -1

13. (3)

15. (2)

17. (4)

19. (2)

21. (4)

23. (1)

25. (2)

28. (a) 13 **(b)** $\sqrt{34}$

Chapter 10

LOCUS AND CONSTRUCTIONS

10.1 SIMPLE LOCUS

KEY IDEAS

A **locus** (plural: loci) may be thought of as a path consisting of the set of all points, and only those points, that satisfy a given set of conditions.

Finding a Simple Locus

Finding a *simple locus* involves identifying and then describing the set of all points in a plane that satisfy a single condition.

Example: To find the locus of points that are 3 inches from point *K*, proceed as follows:

Step 1. Identify the condition that the points must satisfy. *Condition:* All points must be 3 inches from point *K*.

Step 2. Draw a diagram. Indicate point *K* and enough representative points that satisfy the stated condition so that you are able to discover a pattern. Connect these points with a broken line or a broken curve.

Step 3. Write a sentence that describes the locus. *Sentence:* The locus of points that are 3 inches from point *K* is a circle having point *K* as its center and a radius of 3 inches.

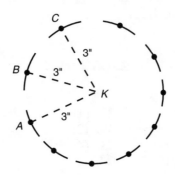

Commonly Encountered Simple Loci

Tables 10.1, 10.2, and 10.3 describe the loci for various given conditions. In each case, the accompanying diagram shows the locus as a broken line or curve.

TABLE 10.1 SIMPLE LOCI INVOLVING CIRCLES

Locus	Diagram
1. Condition: All points d units from a fixed point P. **Locus:** A circle having P as its center and a radius of d units.	
2. Condition: All points d units from a circle having a radius of r units. **Locus:** Two concentric circles having the same center as the original circle, the smaller circle having a radius of $r - d$ units and the larger circle having a radius of $r + d$ units.	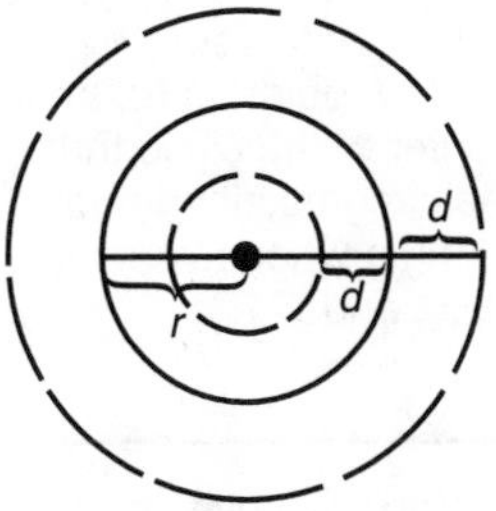
3. Condition: All points equidistant from two concentric circles having radii of p and q units. **Locus:** A circle having the same center as the given circles and a radius of $\dfrac{p + q}{2}$ units.	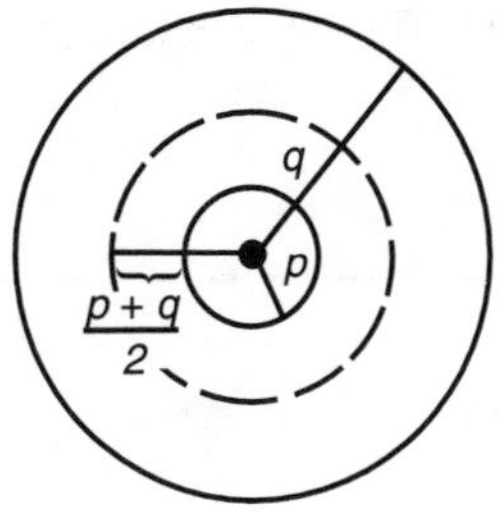

TABLE 10.2 SIMPLE LOCI INVOLVING GIVEN POINTS AND ANGLES

Locus	Diagram
1. **Condition:** All points equidistant from two given points, *A* and *B*. **Locus:** The perpendicular bisector of the line segment determined by points *A* and *B*.	
2. **Condition:** All points equidistant from three given non-collinear points, *A*, *B*, and *C*. **Locus:** The points at which the perpendicular bisectors of $\overline{AB}$ and $\overline{BC}$ intersect. (***Note***: This point represents the center of the circle that can be circumscribed about the triangle whose vertices are *A*, *B*, and *C*.)	
3. **Condition:** All points equidistant from the sides of a given angle. **Locus:** The ray that bisects the angle.	

TABLE 10.3 SIMPLE LOCI INVOLVING GIVEN LINES

Locus	Diagram
1. **Condition:** All points d units from a given line ℓ. **Locus:** Two lines each parallel to line ℓ, one on each side of line ℓ and at a distance of d units from line ℓ.	
2. **Condition:** All points equidistant from two parallel lines. **Locus:** A line that is parallel to the given pair of lines and midway between them.	
3. **Condition:** All points equidistant from two intersecting lines. **Locus:** Two lines, each of which bisects a pair of vertical angles formed by the two intersecting lines.	

Example

1. Find the locus of points:

(a) equidistant from two concentric circles having radii of lengths 3 and 7 centimeters, respectively;

(b) equidistant from two parallel lines that are 8 inches apart.

Solutions: **(a)** The locus of points equidistant from two concentric circles is another circle having the same center as the original circles and a radius length equal to 5 centimeters, which is the average of the lengths of the radii of the two given circles $\left(\dfrac{3+7}{2} = 5\right)$.

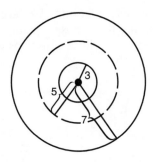

(b) The locus of points equidistant from two parallel lines that are 8 inches apart is a line that is parallel to the given pair of lines and is at a distance of 4 inches from each of them.

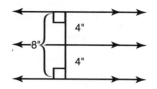

Locus and Coordinates

Coordinates may also be used to specify a locus.

Examples

2. Find an equation that describes the locus of points whose ordinates exceed twice their abscissas by 1.

Solution: Recall that the abscissa of a point is its x-coordinate, while the ordinate of a point is its y-coordinate. Translate the words as follows:

$$\underbrace{ordinates}_{y} \; \overset{exceed}{=} \; \underbrace{twice \; their \; abscissas}_{2x} \; \overset{by \; 1}{+1}$$

The required locus is the set of all points on the line whose equation is $y = 2x + 1$.

3. Find the locus of points that are 2 units from the line whose equation is $x = 3$.

Solution: The required locus con-sists of two lines on either side of $x = 3$ that are parallel to $x = 3$, and each at a distance of 2 units from $x = 3$. As the accompanying diagram shows, the line $x = 1$ is 2 units to the left of $x = 3$ and the line $x = 5$ is 2 units to the right of $x = 3$.

The locus of points that are 2 units from the line whose equation is $x = 3$ is the lines whose equations are $x = 1$ and $x = 5$.

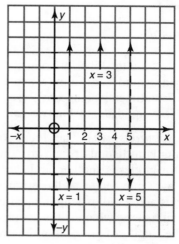

4. Find an equation of a line that describes the locus of points equidistant from the lines whose equations are $y = 3x - 1$ and $y = 3x + 5$.

Solution: The lines given by the equations $y = 3x - 1$ and $y = 3x + 5$ are parallel since the slope of each line is 3. The line parallel to these lines and midway between them must have a slope of 3 and a y-intercept of 2 since 2 is midway between (is the average of) the y-intercepts of the original pair of lines. Hence, the locus of points equidistant from the lines whose equations are $y = 3x - 1$ and $y = 3x + 5$ is the line whose equation is **$y = 3x + 2$**.

5. Find the locus of points equidistant from points $A(4, 5)$ and $B(4, -1)$.

Solution: The required locus is the perpendicular bisector of $\overline{AB}$. Since $\overline{AB}$ is a vertical line segment, the perpendicular bisector of $\overline{AB}$ is a horizontal line that contains the midpoint of $\overline{AB}$, which is $M(4, 2)$. The equation of a horizontal line that contains $M(4, 2)$ is $y = 2$. Therefore, the locus of points equidistant from points A and B is the line whose equation is **$y = 2$**.

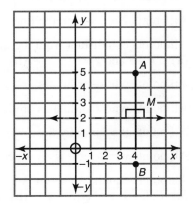

Exercise Set 10.1

1–10. In each case, draw a diagram and describe the locus.

1. The locus of points 1 centimeter from a circle whose radius is 8 centimeters.

2. The locus of points 3 centimeters from a given line.

3. The locus of points that are equidistant from sides $\overline{AB}$ and $\overline{AC}$ of $\triangle ABC$.

4. The locus of points equidistant from two concentric circles having radii of 7 centimeters, and 11 centimeters, respectively.

5. The locus of points 5 inches from vertex B of $\triangle ABC$.

6. The locus of the vertices of isosceles triangles having the same base.

7. The locus of the centers of circles tangent to each of two parallel lines that are 10 inches apart.

8. The locus of the center of a circle that rolls along a flat surface in a plane.

9. The locus of points in the coordinate plane that are equidistant from the *x*- and *y*-axes.

10. The locus of points in the coordinate plane that are 7 units from the origin.

11–21. Find an equation of the line or lines that satisfies each of the following conditions:

11. All points 4 units from the *x*-axis

12. All points 3 units from the *y*-axis

13. All points 5 units from the line $x = 3$

14. All points 2 units from the line $y = -1$

15. All points equidistant from the lines:
    (a) $x = -3$ and $x = 5$ **(b)** $y = -7$ and $y = -1$

16. All points whose ordinates are one-half as great as their abscissas

17. All points whose ordinates are 2 more than three times their abscissas

18. All points the sum of whose ordinates and abscissas is –4

19. All points whose abscissas exceed twice their ordinates by 3

20. All points equidistant from points:
    (a) $P(1, -4)$ and $Q(5, -4)$ **(b)** $R(2, 7)$ and $S(2, -1)$

21. Write an equation or equations that describe the locus of points:
    (a) equidistant from the lines $x = -1$ and $x = 5$
    (b) equidistant from the lines $y = -3$ and $y = -7$
    (c) equidistant from the lines $y = 3x + 1$ and $y = 3x + 9$

22. Prove that any point on the perpendicular bisector of a line segment is equidistant from the endpoints of the segment.

23. Prove that any point on the bisector of an angle is equidistant from the sides of the angle.

10.2 COMPOUND LOCI

KEY IDEAS

To find the number of points that satisfy two or more locus conditions at the same time, use the same diagram to describe the locus for each condition and then locate the points, if any, at which the loci intersect.

Compound Loci That Satisfy Two Conditions

Compound loci are represented by the set of points that satisfy two or more locus conditions at the same time. To determine compound loci having two locus conditions, proceed as follows:

Step 1. Identify the first locus condition, and describe this locus using a diagram.

Step 2. Identify the second locus condition, and describe this locus using the same diagram.

Step 3. Determine the point or points, if any, at which the loci intersect.

Examples

1. Point *P* is on line ℓ. Find the locus of points that are 2 inches from line ℓ and also 2 inches from point *P*.

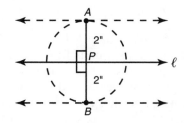

Solution:
Step 1. Locus condition 1: All points 2 inches from line ℓ. The desired locus is a pair of parallel lines on either side of line ℓ, each line at a distance of 2 inches from line ℓ.

Step 2. Locus condition 2: All points 2 inches from point *P*. The desired locus is a circle that has *P* as its center and has a radius of 2 inches. See the accompanying diagram.

Step 3. The required locus is the **2 points, *A* and *B*,** that satisfy both conditions.

2. Two parallel lines are 8 inches apart. Point *P* is located on one of the lines. Find the number of points that are equidistant from the parallel lines and are also at a distance from point *P* of:

(a) 5 inches   **(b)** 4 inches   **(c)** 3 inches

Solutions: **(a)** *Step 1. Locus condition 1:* All points equidistant from the two parallel lines. The desired locus is a line parallel to the original pair of lines and midway between them.

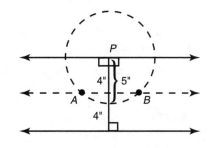

Step 2. Locus condition 2: All points 5 inches from point *P*. The desired locus is a circle that has *P* as its center and has a radius of 5 inches. See the accompanying diagram.

Step 3. Since the loci intersect at points *A* and *B,* there are **2** points that satisfy both conditions.

(b) Since the circle has a radius of 4 inches, it is tangent to the line that is midway between the original pair of parallel lines. The loci intersect at point A. There is **1** point that satisfies both conditions.

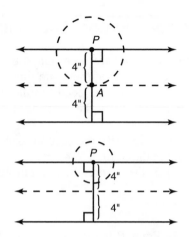

(c) Since the circle has a radius of 3 inches, it does *not* intersect the line that is midway between the original pair of parallel lines. Since the loci do *not* intersect, there is **0** point that satisfies both conditions.

3. How many points are 3 units from the origin and 2 units from the y-axis?

Solution: Step 1. Locus condition 1: All points 3 units from the origin. The desired locus is a circle with the origin as its center and a radius of 3 units. Note that the circle intersects each coordinate axis at 3 and –3.

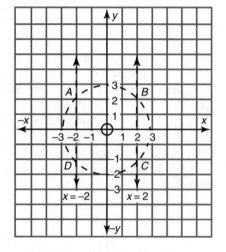

Step 2. Locus condition 2: All points 2 units from the y-axis. The desired locus is a pair of parallel lines; one line is 2 units to the right of the y-axis ($x = 2$), and the other line is 2 units to the left of the y-axis ($x = -2$). See the accompanying diagram.

Step 3. Since the loci intersect at points A, B, C, and D, there are **4** points that satisfy both conditions.

4. Given: points $A(2, 7)$ and $B(6, 7)$.
(a) Write an equation of $\overleftrightarrow{AB}$.
(b) Describe the locus of points equidistant from:
    (1) points A and B (2) the x- and y-axes
(c) How many points satisfy both conditions obtained in part (b)?

Solutions: **(a)** Since the y-coordinates of points A and B are the same, points A and B determine a horizontal line, $\overleftrightarrow{AB}$ (see the accompanying diagram on page 313), whose equation is $y = 7$.

(b) (1) The locus of points equidistant from two points is the perpendicular bisector of the line segment determined by the given points. The midpoint of $\overline{AB}$ is $M(4, 7)$. Since $\overleftrightarrow{AB}$ is a horizontal line, a vertical line that contains $(4, 7)$ will be the perpendicular bisector of $\overline{AB}$ (see the accompanying diagram on page 313). An equation of this line is $x = 4$.

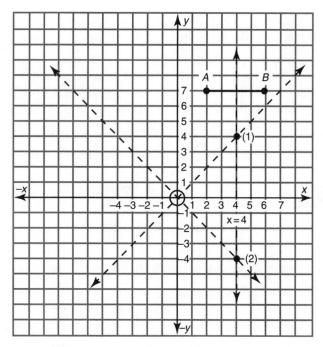

(2) The locus of points equidistant from the *x*- and *y*-axes is the pair of lines that bisect the pairs of vertical angles formed by the intersecting coordinate axes (see the accompanying diagram).

(c) There are **2** points that satisfy the two conditions in part (b).

Exercise Set 10.2

1. How many points are equidistant from points *A* and *B* and also 4 inches from $\overline{AB}$?

2. How many points are equidistant from two intersecting lines and also 3 inches from their points of intersection?

3. Point *A* is 4 inches from line *k*. Find the number of points that are 1 inch from line *k* and also at a distance from point *A* of:
   (a) 1 inch   **(c)** 4 inches   **(e)** 6 inches
   (b) 7 inches   **(d)** 5 inches   **(f)** 3 inches

4. Points *J*, *K*, and *L* are noncollinear. If points *K* and *L* are 8 units apart, find the number of points that are equidistant from points *K* and *L* and also:
   (a) 3 units from *L* **(c)** 2 units from $\overleftrightarrow{KL}$
   (b) 4 units from *K* **(d)** equidistant from the sides of ∠*JKL*

5. Point *P* is *x* inches from line ℓ. If there are exactly 3 points that are 2 inches from line ℓ and also 6 inches from point *P*, find the value of *x*.

6. Point *X* is the midpoint of $\overline{PQ}$. Find the number of points that are

equidistant from points P and Q and also 5 centimeters from point X if:
(a) $PQ = 8$ **(b)** $PQ = 10$ **(c)** $PQ = 12$

7. Lines p and q are parallel and 10 centimeters apart. Point A is between lines p and q and is 2 centimeters from line q. Find the number of points equidistant from lines p and q and also d centimeters from point A if:
   (a) $d = 7$ cm   **(b)** $d = 1$ cm   **(c)** $d = 3$ cm

8. Complete Exercise 7 assuming that point A is *not* between lines p and q.

9. Parallel lines $\overleftrightarrow{AB}$ and $\overleftrightarrow{CD}$ are 6 inches apart. Find the number of points that are equidistant from the two lines and are also:
   (a) 3 inches from point A **(c)** 2 inches from point D
   (b) 4 inches from point C **(d)** equidistant from points A and B

10. How many points are equidistant from the sides of $\angle ABC$ and are also 2 inches from point B?

11. How many points are equidistant from the three vertices of a triangle?

12. Find the number of points that are:
    (a) 2 units from the x-axis and 3 units from the y-axis
    (b) equidistant from points $A(0, 3)$ and $B(4, 3)$ and also 2 units from the origin
    (c) 4 units from the origin and also 4 units from the x-axis
    (d) 3 units from the line $y = -1$ and also 3 units from the origin
    (e) equidistant from the lines $x = -3$ and $x = 1$ and also 2 units from the origin
    (f) equidistant from the lines $y = 5$ and $y = -3$ and also 2 units from the origin
    (g) 2 units from the line $x = 4$ and also 3 units from the origin
    (h) equidistant from points $P(2, 1)$ and $Q(2, 5)$ and also 3 units from the origin

13. Point P is the center of two concentric circles having radii of 4 inches and 10 inches, respectively. If point A lies on the larger circle, find the number of points equidistant from the two circles and also:
    (a) equidistant from points P and A **(b)** 3 units from point A

14. Find the number of points that are 3 inches from point A and 5 inches from point B if:
    (a) $AB = 8$ **(b)** $AB = 6$ **(c)** $AB = 10$

15. What is an equation of the locus of points equidistant from points A $(3, 1)$ and B $(7, 1)$?

16. Find the number of points that are equidistant from points $(-1, 0)$ and $(3, 0)$ and are also 2 units from the origin.

17. **(a)** On graph paper, draw the locus of points 2 units from the line whose equation is $y = 1$.

(b) Write the equation(s) of the locus described in part (a).
(c) Describe fully the locus of points at a distance p from point $(2, 5)$.
(d) How many points satisfy the conditions in parts (a) and (c) simultaneously if:
   (1) $p = 2$ (2) $p = 3$ (3) $p = 4$

10.3   BASIC CONSTRUCTIONS

KEY IDEAS

Geometric constructions, unlike *drawings,* are made only with a straight-edge (for example, an unmarked ruler) and compass. The point at which the pivot point of the compass is placed is sometimes referred to as the **center**, while the fixed compass setting that is used is called the **radius length**. The part of the circle made by the compass is termed an **arc**.

Copying Segments and Angles

Given a line segment or angle, it is possible to construct another line segment or angle that is congruent to the original segment or angle without using a ruler or protractor.

Construction 1
Given line segment $\overline{AB}$, construct a congruent segment.

Step	Diagram
1. Draw any line, and choose any convenient point on it. Label the line as ℓ and the point as C.	$A \bullet$ —╫— $\bullet B$
2. Using a compass, measure $\overline{AB}$ by placing the compass point on A and the pencil point on B.	
3. Using the same compass setting, place the compass point on C and draw an arc that intersects line ℓ. Label the point of intersection as D.	$\ell \longleftarrow\ \overset{\bullet}{C}\ \text{╫}\ \overset{)}{D} \longrightarrow$

Conclusion: $AB \cong CD$.

Construction 2

Given $\angle ABC$, construct a congruent angle.

Step	Diagram
1. Draw any line and choose any point on it. Label the line as ℓ and the point as *S*.	
2. Using any convenient compass setting, place the compass point on *B* and draw an arc intersecting $\overrightarrow{BC}$ at *X* and $\overrightarrow{BA}$ at *Y*.	
3. Using the same compass setting, place the compass point at *S* and draw arc *WT*, intersecting line ℓ at *T*.	
4. Adjust the compass setting to measure the line segment determined by points *X* and *Y* by placing the compass point at *X* and the pencil at *Y*.	
5. Using the same compass setting, place the compass point at *T* and construct an arc intersecting arc *WT* at point *R*.	
6. Using a straightedge, draw $\overrightarrow{SR}$	

Conclusion: $\angle ABC \cong \angle RST$.

Rationale: The arcs were constructed so that $\overline{BX} \cong \overline{ST}$, $\overline{BY} \cong \overline{SR}$, and $\overline{XY} \cong \overline{TR}$. Therefore, $\triangle XYB \cong \triangle TRS$ by the SSS postulate. By CPCTC, $\angle ABC \cong \angle RST$.

Constructing Bisectors of Segments and Angles

To find by construction the locus of points equidistant from two points, construct the line that is the perpendicular bisector of the segment determined by the two points. To find by construction the locus of points equidistant from the sides of an angle, construct the ray that bisects the angle.

Construction 3

Given two points, construct the perpendicular bisector of the segment determined by the two points.

Step	Diagram
1. Label points A and B, and draw $\overline{AB}$. Choose any compass setting (radius length) that is _more_ than one-half the length of $\overline{AB}$.	
2. Using this compass setting, and points A and B as centers, construct a pair of arcs above and below $\overline{AB}$. Label the points at which the pairs of arcs intersect as P and Q.	
3. Draw $\overleftrightarrow{PQ}$, and label the point of intersection of $\overleftrightarrow{PQ}$ and $\overleftrightarrow{AB}$ as M.	

Conclusion: $\overleftrightarrow{PQ}$ is the perpendicular bisector of $\overline{AB}$.

Rationale: The arcs were constructed in such a way that $AP = BP = AQ = BQ$. Since quadrilateral $APBQ$ is equilateral, it is a rhombus. Since the diagonals of a rhombus are perpendicular bisectors, $\overline{AM} \cong \overline{BM}$ and $\overline{PQ} \perp \overline{AB}$.

Construction 4

Given an angle, construct the bisector of the angle.

Step	Diagram
1. Name the angle, $\angle ABC$. Using B as a center, construct an arc, using any convenient radius length, that intersects $\overrightarrow{BA}$ at point P and $\overrightarrow{BC}$ at point Q.	
2. Using points P and Q as centers and the same radius length, draw a pair of arcs that intersect. Label the point at which the arcs intersect as D.	
3. Draw $\overrightarrow{BD}$.	

Conclusion: $\overrightarrow{BD}$ is the bisector of $\angle ABC$.
Rationale: See Exercise 1(a).

317

Constructing Perpendicular Lines

A line can be constructed perpendicular to a given line at a given point on the line or through a given point not on the line.

Construction 5

Given a line ℓ and a point P *not* on the line, construct a line through P and perpendicular to line ℓ.

Step	Diagram
1. Using P as a center and any convenient radius length, construct an arc that intersects line ℓ at two points. Label these points as A and B. **2.** Choose a radius length greater than one-half the length of $\overline{AB}$. Using points A and B as centers, construct a pair of arcs that intersect at point Q. **3.** Draw $\overleftrightarrow{PQ}$, intersecting line ℓ at point M.	

Conclusion: $\overleftrightarrow{PQ}$ is perpendicular to line ℓ at point M.
Rationale: See Exercise 1(b).

Construction 6

Given a line ℓ and a point P on line ℓ, construct a line through P and perpendicular to line ℓ.

Step	Diagram
1. Using P as a center and any convenient radius length, construct an arc that intersects line ℓ at two points. Label these points as A and B. **2.** Choose a radius length greater than one-half the length of $\overline{AB}$. Using points A and B as centers, construct a pair of arcs on either side of line ℓ that intersect at point Q. **3.** Draw $\overleftrightarrow{PQ}$.	

318

Conclusion: $\overleftrightarrow{PQ}$ is perpendicular to line ℓ at point P.
Rationale: See Exercise 1(c).

Constructing Parallel Lines

A line can be constructed parallel to a given line and through a given point not on the line by drawing any convenient transversal through the point and then constructing a congruent corresponding angle, using this point as a vertex.

Construction 7
Given a line $\overleftrightarrow{AB}$ and a point P *not* on the line, construct a line through P and parallel to $\overleftrightarrow{AB}$.

Step	Diagram
1. Through P draw any convenient line, extending it so that it intersects $\overleftrightarrow{AB}$. Label the point of intersection as Q. 2. Using P and Q as centers, draw arcs having the same radius length. Label the point at which the arc intersects the ray opposite $\overrightarrow{PQ}$ as R. 3. Construct an angle at P, one of whose sides is $\overrightarrow{PR}$, congruent to $\angle PQB$. 4. Draw $\overleftrightarrow{PS}$.	

Conclusion: Since $\angle PQB$ and $\angle RPS$ are congruent corresponding angles, $\overleftrightarrow{PS}$ is parallel to $\overleftrightarrow{AB}$.

Example

1. (a) Construct the altitude to side $\overline{RT}$ of acute triangle RST.
(b) Construct the median to side $\overline{ST}$ of acute triangle RST.
(c) Construct a line through vertex T of acute triangle RST and parallel to side $\overline{RS}$.

Solutions: **(a)** Construct a line through S and perpendicular to $\overline{RT}$ (refer to Construction 5). The actual construction is left for you.

(b) Locate the midpoint M of $\overline{ST}$ by constructing the perpendicular bisector of $\overline{ST}$ (refer to Construction 3). Draw the line segment (median) whose endpoints are R and M. The actual construction is left for you.

(c) At vertex T, using $\overrightarrow{RT}$ as a transversal, construct $\angle 1$ congruent to $\angle R$ as shown in the accompanying diagram. Since $\angle 1$ and $\angle R$ are corresponding angles, $\overrightarrow{TA}$ is parallel to $\overline{RS}$.

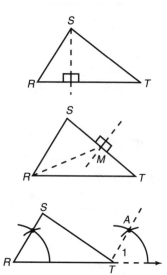

Exercise Set 10.3

1. Provide the rationale for:
   (a) Construction 4 (*Hint:* Draw $\overline{PD}$ and $\overline{QD}$, and prove that $\triangle BPD \cong \triangle BQD$.)
   (b) Construction 5 (*Hint:* Draw segments $\overline{PA}, \overline{PB}, \overline{AQ}$, and $\overline{BQ}$. Prove that $\triangle PAQ \cong \triangle PBQ$. Next, prove that $\triangle PMA \cong \triangle PMB$.)
   (c) Construction 6 (*Hint:* Draw $\overline{AQ}$ and $\overline{BQ}$, and prove that $\triangle QPA \cong \triangle QPB$.)

2. To locate a point equidistant from the vertices of a triangle, construct
   (a) the perpendicular bisectors of the sides
   (b) the angle bisectors
   (c) the altitudes
   (d) the medians

3. Draw obtuse triangle ABC, where $\angle B$ is obtuse. Construct:
   (a) the altitude to side $\overline{BC}$ (extended, if necessary)
   (b) the median to side $\overline{BC}$
   (c) a line through A and parallel to $\overline{BC}$

4. Given ray $\overrightarrow{OP}$, find by construction the segment that represents the dilation of $\overrightarrow{OP}$, having point O as the center of dilation and a constant of dilation of:
   (a) 2   **(b)** $\frac{1}{2}$ **(c)** 1.5   **(d)** -1

5. Given two segments having lengths of a units and b units ($b > a$), respectively, construct a segment whose length is:
   (a) $(a + b)$ units   **(b)** $(b - a)$ units

6. Given two angles having degree measures of a and b ($b > a$), respectively, construct an angle whose degree measure is:
   (a) $(a + b)$ **(b)** $(b - a)$

7. Draw three noncollinear points.
   (a) Construct the locus of points equidistant from the three points.
   (b) Construct the circle that contains the three points.

8. Given a circle, find *by construction* the center of the circle. (*Hint:* Construct the locus of points equidistant from *any* three points on the circle.)

9. Given a triangle, construct the circumscribed circle. (*Hint:* See Exercises 7 and 8.)

10. Given parallelogram *ABCD*:
   (a) Construct an altitude from point B to $\overline{AD}$.
   (b) If point H is between points A and D, construct an altitude at point H.

11. Construct an angle having a degree measure of 45.

12. A *tangent* to a circle is a line that intersects the circle at exactly one point, called *the point of tangency*. A radius drawn to the point of tangency forms a right angle with the tangent. Given a circle whose center is point O and any point P on the circle, construct a line that is tangent to the circle at point P. (*Hint:* Draw $\overline{OP}$, and construct a line perpendicular to $\overline{OP}$ at point P.)

13. Given trapezoid *RSTW*, in which $\overline{RW} \parallel \overline{ST}$, construct the median of the trapezoid.

14. Construct a parallelogram that is:
   (a) *not* a rectangle   **(c)** a rhombus but *not* a square
   (b) a rectangle   **(d)** a square

REGENTS TUNE-UP: CHAPTER 10

Each of the questions in this section has appeared on a previous Course II Regents Examination. Here is an opportunity for you to review the material in Chapter 10 and, at the same time, prepare for the Course II Regents Examination.

---

1. What is the total number of points that are 3 units from line m and also 5 units from P, a point on line m?

2. What is an equation of the locus of points equidistant from points $A(1, 2)$ and $B(5, 2)$?
   (1) $x = 3$ (2) $y = 3$ (3) $x = 2$ (4) $y = 2$

3. In a plane what is the locus of points 8 centimeters from a given line?
    (1) A line   (3) Two intersecting lines
    (2) A circle   (4) Two parallel lines

4. On a coordinate plane, how many points are 5 units from the origin and satisfy the equation $x = 4$?
    (1) 1   (2) 2   (3) 3   (4) 0

5. The accompanying diagram shows the construction of the bisector of $\angle ABC$. Which reason for triangle congruence is used in proving that $\overline{BF}$ bisects $\angle ABC$?

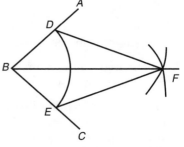

    (1) ASA   (3) SSS
    (2) SAS   (4) SAA

6. Two points, L and P, are 8 units apart. How many points are equidistant from L and P and also 3 units from L?
    (1) 1   (2) 2   (3) 0   (4) 4

7. Point C is 3 centimeters from line $\overleftrightarrow{AB}$. The number of points on $\overleftrightarrow{AB}$ that are also 5 centimeters from C is:
    (1) 1   (2) 2   (3) 3   (4) 0

8. Point P lies between two parallel lines a and b, which are 3 centimeters apart. What is the total number of points equidistant from a and b, and also 2 centimeters from P?
    (1) 1   (2) 2   (3) 3   (4) 0

9. What is the total number of points that are 2 units from the y-axis and also 3 units from the origin?
    (1) 0   (2) 2   (3) 3   (4) 4

10. The equation of the locus of points equidistant from the graphs of $x = 3$ and $x = -5$ is:
    (1) $y = 1$ (2) $y = -1$ (3) $x = 1$ (4) $x = -1$

11. The vertices of $\triangle ABC$ are $A(-4, -2)$, $B(2, 6)$, $C(2, -2)$.
    (a) Write an equation of the locus of points equidistant from vertex B and vertex C.
    (b) Write an equation of the line parallel to $\overline{BC}$ and passing through vertex A.
    (c) Find the coordinates of the point of intersection of the locus in part (a) and the line determined in part (b).
    (d) Write an equation of the locus of points that are 4 units from vertex C.
    (e) What is the total number of points that satisfy the loci described in parts (a) and (d)?

12. (a) Describe completely the locus of points n units from point $P(3, 2)$.
   (b) Describe completely the locus of points 2 units from the line whose equation is $x = 3$.
   (c) What is the total number of points that satisfy the conditions in parts (a) and (b) simultaneously for the following values of $n?$
   (1) $n < 2$ (2) $n = 2$

ANSWERS TO SELECTED EXERCISES: CHAPTER 10

Section 10.1
 4. Locus is a concentric circle with radius of 9 cm.
 7. Locus is a line equidistant between the two parallel lines.
 8. Locus is a line parallel to the surface at a distance equal to the radius of the circle.
 9. Locus is the lines $y = \pm x$.
 10. Locus is a circle with center at the origin and a radius of 7.
 11. $y = \pm 4$
 12. $x = \pm 3$
 13. $x = -2, x = 8$
 14. $y = -3, y = 1$
 15. (a) $x = 1$
    (b) $y = -4$
 16. $y = \frac{1}{2}x$
 17. $y = 3x + 2$
 18. $x + y = -4$
 19. $x = 2y + 3$
 20. (a) $x = 3$ **(b)** $y = 3$
 21. (a) $x = 2$
    (b) $y = -5$
    (c) $y = 3x + 5$

Section 10.2
 1. 2
 3. (a) 0 **(d)** 3
    (b) 4 **(e)** 4
    (c) 2 **(f)** 1
 5. 4
 7. (a) 2 **(b)** 0 **(c)** 1
 9. (a) 1 **(c)** 0
    (b) 2 **(d)** 1
 11. 1
 13. (a) 2 **(b)** 1

Regents Tune-Up: Chapter 10
 1. 2   **4.** (2)   **7.** (2)   **10.** (4)
 2. (1)   **5.** (3)   **8.** (2)   **11. (a)** $y = 2$ **(b)** $x = -4$ **(c)** $(-4, 2)$
 3. (4)   **6.** (3)   **9.** (4)   **(d)** $(x - 2)^2 + (y + 2)^2 = 14$ **(e)** 1
 12. (a) The locus is a circle with center $(3, 2)$ and a radius of length n.
    (b) The locus of points is the pair of lines $x = 1$ and $x = 5$.
    (c) (1) 0   (2) 2

Unit Four ANALYTIC GEOMETRY

## CHAPTER 11

QUADRATIC EQUATIONS IN TWO VARIABLES

11.1 GENERAL EQUATION OF A CIRCLE

KEY IDEAS

The graph of the equation $x^2 + y^2 = r^2$ is a circle whose center is at the origin and whose radius is r. The general equation of a circle whose center is *not* necessarily located at the origin can be derived by using the distance formula to find the length of the segment drawn from the center $O(h, k)$ of the circle to any point $P(x, y)$ on the circle:

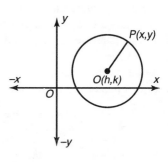

$$\sqrt{(x - h)^2 + (y - k)^2} = OP$$

By substituting the radius length r for OP and then squaring both sides of the equation, the general equation of the circle

$$(x - h)^2 + (y - k)^2 = r^2$$

is obtained.

The dilation of a circle produces another circle that has the same center but a different radius length. The translation of a circle produces another circle that has the same radius length but a different center.

Equations of Circles

The graph of the equation $(x - h)^2 + (y - k)^2 = r^2$ is a circle having a radius of r units and a center located at (h, k). If $h = 0$ and $k = 0$, then the center of the circle is at the origin, and the equation of the circle simplifies to $x^2 + y^2 = r^2$.

Examples

1. Write an equation that describes the locus of points 5 units from point $(2, -1)$.

Solution: The locus of points 5 units from the given point $(2, -1)$ is a circle having $(2, -1)$ as its center and a radius length of 5. An equation of the circle is

$$(x - 2)^2 + (y - [-1])^2 = 5^2$$
$$\mathbf{(x - 2)^2 + (y + 1)^2 = 25}$$

2. Determine the center and the radius length of a circle whose equation is: **(a)** $(x - 1)^2 + y^2 = 13$ **(b)** $(x + 3)^2 + (y - 4)^2 = 36$

Solutions: **(a)** Since $(x - 1)^2 + y^2 = 13$ may be rewritten as

$$(x - 1)^2 + (y - 0)^2 = (\sqrt{13})^2,$$

the center of this circle is **(1, 0)** and the length of its radius is $\sqrt{13}$.
(b) Since $(x + 3)^2 + (y - 4)^2 = 36$ may be rewritten as

$$(x - (-3))^2 + (y - 4)^2 = 6^2,$$

the center of this circle is **(-3, 4)** and the length of its radius is **6**.

3. If point $(t, 5)$ lies in the first quadrant of a circle whose equation is $x^2 + y^2 = 169$, what is the value of t?

Solution: The coordinates of $(t, 5)$ must satisfy the equation of the circle. Therefore,

$$x^2 + y^2 = 169$$
$$t^2 + 5^2 = 169$$
$$t^2 = 169 - 25 = 144$$
$$t = \pm\sqrt{144} = \pm 12$$

Since the point is in the first quadrant, $t = \mathbf{12}$.

4. What is an equation of a circle that is tangent to the y-axis and whose center is $(2, 3)$?

Solution: As the accompanying diagram illustrates, the radius drawn to the point of tangency is a horizontal segment whose length is 2 units.
Hence, an equation of the circle is $\mathbf{(x - 2)^2 + (y - 3)^2 = 4}$.

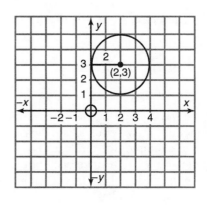

5. The coordinates of the endpoints of a diameter of a circle are $A(1, 2)$ and $B(-7, -4)$.

(a) Find an equation of this circle.

(b) Determine whether the circle passes through point $P(-6, -5)$.

Solutions: **(a)** The center $O(h, k)$ of the circle is found by finding the midpoint of diameter $\overline{AB}$:

$$h = \frac{1 + (-7)}{2} = \frac{-6}{2} = -3, \qquad k = \frac{2 + (-4)}{2} = \frac{-2}{2} = -1$$

The coordinates of the center of the circle are $O(-3, -1)$. To find the length of the radius, find the distance between the center and *any* point on the circle, say point A.

Let $(x_1, y_1) = A(1, 2)$ and $(x_2, y_2) = O(-3, -1)$. Then

$$OA = \sqrt{(x_2 - x_1)^2 + (y_2 - y_1)^2}$$

$$= \sqrt{(-3 - 1)^2 + (-1 - 2)^2}$$

$$= \sqrt{(-4)^2 + (-3)^2}$$

$$= \sqrt{16 + 9}$$

$$= \sqrt{25} = 5$$

An equation of a circle whose center is at $(-3, -1)$ and whose radius is 5 is

$$(x - [-3])^2 + (y - [-1])^2 = 5^2$$
$$(x + 3)^2 + (y + 1)^2 = 25$$

(b) Point $P(-6, -5)$ lies on the circle if its coordinates satisfy the equation of the circle:

$$
\begin{array}{r|l}
(x + 3)^2 + (y + 1)^2 & = 25 \\
(-6 + 3)^2 + (-5 + 1)^2 & \overset{?}{=} 25 \\
(-3)^2 + (-4)^2 & \quad 25 \\
9 + 16 & \quad 25 \\
25 & \overset{}{=} 25
\end{array}
$$

Therefore, **$P(-6, -5)$ lies on the circle**.

Dilations of Circles

If two circles have the same center, then one of the circles may be considered to be the dilation of the other circle. The *center of dilation* is the common center of the two circles, and the *constant of dilation* is the ratio of their radii.

For example, the circle $x^2 + y^2 = 64$ may be considered a dilation of the circle $x^2 + y^2 = 16$ since each circle has the origin as its center. In this case, since the radius of the larger circle is 8 and the radius of the smaller circle 4, the constant of dilation is $8 \div 4$ or 2.

Example

6. Write an equation of the circle that is the dilation of the circle $x^2 + y^2 = 9$, using a constant of dilation of 4.

Solution: The radius of the original circle is 3. The dilation of this circle, using a dilation constant of 4, is a circle whose radius has a length of 3×4 or 12.

Hence, the dilation of the circle $x^2 + y^2 = 9$, using a constant of dilation of 4, is the circle $x^2 + y^2 = \mathbf{144}$.

Translations of Circles

The circles $(x - h)^2 + (y - k)^2 = r^2$ and $x^2 + y^2 = r^2$ have the same size and shape, but differ in their locations in the coordinate plane. Compared to the center of the circle $x^2 + y^2 = r^2$, the center of the circle $(x - h)^2 + (y - k)^2 = r^2$ is shifted h units in the horizontal direction and k units in the vertical direction.

- If $h > 0$, the circle is shifted horizontally to the right; if $h < 0$, the circle is shifted horizontally to the left.
- If $k > 0$, the circle is shifted vertically up; if $k < 0$, the circle is shifted vertically down.

For example, since the center of the circle $(x - 1)^2 + (y + 3)^2 = 100$ is $(1, -3)$, the circle $(x - 1)^2 + (y + 3)^2 = 100$ is a translation of the circle $x^2 + y^2 = 100$, shifted 1 unit horizontally to the right and 3 units vertically down.

Examples

7. Under a certain translation the image of the circle $x^2 + y^2 = 25$ is the circle $(x - 1)^2 + (y - 4)^2 = 25$. What is an equation of the circle that is the image of the circle $(x + 2)^2 + (y - 3)^2 = 49$ under the same translation?

Solution: Since the center of the circle $(x - 1)^2 + (y - 4)^2 = 25$ is $(1, 4)$, the translation shifts the original circle 1 unit horizontally to the right and 4 units vertically up. Therefore, to find the image of the circle $(x + 2)^2 + (y - 3)^2 = 49$ under the same translation, add 1 unit to the x-coordinate of its center, and add 4 units to the y-coordinate of its center. The center of the circle $(x + 2)^2 + (y - 3)^2 = 49$ is $(-2, 3)$, so the center of its image is $(-2 + 1, 3 + 4) = (-1, 7)$.

An equation of the image of this circle is $(x - [-1])^2 + (y - 7)^2 = 49$, or $\mathbf{(x + 1)^2 + (y - 7)^2 = 49}$.

8. (a) On graph paper, draw the locus of points 4 units from point $(4, 2)$. Label the graph **a**.

(b) Write an equation for the locus drawn in part (a).

(c) On the same set of axes, draw the image of the graph drawn in part (a) after a reflection in the y-axis. Label the graph **c**.

(d) On the same set of axes, draw the image of the graph drawn in part (c) after a translation that moves (x, y) to $(x + 4, y - 2)$. Label the graph **d**.

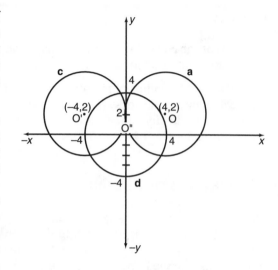

Solution: **(a)** The locus of points 4 units from point $(4, 2)$ is a circle whose center is $(4, 2)$ and whose radius is 4. After labeling the coordinate axes, set the compass radius so that it is equal to 4 units along either axis. Then place the compass point on $(4, 2)$, the center of the circle, and draw a circle. The graph is labeled **a** in the accompanying figure.

(b) Since the circle drawn in part (a) has a radius of 4 units and center at $(4, 2)$, let $h = 4$, $k = 2$, and $r = 4$ in the equation $(x - h)^2 + (y - k)^2 = r^2$. Thus, an equation for the locus drawn in part (a) is $(x - 4)^2 + (y - 2)^2 = 16$.

(c) A reflection of a graph in the y-axis maps each point (x, y) of the original graph onto $(-x, y)$. Under this transformation the image of $(4, 2)$, the center of the circle drawn in part (a), is $(-4, 2)$. On the same set of axes, draw a circle with center at $(-4, 2)$ and a radius length of 4 units. The reflected graph is labeled **c** in the accompanying diagram.

(d) A translation of a graph that moves each point (x, y) to $(x + 4, y - 2)$ will move $(-4, 2)$, the center of the circle drawn in part (c), to $(-4 + 4, 2 - 2)$ $= (0, 0)$. On the same set of axes, draw a circle with center at $(0, 0)$ and a radius length of 4 units. The translated graph is labeled **d** in the accompanying diagram.

Exercise Set 11.1

1. Which is an equation of the circle whose center is at $(4, -2)$ and whose radius is 3?
   (1) $(x + 4)^2 + (y - 2)^2 = 9$ (3) $(x + 4)^2 + (y - 2)^2 = 3$
   (2) $(x - 4)^2 + (y + 2)^2 = 9$ (4) $(x - 4)^2 + (y + 2)^2 = 3$

2. Which is an equation of the circle that is a translation of the circle $x^2 + y^2$ $= 25$ shifted 3 units horizontally to the right and 2 units vertically down?
   (1) $(x + 3)^2 + (y - 2)^2 = 25$ (3) $(x - 3)^2 + (y - 2)^2 = 25$
   (2) $(x - 3)^2 + (y + 2)^2 = 25$ (4) $(x + 3)^2 + (y + 2)^2 = 25$

3. Write an equation that describes the locus of points 7 units from point $(-2, 3)$.

4. Write an equation of the circle that has a diameter whose endpoints are:
   (a) $(0, 3)$ and $(0, -3)$ **(b)** $(-2, 5)$ and $(-8, 5)$

5. For each of the following, state whether point P lies on the given circle:
  (a) $(x-4)^2 + (y+5)^2 = 49$; $P(4, -12)$
  (b) $(x+2)^2 + (y-3)^2 = 37$; $P(-8, 2)$
  (c) $(x-1)^2 + (y+6)^2 = 25$; $P(3, -9)$

6. Point $P(a, -12)$ lies on the circle $x^2 + y^2 = 169$. If point P lies in the third quadrant, find the value of a.

7. Find an equation of the dilation of the circle $x^2 + y^2 = 100$ if the constant of dilation is:
  (a) 2   **(b)** $\frac{1}{2}$ **(c)** 1

8. The center of a circle that has a radius of 4 is the origin. Find an equation of the translation of this circle if the original circle is shifted:
  (a) 2 units to the right and 3 units up
  (b) 1 unit to the left and 4 units up
  (c) 3 units to the left and 1 unit down
  (d) 2 units down

9. Given the circle $(x+1)^2 + (y-2)^2 = 36$, write an equation of the circle that is:
  (a) a translation of the original circle 1 unit horizontally to the left and 3 units vertically down
  (b) a dilation of the original circle with a dilation constant of 3

10. Equations of a circle and of its dilation are $(x-1)^2 + (y+1)^2 = 4$ and $(x-1)^2 + (y+1)^2 = 36$, respectively. If the circle $x^2 + y^2 = 1$ undergoes the same dilation, what is an equation of its image?

11. What is an equation of a circle that is tangent to the line $y = -3$ and whose center is at the origin?

12. What is an equation of a circle that is tangent to the x-axis and whose center is at $(-4, 3)$?

13. How many points, if any, do the graphs of each of the following pairs of equations have in common?
  (a) $x^2 + y^2 = 4$ and $x = -1$ **(c)** $x^2 + y^2 = 25$ and $y = 6$
  (b) $x^2 + y^2 = 9$ and $y = 3$ **(d)** $x^2 + y^2 = 16$ and $y = x$

14–17. In each case, write an equation of the circle that has center O and passes through point P.

14. $O(1, 1)$; $P(7, -7)$ **16.** $O(-3, 5)$; $P(1, 9)$

15. $O(2, -3)$; $P(-2, 0)$ **17.** $O(-1, -4)$; $P(-6, 8)$

18. In how many points does each of the following circles intersect the x-axis?
  (a) $x^2 + y^2 = 16$ **(c)** $(x-3)^2 + y^2 = 4$
  (b) $x^2 + (y-3)^2 = 4$ **(d)** $(x-2)^2 + (y-1)^2 = 1$

19. Find the x- and y-intercepts, if any, of each of the following circles (if appropriate, express answers to the nearest tenth);

(a) $x^2 + y^2 = 49$

(b) $x^2 + (y - 1)^2 = 16$

(c) $(x - 3)^2 + (y - 1)^2 = 4$

(d) $(x - 3)^2 + (y - 4)^2 = 25$

(e) $(x + 2)^2 + (y - 5)^2 = 85$

(f) $(x + 3)^2 + (y - 7)^2 = 45$

20. **(a)** On graph paper, draw the locus of points 5 units from point $(-1, -5)$. Label the graph **a**.

(b) Write an equation for the locus drawn in part (a).

(c) On the same set of axes, draw the image of the graph drawn in part (a) after a reflection in the x-axis. Label the graph **c**.

(d) On the same set of axes, draw the image of the graph drawn in part (c) after a translation that moves (x, y) to $(x + 1, y - 5)$. Label the graph **d**.

11.2 GRAPHING $y = ax^2 + bx + c\,(a \neq 0)$

KEY IDEAS

The graph of the quadratic equation $y = ax^2 + bx + c$ $(a \neq 0)$ is a smooth curve called a **parabola** that has a vertical *axis of symmetry*. The axis of symmetry intersects the parabola at a point called the *turning point* or *vertex* of the parabola.

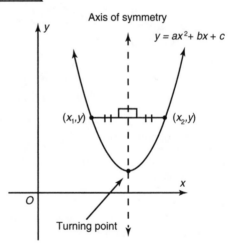

Axis of Symmetry and Turning Point

The graph of $y = ax^2 + bx + c$ $(a \neq 0)$ is a parabola with a vertical axis of symmetry (see Figure 11.1).

• An equation of the axis of symmetry is

$$x = -\frac{b}{2a}.$$

Since the x-coordinate of the turning point is $-\frac{b}{2a}$, substituting this value

for x in $y = ax^2 + bx + c$ gives the y-coordinate of the turning point.

- The sign of a, the coefficient of x^2 in the quadratic equation, determines whether the turning point of a parabola is a minimum point or maximum point on the graph. Observe in Figure 11.2 that:
  1. If $a > 0$, the parabola opens up ("holds water") and the turning point is a *minimum* point of the parabola.
  2. If $a < 0$, the parabola opens down ("spills water") and the turning point is a *maximum* point on the parabola.

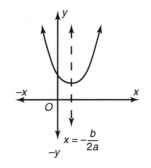

Figure 11.1 Axis of Symmetry of a Parabola

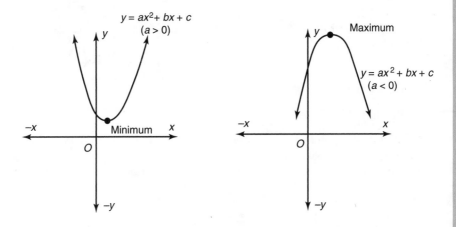

Figure 11.2 Effect of Coefficient a on the Turning Point of a Parabola

Examples

1. For the parabola $y = 3x^2 - 6x + 2$, find:
(a) an equation of the axis of symmetry
(b) the coordinates of the turning point of the parabola

Solutions: **(a)** Let $a = 3$ and $b = -6$. Then

$$x = -\frac{b}{2a} = -\frac{-6}{2 \cdot 3} = \frac{6}{6} = 1.$$

An equation of the axis of symmetry is $x = 1$.

(b) Since the axis of symmetry contains the turning point of the parabola, the x-coordinate of the turning point is 1. To find the y-coordinate of the turning point, replace x by 1 in the quadratic equation $y = 3x^2 - 6x + 2$:

$$y = 3x^2 - 6x + 2$$
$$= 3 \cdot 1^2 - 6 \cdot 1 + 2$$
$$= 3 - 6 + 2$$
$$= -3 \qquad + 2 = -1$$

The coordinates of the turning point are **(1, –1)**.

2. If a parabola intersects the x-axis at $x = 1$ and $x = 5$, what is an equation of its axis of symmetry?

Solution: The axis of symmetry bisects each horizontal segment whose endpoints are two points on the parabola. As shown in the accompanying diagram, since $x = 3$ is midway between $x = 1$ and $x = 5$, the axis of symmetry intersects the x-axis at $x = 3$.

An equation of the axis of symmetry is $x = 3$.

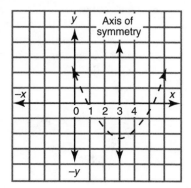

The Graph of $y = ax^2$ $(a \neq 0)$

As illustrated in Figure 11.3:

- The turning point of the parabola $y = ax^2$ is $(0, 0)$, and its axis of symmetry is the y-axis.
- The parabola $y = -ax^2$ is a reflection of the parabola $y = ax^2$ in the x-axis.

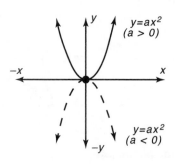

Figure 11.3 Parabola $y = ax^2$

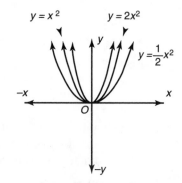

Figure 11.4 Comparing the Width of $y = ax^2$ for Different

Figure 11.4 illustrates that, compared with the parabola $y = x^2$, where coefficient $a = 1$:

- As $|a|$ gets larger, the parabola $y = ax^2$ becomes narrower horizontally.
- As $|a|$ gets smaller, the parabola $y = ax^2$ becomes broader horizontally.

The Graph of $y = ax^2 + c \, (a \neq 0)$

The graph of $y = ax^2 + c$ is a translation of the graph of $y = ax^2$, shifted $|c|$ units in the vertical direction.

- If $c > 0$, the graph of $y = ax^2 + c$ is shifted c units vertically *up*.
- If $c < 0$, the graph of $y = ax^2 + c$ is shifted $|c|$ units vertically *down*. Figure 11.5 illustrates the effect of c for $c = 2$ and $c = -2$

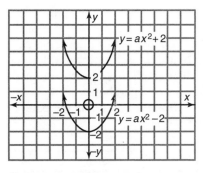

Figure 11.5 Shifting $y = ax^2$

Examples

3. What is an equation of the horizontal line that is tangent to the graph of $y = -2x^2 + 1$?

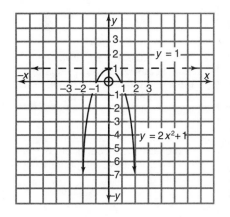

Solution: A horizontal line that contains the turning point of the parabola $y = -2x^2 + 1$ is tangent to the parabola at this point. The turning point of the parabola $y = -2x^2 + 1$ is $(0, 1)$.

The horizontal line **$y = 1$** is tangent to the parabola at its turning point.

4. How many points do the graphs in each of the following have in common?

   (a) $y = -x^2$ and $x^2 + y^2 = 9$

   (b) $y = x^2 + 3$ and $x^2 + y^2 = 4$

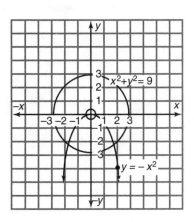

Solutions: **(a)** As the accompanying diagram illustrates, the circle $x^2 + y^2 = 9$ and the parabola $y = -x^2$ intersect at **2** points.

   (b) The length of the radius of the circle $x^2 + y^2 = 4$ is 2, and the turning point of the parabola $y = x^2 + 3$ is $(0, 3)$, which is a minimum point on the graph. Therefore, these graphs have **0** point in common.

Graphing a Parabola

To draw the graph of a parabola, use at least three consecutive integer values of x above the x-coordinate of the turning point of the parabola and the corresponding set of integer values of x below the x-coordinate of the turning point. For each of these values of x, determine the corresponding value of y. Then graph these points and connect them with a smooth curve that has the shape of a parabola.

Example: To graph the parabola whose equation is $y = x^2 - 4x + 1$, follow these steps:

Step	Example
1. Find the x-coordinate of the turning point.	**1.** Since $y = x^2 - 4x + 1$, let $a = 1$ and $b = 4$. $$x = -\frac{b}{2a} = -\frac{(-4)}{2(1)} = \frac{4}{2} = 2$$
2. Make a table of x and y values. Include *at least* seven values of x: the x-coordinate of the turning point and the next three consecutive integer values of x on either side of it. **Note:** Corresponding points above and below the x-coordinate of the turning point have the same y-coordinate.	**2.** <table><tr><th>x</th><th>x² – 4x</th><th>+ 1</th><th>= y</th></tr><tr><td>–1</td><td>(–1)² – 4(–1)</td><td>+ 1</td><td>= 6</td></tr><tr><td>0</td><td>0² – 4 · 0</td><td>+ 1</td><td>= 1</td></tr><tr><td>1</td><td>1² – 4 · 1</td><td>+ 1</td><td>= –2</td></tr><tr><td>2</td><td>2² – 4 · 2</td><td>+ 1</td><td>= –3</td></tr><tr><td>3</td><td>3² – 4 · 3</td><td>+ 1</td><td>= –2</td></tr><tr><td>4</td><td>4² – 4 · 4</td><td>+ 1</td><td>= 1</td></tr><tr><td>5</td><td>5² – 4 · 5</td><td>+ 1</td><td>= 6</td></tr></table>
3. Draw the axis of symmetry, and then plot the points obtained in Step 2. Connect the points with a smooth and continuous curve that is symmetric with respect to the line $x = 2$ (the axis of symmetry). Use arrow heads to indicate that the parabola continues to rise without bound. **4.** Label the parabola with its equation.	

Examples

5. Draw the graph of $y = -x^2 + 3x + 5$, including all values of x such that $-1 \le x \le 4$.

Solution: Begin by finding the equation of the axis of symmetry and, therefore, the x-coordinate of the turning point of the parabola. Since $y = -x^2 + 3x + 5$, let $a = -1$ and $b = 3$. Then

$$x = -\frac{b}{2a} = -\frac{3}{2(-1)} = \frac{-3}{-2} = \frac{3}{2}.$$

In order to include all values of x such that $-1 \le x \le 4$, construct a table of values that contain all integer values in this interval, as well as the x-coordinate of the turning point of the parabola: $-1, 0, 1, \frac{3}{2}, 2, 3, 4$. Notice that there are three pairs of values of x such that the numbers in each pair are on either side of $\frac{3}{2}$ and the same distance from it.

x	$-x^2$	$+$	$3x$	$+5$	$= y$
-1	$-(-1)^2$	$+$	$3(-1)$	$+5$	$=1$
0	0	$+$	$3 \cdot 0$	$+5$	$=5$
1	$-(1)^2$	$+$	$3 \cdot 1$	$+5$	$=7$
$\dfrac{3}{2}$	$-\left(\dfrac{3}{2}\right)^2$	$+$	$3\left(\dfrac{3}{2}\right)$	$+5$	$=\dfrac{29}{4}$
2	$-(2)^2$	$+$	$3 \cdot 2$	$+5$	$=7$
3	$-(3)^2$	$+$	$3 \cdot 3$	$+5$	$=5$
4	$-(4)^2$	$+$	$3 \cdot 4$	$+5$	$=1$

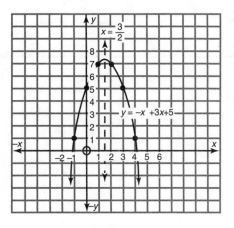

6. (a) On graph paper, draw the graph of the equation $y = (x - 2)^2 - 3$, for all values of x in the interval $-1 \le x \le 5$. Label this graph **a**.

(b) On the same set of axes, draw the graph of the image of the graph drawn in part (a) after a translation moves (x, y) to $(x - 2, y + 3)$. Label this graph **b**.

(c) On the same set of axes, draw the image of the graph drawn in part (b) after a reflection in the x-axis. Label this graph **c**.

Solutions: **(a)** Prepare a table of values using all integer values of x in the interval $-1 \le x \le 5$. Then graph these points, as shown in the accompanying figure.

x	$(x-2)^2 - 3$	$=$	y
-1	$(-1-2)^2 - 3$	$=$	6
0	$(0-2)^2 - 3$	$=$	1
1	$(1-2)^2 - 3$	$=$	-2
2	$(2-2)^2 - 3$	$=$	-3
3	$(3-2)^2 - 3$	$=$	-2
4	$(4-2)^2 - 3$	$=$	1
5	$(5-2)^2 - 3$	$=$	6

(b) Using the translation rule $(x, y) \to (x-2, y+3)$, obtain and then graph on the same set of axes the points that are the images of the points graphed in part (a).

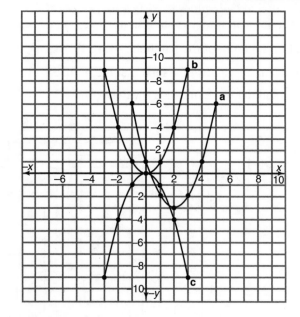

Original Parabola	Translated Parabola
$(-1, 6)$	$(-1-2,\ \ 6+3) = (-3, 9)$
$(0, 1)$	$(0-2,\ \ 1+3) = (-2, 4)$
$(1, -2)$	$(1-2, -2+3) = (-1, 1)$
$(2, -3)$	$(2-2, -3+3) = (0, 0)$
$(3, -2)$	$(3-2, -2+3) = (1, 1)$
$(4, 1)$	$(4-2,\ \ 1+3) = (2, 4)$
$(5, 6)$	$(5-2,\ \ 6+3) = (3, 9)$

The translated graph is labeled **b** in the accompanying diagram.

(c) A reflection of a graph in the x-axis maps each point (x, y) onto $(x, -y)$. Under the transformation rule $(x, y) \to (x, -y)$, the points that are the images of the points graphed in part (c) are $(-3, 9) \to (-3, -9)$, $(-2, 4) \to (-2, -4)$, $(-1, 1) \to (-1, -1)$, $(0, 0) \to (0, 0)$, $(1, 1) \to (1, -1)$, $(2, 4) \to (2, -4)$, $(3, 9) \to (3, -9)$. The graph of these points is shown in the accompanying diagram and is labeled **c**.

Exercise Set 11.2

1–12. On graph paper, draw the graph of each equation, including all values of x in the given interval.

1. $y = x^2 - x - 6; -2 \le x \le 3$

2. $y = -x^2 + 2x - 3; -2 \le x \le 4$

3. $y = -x^2 + 4x - 4; -1 \le x \le 5$

4. $y = -2x^2 + 8x + 3; -1 \le x \le 5$

5. $y = x^2 - 6x + 9; 0 \le x \le 6$

6. $y = x^2 + 4x + 3; -5 \le x \le 1$

7. $y = -x^2 + 3x + 5; -1 \le x \le 4$

8. $y = x^2 - x; -2 \le x \le 3$

9. $y = -x^2 - 2x + 8; -4 \le x \le 2$

10. $y = -x^2 + 3x + 10; -1 \le x \le 4$

11. $y = (x - 1)^2 + 2; -2 \le x \le 4$

12. $y = (x + 1)^2 - 3; -4 \le x \le 2$

13. For the graph of $y = -x^2 + 2x + 5$:
   (a) Find the coordinates of the turning point.
   (b) Write an equation of the line that contains the turning point and is:
      (1) parallel to the *x*-axis
      (2) parallel to the line whose equation is $y = 3x + 4$.
   (c) Write an equation of the locus of points 2 units from the turning point.

14. Write an equation (or equations) of the locus of points 3 units from the axis of symmetry of the graph of $y = x^2 - 4x + 5$

15. Which is an equation of the parabola that has the *y*-axis as its axis of symmetry and its maximum point at (0, –4)?
   (1) $y = x^2 - 4$ (2) $y = -x^2 + 4$ (3) $y = x^2 + 4$ (4) $y = -x^2 - 4$

16. Which is an equation of the parabola that has the *y*-axis as its axis of symmetry and its minimum point at (0, 3)?
   (1) $y = x^2 - 3$ (3) $y = x^2 + 3$
   (2) $y = -x^2 + 3$ (4) $y = -x^2 - 3$

17. Which is an equation of the parabola graphed in the accompanying diagram?
   (1) $y = x^2 + 4$
   (2) $y = x^2 - 4$
   (3) $y = -x^2 + 4$
   (4) $y = -x^2 - 4$

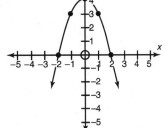

18. If a parabola intersects the *x*-axis at $x = -1$ and $x = 3$, what is an equation of the axis of symmetry?

19. Write an equation of the horizontal line that is tangent to the graph of:
   (a) $y = x^2 - 2$ **(b)** $y = -x^2 + 1$ **(c)** $y = -x^2 - 3$ **(d)** $y = 2x^2 + 8x - 5$

20. (a) Draw the graph of $y = \frac{1}{2}x^2 - 2x + 3$, including all values of *x* such that $-1 \le x \le 5$.

(b) For the graph drawn in part (a):

    (1) Write an equation of the line that passes through the turning point and is perpendicular to the axis of symmetry.

    (2) Write an equation of the locus of points 5 units from the turning point.

    (3) Write an equation (or equations) of the locus of points 3 units from the axis of symmetry.

21. For each of the following pairs of equations, sketch the graphs on the same set of axes and then determine the number of points, if any, the graphs of the two equations have in common:

    (a) $y = 3$ and $y = -x^2 + 3$ **(c)** $y = x^2 + 4$ and $x^2 + y^2 = 16$

    (b) $y = 2$ and $y = x^2 + 1$ **(d)** $y = x^2 - 3$ and $x^2 + y^2 = 9$

22. **(a)** On graph paper, draw the graph of the equation $y = (x + 1)^2 + 2$, including all values of x in the interval $-4 \le x \le 2$.

    (b) Write an equation or equations that describe the locus of points:

        (1) 4 units from the vertex

        (2) 2 units from the axis of symmetry.

    (c) On the same set of axes, draw the graph of the image of the graph drawn in part (a) after a translation moves (x, y) to $(x + 1, y - 2)$. Label this graph **c**.

    (d) On the same set of axes, draw the image of the graph drawn in part (c) after a reflection in the x-axis. Label this graph **d**.

23. **(a)** On graph paper, draw the graph of the equation $y = -x^2 - 2x + 2$, including all values of x from $x = -4$ to $x = 2$.

    (b) On the same set of axes, draw the graph of the image of the graph drawn in part (a) after a translation moves (x, y) to $(x + 4, y - 3)$. Label this graph **b**.

    (c) On the same set of axes, draw the image of the graph drawn in part (b) after a reflection in the x-axis. Label this graph **c**.

24. **(a)** On graph paper, draw the graph of the equation $y = x^2 - 4x + 9$, including all values of x in the interval $-1 \le x \le 5$.

    (b) On the same set of axes, draw the graph of the image of the graph drawn in part (a) after a translation moves (x, y) to $(x - 2, y - 5)$. Label this graph **b**.

    (c) On the same set of axes, draw the image of the graph drawn in part (b) after a reflection in the x-axis. Label this graph **c**.

25. **(a)** On graph paper, draw the graph of the equation $y = x^2 - 6x$, including all values of x in the interval $0 \le x \le 6$.

    (b) After the graph drawn in part (a) is translated, point $(0, 0)$ is the image of the turning point of the graph drawn in part (a). On the same set of axes, draw the graph that is the image of the graph drawn in part (a) after this translation. Label this graph **b**.

    (c) On the same set of axes, draw the image of the graph drawn in part (b) after a reflection in the line $y = x$. Label this graph **c**.

11.3 SOLVING QUADRATIC EQUATIONS GRAPHICALLY

KEY IDEAS

The point or points, if any, at which the parabola $y = ax^2 + bx + c$ $(a \neq 0)$ crosses the x-axis have y-coordinates of 0. The x-coordinates of these points represent the roots of the corresponding quadratic equation,

$$0 = ax^2 + bx + c.$$

If the parabola does not cross the x-axis, then the roots of $ax^2 + bx + c = 0$ are *not* real.

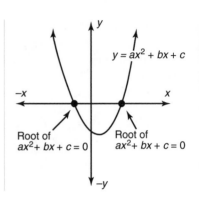

Intercepts of a Parabola

The y-coordinate of the point at which a parabola crosses the y-axis is called the *y-intercept* of the parabola. The x-coordinate of any point at which a parabola crosses the x-axis is called an *x-intercept* of the parabola. As shown in Figure 11.6, a parabola may have no, one, or two x-intercepts.

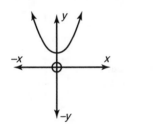 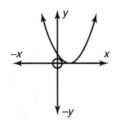 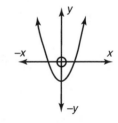

Figure 11.6 Possible Numbers of x-Intercepts of a Parabola

For the parabola whose equation is $y = ax^2 + bx + c$ $(a \neq 0)$:

- The y-intercept is c. For example, the y-intercept of $y = x^2 + x - 6$ is -6.
- The x-intercept(s) are the real roots, if any, of the quadratic equation $ax^2 + bx + c = 0$. For example, the x-intercepts of $y = x^2 + x - 6$ are the real roots, if any, of $x^2 + x - 6 = 0$. Since the roots of $x^2 + x - 6 = 0$ are -3 and 2, $x = -3$ and $x = 2$ are the x-intercepts of the graph of $y = x^2 + x - 6$. If the roots of $ax^2 + bx + c = 0$ are *not* real, then the parabola has no x-intercepts and, as a result, the graph will *not* intersect the x-axis.

Example

1. **(a)** What are the y-intercept and the coordinates of the turning point of the parabola $y = x^2 + 2x - 5$?

(b) Draw the graph of $y = x^2 + 2x - 5$, including all values of x such that $-4 \le x \le 2$.

(c) From the graph drawn in part (b), find the two consecutive integers between which the positive root of $x^2 + 2x - 5 = 0$ lies.

(d) What is the smallest value of k such that the line $y = k$ intersects the graph of $y = x^2 + 2x - 5$?

(e) What is the minimum value of k for which the roots of the equation $x^2 + 2x - 5 = k$ are real?

(f) What is the greatest integer value of k that will make the roots of the equation $x^2 + 2x - 5 = k$ *not* real?

Solutions: **(a)** The y-intercept of $y = x^2 + 2x - 5$ is **–5**. To find the coordinates of the turning point (vertex) of the parabola, first determine the equation of the axis of symmetry. Let $a = 1$ and $b = 2$. Then

$$x = -\frac{b}{2a} = -\frac{2}{2 \cdot 1} = -1.$$

Rewrite the equation of the parabola: $y = \quad x^2 \quad + \quad 2x \quad - 5$
Replace x by –1: $\qquad\qquad\qquad y = (-1)^2 + 2(-1) - 5$
Simplify: $\qquad\qquad\qquad\qquad y = \quad 1 \quad + \quad -2 \quad - 5 = -6$

The coordinates of the turning point are **(–1, –6)**.

(b)

x	$x^2 \quad + \quad 2x \quad\quad - \quad 5$	$= y$
–4	$(-4)^2 + 2(-4) - 5$	$= 3$
–3	$(-3)^2 + 2(-3) - 5$	$=-2$
–2	$(-2)^2 + 2(-2) - 5$	$=-5$
–1	*Turning point*	$=-6$
0	$0^2 \quad + 2 \cdot 0 \; - 5$	$=-5$
1	$1^2 \quad + 2 \cdot 1 \; - 5$	$=-2$
2	$2^2 \quad + 2 \cdot 2 \; - 5$	$= 3$

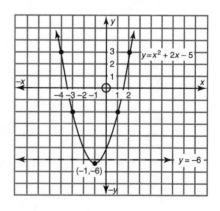

(c) Since the parabola intersects the positive x-axis between $x = 1$ and $x = 2$, the positive root of $x^2 + 2x - 5 = 0$ lies between **1** and **2**.

(d) The lowest point on the parabola is the turning point, whose coordinates are (–1, –6). Therefore, the smallest value of k such that the horizontal line $y = k$ intersects the graph of $y = x^2 + 2x - 5$ is **–6** (the y-coordinate of the turning point).

(e) In general, the point or points at which the parabola $y = ax^2 + bx + c$ and the horizontal line $y = k$ intersect, if any, represent the real roots of the quadratic equation $ax^2 + bx + c = k$, where k is some constant number.

The *minimum* value of k for which the roots of the equation $x^2 + 2x - 5 = k$ are real corresponds to the *smallest* value of k for which the graphs $y = k$ and $y = x^2 + 2x - 5$ intersect, which is **–6**.

(f) In general, if the graphs of $y = k$ and $y = ax^2 + bx + c$ do *not* intersect, then the roots of $ax^2 + bx + c = k$ are *not* real (are imaginary). For all values of k less than –6, the graphs of $y = k$ and $y = x^2 + 2x - 5$ do not intersect.

Therefore, **–7** is the *largest integer* value of k such that the roots of $x^2 + 2x - 5 = k$ are *not* real.

Exercise Set 11.3

1–8. In each case, do the following:
   (a) *Determine the y-intercept and the coordinates of the turning point of the graph of the given equation.*
   (b) *Draw the graph of each equation, including all values of x in the given interval.*
   (c) *Use the graph of $y = ax^2 + bx + c$ drawn in part (b) to find the roots of the corresponding quadratic equation, $ax^2 + bx + c = 0$.*
   (d) *Determine the value of k that will make the roots of $ax^2 + bx + c = k$ real and equal.*
   (e) *Give an integer value of k that will make the roots of $ax^2 + bx + c = k$ not real.*

1. $y = x^2 + 6x + 8;\ -6 \le x \le 0$

2. $y = x^2 - 4x;\ -1 \le x \le 5$

3. $y = x^2 + 4x;\ -5 \le x \le 1$

4. $y = x^2 - 6x - 7;\ 0 \le x \le 6$

5. $y = -x^2 - 2x + 3;\ -4 \le x \le 2$

6. $y = -x^2 + 2x - 1;\ -2 \le x \le 4$

7. $y = x^2 - x - 6;\ -2 \le x \le 3$

8. $y = \frac{1}{2}x^2 - x - 4;\ -2 \le x \le 4$

9. (a) Draw the graph of $y = x^2 - 4x + 2$, including all values of x such that $-1 \le x \le 5$.
   (b) Using the graph drawn in part (a):
   (1) Estimate the roots of $x^2 - 4x + 2 = 0$ to the nearest tenth.
   (2) Find the smallest integral value of k for which the roots of $x^2 - 4x + 2 = 0$ are real.

10. (a) Draw the graph of $y = -2x^2 + 4x - 9$, including all values of x such that $-2 \le x \le 4$.
   (b) Using the graph drawn in part (a):
   (1) Estimate the roots of $-2x^2 + 4x - 9 = 0$ to the *nearest tenth*.
   (2) Find the largest integral value of k for which the roots of $x^2 - 4x + 2 = 0$ are real.

11.4 SOLVING LINEAR-QUADRATIC SYSTEMS OF EQUATIONS

=== ∧ KEY IDEAS ===

Solving a system of equations means finding the sets of all values of the variables that satisfy two or more equations at the same time. A system of equations consisting of one linear equation and one quadratic equation in two variables may be solved in either of two ways:

- *Graphically,* by graphing each equation on the same set of coordinate axes. The coordinates of the point(s) of intersection of the two graphs, if any, represent the solution set of the system of equations.
- *Algebraically,* by using the linear equation and the substitution principle to eliminate one of the two variables in the quadratic equation. The resulting quadratic equation can then be solved by factoring or by using the quadratic formula.

Solving a Linear-Quadratic System of Equations Graphically

As Figure 11.7 illustrates, a line may intersect a parabola (or circle) in no, one, or two points. Therefore, the solution set of a linear-quadratic system of equations may consist of two ordered pairs of numbers, one ordered pair of numbers, or no ordered pairs.

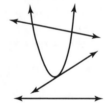

Figure 11.7 Possible Numbers of Points in Which a Line and Parabola May Intersect

Example

1. (a) Draw the graph of $y = -x^2 + 4x - 3$ for all values of x such that $-1 \le x \le 5$.

(b) On the same set of axes, draw the graph of $x + y = 1$.

(c) Determine the solution set of the system

$$y = -x^2 + 4x - 3$$
$$x + y = 1.$$

(d) Check the answer obtained in part (c) *algebraically.*

Solutions:

(a) Make a table of values, using all integral values of x such that $-1 \leq x \leq 5$, and then draw the parabola.

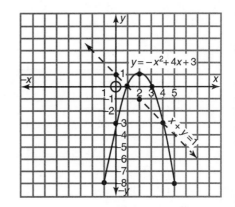

x	$-x^2 + 4x - 3$	$= y$
-1	$-(-1)^2 + 4(-1) - 3$	$= -8$
0	$-0^2 + 4 \cdot 0 - 3$	$= -3$
1	$-(1)^2 + 4 \cdot 1 - 3$	$= 0$
2	$-(2)^2 + 4 \cdot 2 - 3$	$= 1$
3	$-(3)^2 + 4 \cdot 3 - 3$	$= 0$
4	$-(4)^2 + 4 \cdot 4 - 3$	$= -3$
5	$-(5)^2 + 4 \cdot 5 - 3$	$= -8$

Note: $(2, 1)$ is the turning point of the parabola.

(b) Solve for y: $y = -x + 1$. Make a table of values, using any three convenient values for x.

x	$-x + 1$	$= y$
0	$0 + 1$	$= 1$
1	$-1 + 1$	$= 0$
2	$-2 + 1$	$= -1$

(c) Draw the graph of $x + y = 1$. Since the graphs drawn in parts (a) and (b) intersect at $(1, 0)$ and $(4, -3)$, the solution set of the system of equations $y = -x^2 + 4x - 3$ and $x + y = 1$ is $\{(\mathbf{1, 0}), (\mathbf{4, -3})\}$.

(d) In an algebraic check, we must demonstrate that each ordered pair of the solution set satisfies each of the *original* equations.

To check $(1, 0)$, let $x = 1$ and $y = 0$:

$$
\begin{array}{l|l}
y \overset{?}{=} -x^2 + 4x \;\; -3 & x + y \overset{?}{=} 1 \\
0 \;\; -(1)^2 + 4 \cdot 1 - 3 & 1 + 0 \overset{\checkmark}{=} 1 \\
0 \;\;\;\;\; -1 + 4 \;\;\;\; -3 & 1 \overset{\checkmark}{=} 1 \\
0 \;\;\;\;\;\;\;\;\; 3 \;\;\;\;\; -3 & \\
0 \overset{\checkmark}{=} 0 &
\end{array}
$$

To check $(4, -3)$, let $x = 4$ and $y = -3$:

$$
\begin{array}{l|l}
y \overset{?}{=} -x^2 + 4x \;\; -3 & x + y \overset{?}{=} 1 \\
-3 \;\; -(4)^2 + 4 \cdot 4 - 3 & 4 + (-3) \overset{\checkmark}{=} 1 \\
-3 \;\;\;\; -16 + 16 \;\;\; -3 & 1 \overset{\checkmark}{=} 1 \\
-3 \;\;\;\;\;\;\;\;\;\; 0 \;\;\;\;\;\; -3 & \\
-3 \overset{\checkmark}{=} -3 &
\end{array}
$$

Solving a Linear-Quadratic System of Equations Algebraically

A linear-quadratic system of equations such as $x + y = 1$ and $y = -x^2 + 4x - 3$ may be solved algebraically as follows:

Step	Example
1. If necessary, rewrite the linear equation so that one of the variables is expressed in terms of the other. When the quadratic equation has the form $y = ax^2 + bx + c$, it is usually easier to solve the system by solving the linear equation for y in terms of x.	**1.** $x + y = 1$ $\quad\quad y = -x + 1$
2. Substitute into the quadratic equation the expression obtained by solving for the variable in the linear equation.	**2.** Since $y = -x + 1$, replace y by $-x + 1$: $y = -x^2 + 4x - 3$ $-x + 1 = -x^2 + 4x - 3$
3. Express the quadratic equation in standard form. Solve the resulting quadratic equation, usually by factoring.	**3.** $0 = -x^2 + 4x + x - 3 - 1$ $0 = -x^2 + 5x - 4$ Multiply each term by -1: $0 = x^2 - 5x + 4$ $0 = (x - 1)(x - 4)$ $(x - 1 = 0) \quad$ or $(x - 4 = 0)$ $\quad\ x = 1 \quad\quad$ or $x = 4$
4. Find the value of the remaining variable of each ordered pair by substituting each root of the quadratic equation into the linear equation.	**4.** Let $\ \ x = 1$. $\quad$ Let $x = 4$. $\quad$ Then $y = -x + 1 \quad\quad$ Then $y = -x + 1$ $\quad\quad\quad = -1 + 1 \quad\quad\quad\quad\quad\ = -4 + 1$ $\quad\quad\quad = 0 \quad\quad\quad\quad\quad\quad\quad\ = -3$ The solution set is $\{(\mathbf{1, 0}), (\mathbf{4, -3})\}$.
5. Check algebraically by verifying that each ordered pair satisfies each of the *original* equations.	**5.** The check is left for you. (See solution by graphing in Example 1 on page 343.)

Example

2. Solve the following system of equations algebraically and check:

$$x^2 + y^2 = 50$$
$$y + 10 = 3x$$

Solution:

Solve for y in the linear equation: $\qquad\qquad y = 3x - 10$

Substitute for variable y in the $\qquad\qquad x^2 + y^2 = 50$
quadratic equation: $\qquad\qquad x^2 + (3x - 10)^2 = 50$

Simplify and express the quadratic $\qquad x^2 + 9x^2 - 60x + 100 = 50$
equation in standard form: $\qquad 10x^2 - 60x + 100 = 50$

$$10x^2 - 60x + 100 - 50 = 0$$
$$10x^2 - 60x + 50 = 0$$
$$\frac{10x^2}{10} - \frac{60x}{10} + \frac{50}{10} = 0$$
$$x^2 - 6x + 5 = 0$$

Solve by factoring: $\qquad\qquad (x - 1)(x - 5) = 0$
$$(x - 1 = 0) \text{ or } (x - 5 = 0)$$

Find the corresponding value $\qquad x = 1 \qquad\qquad\quad x = 5$
of y by substituting each value $\quad y = 3x - 10 \qquad\quad y = 3x - 10$
of x into the linear equation: $\qquad = 3(1) - 10 \qquad\quad = 3(5) - 10$

Write the solution as a set of $\qquad = 3 - 10 \qquad\qquad = 15 - 10$
ordered pairs: $\qquad\qquad\qquad = -7 \qquad\qquad\quad = 5$

The check is left for you. $\quad$ The solution set is $\{(1, -7), (5, 5)\}$.

Exercise Set 11.4

1–15. Solve each of the following systems of equations algebraically and check. If the quadratic equation in one variable cannot be factored, find the discriminant. If the discriminant is less than 0, write, "The system does not have real roots."

1. $y = x^2 - 2$
$\quad y = 2x + 1$

2. $y = x^2 - x$
$\quad y = 3x$

3. $y = -x^2 + 3x$
$\quad y + 3 = x$

4. $y = 3x - 2$
$\quad y = x^2 + 2x$

5. $y = x^2 - 2x + 3$
$\quad y = 2x - 1$

6. $y = x + 9$
$\quad y = x^2 - 4x + 3$

7. $y = x^2 - 6x - 1$
$\quad y - x = 7$

8. $y + 7x = 3$
$\quad y = 2x^2 - 4x + 1$

9. $y = -x^2 - 2x + 9$
$\quad y = 2x - 3$

10. $y = x^2 + 3x - 5$
$\quad y - 2x = 1$

11. $y = -x^2 + 4x - 2$
$\quad y + 5 = 2x$

12. $y = x^2 - 6x + 9$
$\quad y + 2x = 5$

13. $y = \frac{1}{2}x^2 - 2x + 1$
$\quad y + 3 = x$

14. $y = -x^2 - 2x + 3$
$\quad y + x = 6$

15. $y = x^2 + 3x + 2$
$\quad y + x + 2 = 0$

16–30. For each system of equations given in Exercises 1–15, do the following:

    (a) Draw the graph of the quadratic equation, using the turning point and three consecutive integer values of x on either side of it.

    (b) On the same set of axes used in part (a), draw the graph of the linear equation.

    (c) Using the graphs drawn in parts (a) and (b), determine the solution set of the system of equations.

31–40. Solve each of the following systems of equations algebraically, and check.

31. $y = 2x^2 - 5x + 5$
$\quad\;\, y - x = 5$

36. $x^2 + y^2 = 25$
$\quad\;\, x + 2y = 10$

32. $x^2 + y^2 = 50$
$\quad\;\, x - y = 8$

37. $x^2 + y^2 - 8 = 0$
$\quad\;\, x + 3y = 4$

33. $y + 11 = 3x$
$\quad\;\, x^2 - 4x - y - 5 = 0$

38. $x - y = 1$
$\quad\;\, x^2 + y^2 - 4y = 5$

34. $x^2 + y^2 = 20$
$\quad\;\, y + 2x = 10$

39. $x^2 - 3y^2 = 6$
$\quad\;\, x + 2y = -1$

35. $x^2 + y^2 = 17$
$\quad\;\, x - y = 5$

40. $(x - 2)^2 + (y - 3)^2 = 25$
$\quad\;\, x - y + 2 = 0$

41. (a) Using a compass, draw the graph of $x^2 + y^2 = 25$.

    (b) On the same set of axes used in part (a), draw the graph of $x + y = -1$.

    (c) On the basis of the graphs drawn in parts (a) and (b), determine the solution set of the system of equations $x^2 + y^2 = 25$ and $x + y = -1$.

42. (a) Using a compass, draw the graph of $x^2 + y^2 = 100$.

    (b) On the same set of axes used in part (a), draw the graph of $x + y = 2$.

    (c) On the basis of the graph drawn in parts (a) and (b), determine the solution set of the system of equations $x^2 + y^2 = 100$ and $x + y = 2$.

REGENTS TUNE-UP: CHAPTER 11

Each of the questions in this section has appeared on a previous Course II Regents Examination. Here is an opportunity for you to review the material in Chapter 11 and, at the same time, prepare for the Course II Regents Examination.

1. Which are the coordinates of the turning point of the parabola whose equation is $y = x^2 - 2x - 3$?
(1) $(1, -4)$ (2) $(-1, 0)$ (3) $(1, 2)$ (4) $(-1, -2)$

2. Which is an equation of the circle with center at $(-3, 1)$ and radius of 5?
(1) $(x + 3)^2 + (y - 1)^2 = 5$ (3) $(x + 3)^2 + (y - 1)^2 = 25$
(2) $(x - 3)^2 + (y + 1)^2 = 5$ (4) $(x - 3)^2 + (y + 1)^2 = 25$

3. Which is an equation of the axis of symmetry of the graph of the equation $y = 2x^2 - 3x - 1$?
(1) $x = \dfrac{3}{2}$ (2) $y = -\dfrac{3}{2}$ (3) $x = \dfrac{3}{4}$ (4) $y = \dfrac{3}{4}$

4. The graphs of the equations $y = x^2$ and $x = 2$ intersect in
(1) 1 point   (2) 2 points   (3) 3 points   (4) 0 point

5. Which is a solution for the following system of equations?
$$y = x^2$$
$$y = -4x + 12$$
(1) $(-2, 4)$ (2) $(6, 36)$ (3) $(2, 4)$ (4) $(-6, 24)$

6. The graphs of the equations $y = x^2 - 5x + 6$ and $x + y = 6$ are drawn on the same set of axes. At which point do the graphs intersect?
(1) $(4, 2)$ (2) $(5, 1)$ (3) $(3, 3)$ (4) $(2, 4)$

7. How many points do the graphs of $x^2 + y^2 = 9$ and $y = 4$ have in common?
(1) 1   (2) 1   (3) 0   (4) 4

8. Which is a solution for the system of equations $y = 2x - 15$ and $y = x^2 - 6x$?
(1) $(3, -9)$ (2) $(0, 0)$ (3) $(5, 5)$ (4) $(6, 0)$

9. Which is a point of intersection of the graphs of the line $y = x$ and the parabola $y = x^2 - 2$?
(1) $(1, 1)$ (2) $(2, 2)$ (3) $(0, 0)$ (4) $(2, -1)$

10. (a) Draw the graph of the equation $y = \dfrac{1}{2} x^2 - 4x + 4$, including all values of x such that $0 \le x \le 8$.

(b) Write the coordinates of the turning point.

(c) Between which pair of consecutive integers does one root of the equation $\dfrac{1}{2} x^2 - 4x + 4 = 0$ lie?

(1) 0 and 1   (2) 1 and 2   (3) 2 and 3   (4) -1 and 0

11. Solve the following system of equations algebraically and check:
$$y = 3x^2 - 8x + 5$$
$$x + y = 3.$$

12. **(a)** Draw a graph of the equation $y = -x^2 + 4x - 3$ for all values of x such that $-1 \le x \le 5$.
    (b) On the same set of axes, draw the graph of $y + 1 = x$.
    (c) Using the graphs drawn in parts (a) and (b), determine the solution of the system:
    $$y = -x^2 + 4x - 3$$
    $$y + 1 = x.$$

13. **(a)** On graph paper, draw the graph of the parabola $y = x^2 + 6x + 5$, including all values of x in the interval $-6 \le x \le 0$.
    (b) On the same set of axes, draw the image of the parabola drawn in part (a) after a translation of $(x, y) \to (x + 3, y - 3)$.
    (c) Using the graph, write the coordinates of the point of intersection of the parabolas drawn in parts (a) and (b).

14. Solve the following system of equations and check. [*Either an algebraic or a graphic method will be accepted.*]
    $$x^2 + y^2 = 25$$
    $$3x - 4y = 0$$

15. **(a)** On graph paper, draw the graph of the parabola $y = (x + 3)^2 - 2$ for all values of x in the interval $-6 \le x \le 0$.
    (b) On the same set of axes, draw the image of the graph drawn in part (a) after a translation that maps (x, y) to $(x + 3, y + 2)$.
    (c) On the same set of axes, draw the image of the graph drawn in part (b) after a reflection in the x-axis.

ANSWERS TO SELECTED EXERCISES: CHAPTER 11

Section 11.1

1. (2)

3. $(x + 2)^2 + (y - 3)^2 = 49$ (b)

5. (a) on circle
   (b) on circle
   (c) not on circle

7. (a) $x^2 + y^2 = 400$
   (b) $x^2 + y^2 = 25$
   (c) $x^2 + y^2 = 100$

9. (a) $x^2 + (y + 1)^2 = 36$
   (b) $(x + 1)^2 + (y - 2)^2 = 324$

11. $x^2 + y^2 = 9$

13. (a) 2   **(b)** 1   **(c)** 0   **(d)** 2

15. $(x - 2)^2 + (y + 3)^2 = 25$

17. $(x + 1)^2 + (y + 4)^2 = 169$

19. (a) $(\pm 7, 0), (0, \pm 7)$
   (c) $(4.7, 0)$ and $(1.3, 0)$
   (e) $(-5.7, 0)$ and $(-9.7, 0)$; $(0, -4)$ and $(0, 14)$

Section 11.2

13. (a) $(1, 6)$
   (b) (1) $y = 6$
      (2) $y = 3x + 3$
14. $x = -1, 5$
15. (4)
16. (3)
17. (3)
18. $x = 1$

19. (a) $y = -2$ **(c)** $y = -3$
   (b) $y = 1$ **(d)** $y = -13$
20. (b) (1) $y = 1$
     (2) $(x - 2)^2 + (y - 1)^2 = 25$
     (3) $x = -1, 5$
21. (a) 1   **(b)** 2   **(c)** 1   **(d)** 3
22. (b) (1) $(x + 1)^2 + (y - 2)^2 = 16$
     (2) $x = -3, 1$

Section 11.3

1. (a) y-intercept $= (0, 8)$
   turning point $= (-3, -1)$
   (c) $x = -4, -2$
   (d) -1 **(e)** -2
3. (a) y-intercept $= (0, 0)$
   turning point $= (-2, -4)$
   (c) $x = 0, -4$
   (d) -4 **(e)** -5
5. (a) y-intercept $= (0, 3)$, turning point $= (-1, 4)$
   (c) $-3, 1$ **(d)** 4   **(e)** 5

7. (a) y-intercept $= (0, -6)$
   turning point $= \left(\frac{1}{2}, -6\frac{1}{4}\right)$
   (c) $x = -2, 3$
   (d) $-6\frac{1}{4}$ **(e)** -7
9. (b) (1) $x = 0.6, 3.4$ (2) -2

Section 11.4

1. $(-1, -1), (3, 7)$
3. $(-1, -4), (3, 0)$
5. $(2, 3)$
7. $(-1, 6), (8, 15)$

9. $(-6, -15), (2, 1)$
11. $(3 \pm \sqrt{3}, 1 \pm 2\sqrt{3})$
13. $(2, -1), (4, 1)$
15. $(2, -4)$

31. $(0, 5), (3, 8)$
33. $(1, -8), (6, 7)$
35. $(4, -1), (1, -4)$
37. $\left(\frac{14}{5}, \frac{2}{5}\right), (-2, 2)$
39. $(9, -5), (3, -1)$

Regents Tune-Up: Chapter 11

1. (1)
2. (1)
3. (3)

4. (1)
5. (3)
6. (1)

7. (3)
8. (1)
9. (2)

11. $\left(\frac{1}{3}, \frac{8}{3}\right), (2, 1)$
12. (c) $(1, 0), (2, 1)$
14. (d) $(4, 3), (-4, -3)$

PROBABILITY AND COMBINATIONS

CHAPTER 12

PROBABILITY AND COMBINATIONS

12.1 PROBABILITY CONCEPTS

KEY IDEAS

The mathematical **probability** of an event expresses the likelihood that the event will occur as a fraction whose value ranges from 0 to 1. The closer this fractional value is to 1, the greater the certainty that the event will occur.

If an event can happen in r of n equally likely ways, then the probability that this event will occur is $\frac{r}{n}$.

Definition of Probability

The set of all possible ways in which a probability experiment can turn out is called the **sample space**. The outcomes in the sample space that will make an event occur are the **favorable outcomes** or **successes** for that event. If event E represents some event from a sample space that contains only equally likely outcomes, then the probability that event E will occur is denoted by $P(E)$ and defined as

$$P(E) = \frac{\textbf{Number of favorable outcomes}}{\textbf{Total number of possible outcomes}}.$$

For example, consider the probability experiment of rolling a six-sided die and obtaining a number greater than 4. The sample space is the set of all the possible numbers of dots that may appear on the side of the die that faces up: $\{1, 2, 3, 4, 5, 6\}$. Since 5 and 6 are each greater than 4, two out of the six possible outcomes in the sample space are favorable outcomes. Thus,

$$P \text{ (rolling a number} > 4) = \frac{2}{6}.$$

Some Probability Facts

Since the numerator of the probability fraction for an event E must always be less than or equal to the denominator, $P(E)$ ranges in value from 0 to 1.

- $P(E) = 0$ if event E is impossible.
- $P(E) = 1$ if event E is certain to occur.
- $P(\text{not } E) = 1 - P(E)$. For example, since the probability of rolling a die and getting a number greater than 4 is $\frac{2}{6}$, the probability of rolling a number less than or equal to 4 is $1 - \frac{2}{6} = \frac{4}{6}$.

Probability Involving *or*

In probability problems involving two (or more) events, the events may or may not have outcomes that are successes for both events.

- If events A and B have no successful outcomes in common, then

$$P(A \text{ or } B) = P(A) + P(B).$$

Example: What is the probability of obtaining a 1 or an even number on a single roll of a die?

Let A = event of rolling a 1;
B = event of rolling an even number.

Since there are six possible outcomes and three even numbers, $P(A) = \frac{1}{6}$ and $P(B) = \frac{3}{6}$.

$$P(A \text{ or } B) = P(A) + P(B)$$
$$= \frac{1}{6} + \frac{3}{6} = \frac{4}{6} = \frac{2}{3}$$

- If events A and B have outcomes in common that are successes for both events, then

$$P(A \text{ or } B) = P(A) + P(B) - P(A \text{ and } B).$$

Example: What is the probability of obtaining a 2 or an even number on a single roll of a die?

Let A = event of rolling a 2;
B = event of rolling an even number.

Since there are six possible outcomes, $P(A) = \frac{1}{6}$. There are three even numbers, so $P(B) = \frac{3}{6}$. Since 2 is an even number, it is counted in both $P(A)$ and in $P(B)$. Events A and B have one successful outcome in common, so $P(A \text{ and } B) = \frac{1}{6}$.

$$P(A \text{ or } B) = P(A) + P(B) - P(A \text{ and } B)$$
$$= \frac{1}{6} + \frac{3}{6} - \frac{1}{6} = \frac{3}{6} = \frac{1}{2}$$

Probability Involving *and*

Multiplying the probability that event A will occur by the probability that event B will occur gives the probability that events A and B will both occur. Thus,

$$P(A \text{ and } B) = P(A) \cdot P(B).$$

For example, the probability of tossing a fair coin two times and getting two heads is the product of the probabilities of obtaining a head on each of the two tosses. Thus,

$$P(\text{head and head}) = \tfrac{1}{2} \cdot \tfrac{1}{2} = \tfrac{1}{4}.$$

Sometimes the notation $P(A, B)$ is used to indicate the probability that event B occurs after event A.

Examples

1. If a coin is tossed and then a die is rolled, what is the probability of getting a head and a number less than 3?

Solution: $P(H) = \tfrac{1}{2}$. There are two numbers less than 3 (1 and 2), so $P(N < 3) = \tfrac{2}{6} = \tfrac{1}{3}$.

$$
\begin{aligned}
P(H \text{ and } N > 3) &= P(H) \times P(N < 3) \\
&= \tfrac{1}{2} \times \tfrac{1}{3} \\
&= \tfrac{1}{6}
\end{aligned}
$$

2. (a) What is the probability of rolling a number greater than 4 on two successive rolls of a die?

(b) What is the probability of rolling a 6 and then a different number on the second roll?

Solutions: The sample space for each roll is $\{1, 2, 3, 4, 5, 6\}$, so the total number of possible outcomes is six. Let $x =$ the number that is rolled.

(a) Since the favorable outcomes are 5 and 6, $P(x > 4) = \tfrac{2}{6} = \tfrac{1}{3}$. To find the probability of rolling a number greater than 4 on the first roll and on the second roll, you need to multiply probabilities. Thus,

$$P(x > 4 \text{ and } x > 4) = P(x > 4) \, P(x > 4) = \tfrac{1}{3} \cdot \tfrac{1}{3} = \tfrac{1}{9}.$$

(b) Since $P(x = 6) = \tfrac{1}{6}$ and $P(x \neq 6) = \tfrac{5}{6}$,

$$P(x = 6 \text{ and } x \neq 6) = \tfrac{1}{6} \cdot \tfrac{5}{6} = \tfrac{5}{36}.$$

3. Find the probability of picking two kings from a deck of cards when the first card: **(a)** is not replaced   **(b)** is replaced

Solution: **(a)** When the first card is not replaced in the deck, assume that a favorable outcome is removed from the original sample space of 52 cards. For the second draw 51 cards are left in the deck, three of which are kings. Thus,

$$P(\text{king, king}) = P(\text{first king}) \times P(\text{second king})$$
$$= \frac{4}{52} \times \frac{3}{51}$$
$$= \frac{1}{13} \times \frac{1}{17}$$
$$= \frac{1}{221}.$$

(b) Since the first card is replaced, the two selections are independent events and have the same sample space. Thus,

$$P(\text{king, king}) = P(\text{first king}) \times P(\text{second king})$$
$$= \frac{4}{52} \times \frac{4}{52}$$
$$= \frac{1}{13} \times \frac{1}{13}$$
$$= \frac{1}{169}.$$

4. A jar contains three red marbles, two white marbles, and four blue marbles. A marble is chosen at random from the jar and then replaced. Another marble is chosen.

(a) Find the probability that both marbles are white.

(b) If the first marble is not replaced, find the probability that both marbles are the same color.

Solutions: **(a)** There are nine marbles in the jar, so the sample space for each selection with replacement is 9. On each selection from the jar, two white marbles are available to be picked. The probability that a white marble is selected on the first try is $\frac{2}{9}$, and with replacement the probability that a white marble is picked on the second try is also $\frac{2}{9}$. The probability that these events will occur jointly is, therefore,

$$P(\text{both white}) = P(\text{first white}) \times P(\text{second white})$$
$$= \frac{2}{9} \times \frac{2}{9} = \frac{4}{81}.$$

(b) $P(\text{same color}) = P(\text{both red}) + P(\text{both white}) + P(\text{both blue})$. Since there is no replacement, there are nine outcomes in the sample space for the first pick, and eight possible outcomes for the second pick. The outcome that is removed is assumed to be the color that the second pick is trying to match.

$$P(\text{both red}) = \frac{3}{9} \times \frac{2}{8} = \frac{6}{72}$$
$$P(\text{both white}) = \frac{2}{9} \times \frac{1}{8} = \frac{2}{72}$$
$$\underline{P(\text{both blue}) = \frac{4}{9} \times \frac{3}{8} = \frac{12}{72}}$$
$$P(\text{same color}) \qquad = \frac{20}{72} = \frac{5}{18}$$

Exercise Set 12.1

1. If $P(A) = 0.7$, $P(B) = 0.5$, and $P(A$ and $B) = 0.35$, what is $P(A$ or $B)$?

2. What is the probability that the average of two consecutive even integers is also an even integer?

   (1) 0   (2) $\frac{1}{2}$ (3) 1   (4) Impossible to determine

3. Express, in terms of x, the probability that an event will *not* happen if the probability that the event will happen is represented by:

   (a) x **(b)** $\frac{x}{4}$ **(c)** $x + 4$ **(d)** $4x - 1$

4. A jar contains x red marbles, $2x - 1$ blue marbles, and $2x + 1$ white marbles. One marble is drawn at random.
   (a) Express, in terms of x, the total number of marbles in the jar.
   (b) Express, in terms of x, the probability of drawing a blue marble.
   (c) If the probability of drawing a blue marble is $\frac{1}{3}$, find the value of x.
   (d) What is the probability of *not* drawing a red marble?

5. A softball team plays two games each weekend, one on Saturday and the other on Sunday. The probability of winning on Saturday is $\frac{3}{5}$, and the probability of winning on Sunday is $\frac{4}{7}$. Find the probability of
   (a) losing a Saturday game and winning a Sunday game
   (b) losing a Sunday game after winning a Saturday game
   (c) winning both games
   (d) losing both games

6. A jar contains three yellow marbles, five white marbles, and two black marbles. Two marbles are randomly selected, and their colors are noted. Find the probability of selecting without replacement:
   (a) one white and one black marble
   (b) two white marbles
   (c) two marbles having the same color
   (d) two marbles having different colors

7. Answer each part of Exercise 6 assuming replacement.

8. Two cards are drawn at random without replacement from a standard deck of 52 playing cards. Find the probability that the two cards:
   (a) are both spades   **(c)** are picture cards
   (b) are in different suits   **(d)** have the same face value

9. Answer each part of Exercise 8 assuming replacement.

10. John has 10 navy blue socks and 14 black socks in a drawer. If he selects two socks at random, what is the probability they will be the same color?

12.2 COUNTING ARRANGEMENTS OF OBJECTS: PERMUTATIONS

=== **KEY IDEAS** ===

A **permutation** is an arrangement of objects in which order matters. A special notation is useful when discussing permutations. The product of the integers from n to 1, inclusive, is called n **factorial** and is written as $n!$ For example,

$$5! = 5 \cdot 4 \cdot 3 \cdot 2 \cdot 1 = 120.$$

Note that n is defined only if n is a positive integer. 0! is defined to be equal to 1.

Alternatively, $n!$ may be written as $_nP_n$. For example,

$$_4P_4 = 4! = 4 \cdot 3 \cdot 2 \cdot 1 = 24.$$

Arranging Objects

When finding the number of possible different arrangements of a set of objects in which the order of the objects is considered, two important situations arise:

1. *All of the objects are used in each arrangement.* If every object is used in each arrangement, then the number of different arrangements possible is $n!$, where n represents the number of objects being arranged. This situation is sometimes symbolized by the notation $_nP_n$, which is read as "the permutation of n objects taken n at a time." The notations $n!$ and $_nP_n$ are mathematically equivalent.

Example: **(a)** In how many different ways can an algebra book, a geometry book, a trigonometry book, and a calculus book be arranged on a bookshelf?
(b) In how many different ways can these books be arranged if the geometry book must appear first?

(a) Since there are four different books, they can be arranged on a shelf in

$$_4P_4 = 4 \cdot 3 \cdot 2 \cdot 1 = \mathbf{24} \text{ ways.}$$

(b) If the geometry book must come first, then there is only one choice for the first position on the shelf; the next three positions may be filled by any of the *three* remaining books. Therefore, the books can be arranged in

$$1 \cdot {_3P_3} = 1 \cdot 3! = 1 \cdot 3 \cdot 2 \cdot 1 = 6 \text{ ways.}$$

2. *Not all of the objects are used in each arrangement.* If n objects are being used to fill r positions and $r < n$, then every object is not used in each arrangement. The process of arranging n objects in r positions ($r \leq n$) is symbolized by the notation $_nP_r$, which is read as "the permutation of n objects taken r at a time" and is defined as the product of the r greatest factors of $n!$:

$$_nP_r = n(n-1)(n-2)(n-3) \ldots (n-r+1).$$

Example: In how many ways can five students be seated in a row that has three chairs?
The students can be seated in

$$\begin{array}{c} _5P_3 = \underset{Chair \to}{} \underset{1st}{5} \cdot \underset{2nd}{4} \cdot \underset{3rd}{3} = 60 \text{ ways} \end{array}$$

Examples

1. In how many different ways can the digits 1, 3, 5, and 7 be arranged to form a four-digit number if repetition of digits:
(a) is *not* allowed?   **(b)** is allowed?

Solutions: **(a)** Since each digit can be used only once, the number of ways in which the four digits can be used to form a four-digit number is

$$_4P_4 = 4 \cdot 3 \cdot 2 \cdot 1 = 24.$$

(b) Each position of the number may be filled by any of the four original digits, so a four-digit number can be formed from the original four digits in

$$4 \cdot 4 \cdot 4 \cdot 4 = 256 \text{ ways.}$$

2. How many even four-digit numbers can be formed using the digits 1, 2, 3, and 9 if repetition of digits is *not* allowed?

Solution: An integer is even if it ends in an even number. Therefore, in this case the last digit of the number must be 2. The first three positions of the number can be filled in $_3P_3$ ways, so the number of different even numbers that can be formed using these digits is

$$_3P_3 \cdot 1 = 3 \cdot 2 \cdot 1 \cdot 1 = 6.$$

3. How many three-digit numbers greater than 500 can be formed from the digits 1, 2, 3, 4, 5, and 6:
(a) without repetition of digits?   **(b)** with repetition of digits?

Solutions: **(a)** The first digit of the number must be greater than or equal to 5. Since two digits in the set of digits are greater than or equal to 5, the first position of the number can be filled in $_2P_1$ ways. After the digit for the first position is chosen, the middle and last positions of the three-digit number can be filled from the remaining five digits in $_5P_2$ ways. Using the counting principle, you find that the number of three-digit numbers greater than 500 that can be formed without repetition of digits is

$$_2P_1 \cdot {}_5P_2 = 2 \cdot (5 \cdot 4) = \mathbf{40}.$$

(b) Again, the first position of the number can be filled in $_2P_1$ ways. After this digit is chosen, any one of the original six digits can be used to fill both the middle and the last position since repetition of digits is allowed. Therefore, the number of different three-digit numbers greater than 500 that can be formed when repetition of digits is allowed is

$$_2P_1 \cdot 6 \cdot 6 = 2 \cdot (6 \cdot 6) = \mathbf{72}.$$

Arrangements of Objects with Some Identical

If in a set of n objects some are exactly alike, then the n objects can be arranged in *fewer* different ways than n objects that are all different.

- If in a set of n objects, a objects are identical, then the n objects taken all at a time can be arranged in

$$\frac{n!}{a!} \text{ different ways.}$$

Example: The word BETWEEN has seven letters, and three of these letters (E) are identical. The number of possible different arrangements of these seven letters is

$$\frac{7!}{3!} = \frac{7 \cdot 6 \cdot 5 \cdot 4 \cdot \cancel{3} \cdot \cancel{2} \cancel{1}}{\cancel{3} \cdot \cancel{2} \cancel{1}} = \mathbf{840}.$$

- If, in a set of n objects, a objects are identical, b objects are identical, c objects are identical, and so forth, then the number of different ways in which the n objects taken all at a time can be arranged is

$$\frac{n!}{a!b!c! \ldots}.$$

Examples

4. In how many different ways can four red flags, three blue flags, and one green flag be arranged on a vertical flagpole?

Solution: The eight flags include four alike and three alike, so they can be arranged in

$$\frac{8!}{4! \cdot 3!} = \frac{8 \cdot 7 \cdot 6 \cdot 5 \cdot 4 \cdot 3 \cdot 2 \cdot 1}{(4 \cdot 3 \cdot 2 \cdot 1)(3 \cdot 2 \cdot 1)} = \textbf{280} \text{ ways.}$$

5. The letters of the word CIRCLE are randomly rearranged.
(a) In how many different ways can the six letters be arranged?
(b) In how many different ways can the six letters be arranged if:
(1) the letter E is first?　　(2) the first and last letters are C?

Solutions: **(a)** Six letters, two of which are identical, can be arranged in

$$\frac{6!}{2!} = \textbf{360} \text{ ways.}$$

(b) (1) If the letter E is first, then the remaining five letters include two C's. Five letters, two of which are identical, can be arranged in

$$\frac{5!}{2!} = \textbf{60} \text{ ways.}$$

(2) If one letter C is first and the other letter C is last, then the remaining four letters can be arranged in $4! = \textbf{24}$ ways.

Probability and Permutations

It may be helpful to express a probability in terms of permutations.

Examples

6. The letters L, O, G, I, and C are randomly arranged to form a five-letter word. What is the probability that the word LOGIC will be formed?

Solution: The five letters L, O, G, I, and C can be arranged in $_5P_5$ different ways. Since exactly one of these $_5P_5$ arrangements is the word LOGIC,

$$P(\text{LOGIC}) = \frac{1}{_5P_5} = \frac{1}{\textbf{120}}.$$

7. A jar contains three red marbles, two white marbles, and four blue marbles. Two marbles, one at a time, are to be chosen from the jar without replacement.
(a) What is the total number of ways in which the two marbles can be selected?
(b) What is the probability that the two marbles selected will be the same color?

Solutions: **(a)** Two marbles can be selected without replacement from the nine marbles in the jar in $_9P_2 = \textbf{72}$ ways.

(b) Two red marbles can be selected from three red marbles, without replacement, in $_3P_2$ ways.

Two white marbles can be selected from two white marbles, without replacement, in $_2P_2$ ways.

Two blue marbles can be selected from four blue marbles, without replacement, in $_4P_2$ ways. Therefore,

$$P(\text{same color}) = P(\text{both red}) + P(\text{both white}) + P(\text{both blue})$$

$$= \frac{_3P_2}{_9P_2} + \frac{_2P_2}{_9P_2} + \frac{_4P_2}{_9P_2}$$

$$= \frac{_3P_2 + {_2P_2} + {_4P_2}}{_9P_2}$$

$$= \frac{3 \cdot 2 + 2 \cdot 1 + 4 \cdot 3}{9 \cdot 8}$$

$$= \frac{20}{72} = \frac{5}{18}.$$

You should compare this solution to the solution of Example 4(b) of Section 12.1 on page 353, where the same problem is solved without using permutations.

8. From the set $\{1, 2, 3, 4, 5\}$, a three-digit number is formed by randomly selecting three digits, one at a time, without repetition of digits.

(a) How many different three-digit numbers can be formed?

(b) What is the probability that an odd number is formed?

Solutions: **(a)** A three-digit number can be formed from five digits, without the same digit being used more than once, in $_5P_3 = \mathbf{60}$ ways.

(b) An odd number must end in an odd digit. Since there are three odd digits in the given set of numbers, there are $_3P_1$ ways in which the last digit of the number can be selected.

The first two digits of the number can be selected from the remaining four digits in $_4P_2$ ways.

Using the counting principle, you find that the number of ways in which an odd number can be formed is $_4P_2 \cdot {_3P_1}$. Therefore,

$$P(\text{forming an odd number}) = \frac{_4P_2 \cdot {_3P_1}}{_5P_3} = \frac{(4 \cdot 3) \cdot 3}{5 \cdot 4 \cdot 3} = \frac{3}{5}.$$

9. Two cards are randomly drawn, one at a time without replacement, from a standard deck of 52 playing cards. Find the probability of each of the following events:

(a) Two hearts are drawn.

(b) The ace of spades and a red card are drawn in that order.

Solutions: **(a)** Method 1: Using Permutations. Two cards can be selected from 52 cards, without replacement, in $_{52}P_2$ ways. Two hearts, one followed by another, can be selected from a total of 13 hearts in $_{13}P_2$ ways. Therefore,

$$P\text{(two hearts are drawn)} = \frac{_{13}P_2}{_{52}P_2} = \frac{\overset{1}{\cancel{13}} \cdot 12}{\underset{4}{\cancel{52}} \cdot 51} = \frac{3}{51} = \frac{1}{\mathbf{17}}.$$

Method 2: Without Permutations. To find the joint probability of drawing a heart on the first pick *and* drawing a heart on the second pick, multiply the probabilities of drawing a heart on the two card selections.

$$P\text{(two hearts)} = P\text{(one heart)} \times \quad P\text{(second heart)}$$

$$= \frac{13\text{(hearts)}}{52\text{(cards)}} \times \frac{12\text{(hearts remaining)}}{51\text{(cards remaining)}}$$

$$= \frac{1}{\cancel{4}} \times \frac{\overset{1}{\cancel{4}}}{17} = \frac{1}{17}$$

(b) Method 1: Using Permutations. The ace of spades can be selected in only one way, and one red card can be selected from a total of 26 red cards (13 hearts + 13 diamonds) in $_{26}P_1$ ways. Using the counting principle, you find that the ace of spades and one red card can be drawn in $1 \cdot {_{26}P_1} =$ ways. Therefore,

$$P\text{(ace of spades, a red card)} = \frac{_{26}P_1}{_{52}P_2} = \frac{\overset{1}{\cancel{26}}}{\underset{2}{\cancel{52}} \cdot 51} = \frac{1}{\mathbf{102}}.$$

Method 2: Without Permutations. To find the joint probability of drawing the ace of spades on the first pick *and* drawing a red card on the second pick, multiply the probability of selecting the ace of spades on the first pick by the probability of selecting a red card on the second pick.

$$P\text{(ace of spades, a red card)} = P\text{(ace of spades)} \times P\text{(red card)}$$

$$= \frac{1}{52} \times \frac{26}{51}$$

$$= \frac{1}{\underset{2}{\cancel{52}}} \times \frac{\overset{1}{\cancel{26}}}{51} = \frac{1}{102}$$

Evaluating *x*! and $_nP_r$ Using a Scientific Calculator

Some scientific calculators have "second" function keys that can evaluate factorials [*x*!] and permutations [$_nP_r$].

Example 1: To calculate 7!, follow these steps:
Step 1. Enter 7.

Step 2. Press the [INV] or [2nd] key or [SHIFT] key followed by the [*x*!] key. Since the display window shows 5040, 7! = **5040**.

Example 2: To calculate $_7P_3$, follow these steps:
Step 1. Enter 7.
Step 2. Press the [INV] or [2nd] key or [SHIFT] key followed by the [$_nP_r$] key.
Step 3. Enter 3.
Step 4. Press the [=] key.

Since the display window shows 210, $_7P_3$ = **210**. Not all calculators work in the same way. If this procedure does not work, you need to read the manual that comes with your calculator.

Exercise Set 12.2

1. Show that $_8P_3$ and $\dfrac{8!}{(8-3)!}$ are equivalent.

2–10. Find the number of ways in which each of the following activities can be performed:

2. Arranging a chemistry book, a calculus book, a history book, a poetry book, and a dictionary on a shelf so that:
(a) the dictionary appears last
(b) the chemistry or history book appears first

3. Forming a three-digit number (without using the same digit more than once) using the digits:
(a) 1, 3, 5   (b) 2, 4, 6, 8   (c) 0, 1, 2, 3, 4, 5

4. Seating seven students in a row of:
(a) seven chairs   (b) five chairs

5. Arranging in random order the letters of the word:
(a) FREEZE   (c) ELLIPSE
(b) ARRAY   (d) COMMITTEE

6. Using the digits 2, 4, 6, and 8 to form a three-digit number less than 500:
(a) without repetition of digits   (b) with repetition of digits

7. Arranging the letters of the word TRIANGLE so that a vowel comes first.

8. Arranging three black flags, two red flags, and one green flag on a vertical flagpole.

9. Arranging three black flags, two red flags, and one green flag on a vertical flagpole so that:
(a) the green flag is first   (b) a black flag is last

10. Arranging the letters of the word PARABOLA so that:
    (a) a vowel is *not* the first letter
    (b) the three A's are consecutive

11. How many three-digit numbers can be formed from the digits 1, 2, 3, 4, and 5 if:
    (a) each number must be less than 400 and no digit may be repeated?
    (b) each number must be less than 400 and digits may be repeated?
    (c) the middle digit of each number must be an odd number and no digit may be repeated?

12. Find the probability that an odd number will be formed from the digits 2, 4, 5, 6, and 8 if:
    (a) all the digits are used without repetition
    (b) all the digits are used with repetition of digits allowed
    (c) three of the digits are used without repetition
    (d) a three-digit number is formed with repetition of digits allowed

13. What is the probability that, when Allan, Barbara, José, Steve, George, and Maria line up:
    (a) Barbara is first?
    (b) all four boys are before the girls?
    (c) a girl is first and last?

14. Two cards are randomly drawn from a standard deck of 52 playing cards. Find the probability of each of the following events:
    (a) Two kings are drawn.
    (b) A heart and then a club are drawn.
    (c) A spade followed by a card of a different suit is drawn.

15. A jar contains three orange marbles, four brown marbles, and two red marbles. Three marbles are drawn in sequence, without replacement. Find the probability of each of the following events:
    (a) Two orange marbles and a red marble are drawn in that order.
    (b) Three marbles having the same color are drawn.

16. If three black flags, two red flags, and one green flag are randomly arranged on a vertical flagpole, find the probability that:
    (a) the first and last flags are red
    (b) the three black flags are next to each other

12.3 COMBINATIONS

If from a group of five people a committee consisting of Joe, Susan, and Elizabeth is selected, then this *combination* of three people is the *same* as a committee consisting of Elizabeth, Joe, and Susan. A **combination** is a selection of people or objects in which the *identity,* rather than the order, of the people or objects is important.

In a *permutation,* unlike a combination, order is considered. For example, the arrangement in a line of Joe followed by Susan followed by Elizabeth is *different* from the arrangement in a line of Elizabeth followed by Joe followed by Susan.

Combination Versus Permutation

The letters A, B, and C may be arranged in six different ways: (1) ABC, (2) ACB, (3) BAC, (4) BCA, (5) CAB, (6) CBA. Although there are six permutations of the letters A, B, and C, there is only one distinct set, or combination of the three letters: $\{A, B, C\}$. A *combination* is an unordered set of objects, while a *permutation* is any ordered arrangement of the objects in that set.

Combination Notation

If a set consists of n objects, then the different *number* of subsets that contain r of those n objects, without regard to their order, is denoted by $_nC_r$. The notation $_nC_r$ is read as "the number of combinations of n objects selected r at a time." The different combinations of the three letters A, B, and C ($n = 3$) selected two at a time ($r = 2$) are the subsets $\{A,B\}$, $\{A,C\}$, and $\{B,C\}$. Since there are three subsets for $n = 3$ and $r = 2$, $_3C_2 = 3$.

Combination Formula

It is usually not practical to evaluate $_nC_r$ by listing and then counting the number of different subsets with r objects that can be formed from a set of n objects. Instead, the following formula can be used to evaluate $_nC_r$:

MATH FACTS

If $0 \le r \le n$, then

$$_nC_r = \frac{n!}{r!(n-r)!} = \frac{_nP_r}{r!}.$$

Example: To find the total number of three-member committees that can be formed from five people, evaluate $_5C_3$ by letting $n = 5$ and $r = 3$ in the combination formula:

$$_nC_r = \frac{_nP_r}{r!}$$

$$_5C_3 = \frac{_5P_3}{3!} = \frac{5 \cdot 4 \cdot 3}{3 \cdot 2 \cdot 1} = 5 \cdot 2 = 10.$$

Combinatorial Relationships

The following formulas can often save you time in evaluating combinations that have the indicated forms:

MATH FACTS

- $_nC_n = 1$ *Example:* $_9C_9 = 1$
- $_nC_1 = n$ *Example:* $_{13}C_1 = 13$
- $_nC_0 = 1$ *Example:* $_8C_0 = 1$
- $_nC_k = {_nC_{n-k}}$ $(n \ge k)$ *Example:* $_{15}C_{13} = {_{15}C_2}$

Examples

1. A jar contains two red marbles, three white marbles, and five blue marbles. In how many ways can a set of seven marbles be selected?

Solution: A group of seven marbles ($r = 7$) can be selected from a group of 10 marbles ($n = 2 + 3 + 5 = 10$) in

$$_{10}C_7 = {_{10}C_{10-7}} = \frac{_{10}P_3}{3!} = \frac{10 \cdot \overset{3}{\cancel{9}} \cdot \overset{4}{\cancel{8}}}{\cancel{3} \cdot \cancel{2} \cdot 1} = \mathbf{120} \text{ ways.}$$

2. The coach of a team is going to select five players at random from a group of 11 students trying out for the team. If Lois is one of the 11 students trying out, how many five-player combinations will:
(a) include Lois?   **(b)** *not* include Lois?

Solutions: **(a)** Since Lois must be on the team, the other four team players can be selected from the remaining 10 players in $_{10}C_4$ ways. Therefore, the number of five-player combinations that include Lois is:

$$_{10}C_4 = \frac{_{10}P_4}{4!} = \frac{10 \cdot \overset{3}{\cancel{9}} \cdot \overset{2}{\cancel{8}} \cdot 7}{\underset{1}{\cancel{4} \cdot \cancel{3} \cdot \cancel{2} \cdot 1}} = \mathbf{210}.$$

(b) Since Lois cannot be on the team, the five team players must be selected from the remaining 10 students. Therefore, the number of five-player combinations that do *not* include Lois is:

$$_{10}C_5 = \frac{_{10}P_5}{5!} = \frac{\overset{2}{\cancel{10}} \cdot 9 \cdot \overset{2}{\cancel{8}} \cdot 7 \cdot \cancel{6}}{\cancel{5} \cdot \cancel{4} \cdot 3 \cdot \cancel{2} \cdot 1} = \mathbf{252}.$$

3. Solve for x: $_{x}C_2 = 21$.

Solution: $_{x}C_2 = \dfrac{x(x-1)}{2!} = 21$

$$\frac{x^2 - x}{2} = 21$$
$$x^2 - x = 2 \cdot 21$$
$$x^2 - x - 42 = 0$$
$$(x - 7)\ (x + 6) = 0$$
$$(x - 7 = 0) \text{ or } (x + 6 = 0)$$
$$x = \mathbf{7} \quad | \qquad x = -6 \text{ (Reject since } x \text{ must be positive.)}$$

Evaluating $_{n}C_r$ Using a Scientific Calculator

Some scientific calculators have a "second" function key $[_{n}C_r]$ that can evaluate combinations. To calculate $_{6}C_3$, follow these steps:

Example:
Step 1. Enter 6.
Step 2. Press the [INV] or [2nd] key or [SHIFT] key followed by the $[_{n}C_r]$ key.
Step 3. Enter 3.
Step 4. Press the [=] key.
Since the display window shows 20, $_{6}C_3 = \mathbf{20}$. Not all calculators work in the same way. If this procedure does not work, you need to read the manual that comes with your calculator.

Multiplication Principle of Counting

If event A can occur in a ways and event B can occur in b ways, then event A and event B can occur in $a \times b$ ways.

Examples

4. There are six pens and seven books on a desk. In how many different ways can four pens *and* three books be chosen from the desk?

Solution: Four pens can be selected from six pens (event A) in $_6C_4$ ways. Three books can be selected from seven books (event B) in $_7C_3$ ways. The number of different selections that include four pens *and* three books is the product $_6C_4 \cdot {_7C_3}$.

- Without a calculator, proceed as follows:

$$\begin{aligned}
_6C_4 \cdot {_7C_3} &= \frac{_6P_4}{4!} \cdot \frac{_7P_3}{3!} \\
&= \left(\frac{6 \cdot 5 \cdot 4 \cdot 3}{4 \cdot 3 \cdot 2 \cdot 1}\right) \cdot \left(\frac{7 \cdot 6 \cdot 5}{3 \cdot 2 \cdot 1}\right) \\
&= (5 \cdot 3) \cdot (7 \cdot 5) \\
&= (15) \cdot (35) \\
&= \mathbf{525}
\end{aligned}$$

- Using a scientific calculator, evaluate $_6C_4$ and $_7C_3$. Then multiply the results.

$$_6C_4 \cdot {_7C_3} = (15) \times (35) = \mathbf{525}$$

5. From a group of six boys and three girls, how many six-member committees can be formed if:
   (a) each committee must have four boys and two girls?
   (b) each committee must have the same number of boys and girls?
   (c) each committee must have *at least* one girl?

Solutions: **(a)** Four boys can be selected from six boys in $_6C_4$ ways. Two girls can be selected from three girls in $_3C_2$ ways.
   Use the counting principle: the number of ways in which four boys *and* two girls can be selected for a six-member committee is

$$_6C_4 \cdot {_3C_2} = 15 \cdot 3 = \mathbf{45}.$$

(b) Each committee must have three boys and three girls.
Three boys can be selected from six boys in $_6C_3$ ways.
Three girls can be selected from three girls in $_3C_3$ ways.
   Use the counting principle: the number of ways in which equal numbers of boys *and* girls can be selected for each committee is

$$_6C_3 \cdot {_3C_3} = 20 \cdot 1 = \mathbf{20}.$$

(c) Here are the possible compositions of the committee:

Committee	Number of Different Committees
1 girl and 5 boys	$_3C_1 \cdot {_6}C_5 = 3 \cdot 6 = 18$
2 girls and 4 boys	$_3C_2 \cdot {_6}C_4 = 3 \cdot 15 = 45$
3 girls and 3 boys	$_3C_3 \cdot {_6}C_3 = 1 \cdot 20 = 20$

The number of possible committees with *at least* one girl $= 18 + 45 + 20 = \textbf{83}$.

Probability and Combinations

Combinations can also be used to solve probability problems involving selections in which order does not matter.

Examples

6. A drawer contains six navy socks, four brown socks, and two black socks. The drawer does not contain any other socks. If two socks are selected from the drawer without looking, find:
    (a) the number of different ways in which two socks can be chosen
    (b) the probability that the color of the two socks is the same

Solutions: **(a)** The number of ways in which two socks can be selected from 12 socks (6 navy + 4 brown + 2 black) is $_{12}C_2 = \textbf{66}$.
    (b) $P(\text{same color}) = P(2 \text{ navy}) + P(2 \text{ brown}) + P(2 \text{ black})$

Color	Number of Ways Can Be Selected
2 navy	$_6C_2 = 15$
2 brown	$_4C_2 = 6$
2 black	$_2C_2 = 1$

$$P(\text{same color}) = \frac{15 + 6 + 1}{66} = \frac{\textbf{22}}{\textbf{66}}$$

7. From a group of six boys and three girls, a six-member committee is formed.
    (a) How many six-member committees can be formed?
    (b) If Maria is one of the girls, what is the probability that Maria is *not* selected for the committee?
    (c) What is the probability that the six-member committee will *not* include a girl?

(d) What is the probability that a six-member committee will include a boy?

Solutions: **(a)** The number of six-member committees that can be selected from nine people (6 boys + 3 girls) is $_9C_6$ or **84**.

(b) If Maria is excluded, then the number of ways in which a six-member committee can be selected from the remaining eight students is $_8C_6$.

$$P \text{ (Maria is } not \text{ selected)} = \frac{_8C_6}{_9C_6} = \frac{28}{84} = \frac{1}{3}$$

(c) $P(\text{no girl}) = P(6 \text{ boys}) = \dfrac{1}{84}$.

(d) Since there are only three girls, a six-member committee must include a boy, so $P(\text{committee includes a boy}) = \mathbf{1}$.

8. From a U.S. Senate committee consisting of five Republicans and three Democrats, a four-member subcommittee is formed at random by drawing lots.

(a) How many four-member subcommittees can be formed?

(b) What is the probability that the four-member subcommittee will include only Republicans?

(c) What is the probability that the four-member subcommittee will include only Democrats?

(d) What is the probability that the four-member subcommittee will include the same number of Democrats as Republicans?

(e) What is the probability that the four-member subcommittee will include *at least* two Democrats?

(f) What is the probability that the four-member subcommittee will include *at most* three Republicans?

Solutions: **(a)** The number of four-member subcommittees that can be formed from eight people (5 Republicans + 3 Democrats) is $_8C_4 = \mathbf{70}$.

(b) The number of ways in which four Republicans can be chosen from five Republicans is $_5C_4$. Hence,

$$P(\text{all Republicans}) = \frac{_5C_4}{70} = \frac{5}{70}.$$

(c) Since there are three Democrats, it is an impossibility that the four-member subcommittee will include only Democrats. Hence, the probability is **0** that the four-member subcommittee will include only Democrats.

(d) The subcommittee will include the same number of Democrats as Republicans if it has two Democrats *and* two Republicans. The number of ways in which two Democrats can be selected from three Democrats is $_3C_2$. The number of ways in which two Republicans can be selected from five Republicans is $_5C_2$. Thus:

$$P(2 \text{ Democrats and 2 Republicans}) = \frac{{}_5C_2 \cdot {}_3C_2}{70} = \frac{10 \cdot 3}{70} = \frac{30}{70}.$$

(e) The four-member subcommittee will include at *least* two Democrats if it consists of two Democrats and two Republicans *or* three Democrats and one Republican.

Committee	Number of Committees
2 Democrats and 2 Republicans	${}_5C_2 \cdot {}_3C_2 = 10 \cdot 3 = 30$
3 Democrats and 1 Republican	${}_3C_3 \cdot {}_5C_1 = 1 \cdot 5 = 5$

Thus,

$$P(\text{at least 2 Democrats}) = \frac{30 + 5}{70} = \frac{35}{70}.$$

(f) <u>Solution Method 1</u>: The four-member subcommittee will include *at most* three Republicans if it consists of no Republican, one Republican, two Republicans, or three Republicans. Recall from part (c) that it is an impossibility for the four-member subcommittee to include no Republicans and four Democrats.

Committee	Number of Committees
0 Republican and 4 Democrats	0
1 Republican and 3 Democrats	${}_5C_1 \cdot {}_3C_3 = 5 \cdot 1 = 5$
2 Republicans and 2 Democrats	${}_5C_2 \cdot {}_3C_2 = 10 \cdot 3 = 30$
3 Republicans and 1 Democrat	${}_5C_3 \cdot {}_3C_1 = 10 \cdot 3 = 30$

Thus,

$$P(\text{at most 3 Republicans}) = \frac{5 + 30 + 30}{70} = \frac{65}{70}.$$

<u>Solution Method 2</u>: The sum of the probability that the four-member subcommittee will include *at most* three Republicans and the probability that the four-member subcommittee will include exactly four Republicans must be equal to 1. Since $P(4 \text{ Republicans}) = \frac{{}_5C_4}{70} = \frac{5}{70}$,

$$P(\text{at most 3 Republicans}) = 1 - \frac{5}{70} = \frac{65}{70}.$$

Exercise Set 12.3

1. In each case, find x:

(a) $_6C_x = 1$ (c) $_xC_7 = {_xC_2}$ (e) $_xC_2 = x$

(b) $_xC_2 = 15$ (d) $_xC_2 = 45$ (f) $6(_xC_5) = {_{(x+2)}C_5}$

2. How many committees of three can be chosen from a class of 10 students?

3. How many triangles can be formed using as vertices nine points, no three of which are collinear?

4. How many different diagonals can be drawn in a polygon having nine sides?

5. The expression $_{25}C_{20}$ is equivalent to:

(1) $_{25}P_{20}$ (2) $_{25}C_5$ (3) $_{25}P_5$ (4) $5!$

6. In how many ways can a committee of four be selected from five women and three men if

(a) the same person is *always* included in the committee?

(b) the same person is *always* excluded from the committee?

(c) the committee includes more women than men?

(d) the committee includes all men?

(e) the committee has *at most* two men?

7. A three-person committee is selected from three men and four women. What is the probability that:

(a) the members of the committee are all men or all women?

(b) Juan, one of the men, is *always* selected for the committee?

(c) Christine, one of the women, is *never* included on the committee?

(d) *at least* two women are selected?

8. If a committee of two boys and two girls is seated in a line, in how many different ways can the line be arranged so that two members of the same sex do *not* sit next to each other?

9. A drawer holds five navy socks, seven brown socks, and six black socks. If two socks are selected without looking, what is the probability that they do *not* match?

10–11. Three marbles are randomly selected without replacement from a jar that contains seven red, five blue, and three white marbles.

10. In how many different ways can:

(a) the three marbles be selected?

(b) a blue marble *not* be selected?

(c) three marbles of the same color be selected?

(d) three marbles of different colors be selected?

11. Find the probability of each of the following events:
    (a) Three red marbles are selected.
    (b) One red and two white marbles are selected.
    (c) *At least* one of the marbles is blue.
    (d) *At most* two marbles are red.

12. Coach Euclid will select six players at random from a group of 10 students trying out for a team.
    (a) How many different six-player combinations are possible?
    (b) If Jill is one of the 10 students trying out for the team, how many of the six-player combinations will include Jill?
    (c) What is the probability that Jill will be selected as one of the six players?
    (d) After selecting the team, Coach Euclid asked the six members to stand in a straight line. How many different lineups are possible?
    (e) If Jill is on the team, what is the probability that she will be standing first in the lineup?

13. A committee of five people chosen for a class function has three male and two female members.
    (a) How many three-person subcommittees having *at least* two males can be formed?
    (b) What is the probability of a three-person subcommittee having exactly one male member?

14. The student government at Central High School consists of four seniors, three juniors, three sophomores, and two freshmen.
    (a) How many committees of four students can be formed?
    (b) How many committees of four students will have exactly one student from each grade?
    (c) What is the probability that a committee of four students will have exactly one student from each grade?
    (d) Nine students will be chosen from the student government to go to a convention. What is the probability that no senior will be chosen to go?

15. On an examination a student is to select any four out of nine problems. All of the problems are of equal difficulty. The examination contains one geometry, three logic, one locus, and four probability problems.
    (a) How many four-problem selections can be made?
    (b) How many of those selections will contain one logic, one locus, and two probability problems?
    (c) What is the probability that a four-problem selection contains one logic, one locus, and two probability problems?
    (d) What is the probability that a four-problem selection will contain all logic problems?

REGENTS TUNE-UP: CHAPTER 12

Each of the questions in this section has appeared on a previous Course II Regents Examination. Here is an opportunity for you to review the material in Chapter 12 and, at the same time, prepare for the Course II Regents Examination.

1. How many different five-person committees can be selected from nine people?

2. How many different arrangements of seven letters can be made using the letters in the word ULYSSES?

3. Evaluate: $\dfrac{_4P_2}{_4C_2}$.

4. From a menu of five sandwiches and five beverages, how many different lunches consisting of two different sandwiches and one, beverage can be selected?

5. A bag of marbles contains two green, one blue, and three red marbles. If two marbles are chosen at random without replacement, what is the probability that both will be red?

   (1) $\frac{1}{5}$ (2) $\frac{1}{6}$ (3) $\frac{1}{10}$ (4) $\frac{1}{12}$

6. Which expression is *not* equivalent to $_8C_5$?

   (1) 56   (2) $_8P_5$ (3) $_8C_3$ (4) $\dfrac{8 \cdot 7 \cdot 6}{3 \cdot 2 \cdot 1}$

7. A jar contains four red marbles and five blue marbles. What is the probability of selecting at random, without replacement, two blue marbles?

   (1) $\frac{20}{81}$ (2) $\frac{16}{81}$ (3) $\frac{20}{72}$ (4) $\frac{16}{72}$

8. If one card is selected at random from a standard deck of 52 cards, what is the probability of choosing a black card or a king?

   (1) $\frac{30}{52}$ (2) $\frac{22}{52}$ (3) $\frac{28}{52}$ (4) $\frac{4}{52}$

9. How many different ten-letter permutations can be formed from the letters of the word CALIFORNIA?

   (1) $\dfrac{10!}{2!\,2!}$ (2) $\dfrac{10!}{2!}$ (3) $\dfrac{10!}{4!}$ (4) $\dfrac{8!}{2!\,2!}$

10. Which statement is true?

    (1) $_{10}C_3 = 30$ (2) $_{10}C_3 = {_{10}C_7}$ (3) $_{10}C_3 = {_{10}P_3}$ (4) $_{10}C_3 = \dfrac{10!}{3!}$

11. The expression $_{15}C_1 + {}_{15}C_{15}$ is equivalent to
(1) 16   (2) 2   (3) 3   (4) 15

12. A pencil holder contains six blue pencils and three red pencils. If two pencils are drawn at random, what is the probability that both are blue?
(1) $\frac{2}{9}$ (2) $\frac{6}{9}$ (3) $\frac{30}{72}$ (4) $\frac{30}{81}$

13. A math test contains only geometry questions and logic questions. The number of logic questions is 2 less than the number of geometry questions.
   (a) If the probability of selecting a logic question is $\frac{2}{5}$, how many questions are on the test?
   (b) If five questions are selected at random from this test, find the probability that all five will be:
   (1) geometry questions   (2) logic questions

14. There are five boys and three girls in a math class.
   (a) In how many different ways may the eight students be arranged in a line?
   (b) In how many different ways may the eight students be arranged in a line if all three girls are to precede the five boys?
   (c) How many six-member committees can be formed from the eight students?
   (d) How many of these committees consist of exactly four boys and two girls?
   (e) What is the probability that one of the six-member committees consists of exactly four boys and two girls?

15. From the members of a band consisting of five clarinet players, four trumpet players, and three tuba players, a three-member group is to be formed.
   (a) How many three-member groups can be formed?
   (b) What is the probability that the three-member group formed consists of one clarinet player, one trumpet player, and one tuba player?
   (c) What is the probability that the three-member group formed consists of three clarinet players, three trumpet players, or three tuba players?

16. There are seven boys and three girls on a school tennis team. The coach must select four people from this group to participate in a county championship.
   (a) How many four-person teams can be formed from the group of 10 students?
   (b) In how many ways can two boys and two girls be chosen to participate in the county championship?
   (c) What is the probability that two boys and two girls are chosen for the team?
   (d) What is the probability that a four-member team will contain at least one boy?

Answers to Selected Exercises: Chapter 12

Section 12.1

1. 0.85

2. (1)

3. (a) $1 - x$

   (b) $\frac{3}{4}x$

   (c) $-x - 3$

   (d) $-4x + 2$

4. (a) $5x$

   (b) $\frac{2x-1}{5x}$

   (c) 3   (d) $\frac{4}{5}$

5. (a) $\frac{8}{35}$ (c) $\frac{12}{35}$

   (b) $\frac{9}{35}$ (d) $\frac{6}{35}$

6. (a) $\frac{10}{90}$ (c) $\frac{28}{90}$

   (b) $\frac{20}{90}$ (d) $\frac{62}{90}$

9. (a) $\frac{1}{16}$ (c) $\frac{9}{169}$

   (b) $\frac{12}{16}$ (d) $\frac{16}{52}$

10. $\frac{272}{552}$

Section 12.2

2. (a) 24   (b) 48

3. (a) 6   (c) 100

   (b) 24

4. (a) 5040 (b) 210

5. (a) 120 (c) 1260

6. (a) 12   (b) 32

7. 15,120

8. 60

9. (a) 10   (b) 30

10. (a) 3360 (b) 720

11. (a) 36 (b) 75 (c) 36

13. (a) $\frac{1}{720}$

   (b) $\frac{1}{15}$

15. (a) $\frac{12}{504}$

   (b) $\frac{30}{504}$

Section 12.3

1. (a) 6   (b) 9   (c) 3

3. 84

5. (2)

7. (a) $\frac{5}{35}$ (b) $\frac{15}{35}$ (c) $\frac{22}{35}$

9. $\frac{107}{153}$

11. (a) $\frac{35}{455}$ (b) $\frac{21}{455}$ (c) $\frac{335}{455}$

13. (a) 4   (b) $\frac{3}{10}$

15. (a) 126 (b) 18   (c) $\frac{18}{126}$ (d) 0

Regents Tune-Up: Chapter 12

1. 126

2. 840

3. 2

4. 50

5. (1)

6. (2)

7. (3)

8. (3)

9. (1)

10. (2)

11. (1)

12. (3)

13. (a) 18

   (b) (1) $\frac{252}{8568}$ (2) $\frac{56}{8568}$

15. (a) 220

   (b) $\frac{60}{220}$ (c) $\frac{15}{220}$

16. (a) 210 (c) $\frac{63}{210}$

   (b) 63   (d) 1

GLOSSARY

Abscissa The x-coordinate of a point in the coordinate plane.

Absolute value The absolute value of a number x, denoted by $|x|$, is its distance from zero on the number line. Thus, $|x|$ always represents a nonnegative number.

Acute angle An angle whose degree measure is less than 90.

Acute triangle A triangle that contains three acute angles.

Additive inverse The opposite of a number. The additive inverse of a number x is $-x$ since $x + (-x) = 0$.

Adjacent angles Two angles that have the same vertex, share a common side, but do not have any interior points in common.

Alternate interior angles Two interior angles that lie on opposite sides of a transversal.

Altitude A segment that is perpendicular to the side to which it is drawn.

Angle The union of two rays that have the same endpoint.

Angle of depression The angle formed by a horizontal line of vision and the line of sight when viewing an object beneath the horizontal line of vision.

Angle of elevation The angle formed by a horizontal line of vision and the line of sight when viewing an object above the horizontal line of vision.

Antecedent The part of a conditional statement that follows the word "if." Sometimes the term "hypothesis" is used in place of "antecedent."

Associative property The mathematical law that states that the order in which three numbers are added or multiplied does not matter.

Average See *Mean*.

Axis of symmetry For the parabola $y = ax^2 + bx + c$, the vertical line that contains the vertex, an equation of which is $x = -\dfrac{b}{2a}$.

Base angles of an isosceles triangle The two congruent angles that include the base of an isosceles triangle.

Biconditional A statement of the form p if and only if q, denoted by $p \leftrightarrow q$, which is true only when p and q have the same truth value.

Binary operation An operation that is performed on two members of a set at a time.

Binomial A polynomial with two unlike terms.

Bisector of an angle A ray that divides the angle into two angles that have the same degree measure.

Bisector of a segment A line, ray, or segment that contains the midpoint of the given segment.

Chain Rule See *Law of Syllogism*

Circle The set of points (x, y) in a plane that are a fixed distance r from a given point (h, k) called the *center*. Thus, $(x - h)^2 + (y - k)^2 = r^2$.

Closure property A set is closed under a binary operation if performing that operation on any two members of the set always produces a result that is a member of the same set.

Coefficient The number that multiplies the literal factors of a monomial. The coefficient of $-5x^2y$ is -5.

Collinear points Points that lie on the same line.

Combination A subset of a set of objects in which their order is not considered.

Combination formula The combination of n objects taken r at a time, denoted by $_nC_r$, is given by the formula $_nC_r = \dfrac{_nP_r}{r!} = \dfrac{n!}{r!(n-r)!}$.

Commutative property The mathematical law that states that the order in which two numbers are added or multiplied does not matter.

Complementary angles Two angles whose degree measures add up to 90.

Compound loci   The set of points that satisfy two or more locus conditions.

Compound statement   A statement in logic that is formed by combining two or more simple statements using logical connectives.

Conditional statement   A statement that has the form "If p then q," denoted by $p \rightarrow q$, which is always true except in the case in which p is true and q is false.

Congruent angles   Angles that have the same degree measure.

Congruent figures   Figures that have the same size and the same shape. The symbol for congruence is $\cong$.

Congruent polygons   Two polygons having the same number of sides are congruent if their vertices can be paired so that all corresponding sides have the same length and all corresponding angles have the same degree measure.

Congruent triangles   Two triangles are congruent if any one of the following conditions is true: (1) the sides of one triangle are congruent to the corresponding sides of the other triangle ($SSS \cong SSS$); (2) two sides and the included angle of one triangle are congruent to the corresponding parts of the other triangle ($SAS \cong SAS$); (3) two angles and the included side of one triangle are congruent to the corresponding parts of the other triangle ($ASA \cong ASA$); (4) two angles and the side opposite one of these angles of one triangle are congruent to the corresponding parts of the other triangle ($AAS \cong AAS$).

Congruent segments   Line segments that have the same length.

Conjugate pair   The sum and difference of the same two terms, as in $a + b$ and $a - b$.

Conjunct   Each of the individual statements that comprise a conjunction.

Conjunction   A statement of the form p and q, denoted by $p \wedge q$, which is true only when p and q are true at the same time.

Consequent   The part of a conditional statement that follows the word "then." Sometimes the word "conclusion" is used in place of "consequent."

Constant   A quantity that is fixed in value. In the equation $y = x + 3$, x and y are variables and 3 is a constant.

Contradiction   A compound statement that is always false. The statement $p \wedge \sim p$ is a contradiction.

Contrapositive   The conditional statement formed by negating and then interchanging both parts of a conditional statement. The contrapositive of $p \rightarrow q$ is $\sim q \rightarrow \sim p$.

Converse   The conditional statement formed by interchanging both parts of another conditional statement. The converse of $p \rightarrow q$ is $q \rightarrow p$.

Coordinate   The real number that corresponds to the position of a point on a number line.

Coordinate plane   The region formed by a horizontal number line and vertical number line intersecting at their zero points.

Corresponding angles   A pair of angles that lie on the same side of the transversal, one of which is an interior angle and the other an exterior angle.

Cosine ratio   In a right triangle, the ratio of the length of the leg that is adjacent to a given acute angle to the length of the hypotenuse.

Degree   A unit of angle measure. One degree is the measure of an angle formed by 1/360th of one complete rotation of a ray about its endpoint.

Degree of a monomial   The sum of the exponents of the variable factors in the monomial.

Degree of a polynomial   The greatest degree of its monomial terms.

DeMorgan's laws   (1) $\sim (p \vee q) = \sim p \wedge \sim q$ and (2) $\sim (p \wedge q) = \sim p \vee \sim q$.

Dilation   A transformation in which a figure is enlarged or reduced in size based on a center and a scale factor.

Discriminant The quantity $b^2 - 4ac$ that is underneath the radical sign in the quadratic formula.

Disjunct Each of the statements that comprise a disjunction.

Disjunction A statement of the form p or q, denoted by $p \lor q$, which is true when p is true, q is true, or both p and q are true.

Distance formula The distance d between points (x_1, y_1) and (x_2, y_2) is given by the formula
$$d = \sqrt{(x_2 - x_1)^2 + (y_2 - y_1)^2}.$$

Distributive property of multiplication over addition For any real numbers a, b, and c, $a(b + c) = ab + ac$ and $(b + c)a = ba + ca$.

Domain The set of all possible replacements for a variable.

Equation A statement that two quantities have the same value.

Equilateral triangle A triangle whose three sides have the same length.

Equivalent equations Two equations that have the same solution set. Thus, $2x = 6$ and $x = 3$ are equivalent equations.

Event A particular subset of outcomes from the set of all possible outcomes of a probability experiment. In flipping a coin, one event is getting a head; another event is getting a tail.

Exponent In x^n, the number n is the exponent and tells the number of times the base x is used as a factor in a product. Thus, $x^3 = (x)(x)(x)$.

Extremes In the proportion $\frac{a}{b} = \frac{c}{d}$ the terms a and d are the *extremes*.

Factor A number or variable that is being multiplied in a product.

Factoring The process by which a number or polynomial is written as the product of two or more terms.

Factoring completely Factoring a number or polynomial into its prime factors.

Factorial n Denoted by $n!$ and defined for any positive integer n as the prod-

uct of consecutive integers from n to 1. Thus, $5! = 5 \cdot 4 \cdot 3 \cdot 2 \cdot 1 = 120$.

FOIL The rule for multiplying two binomials horizontally by forming the sum of the products of the first terms (F), the outer terms (O), the inner terms (I), and the last terms (L) of each binomial.

Formula An equation that shows how one quantity depends on one or more other quantities.

Fundamental counting principle If event A can occur in m ways and event B can occur in n ways, then both events can occur in m times n ways.

Greatest common factor (GCF) The GCF of two or more monomials is the monomial with the greatest coefficient and the variable factors of the greatest degree that are common to all the given monomials. The GCF of $8a^2b$ and $20ab^2$ is $4ab$.

Hypotenuse The side of a right triangle that is opposite the right angle.

Image In a geometric transformation, the point or figure that corresponds to the original point or figure.

Inequality A sentence that uses an inequality relation such as $<$ (is less than), $\leq$ (is less than or equal to), $>$ (is greater than), $\geq$ (is greater than or equal to), or $\neq$ (is unequal to).

Integer A number from the set $\{\ldots -3, -2, -1, 0, 1, 2, 3, \ldots\}$.

Inverse The statement formed by negating both the antecedent and consequent of a conditional statement. Thus, the inverse of $p \to q$ is $\sim p \to \sim q$.

Irrational number A number that cannot be expressed as the quotient of two integers.

Isosceles triangle A triangle in which at least two sides have the same length.

Law of Contrapositive Inference A conditional statement and its contrapositive have the same truth value. Thus, $p \rightarrow q$ and $\sim q \rightarrow \sim p$ are logically equivalent statements.

Law of Disjunctive Inference If a disjunction is true, then at least one of the disjuncts is true. Thus, if $p \vee q$ and $\sim p$ are true statements, then q is true.

Law of Conjunctive Simplification If a conjunction is true, then each conjunct is true. Thus, if $p \wedge q$ is true, then p and q are both true.

Law of Detachment (*Modus Ponens*) If a conditional statement and its antecedent are true, then its consequent is true. Thus, if $p \rightarrow q$ and p are true, then q is true.

Law of Double Negation The statements p and $\sim(\sim p)$ always have the same truth value.

Law of *Modus Tollens* If a conditional statement is true and its consequent is false, then its antecedent is false. Thus, if $p \rightarrow q$ is true and q is false, then p is false.

Law of Syllogism (Chain Rule) If the conditionals $p \rightarrow q$ and $q \rightarrow r$ are both true, then $p \rightarrow r$ is true.

Leg of a right triangle Either of the two sides of a right triangle that is not opposite the right angle.

Line Although an undefined term in geometry, it can be described as a continuous set of points that describes a straight path extending indefinitely in two opposite directions.

Linear equation An equation in which the greatest exponent of a variable is 1. A linear equation can be put into the form $Ax + By = C$, where A, B, and C are constants and A and B are not both zero.

Line reflection A transformation in which each point P that is not on line ℓ is paired with a point P' on the opposite side of line ℓ so that line ℓ is the perpendicular bisector of $\overline{PP'}$. If P is on line ℓ, then P is paired with itself:

Line segment Part of a line that consists of two different points on the line, called *endpoints,* and all points on the line that are between them.

Line symmetry A figure has line symmetry when a line ℓ divides the figure into two parts such that each part is the reflection of the other part in line ℓ.

Locus The set of all points, and only those points, that satisfy a given condition.

Logical connectives The conjunction $(\wedge)$, disjunction $(\vee)$, conditional $(\rightarrow)$, and biconditional $(\leftrightarrow)$ of two statements.

Logically equivalent statements Statements that always have the same truth value.

Mean (Average) The sum of the data values in a set divided by n.

Mean proportional between *a* and *b* The number x such that $\frac{a}{x} = \frac{x}{b}$.

Means In the proportion $\frac{a}{b} = \frac{c}{d}$, the terms b and c are the means. If b and c have the same value, then either b or c is the mean proportional between a and d.

Median of a triangle A line segment whose endpoints are a vertex of the triangle and the midpoint of the opposite side.

Midpoint The point M that lies between the endpoints of line segment AB such that $AM = BM$ and points A, B, and M are collinear.

Midpoint formula The midpoint of the line segment whose endpoints are (x_1, y_1) and (x_2, y_2) is
$$\left(\frac{x_1 + x_2}{2}, \frac{y_1 + y_2}{2} \right).$$

Monomial A number, variable, or the product of a number and a variable.

Multiplicative inverse The reciprocal of a nonzero number.

Negation The negation of statement p is the statement, denoted by $\sim p$, that has the opposite truth value of p.

Obtuse angle An angle whose degree measure is greater than 90 and less than 180.

Obtuse triangle A triangle that contains an obtuse angle.

Open sentence A sentence whose truth value cannot be determined until its placeholders are replaced with values from the replacement set.

Opposite rays Two rays that have the same endpoint and form a line.

Ordered pair Two numbers that are written in a definite order.

Ordinate The y-coordinate of a point in the coordinate plane.

Origin The zero point on a number line.

Outcome A possible result in a probability experiment.

Parabola The graph of a quadratic equation in which either x or y, but not both, are squared. The graph of an equation of the form $y = ax^2 + bx + c$ $(a \neq 0)$ is a parabola that has a vertical axis of symmetry, an equation of which is $x = -\frac{b}{2a}$.

Parallel lines Lines in the same plane that do not intersect.

Parallelogram A quadrilateral that has two pairs of parallel sides.

Perfect square A rational number whose square root is rational.

Permutation An ordered arrangement of objects.

Perpendicular lines Lines that intersect at right angles.

Plane Although undefined in geometry, a plane can be described as a flat surface that extends indefinitely in all directions.

Point Although undefined in geometry, a point can be described as indicating location with no size.

Point symmetry A figure has point symmetry if after being rotated 180° the image coincides with the original figure.

Polygon A simple closed curve whose sides are line segments.

Polynomial A monomial or the sum or difference of two or more monomials.

Power A number written with an exponent, as in 2^4, which is read "2 raised to the fourth power."

Prime factorization The factorization of a polynomial into factors each of which is divisible only by itself and 1.

Probability of an event The number of ways in which the event can occur divided by the total number of possible outcomes.

Proportion An equation that states that two ratios are equal. In the proportion $\frac{a}{b} = \frac{c}{d}$, the product of the means equals the product of the extremes. Thus, $b \cdot c = a \cdot d$.

Pythagorean theorem In a right triangle, the square of the length of the hypotenuse is equal to the sum of the squares of the lengths of the legs.

Quadrant One of four rectangular regions into which the coordinate plane is divided.

Quadratic equation An equation that can be put into the form $ax^2 + bx + c = 0$, provided that $a \neq 0$.

Quadratic formula The roots of the quadratic equation $ax^2 + bx + c = 0$ are given by the formula
$$x = \frac{-b \pm \sqrt{b^2 - 4ac}}{2a} \quad (a \neq 0).$$

Quadratic polynomial A polynomial whose degree is 2.

Quadrilateral A polygon with four sides.

Radical (square root) sign The symbol $\sqrt{}$ that denotes the positive square root of a nonnegative number.

Radicand The expression that appears underneath a radical sign.

Ratio A comparison of two numbers by division. The ratio of a to b is the fraction $\frac{a}{b}$, provided that $b \neq 0$.

Rational number A number that can be written in the form $\frac{a}{b}$, where a and b are integers and $b \neq 0$. Decimals in which a set of digits endlessly repeat, such as $.25000 \ldots$ $(= \frac{1}{4})$ and $.33333 \ldots$ $(= \frac{1}{3})$, represent rational numbers.

Ray The part of a line that consists of a point, called an *endpoint*, and the set of points on one side of the endpoint.

Real number A number that is either rational or irrational.

Reciprocal The reciprocal of a nonzero number x is $\frac{1}{x}$.

Rectangle A parallelogram with four right angles.

Reflection in the origin A transformation that maps $P(x, y)$ onto $P'(-x, -y)$

Replacement set The set of values that a variable may have.

Rhombus A parallelogram with four sides that have the same length.

Right angle An angle whose degree measure is 90.

Right triangle A triangle that contains a right angle.

Root A number that makes an equation a true statement.

Rotation A transformation in which a point or figure is moved about a fixed point a given number of degrees.

Scalene triangle A triangle in which the three sides have different lengths.

Similar polygons Two polygons with the same number of sides are similar if their vertices can be paired so that corresponding angles have the same measure and the lengths of corresponding sides are in proportion.

Similar triangles If two triangles have two pairs of corresponding angles that have the same degree measure, then the triangles are similar.

Sine ratio In a right triangle, the ratio of the length of the leg that is opposite a given acute angle to the length of the hypotenuse.

Slope A measure of the steepness of a nonvertical line. The slope of a horizontal line is 0, and the slope of a vertical line is undefined.

Slope formula The slope m of a nonvertical line that contains the points (x_1, y_2) and (x_2, y_2) is given by the formula

$$m = \frac{y_2 - y_1}{x_2 - x_1}.$$

Slope-intercept form An equation of a line that has the form $y = mx + b$, where m is the slope of the line and b is the y-intercept.

Solution Any value from the replacement set of a variable that makes an open sentence true.

Solution set The collection of all values from the replacement set of a variable that makes an open sentence true.

Square A rectangle whose four sides have the same length.

Square root The square root of a nonnegative number n is one of two identical numbers whose product is n. Thus, $\sqrt{9} = 3$ since $3 \times 3 = 9$.

Statement Any sentence that is true or false, but not both.

Success Any favorable outcome of a probability experiment.

Supplementary angles Two angles whose degree measures add up to 180.

System of equations A set of equations whose solution is the set of values that make each of the equations true at the same time.

Tangent ratio In a right triangle, the ratio of the length of the leg that is opposite a given acute angle to the length of the leg that is adjacent to the same angle.

Tautology A compound statement that is true regardless of the truth values of its component statements.

Theorem A generalization in mathematics that can be proved.

Transformation The process of "moving" each point of a figure according to some given rule.

Translation A transformation in which each point of a figure is moved the same distance and in the same direction.

Transversal A line that intersects two other lines in two different points.

Trapezoid A quadrilateral with exactly one pair of parallel sides.

Triangle A polygon with three sides.

Trinomial A polynomial with three terms.

Truth value Either true or false, but not both.

Turning point of a parabola   See *Vertex of a parabola*.

Undefined term   A term that can be described but not defined. The terms "point," "line," and "plane" are undefined in geometry.

Variable   The symbol, usually a letter, that represents an unspecified member of the replace set.

Vertex of a parabola (Turning point of a parabola)   The point at which the axis of symmetry intersects a parabola.

Vertical angles   A pair of nonadjacent angles formed by two intersecting lines.

x-axis   The horizontal axis in the coordinate plane.

x-coordinate   The first number in an ordered pair.

y-axis   The vertical axis in the coordinate plane.

y-coordinate   The second number in an ordered pair.

y-intercept   The y-coordinate of the point at which the graph of an equation intersects the y-axis.

REGENTS EXAMINATION

Examination June 1994

Three Year Sequence for High School Mathematics — Course II

Part I

Answer 30 questions from this part. Each correct answer will receive 2 credits. No partial credit will be allowed. Write your answers in the spaces provided on the separate answer sheet. Where applicable, answers may be left in terms of π or in radical form.   [60]

1 Segment $\overline{AB}$ is parallel to segment $\overline{CD}$. If the slope of $\overline{AB} = -\frac{3}{7}$ and the slope of $\overline{CD} = -\frac{x}{14}$, find the value of x.

2 Lines $\overleftrightarrow{AB}$ and $\overleftrightarrow{CD}$ intersect at point F. What is the total number of points 4 centimeters from point F and also equidistant from $\overleftrightarrow{AB}$ and $\overleftrightarrow{CD}$?

3 In the following system, determine the value of $(a \circledcirc b) \circledcirc c$.

$\circledcirc$	a	d	b	c
a	b	a	c	d
d	a	d	b	c
b	c	b	d	a
c	d	c	a	b

4 If a translation maps $(x,y) \rightarrow (x + 2, y + 3)$, what are the coordinates of B', the image of point $B(-3,5)$ after this translation?

5 In the accompanying diagram, $\ell \parallel m$, t and s are intersecting transversals, $m\angle 1 = 130$, and $m\angle 2 = 60$. Find $m\angle 3$.

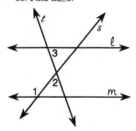

6 In $\triangle ABC$, $m\angle A = 65$ and $m\angle C = 60$. Which is the *shortest* side of the triangle?

7 If $\tan A = \frac{3}{4}$, find $m\angle A$ to the *nearest degree*.

8 In the accompanying diagram, the altitude to the hypotenuse of the right triangle divides the hypotenuse into two segments of lengths 3 and 12. What is the length of the altitude?

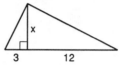

9 What are the coordinates of P', the image of $P(1,2)$ after a reflection in the origin?

10 The coordinates of A and B are $(2a,4b)$ and $(8a,6b)$, respectively. Express, in terms of a and b, the coordinates of the midpoint of $\overline{AB}$.

11 In isosceles triangle ABC, $\overline{AB} \cong \overline{CB}$. Find $m\angle B$, if $m\angle A = 5x - 4$ and $m\angle C = 2x + 20$.

12 In the accompanying diagram, $WXYZ$ is a parallelogram, line $\overline{YZ}$ is extended to point V, $\overline{WZ} \cong \overline{VZ}$, and $m\angle V = 50$. Find $m\angle ZWX$.

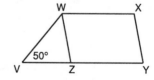

13 In $\triangle ABC$, $\overline{AB} \perp \overline{BC}$ and $\overline{DE} \perp \overline{CA}$. If $DE = 8$, $CD = 10$, and $CA = 30$, find AB.

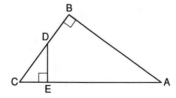

14 Write an equation of the line that passes through points (2,3) and (4,5).

15 What is the positive root of the equation $c^2 - 6c = 27$?

16 If the length of one side of a rectangle is 8 and the length of a diagonal is 10, find the area of the rectangle.

Directions (17–34): For *each* question chosen, write on the separate answer sheet the *numeral* preceding the word or expression that best completes the statement or answers the question.

17 Two consecutive angles of a parallelogram measure $2x + 10$ and $x - 10$. What is the value of x?
(1) 30   (3) 120
(2) 60   (4) –20

18 What is the length of the line segment joining points $J(1,5)$ and $K(3,9)$?
(1) $2\sqrt{5}$ (3) $13\sqrt{2}$
(2) $\sqrt{13}$ (4) $2\sqrt{13}$

19 Which statement is logically equivalent to $\sim(a \wedge \sim b)$?
(1) $\sim a \wedge b$ (3) $\sim a \vee \sim b$
(2) $\sim a \wedge \sim b$ (4) $\sim a \vee b$

20 Which statement is equivalent to the inequality $9 - 4x \leq 3x - 5$?
(1) $x > -2$ (3) $x \leq -2$
(2) $x < 2$ (4) $x \geq 2$

21 Which polygon must have congruent diagonals?
(1) parallelogram   (3) trapezoid
(2) rectangle   (4) rhombus

22 What is the y-intercept of the graph of the equation $y = 2x^2 - 5x + 7$?
(1) –5   (3) 7
(2) 2   (4) –7

23 If the statements $m \rightarrow n$ and $\sim m \rightarrow s$ are true, then which statement is a logical conclusion?
(1) $n \rightarrow s$ (3) s
(2) $s \rightarrow n$ (4) $\sim n \rightarrow s$

24 Which equation describes the locus of points 5 units from point (3,–4)?
(1) $(x + 3)^2 + (y - 4)^2 = 5$
(2) $(x - 3)^2 + (y + 4)^2 = 5$
(3) $(x - 3)^2 + (y + 4)^2 = 25$
(4) $(x + 3)^2 + (y - 4)^2 = 25$

25 In the solution of this problem, which property of real numbers justifies statement 5?

Statements	Reasons
1. $3x = 6$	1. Given
2. $\frac{1}{3}(3x) = \frac{1}{3}(6)$	2. Multiplication axiom
3. $\left(\frac{1}{3} \cdot 3\right)x = 2$	3. Associative property
4. $1 \cdot x = 2$	4. Multiplicative inverse
5. $x = 2$	5. _____

(1) Closure   (3) Commutative
(2) Identity   (4) Inverse

26 How many 9-letter arrangements can be formed from the letters in the word "SASSAFRAS"?
(1) $\frac{4!}{3!}$ (3) $\frac{9!}{7!}$
(2) $\frac{9!}{4!3!}$ (4) $9!$

27 If the length of each leg of an isosceles triangle is 17 and the base is 16, the length of the altitude to the base is
(1) 8   (3) 15
(2) $8\frac{1}{2}$ (4) $\sqrt{32}$

28 Which equation represents the line that passes through point (0,6) and is perpendicular to the line whose equation is $y = 3x - 2$?
(1) $y = -\frac{1}{3}x + 6$ (3) $y = -3x + 6$
(2) $y = \frac{1}{3}x + 6$ (4) $y = 3x + 6$

29 Expressed as a fraction in lowest terms, $\dfrac{1}{x^2 - 4} \div \dfrac{x}{x - 2}$, $x \neq 2, 0, -2$, is equivalent to
(1) $\dfrac{1}{x(x + 2)}$ (3) $\dfrac{1}{x(x - 2)}$
(2) $\dfrac{-2}{x^2 - 4}$ (4) $\dfrac{1}{2}$

30 The lengths of two sides of a triangle are 7 and 10. The length of the third side may be
(1) 17   (3) 3
(2) 20   (4) 8

31 Which expression is *not* equivalent to $_7C_5$?

(1) $_7P_5$

(3) $\frac{7 \cdot 6 \cdot 5 \cdot 4 \cdot 3}{5 \cdot 4 \cdot 3 \cdot 2 \cdot 1}$

(2) 21

(4) $_7C_2$

32 What are the roots of the equation $2x^2 - 6x + 3 = 0$?

(1) $\frac{-3 \pm \sqrt{3}}{2}$

(3) $\frac{3 \pm \sqrt{3}}{2}$

(2) $\frac{-3 \pm \sqrt{15}}{2}$

(4) $\frac{3 \pm \sqrt{15}}{2}$

33 The sum of $\frac{x+4}{x}$ and $\frac{x-4}{4}$ is

(1) $\frac{1}{2}$

(3) $\frac{x^2 + 16}{4x}$

(2) $4 + x$

(4) $\frac{2x}{x+4}$

34 In the accompanying diagram, $\triangle ABC$ is a scalene triangle.

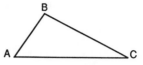

If the median is drawn from vertex B, what is the probability that its length will be greater than the length of the altitude?

(1) 1

(3) $\frac{1}{2}$

(2) 0

(4) $\frac{2}{3}$

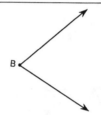

Directions (35): Leave all construction lines on the answer sheet.

35 *On the answer sheet*, construct the ray that bisects $\angle B$.

Part II

Answer three questions from this part. Clearly indicate the necessary steps, including appropriate formula substitutions, diagrams, graphs, charts, etc. Calculations that may be obtained by mental arithmetic or the calculator do not need to be shown. [30]

36 Answer both *a* and *b* for all values of x for which these expressions are defined.

a Express the product in simplest form: $\frac{x^2 - 9}{x^2 - x - 20} \cdot \frac{4x^2 - 20x}{4x^2 - 12x}$ [6]

b Solve for x: $\frac{x - 3}{2} = \frac{6}{x + 8}$ [4]

37 *a* On graph paper, draw the graph of the equation $y = x^2 - 4x + 4$, including all values of x from $x = -1$ to $x = 5$. Label the graph *a*.

b On the same set of axes, draw the image of the graph drawn in part *a* after a translation that maps $(x,y) \rightarrow (x - 2, y + 3)$. Label the image *b*. [2]

c On the same set of axes, draw the image of the graph drawn in part *b* after a reflection in the *x*-axis. Label the image *c*. [2]

d Which equation could represent the graph drawn in part *c*? [2]

(1) $y = -x^2 + 4x - 4$

(3) $y = -x^2 - 3$

(2) $y = x^2 - 3$

(4) $y = -x^2 + 3$

38 Alan has three detective books, two books about cars, and five comic books. He plans to lend three books to his friend David.

  a How many different selections of three books can Alan lend his friend? [2]

  b Find the probability that a three-book selection will contain
  (1) one book of each type [3]
  (2) comic books, only [3]
  (3) books about cars, only [2]

39 Trapezoid *ABCD* has coordinates *A*(–6,0), *B*(17,0), *C*(2,8), and *D*(0,8). Find the

  a area of trapezoid *ABCD* [3]

  b perimeter of trapezoid *ABCD* [4]

  c measure of ∠*B* to the *nearest degree* [3]

40 *On your answer paper*, write the numerals 1 through 8, and next to each numeral, give a reason for each statement in the proof. For statement 1, write "Given."

Given: △*ABC*, $\overline{AC} \cong \overline{BC}$, $\overline{AD}$ and $\overline{BE}$ intersect at *G*, and ∠1 ≅ ∠2.

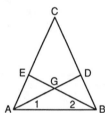

Prove: $\overline{EG} \cong \overline{DG}$

Statements	Reasons	
(1) △*ABC*, $\overline{AC} \cong \overline{BC}$, ∠1 ≅ ∠2	(1) Given	
(2) ∠*CAB* ≅ ∠*CBA*	(2)	[2]
(3) $\overline{AB} \cong \overline{BA}$	(3)	[1]
(4) △*EAB* ≅ △*DBA*	(4)	[2]
(5) ∠*AEB* ≅ ∠*BDA*, $\overline{AE} \cong \overline{BD}$	(5)	[1]
(6) ∠*EGA* ≅ ∠*DGB*	(6)	[1]
(7) △*EGA* ≅ △*DGB*	(7)	[2]
(8) $\overline{EG} \cong \overline{DG}$	(8)	[1]

Part III

Answer one question from this part. Clearly indicate the necessary steps, including appropriate formula substitutions, diagrams, graphs, charts, etc. Calculations that may be obtained by mental arithmetic or the calculator do not need to be shown. [10]

41 Given: If pro basketball players compete in the Olympics, then college players do not play.
If college players do not play, then the team is not an amateur team.
If the team is not an amateur team and the team does not win the gold medal, then the people are not happy.
Pro basketball players compete in the Olympics.
The people are happy.

Let *P* represent: "Pro basketball players compete in the Olympics."
Let *C* represent: "College players play."
Let *A* represent: "The team is an amateur team."
Let *G* represent: "The team wins the gold medal."
Let *H* represent: "The people are happy."

Prove: The team wins the gold medal. [10]

42 The coordinates of the vertices of △*TAG* are *T*(1,3), *A*(8,2), and *G*(5,6). Prove that △*TAG* is an isosceles right triangle. [10]

REGENTS EXAMINATION

Examination January 1995

Three Year Sequence for High School Mathematics — Course II

Part I

Answer 30 questions from this part. Each correct answer will receive 2 credits. No partial credit will be allowed. Write your answers in the spaces provided on the separate answer sheet. Where applicable, answers may be left in terms of π or in radical form. [60]

1 In the accompanying diagram, $\overleftrightarrow{RS} \parallel \overleftrightarrow{TU}$ and $\overleftrightarrow{GH} \parallel \overleftrightarrow{MN}$. If $m\angle x = 115$, find $m\angle y$.

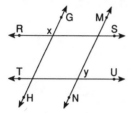

2 In the accompanying diagram, $ABCD$ is a parallelogram with altitude $\overline{DE}$ drawn to side $\overline{AB}$. If $DE = AE$, find the measure of $\angle A$.

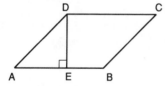

3 The sides of $\triangle ABC$ are 6.8, 6.8, and 8.4 meters. Find the perimeter of the triangle that is formed by joining the midpoints of the sides of $\triangle ABC$.

4 Point $A(6,3)$ is reflected in the x-axis. Find the coordinates of A', its image.

5 If $a \spadesuit b$ is defined as $\dfrac{a - b}{a + b}$, find the value of $-3 \spadesuit 1$.

6 In $\triangle ABC$, side $\overline{AC}$ is extended through C to D and $m\angle DCB = 60$. Which is the longest side of $\triangle ABC$?

7 What is the length of a diagonal of a rectangle whose sides are 3 and 7?

8 Two sides of an isosceles triangle have lengths 2 and 12, respectively. Find the length of the third side.

9 The sides of a triangle have lengths 3, 5, and 7. In a similar triangle, the shortest side has length $x - 3$, and the longest side has length $x + 5$. Find the value of x.

10 Find the number of square units in the area of a triangle whose vertices are $A(2,0)$, $B(6,0)$, and $C(4,5)$.

11 Find, in radical form, the distance between points $(-1,-2)$ and $(5,0)$.

12 What are the coordinates of the center of a circle if the endpoints of a diameter are $(-6,2)$ and $(4,6)$?

13 In equilateral triangle ABC, $AB = 3x$ and $BC = 2x + 12$. Find the numerical value of the perimeter of $\triangle ABC$.

Directions (14–35): For *each* question chosen, write on the separate answer sheet the *numeral* preceding the word or expression that best completes the statement or answers the question.

14 Which coordinate pair is a solution for the following system of equations?

$$x^2 + y^2 = 8$$
$$x = 2$$

(1) $(2,4)$ (3) $(2,\sqrt{8})$
(2) $(2,2)$ (4) $(4,2)$

15 In parallelogram $ABCD$, diagonal $\overline{BD}$ is drawn. Which statement must be true?

(1) $\triangle ABD$ must be an obtuse triangle.
(2) $\triangle CDB$ must be an acute triangle.
(3) $\triangle ABD$ must be an isosceles triangle.
(4) $\triangle ABD$ must be congruent to $\triangle CDB$.

16 In the accompanying diagram, AB intersects $\overleftrightarrow{CE}$ and $\overrightarrow{CD} \perp \overleftrightarrow{AB}$.

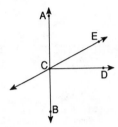

Which statement is true?

(1) $\angle ACE \cong \angle BCD$.
(2) B, C, and D are collinear.
(3) $\angle ACE$ and $\angle ECD$ are complementary.
(4) $\angle ACE$ and $\angle ECD$ are supplementary.

17 Which property is illustrated by $\square(\triangle + O) = \square\triangle + \square O$?
(1) distributive   (3) commutative
(2) associative   (4) transitive

18 From a deck of 52 cards, two cards are randomly drawn without replacement. What is the probability of drawing two hearts?

(1) $\frac{2}{52}$ (3) $\frac{13}{52} \cdot \frac{12}{51}$

(2) $\frac{13}{52} \cdot \frac{13}{51}$ (4) $\frac{13}{52} \cdot \frac{13}{52}$

19 Which is logically equivalent to $\sim(\sim p \vee q)$?
(1) $p \wedge \sim q$ (3) $\sim p \vee \sim q$
(2) $\sim p \wedge \sim q$ (4) $p \vee \sim q$

20 Which is an equation of the circle whose center is the origin and whose radius is 4?
(1) $y = x^2 + 8$ (3) $x^2 + y^2 = 16$
(2) $x^2 + y^2 = 4$ (4) $x + y = 8$

21 Expressed in simplest form, $\frac{x}{2} - \frac{x}{3} + \frac{x}{4}$ is equivalent to

(1) $\frac{x}{3}$ (3) $\frac{3x}{24}$

(2) $\frac{x}{24}$ (4) $\frac{5x}{12}$

22 If a translation maps point $A(-3,1)$ to point $A'(5,5)$, the translation can be represented by
(1) $(x + 8, y + 4)$ (3) $(x + 2, y + 6)$
(2) $(x + 8, y + 6)$ (4) $(x + 2, y + 4)$

23 When the statement "If A, then B" is true, which statement must also be true?
(1) If B, then A.
(2) If not A, then B.
(3) If not B, then A.
(4) If not B, then not A.

24 In right triangle ABC, altitude $\overline{CD}$ is drawn to hypotenuse $\overline{AB}$. If $AD = 5$ and $DB = 24$, what is the length of $\overline{CD}$?
(1) 120   (3) $2\sqrt{30}$
(2) $\sqrt{30}$ (4) $4\sqrt{30}$

25 The graph of which equation has a *negative* slope?
(1) $y = 5x - 3$ (3) $y - 2 = 4x$
(2) $x + y = 5$ (4) $y = 0$

26 What is the equation of the locus of points passing through point $(3,-2)$ and 3 units from the y-axis?
(1) $x = -2$ (3) $x = 3$
(2) $y = -2$ (4) $y = 3$

27 Which expression is a perfect square?
(1) $x^2 - 4x + 4$ (3) $x^2 - 9x + 9$
(2) $x^2 - 4x - 4$ (4) $x^2 - 9x - 9$

28 The roots of the equation $2x^2 + 5x - 2 = 0$ are
(1) $\frac{5 \pm \sqrt{41}}{2}$ (3) $2, \frac{1}{2}$

(2) $-\frac{1}{2}, -2$ (4) $\frac{-5 \pm \sqrt{41}}{4}$

29 How many different 13-letter permutations can be formed from the letters of the word "QUADRILATERAL"?

(1) 13!

(3) $\frac{13!}{3!2!2!}$

(2) $\frac{13!}{7!}$

(4) $\frac{13!}{6!}$

30 The hypotenuse of right triangle ABC is 10 and $m\angle A = 60$. What is the measure, to the *nearest tenth*, of the leg opposite $\angle A$?

(1) 5.0   (3) 7.1

(2) 5.8   (4) 8.7

31 Which equation represents a line parallel to the line whose equation is $y = 2x - 7$?

(1) $y = 2x$

(3) $y = -7$

(2) $y = \frac{1}{2}x - 7$

(4) $y = -\frac{1}{2}x + 7$

32 Expressed in simplest form, $\frac{2x^2}{x^2 - 1} \cdot \frac{x - 1}{x}$, $x \neq 1, 0, -1$, is equivalent to

(1) $\frac{2x}{x - 1}$

(3) $\frac{2}{x}$

(2) 2

(4) $\frac{2x}{x + 1}$

33 A set contains five isosceles trapezoids, three squares, and a rhombus that is not a square. A figure is chosen at random. What is the probability that its diagonals will be congruent?

(1) 1

(3) $\frac{5}{9}$

(2) $\frac{8}{9}$

(4) $\frac{3}{9}$

34 Which graph could represent the equation $y = x^2 - 4$?

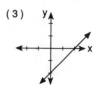

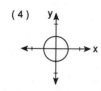

35 In the accompanying diagram, $\triangle ABC$ is scalene.

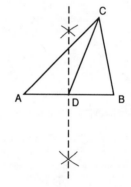

The construction on this triangle shows that $\overline{CD}$ is the

(1) median to side $\overline{AB}$
(2) bisector of angle C
(3) altitude to side $\overline{AB}$
(4) perpendicular bisector of side $\overline{AB}$

Part II

Answer three questions from this part. Clearly indicate the necessary steps, including appropriate formula substitutions, diagrams, graphs, charts, etc. Calculations that may be obtained by mental arithmetic or the calculator do not need to be shown.   [30]

36 Answer both *a* and *b* for all values of *x* for which these expressions are defined.

 a Solve for *x*: $\dfrac{x + 3}{3x} = \dfrac{x}{12}$ [5]

 b Express the product as a single fraction in lowest terms:

$$\frac{x}{3x + 15} \cdot \frac{2x^2 + 11x + 5}{2x^2 + x}$$ [5]

37 *a* On graph paper, draw the graph of the equation $y = -x^2 + 4x - 1$, including all values of *x* in the interval $-1 \le x \le 5$.   [5]

 b On the same set of axes, draw the graph of the equation $x - y = 5$.   [3]

 c From the graphs drawn in parts *a* and *b*, determine the solution(s) of this system of equations:

$$\begin{aligned} y &= -x^2 + 4x - 1 \\ x - y &= 5 \end{aligned}$$ [2]

38 There are seven boys and three girls on a school tennis team. The coach must select four people from this group to participate in a county championship.

 a How many four-person teams can be formed from the group of ten students?   [3]

 b In how many ways can two boys and two girls be chosen to participate in the county championship?   [3]

 c What is the probability that two boys and two girls are chosen for the team?   [2]

 d What is the probability that a four-member team will contain at least one boy?   [2]

39 In the accompanying diagram of rhombus *ABCD*, $m\angle BAD = 36$ and the length of diagonal $\overline{AEC} = 16$.

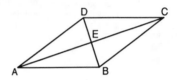

 a Find the length of diagonal $\overline{BD}$ to the *nearest tenth*.   [4]

 b Find the perimeter of rhombus *ABCD* to the *nearest integer*.   [6]

40 The endpoints of $\overline{AB}$ are $A(1,4)$ and $B(5,1)$.

 a On graph paper, draw and label $\overline{AB}$.   [1]

 b Graph and state the coordinates of $\overline{A'B'}$, the image of $\overline{AB}$ under a reflection in the *y*-axis.   [2]

 c Graph and state the coordinates of $\overline{A''B''}$, the image of $\overline{AB}$ under a dilation of 2 with respect to the origin.   [2]

 d Using coordinate geometry, show that a line segment and its image are congruent under a line reflection and are *not* congruent under a dilation.   [5]

Part III

Answer one question from this part. Clearly indicate the necessary steps, including appropriate formula substitutions, diagrams, graphs, charts, etc. Calculations that may be obtained by mental arithmetic or the calculator do not need to be shown.   [10]

41 Given: $B \rightarrow D$
     $D \rightarrow \sim E$
     $(\sim A \wedge \sim B) \rightarrow C$
     $\sim F \rightarrow E$
     $\sim A$
     $\sim C$

 Prove: F [10]

42 Prove: In an isosceles triangle, the line segment that bisects the vertex angle bisects the base.   [10]

REGENTS EXAMINATION

Examination June 1995

Three Year Sequence for High School Mathematics --- Course II

Part I

Answer 30 questions from this part. Each correct answer will receive 2 credits. No partial credit will be allowed. Write your answers in the spaces provided on the separate answer sheet. Where applicable, answers may be left in terms of π or in radical form.   [60]

1 In the accompanying diagram, $\overleftrightarrow{AB}$ is parallel to $\overleftrightarrow{CD}$, and transversal $\overleftrightarrow{EH}$ intersects $\overleftrightarrow{AB}$ and $\overleftrightarrow{CD}$ at F and G, respectively. If $m\angle AFG = 2x + 10$ and $m\angle FGD = x + 20$, find the value of x.

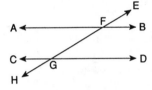

2 In the accompanying diagram, $ABCD$ is a parallelogram, $\overline{DA} \cong \overline{DE}$, and $m\angle B = 70$. Find $m\angle E$.

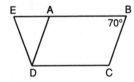

3 In $\triangle ABC$, $m\angle A = 35$ and $m\angle C = 77$. Which is the longest side of the triangle?

4 The sides of a triangle measure 6, 8, and 10. The shortest side of a similar triangle is 15. Find the perimeter of the larger triangle.

5 Rectangle $PROM$ has coordinates $P(2,1)$, $R(8,1)$, $O(8,5)$, and $M(2,5)$. What are the coordinates of the point of intersection of the diagonals?

6 Find, to the *nearest tenth*, the distance between points $(1,3)$ and $(-2,0)$.

7 Solve for x: $\dfrac{2x - 4}{3} = \dfrac{3x + 4}{2}$

8 In the accompanying diagram of right triangle MNQ, $\overline{NP}$ is the altitude to hypotenuse $\overline{MQ}$. If $QP = 16$ and $PM = 9$, find the length of $\overline{NP}$.

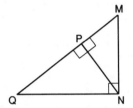

9 How many distinct five-letter permutations can be formed using the letters of the word "GAUSS"?

10 Under a translation, the image of point $(3,2)$ is $(-1,3)$. What are the coordinates of the image of point $(-2,6)$ under the same translation?

11 In $\triangle BAT$, M is the midpoint of $\overline{BA}$ and N is the midpoint of $\overline{BT}$. If $AT = 3x + 12$ and $MN = 15$, find x.

12 How many different bowling teams of five persons can be formed from a group of ten persons?

13 A 20-foot ladder is leaning against a wall. The foot of the ladder makes an angle of 58° with the ground. Find, to the *nearest foot*, the vertical distance from the top of the ladder to the ground.

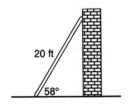

14 In quadrilateral $ABCD$, $m\angle A = 57$, $m\angle B = 65$, and $m\angle C = 118$. What is the measure of an exterior angle at D?

15 Under a dilation with constant of dilation k, the image of the point $(2,3)$ is $(8,12)$. What is the value of k?

Directions (16–34): For *each* question chosen, write on the separate answer sheet the *numeral* preceding the word or expression that best completes the statement or answers the question.

16 An equation of the line that passes through point $(0,3)$ and whose slope is -2 is
(1) $y = -2x + 3$ (3) $y = 2x + 3$
(2) $y = -2x - 3$ (4) $y = 2x - 3$

17 Given: $p \rightarrow q$
         $\underline{\quad p \quad}$
         $\therefore q$

What is this argument called?

(1) DeMorgan's Law
(2) Law of Detachment
(3) Law of Disjunctive Inference
(4) Law of Contrapositive

18 If $x \clubsuit y = \dfrac{x^2 - 2xy + y^2}{x - y}$ defines the binary

operation $\clubsuit$, what is the value of $5 \clubsuit 3$?

(1) 1   (3) 9
(2) 2   (4) 32

19 If $(x - 3)$ and $(x + 7)$ are the factors of the trinomial $x^2 + ax - 21$, what is the value of a?

(1) -3 (3) 7
(2) -4 (4) 4

20 Which statement is *not* always true about a parallelogram?

(1) Opposite sides are parallel.
(2) Opposite sides are congruent.
(3) Opposite angles are congruent.
(4) Diagonals are congruent.

21 The parabola shown in the diagram is reflected in the x-axis.

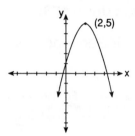

What is the image of the turning point after the reflection?

(1) $(2,-5)$ (3) $(-2,-5)$
(2) $(-2,5)$ (4) $(5,2)$

22 If $\angle C$ is the complement of $\angle A$, and $\angle S$ is the supplement of $\angle A$, which statement is *always* true?

(1) $m\angle C + m\angle S = 180$
(2) $m\angle C + m\angle S = 90$
(3) $m\angle C > m\angle S$
(4) $m\angle C < m\angle S$

23 Which equation describes the locus of points equidistant from points $(2,2)$ and $(2,6)$?

(1) $y = 8$ (3) $x = 8$
(2) $y = 4$ (4) $x = 4$

24 In equilateral triangle ABC, the bisectors of angles A and B intersect at point F. What is $m\angle AFB$?

(1) 60   (3) 120
(2) 90   (4) 150

25 Two sides of a triangle have lengths 5 and 8. Which length can *not* be the length of the third side?

(1) 5   (3) 3
(2) 6   (4) 4

26 In the accompanying diagram of right triangle *ABC*, what is tan *C*?

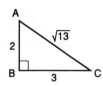

(1) $\frac{2}{3}$ (3) $\frac{\sqrt{13}}{3}$

(2) $\frac{3}{2}$ (4) $\frac{2}{\sqrt{13}}$

27 In the accompanying diagram, $\overleftrightarrow{ACE}$ is parallel to $\overleftrightarrow{DB}$, m$\angle DBA$ = 40, and m$\angle BCE$ = 105.

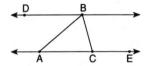

Which statement is true?

(1) $\overline{AB}$ is the longest side of $\triangle ABC$.

(2) $\overline{AC}$ is the longest side of $\triangle ABC$.

(3) $\triangle ABC$ is an isosceles triangle.

(4) $\triangle ABC$ is an obtuse triangle.

28 Which equation represents the circle whose center is (–4,2) and whose radius is 3?

(1) $(x + 4)^2 + (y - 2)^2 = 9$
(2) $(x + 4)^2 + (y - 2)^2 = 3$
(3) $(x - 4)^2 + (y + 2)^2 = 9$
(4) $(x - 4)^2 + (y + 2)^2 = 3$

29 If two legs of a right triangle measure 3 and $\sqrt{10}$, then the hypotenuse must measure

(1) 1   (3) 10
(2) $\sqrt{19}$ (4) 19

30 Which statement is equivalent to "If a quadrilateral is a rectangle, the diagonals are congruent"?

(1) If the diagonals of a quadrilateral are congruent, the quadrilateral is a rectangle.
(2) If a quadrilateral is not a rectangle, the diagonals of the quadrilateral are not congruent.
(3) If the diagonals of a quadrilateral are not congruent, the quadrilateral is not a rectangle.
(4) If a quadrilateral is a parallelogram, the diagonals are congruent.

31 In how many points do the graphs of the equations $x^2 + y^2 = 9$ and $y = 2x - 1$ intersect?

(1) 1   (3) 3
(2) 2   (4) 4

32 Which quadratic equation has irrational roots?

(1) $x^2 + 2x - 8 = 0$ (3) $x^2 - 3x + 2 = 0$
(2) $x^2 - x - 30 = 0$ (4) $x^2 - 4x - 7 = 0$

33 Which equation represents the axis of symmetry of the graph of the equation $y = x^2 - 6x + 5$?

(1) $x = -3$ (3) $x = 3$
(2) $y = -3$ (4) $y = 3$

34 Which equation represents a line that is parallel to the line whose equation is $y = \frac{1}{2}x - 2$?

(1) $y = 2x - 3$ (3) $2y = x - 3$
(2) $y = -2x - 3$ (4) $2y = -x - 3$

Directions (35): Leave all construction lines on the answer sheet.

35 *On the answer sheet*, construct the angle bisector of $\angle C$ of $\triangle ABC$.

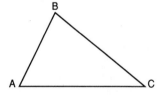

Part II

Answer three questions from this part. Clearly indicate the necessary steps, including appropriate formula substitutions, diagrams, graphs, charts, etc. Calculations that may be obtained by mental arithmetic or the calculator do not need to be shown.   [30]

36 *a* On graph paper, draw the graph of the equation $y = x^2 - 2x - 3$ for all values of x in the interval $-2 \leq x \leq 4$.   [6]

b What are the roots of the equation $x^2 - 2x - 3 = 0$?   [2]

c On the same set of axes, draw the image of the graph drawn in part *a* after a reflection in the y-axis.   [2]

37 Answer both *a* and *b* for all values of x for which these expressions are defined.

a Simplify: $\dfrac{x^2 + 9x + 20}{x^2 - 16} \div \dfrac{x^2 + 5x}{4x - 16}$ [6]

b Solve for x: $\dfrac{2}{x} = \dfrac{x - 3}{5}$ [4]

38 A debating team of four persons is to be chosen from five juniors and three seniors.

a How many different four-member teams are possible?   [2]

b How many of these teams will consist of exactly two juniors and two seniors?   [3]

c What is the probability that one of the four-member teams will consist of exactly one junior and three seniors?   [3]

d What is the probability that one four-member team will consist of juniors only?   [2]

39 In the accompanying diagram of right triangle ABD, $AB = 6$ and altitude $\overline{BC}$ divides hypotenuse $\overline{AD}$ into segments of lengths x and 8.

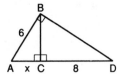

a Find AC to the *nearest tenth*.   [7]

b Using the answer from part *a*, find the measure of $\angle A$ to the *nearest degree*.   [3]

40 An 8- by 10-inch photo has a frame of uniform width placed around it.

a If the uniform width of the frame is x inches, express the outside dimensions of the picture frame in terms of x.   [4]

b If the area of the picture and frame is 143 in^2, what is the uniform width of the frame?   [6]

Part III

Answer one question from this part. Clearly indicate the necessary steps, including appropriate formula substitutions, diagrams, graphs, charts, etc. Calculations that may be obtained by mental arithmetic or the calculator do not need to be shown.   [10]

41 *a* Given:
   Either I go to camp or I get a summer job.
   If I get a summer job, then I will earn money.
   If I earn money, then I will buy new sneakers.
   I do not buy new sneakers.

   Let C represent: "I go to camp."
   Let J represent: "I get a summer job."
   Let M represent: "I earn money."
   Let S represent: "I buy new sneakers."

   Prove: I go to camp.   [8]

b Given the true statements:
   If Michael is an athlete and he is salaried, then Michael is a professional.
   Michael is not a professional.
   Michael is an athlete.

   Which statement must be true?   [2]

   (1) Michael is an athlete and he is salaried.
   (2) Michael is a professional or he is salaried.
   (3) Michael is not salaried.
   (4) Michael is not an athlete.

42 Given: quadrilateral $PQRT$, $\overline{QSV}$, $\overline{RST}$, $\overline{PTV}$, $\overline{QV}$ bisects $\overline{RT}$, and $\overline{QR} \parallel \overline{PV}$.

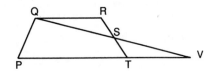

Prove: $\overline{QS} \cong \overline{VS}$ [10]

REGENTS EXAMINATION

Examination August 1995

Three Year Sequence for High School Mathematics — Course II

Part I

Answer 30 questions from this part. Each correct answer will receive 2 credits. No partial credit will be allowed. Write your answers in the spaces provided on the separate answer sheet. Where applicable, answers may be left in terms of π or in radical form. [60]

1 What is the value of $a * (b * d)$ in the system defined below?

$*$	a	b	c	d
a	c	d	a	b
b	d	c	b	a
c	a	b	c	d
d	b	a	d	c

2 If $\tan A = 0.4548$, find the measure of $\angle A$ to the *nearest degree*.

3 If $\dfrac{3}{a + 4} = \dfrac{a - 1}{a}$, what is the positive value of a?

4 Write an equation of the line whose slope is -2 and whose y-intercept is 1.

5 A student council consists of ten members. How many different four-member subcommittees can be formed from the student council?

6 In parallelogram $DATE$, $m\angle D = 8x - 20$ and $m\angle A = 2x + 30$. Find x.

7 In $\triangle ABC$, $m\angle A$ is three times $m\angle B$. An exterior angle at vertex C measures $100°$. What is $m\angle B$?

8 In the accompanying diagram, $\overline{SV}$ is the altitude to hypotenuse $\overline{RT}$ of right triangle RST. If $RV = 3$ and $VT = 12$, find the length of $\overline{SV}$.

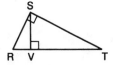

9 Solve for x: $\dfrac{x}{6} + \dfrac{2x}{3} = 5$

10 Find the coordinates of the image of point $T(-7,3)$ under a reflection in the origin.

11 Find, to the *nearest tenth*, the distance between two points whose coordinates are $(-2,5)$ and $(3,-4)$.

12 Express $\dfrac{2x - 10}{x^2 - 2x - 15}$ in simplest form.

13 What are the coordinates of the center of a circle whose equation is $(x + 3)^2 + (y - 1)^2 = 16$?

14 In the accompanying diagram of isosceles triangle ABC, $\overline{BA} \cong \overline{BC}$ and altitude $\overline{BD}$ is drawn. If $BD = 4$ and $AD = 3$, find the perimeter of $\triangle ABC$.

15 In the accompanying diagram of isosceles triangle ABC, $\overline{BA} \cong \overline{BC}$ and $\overline{DC}$ bisects $\angle ACB$. If $m\angle A = 40$, find $m\angle CDB$.

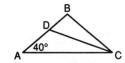

Directions (16–34): For *each* question chosen, write on the separate answer sheet the *numeral* preceding the word or expression that best completes the statement or answers the question.

16 If x and y are any two whole numbers, which statement is *always* true?

(1) $xy = yx$ (3) $x - y = y - x$

(2) $\dfrac{x}{y} = \dfrac{y}{x}$ (4) $x + 3y = y + 3x$

17 After a reflection in the line $y = x$, the image of $(-3,2)$ lies in Quadrant

(1) I   (3) III

(2) II   (4) IV

18 What is the negation of the statement $\sim c \wedge d$?

(1) $c \wedge d$ (3) $c \wedge \sim d$

(2) $c \vee d$ (4) $c \vee \sim d$

19 In the accompanying diagram of $\triangle ABC$, $\overline{DE} \parallel \overline{AB}$, $\overline{CFG} \perp \overline{AB}$, $CD = 6$, $DA = 4$, and $CF = 5$.

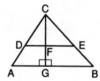

What is the length of $\overline{FG}$?

(1) $1\frac{1}{3}$ (3) $5\frac{1}{3}$

(2) $3\frac{1}{3}$ (4) $10\frac{1}{3}$

20 Given the true statements, $a \rightarrow b$, $a \vee c$, and $\sim b$. Which statement is logically true?

(1) $a \wedge b$ (3) c

(2) b (4) $\sim c \wedge \sim b$

21 Line segment $\overline{AB}$ has midpoint M. If the coordinates of A are $(2,3)$ and the coordinates of M are $(-1,0)$, what are the coordinates of B?

(1) $(1,3)$ (3) $(-4,-3)$

(2) $\left(\frac{1}{2},\frac{3}{2}\right)$ (4) $(-4,6)$

22 In the accompanying diagram, $\overline{PR} \cong \overline{SQ}$, $\overline{PR} \perp \overline{RQ}$, and $\overline{SQ} \perp \overline{RQ}$. Which statement can be used to prove that $\triangle PQR \cong \triangle SRQ$?

(1) AAS $\cong$ AAS   (3) HL $\cong$ HL

(2) SAS $\cong$ SAS   (4) SSS $\cong$ SSS

23 Given points $A(0,0)$, $B(3,2)$, and $C(-2,3)$, which statement is true?

(1) $\overline{AB}$ is parallel to $\overline{AC}$.

(2) $\overline{AB}$ is perpendicular to $\overline{AC}$.

(3) AB is greater than BC.

(4) $\overline{BC}$ is perpendicular to $\overline{CA}$.

24 Which equation represents the locus of all points 3 units to the right of the y-axis?

(1) $x = 3$ (3) $y = 3$

(2) $x = -3$ (4) $y = -3$

25 In the accompanying diagram of $\triangle ABC$, D is a point on $\overline{AC}$, $\overline{AB}$ is extended to E, and $\overline{DE}$ is drawn so that $\triangle ADE \sim \triangle ABC$.

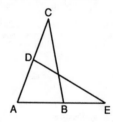

If $m\angle C = 30$ and $m\angle A = 70$, what is $m\angle ADE$?

(1) 30   (3) 80

(2) 70   (4) 100

26 A gumball machine contains six yellow gumballs and five orange gumballs. What is the probability of obtaining, at random and without replacement, two yellow gumballs?

(1) $\frac{36}{110}$

(2) $\frac{36}{121}$

(3) $\frac{30}{110}$

(4) $\frac{30}{121}$

27 In the accompanying diagram of rhombus $QRST$, diagonals $\overline{QS}$ and $\overline{RT}$ intersect at M.

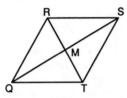

Which statement *must* be true?

(1) Triangle QRM is an isosceles right triangle.

(2) $\triangle QRM \cong \triangle SRM$.

(3) Triangle QRM is an obtuse triangle.

(4) $\overline{QS} \cong \overline{RT}$.

28 Which graph represents the equation
$y = -x^2 + 4$?

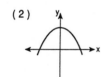

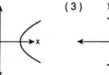

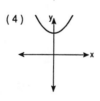

29 In $\triangle ABC$, if $AB = 14$ and $BC = 9$, AC may be equal to

(1) 5
(2) 13

(3) 23
(4) 25

30 The straight string of a kite makes an angle of elevation from the ground of 60°. The length of the string is 400 feet. What is the best approximation of the height of the kite?

(1) 200 ft
(2) 250 ft

(3) 300 ft
(4) 350 ft

31 In $\triangle ABC$, $m\angle A = 3x$, $m\angle B = 4x - 19$, and $m\angle C = 3x - 1$. Which statement is true?

(1) $\overline{AB}$ is the longest side of $\triangle ABC$.

(2) $\triangle ABC$ is an isosceles triangle.

(3) $\overline{AC}$ is the longest side of $\triangle ABC$.

(4) $\triangle ABC$ is an obtuse triangle.

32 The statement $(A \rightarrow \sim R) \wedge (C \rightarrow R)$ is logically equivalent to

(1) $\sim C \rightarrow \sim A$
(2) $C \rightarrow A$

(3) $A \rightarrow C$
(4) $A \rightarrow \sim C$

33 How many different seven-letter arrangements can be formed from the letters in the word "SUCCESS"?

(1) $\frac{7!}{2!3!}$

(2) $7!$

(3) $\frac{7!}{3!}$

(4) $\frac{7!}{2!}$

34 The intersection of the graphs of the functions $y = x^2$ and $y = 2x$ includes the point

(1) (2,4)
(2) (1,1)

(3) (0,2)
(4) (−2,4)

Directions (35): Leave all construction lines on the answer sheet.

35 *On the answer sheet*, construct the median $\overline{AP}$ to $\overline{BC}$ of $\triangle ABC$.

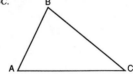

Part II

Answer three questions from this part. Clearly indicate the necessary steps, including appropriate formula substitutions, diagrams, graphs, charts, etc. Calculations that may be obtained by mental arithmetic or the calculator do not need to be shown.   [30]

36 a On graph paper, draw the graph of the equation $y = x^2 - 6x + 8$ for all values of x in the interval $0 \leq x \leq 6$.   [6]

b On the same set of axes, draw the image of the graph drawn in part a after a translation of $(x - 3, y + 1)$ and label it b.   [2]

c Write an equation of the graph drawn in part b.   [2]

37 The length of a rectangle is 4 less than twice its width. If the area of the rectangle is 20, find the width of the rectangle to the *nearest tenth*.   [5,5]

38 a Triangle PQR is congruent to triangle $P'Q'R'$. If $PQ = x + y$, $P'Q' = 10$, $Q'R' = 3x - y$, and $QR = 14$, find the values of x and y.   [5]

b For all values for which the expression is defined, solve for x: $\dfrac{3}{x} = \dfrac{x + 5}{2}$ [5]

39 In the accompanying diagram of parallelogram *MATH*, $\overline{AH}$ is a diagonal, altitude $\overline{AV}$ is drawn to side $\overline{MH}$, $AT = 18$, $VH = 10$, and m$\angle M = 42$.

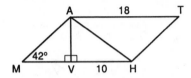

a Find AV to the *nearest tenth*.   [4]

b Find the area of parallelogram *MATH* to the *nearest integer*.   [2]

c Find the perimeter of parallelogram *MATH* to the *nearest integer*.   [4]

40 Solve the following system of equations algebraically and check:

$$x^2 + y^2 = 100$$
$$y = x - 2 \qquad [8,2]$$

Part III

Answer one question from this part. Clearly indicate the necessary steps, including appropriate formula substitutions, diagrams, graphs, charts, etc. Calculations that may be obtained by mental arithmetic or the calculator do not need to be shown.   [10]

41 Given: $\triangle EAD$, $\overline{ABCD}$, $\overline{AB} \cong \overline{DC}$, and $\angle EBC \cong \angle ECB$.

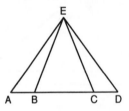

Prove that $\triangle EAD$ is an isosceles triangle.   [10]

42 Quadrilateral *ABCD* has vertices $A(-8,2)$, $B(0,6)$, $C(8,0)$, and $D(-8,-8)$. Prove that quadrilateral *ABCD* is an isosceles trapezoid.   [10]

ANSWERS TO REGENTS EXAMINATIONS

JUNE 1994

1. 6
2. 4
3. b
4. $(-1,8)$
5. 70
6. $\overline{AC}$
7. 37
8. 6
9. $(-1,-2)$
10. $(5a,5b)$
11. 108
12. 80
13. 24
14. $y = x + 1$
15. 9
16. 48
17. 2
18. 1
19. 4
20. 4
21. 2
22. 3
23. 4
24. 3
25. 2
26. 2
27. 3
28. 1
29. 1
30. 4
31. 1
32. 3
33. 3
34. 1
35. construction
36. a $\dfrac{x+3}{x+4}$

    b $-9, 4$
37. d 3
38. a 120

    b (1) $\dfrac{30}{120}$

    (2) $\dfrac{10}{120}$

    (3) 0
39. a 100

    b 52

    c 28

JANUARY 1995

1. 65
2. 45°
3. 11
4. $(6,-3)$
5. 2
6. $\overline{AB}$
7. $\sqrt{58}$
8. 12
9. 9
10. 10
11. $2\sqrt{10}$
12. $(-1,4)$
13. 108
14. 2
15. 4
16. 3
17. 1
18. 3
19. 1
20. 3
21. 4
22. 1
23. 4
24. 3
25. 2
26. 3
27. 1
28. 4
29. 3
30. 4
31. 1
32. 4
33. 2
34. 2
35. 1
36. a 6 and -2

    b $\dfrac{1}{3}$
37. c $(-1,-6)$ and $(4,-1)$
38. a 210

    b 63

    c $\dfrac{63}{210}$

    d 1
39. a 5.2

    b 34
40. b $A'(-1,4)$, $B'(-5,1)$

    c $A''(2,8)$, $B''(10,2)$

JUNE 1995

1. 10
2. 70
3. $\overline{AB}$
4. 60
5. (5,3)
6. 4.2
7. −4
8. 12
9. 60
10. (−6,7)
11. 6
12. 252
13. 17

14. 60°
15. 4
16. 1 ✓
17. 2
18. 2
19. 4
20. 4
21. 1
22. 4
23. 2
24. 3
25. 3
26. 1

27. 1
28. 1
29. 2
30. 3
31. 2
32. 4
33. 3
34. 3
35. construction
36. b −1 and 3
37. a $\frac{4}{x}$
   b 5 and −2

38. a 70
   b 30
   c $\frac{5}{70}$
   d $\frac{5}{70}$
39. a 3.2
   b 58°
40. a $\ell = 10 + 2x$
   $w = 8 + 2x$
   b 1.5
41. b 3

AUGUST 1995

1. c
2. 24
3. 2
4. $y = -2x + 1$
5. 210
6. 17
7. 25
8. 6
9. 6
10. (7,−3)
11. 10.3
12. $\frac{2}{x + 3}$

13. (−3,1)
14. 16
15. 60
16. 1
17. 4
18. 4
19. 2
20. 3
21. 3
22. 2
23. 2
24. 1
25. 3

26. 3
27. 2
28. 2
29. 2
30. 4
31. 3
32. 4
33. 1
34. 1
35. construction
36. c $y = x^2$
37. 4.3
38. a (6,4)

   b {−6,1}
39. a 7.2
   b 130
   c 58
40. (−6,−8)
   (8,6)

INDEX